Across the Creek:
Black Powder Explosions On the Brandywine

Richard D. Templeton

Blue Rock Publishing
Wilmington, Delaware

Copyright © 2020 by Blue Rock Publishing

All rights reserved. No part of this publication may be reproduced or transmitted in any form or by any means, electronic or mechanical, including photocopying, recording, or any information storage and retrieval system, without permission in writing from the publisher, except in the case of brief quotations embodied in critical articles and reviews.

Across the Creek:
Black Powder Explosions on the Brandywine
By Richard D. Templeton
Print ISBN: 978-1-7351079-0-5
eBook ISBN: 978-1-7351079-1-2

Printed in the United States of America

Blue Rock Publishing
Wilmington, Delaware
19803
www.bluerockpublishing.com

Designed by Dave Templeton
Edited by Ann McKelvie
Text set in 12 point Times New Roman

Excerpt from PADDY'S LAMENT: IRELAND 1846-1847, PRELUDE TO HATRED by Thomas Gallagher. Copyright © 1982 by Thomas Gallagher and Michael Gallagher Reprinted by permission of Houghton Mifflin Harcourt Publishing Company. All rights reserved.
Excerpt from The Great Explosion by Brian Dillon. Published by Penguin, 2015. Copyright © Brian Dillon. Reproduced by permission of the author c/o Rogers, Coleridge & White Ltd., 20 Powis Mews, London W11 1JN.
Excerpt from Creating Southern Thunder: The Evolution of Confederate Gunpowder Production During the American Civil War, The Welebaethan: A Journal of History, by Derek Taylor, used by permission of the author.

Library of Congress Control Number: 2020911191

For Lynn

Dedicated to the powdermen and their families

Table of Contents

A Word From the Author vi
Introduction. viii
Prolog xiii
1 Immigrants 1
2 Great Rain All Morning 12
3 Seducing the Workers 24
4 Epitaph to a Perfect Workman 39
5 Blown to Atoms 52
6 A Blast in Town 65
7 No Powder for Johnny Reb 82
8 Patriotic Pissing 98
9 Explosions Are Seldom Serious, Nowadays 112
10 The Big One. 124
11 Risky Solder. 138
12 A Gift of Diamonds 151
13 Men at War. 165
14 Sabotage Jitters 177
15 The (Not So) Old Woman Who Lived in a Shoe 193
Epilog 200
Appendix A-Persons Killed in du Pont
   Powder Yard Explosions on the Brandywine 201
Appendix B—James Hodge's Great War 207
Appendix C—Alan Thaxter's Obituary 214
Acknowledgements. 216
Bibliography 219
Notes. 234
Index 293

A Word from the Author

The chain migration of the Irish to work in the Delaware powder mills, the isolated society on the Brandywine, and European family naming patterns combine to cause a phenomenon found in many manufacturing communities. Sons followed fathers, whose sons followed their fathers, and so on. The families intermarried, and a rather rigid system for giving names to children, based on the old country mores, existed. These factors make it difficult to ensure the persons an author is writing about are the same individuals from one year or era to the next.

A perfect example occurs in DuPont Company petit ledgers, which started when the company began in 1802 and continued through its centennial year. The DuPont petit ledgers are records of pay, seen as credits, and employee disbursements, recorded as debits in the company's employee accounts. Most of the workers kept their money with the DuPont bookkeepers. The petit ledger for 1863 lists four Michael Doughertys receiving pay. Michael Dougherty, Michael Dougherty 3rd, Michael Dougherty Junior, and Michael Dougherty 'boy,' appear among Patricks, Hughs, Williams, and many more Doughertys. The ledger lists twenty-two Doughertys, including the widows of several who had died. Keeping the Doughertys (and Hollands, Donahues, and Toys, among others) straight is a challenge for the researcher.

Most of these single-named people were from different families; the familiar (to the Irish and Italian) naming pattern wherein the first son gets the paternal grandfather's name, the first daughter is named for the maternal grandmother, and so forth, makes an already laborious task that much more difficult. For instance, three Irish brothers working in the mills might all name a first-born son for their father, the child's grandfather. If that grandfather also worked in the mills, there could be four, say, Patrick Xs and, unless their father is identified, it is impossible to know which one is being referenced.

It is also necessary to regard the spelling of names in newspaper accounts as suspect, because of the (often) self-imposed deadlines for reporters and the fact that, in the heat of the moment, they sometimes scribbled their notes. When transcribing, they found them unreadable and copied them incorrectly or made up spellings.

A further note about the practice of using newspapers in this book. I use them extensively to build the stories of the powder-making families. Joyce Longworth and Margery McNinch explain: "When trying to find out about those who lived in the last [20th] century, one invariably runs into an 'Upstairs-Downstairs' situation. Letters, diaries, other written accounts, portraits can document lives of employers... It is much more difficult to delineate the lives of the more humble." The authors continue: "The lives of workers, many of whom were illiterate in the earliest times, are elusive."[1] The writers do not mention newspapers, but the idea is the same—a dearth of primary sources faces the researcher when writing the history of working-class families in 19th century America. Spectacular death, such as occurred in gun powder explosions, was well documented in the papers.

Most of the name spellings throughout this book are from the DuPont Company records. I include some surname variations. One researcher has found 145 varieties of the name Dougherty but, fear not, this book is not about surnames and their deviations; it is, however, in significant respect, about Doughertys.

The name "DuPont" brings up an added issue. In this work, if the name refers to the company, I use "DuPont." If used in the name of a family member, the convention is "du Pont."

And, finally, a word about the use of [sic]. It will not be found in this manuscript as it interrupts reading and is not needed. I have taken great pains to ensure that I have written quoted material exactly as it appears in the original text.

—Richard D. Templeton

Introduction

Inishowen, Clonmany, Tullaghobegly, Clondahorky, Rochetta Cairo, Alessandria. These were place-names dear to the men and women who made up the isolated society of DuPont powder mill workers in Delaware in 19th century America. They were birthplaces and homelands and abandoned places of the past in the Europe they left.

Immigrants came to the New World full of worry and confidence, fear and promise, despair and optimism, carrying with them tales of vibrant futures in a country with streets of gold and endless possibilities. Gathering what few possessions and hopes they had in the land of their birth, cowering in leaky vessels of woe, they made their way to the idyllic Brandywine Valley to start a fresh life.

Most times, kith and kin who preceded them to America saved enough money to pay for their sea transport, the newcomers all but guaranteed a job with the DuPont Company or other manufacturers.

Dirty, smelly, noisy workplaces filled their lives but so did kinship and friendship brought from the Old World. They shared good times and bad, including the loss of fathers and brothers, uncles and nephews, even wives and mothers to black powder explosions. They could not identify the causes of the detonations because the key witnesses were dead.

They could, however, name the result: a hole-in-the-heart grief, leaving a void of deep despair and desolation. Sometimes they named a cause—bad luck, technical breakdown, carelessness, even drunkenness. Doing so did little to ease the pain of the gut-punch they had suffered.

The story of these men and women is not just about explosions, death, destruction, loss. The people who died making black powder came from somewhere, played hard and worked hard, enjoyed themselves, educated their children, and raised loving, close-knit families.

It is a chronicle of American manufacturing and those who made it possible. It is the history of the men and women killed in explosions in the valley of the Brandywine.

While this story is about the powder makers and their families, we must include another family in the recounting. The du Pont family stands out in the account of American manufacturing, beginning at the cusp of a new century.

Pierre Samuel du Pont de Nemours was a leading light of late 18th century France. A French protestant, or Huguenot, also a physiocrat (someone who believed that land was the source of all wealth and that natural economic laws should determine government policy), du Pont was an economist, a publisher, a writer, and a government official. Through his many writings, he became known to Thomas Jefferson, who called him "one of the very great men of the age,"[1] and "the ablest man in France."[2]

Du Pont's close relationship with America's minister to France and future United States president led him to cast his eyes on the New World as a potential test tube for his physiocratic leanings. The jailing of du Pont fils et père during part of the decade-long French Revolution and escaping the guillotine in 1794; the ransacking of the family's home by a mob in 1797; and Pierre Samuel's desire to invest in Virginia land and colonize it for profit, all led to the decision to emigrate to the United States in 1799.

In addition to the plan to colonize Virginia land, the family had several other money-making plans, including import/export, intra-coastal transportation, and international mail service. All the ventures failed to survive.

The du Pont family originally settled near present-day Bayonne, New Jersey, and named their residence Goodstay. One day, Pierre Samuel's younger son, Éleuthère Irénée, was hunting with a French native, Colonel Louis de Tousard. The Colonel had journeyed to North America with the Marquis de LaFayette during the Revolutionary War and became an American army officer. When the two ran out of gunpowder, they found the powder they bought at a country store inferior and expensive.

E.I., as family and friends called Èleuthére, (they also called him Irénée) had apprenticed with Antoine Lavoisier, the so-called "Father of Modern Chemistry," when a teenager in France. The training at Essonne, the French powder-making factory south of Paris, included the manufacturing process.

Why not replace the poorly made American gunpowder with powder made by using French techniques learned at Essonne?

E.I. found investors in France who fronted him the start-up money for a powder facility. Family friend Jefferson touted the area near the nation's new capital as a location; Pierre Samuel was of a like mind. Irénée also looked for a suitable spot in other east coast states.

Colonel Tousard was a member of the small French community in Wilmington, Delaware, and would have made E.I. aware of the area's potential for making high-quality powder: its proximity to a port; its abundance of a very dense rock called "gneiss"[3] for building sturdy mill buildings; and its profusion of black willow trees with which to make charcoal, one of the ingredients of black powder. Other important features were the serene Brandywine Creek, which could be used as motive power for machinery, and the Gallic circle in the city, from which he could draw workers.

The family settled on Wilmington as their home and the location for the first DuPont factory in North America, moving from Goodstay in 1802. After rejecting his father's naming the mills Thunder Mills, E.I. settled, for a brief time, on Lavoisier Mills. He hoped the widow of his former mentor would not object. It is not known if she did, but he reverted to calling his factory Eleutherian Mills.

The year before the du Ponts settled in Delaware, Jefferson had become president of the United States in what would be a fortuitous election for the du Ponts. They continued to correspond with the president, particularly when it concerned United States government gunpowder purchases. Six months after the du Ponts made the first grains of powder, President Jefferson sent a letter to E.I. He told the entrepreneur that, "it is with real pleasure I inform you that it is concluded to be for the public interest to apply to your establishment for whatever can be had from that for the use either of the naval or military department."[4]

Referring to Jefferson as "His Excellency," E.I. wrote the president a long missive, telling the chief executive the government should consider peacetime powder purchases as well as those during war. His reasoning was that, if the government only came to him during times of war, he might not have time to make all the powder required.[5]

War Secretary Henry Dearborn was impressed with the quality of DuPont Company powder, telling his officers on July 4, 1805, that, henceforth, DuPont would be the federal government's only supplier. Despite the federal government's promises, in the years 1805 to 1809, it purchased seven times as much powder from other businesses as it bought from DuPont. Irénée wrote another letter to the president during this time, criticizing the government for its purchasing procedures.

By the eve of the War of 1812, the government fulfilled its promise. By the middle of the war, the United States bought a half million pounds of DuPont powder.

As measured by the number of workers and their payroll, the company grew in those first years. For example, the payroll for the eight months of operation in the first year of production, averaged $80; based on the average monthly pay, this would indicate about eight men on the wage rolls. In 1805, the first full year of operations, the average monthly payroll had climbed to $200. By 1809 the figure had risen to $341.

Growth is also seen in the amount of powder produced. The 1804 figure was over 38,000 pounds, a figure which quadrupled in the first full year of powder production, and continued to climb. But growth did not mean the family was out of debt during this period. It wasn't until the third generation of the family took over the mills that they were finally able to climb into the black.

Despite a few stumbling blocks (the Panics of 1819 and 1837, a poor performance of Du Pont powder at an 1819 test in New York, for example), even in peacetime, the company expanded production.

As the nation spread westward, so did the need for powder. Blasting powder was needed to blow tree stumps out of the ground so farmers had smooth, plantable fields. Coal mines in West Virginia required the larger-grained powders to access coal seams deep underground. Powder was essential for road and canal builders. Hunters and sportsmen wanted top quality, smaller-grained black powder. To feed this voracious need, the DuPont Company manufactured increasing quantities of powder, with sales into the millions of pounds by mid-century.

While periods of peace rewarded the company much more than those of war,[6] the conflicts of the 19th century kept the mills busy. The Mexican-American War of the 1840s, the Crimean War in the mid-1850s, and America's Civil War in the 1860s required nose-to-the-grindstone efforts from the du Pont family and their employees.

During the following decades and into the 20th Century, the Du Pont family name would become a byword for the manufacture of superior brands of American explosives, for family squabbles over the direction and control of the company, and for its domination of the explosives and chemical industries to come. As we will see, these Herculean manufacturing efforts came with the price of a century-and-a-quarter-long series of explosions that would kill 235 men, women, and children, resulting in tragedy for both the du Pont family and the powder makers and their kin. ■

"I am bound to them, though I cannot look into their eyes
or hear their voices.

I honor their history. I cherish their lives. I will tell their story.

I will remember them."

—Unknown author

Prolog

On a bone-chilling winter's day, the penultimate day of the season in 1818, the teenager bundled up his few belongings and set out from home to find work. He waited patiently for the ferry to return to his side of a narrow river so he could continue to the other side and carry on his search.

He was joined by a trio of older men, one not that much older than he, the other two appearing to be in their forties or fifties, and both of them having that air of nobility rarely seen in this part of Delaware, the young state that had separated itself from the colony immediately to the north a few decades before.

The rock-strewn waterway, more creek than river, flowed at an easy pace as it meandered south toward the bustling enclave of Wilmington, and it didn't take long for the four to make it to the center of the green water when they were startled by a loud rumble to the north. One of the men immediately recognized the source of the blast, and his older companion had heard the sound many times in the past, as he was a military man of some note, a former artillerist and cavalry officer in the French army of Napoleon.

After alighting on the west side of the creek, the teenager tagged along with the other men towards the source of the thunderous sound. Children of the era, particularly teens, often supplemented the family income with a dollar or two a month, working in cotton mills, leather tanneries, paper mills, and other factories along the Brandywine. It is likely young Jonas Miller, the lad among the ferry passengers that day, was used to hard work. Hard work was to benefit Miller that awful day and for many years beyond.

The scene that Jonas and the other three men came upon that morning was one of utter devastation: trees were stripped of their limbs, and other kinds of limbs, the kinds that formerly had fingers or toes attached, were strewn haphazardly about the ground. They were mingled with flaming timbers, stones that had once been part of massive-walled mill buildings, and the kinds of detritus the apparent leader of the quartet had seen just three years before in another fatal explosion of gunpowder in the powder mills on the Brandywine. He was Victor du Pont, the older brother of Éleuthère Irénée du Pont, and the first son of Pierre Samuel du Pont, the patriarch of the family.

On that March morning, Jonas and Victor were joined by Marechal Emmanuel de Grouchy, a self-exiled French military officer, and his son Alphonse, a colonel in the French army. The senior de Grouchy had been near Waterloo in a supporting role for Napoleon and his elder son had directed a regiment at the fateful battle.

Victor, Emmanuel, Alphonse, all good Frenchmen, and Jonas, American-born son of Irish parents, immediately set to doing what they could in the powder yard. By this time, the most they could do was to help to free the injured and the mangled bodies of those killed by the explosion from the rubble using axes and their bare hands.

Later, the newspapers reported the marshal and his son had saved many lives in the immediate aftermath of the explosion, but there was no mention of Jonas Miller. A diary kept by a local Wilmington man, William P. Brobson, details his jaded recollection a few years later, of the events of the day: "The Marshal was said to have exerted himself much in preventing the further extension of the ravages caused by the explosion, and to have displayed a courage "worthy of the hero of Borodino" in removing a large quantity of powder from the vicinity of danger. A puff extraordinary was published in the Philadelphia paper detailing his exploits on this occasion in the most bombastic and ridiculous terms. As well as I could learn the facts, however, the Marshal's gallantry on this occasion existed only in the imagination of the author of the puff."[1]

Regardless of de Grouchy's heroism, or lack of it, either at Borodino or on the Brandywine, Jonas Miller's help in the aftermath of the explosion on the Brandywine earned him the offer of a job at the works of E.I. du Pont de Nemours and Company gun powder mills, a position he eagerly accepted.

The 1818 explosion, however, was not the first in the yards, nor would it be the last, as Jonas was to discover during the next fifty-five years, three months and fourteen days of employment at the du Pont works on the Brandywine. ■

• 1 •
Immigrants

> The road from Liverpool to New York, as they who have traveled it well know, is very long, crooked, rough, and eminently disagreeable.
> —*Ralph Waldo Emerson*

The DuPont Company story cannot be told without acknowledging the sacrifices made by the powdermen who provided the backbone of the company from its beginnings and throughout its black powder-making history. Among the sacrifices the men and their families made were leaving their homes, friends, and relatives in the old country and traversing the Atlantic Ocean on leaky, crowded, poorly provisioned ships. They found their way through the ports and teeming streets of a foreign land; started anew in an unfamiliar place; and, as this work will show, died in the explosions that became a regular part of their lives.

Relatives who came before helped them get to the Brandywine. The company encouraged the rush of (mostly) Irish workers by providing passage expenses paid back by deductions from monthly pay once they worked "in the powder."

Family and friends feted the emigrant with a so-called "American wake," a ceremony that mirrored the customs accompanying death.

Wakes were a regular part of life, because death was a regular part of life. They were parties of sorts meant to honor the lamented, to celebrate a life well-lived for an older person, but a mournful event for one younger. In contrast to the farewell American wake, the Irish wake for the dead might see a bottle in the hands of the deceased, or a smoking pipe. Sometimes celebrants took the corpse onto the dance floor, a sign of respect for the departed. The wake included games (often obscene), such as Horse Fair, Fronsey Fronsey, and Shuffle the Brogue; dancing, story-telling and practical jokes; and lots of drinking. The period after death was a time for ritual. Customs included stopping the clocks in the deceased's home so that no one needed to ask the time of death, always having someone sitting with the corpse (in part so grave robbers could not steal it and sell it to a medical school) and keening.

This last was not peculiar to Eire; many countries have keening. It involves a ceremony in which an old woman sings a discordant wailing song, extolling the positive attributes of the dead, and reciting his or her genealogy. They called these women *mna caoine*[1] in the Irish language.

The American wake, though, was unique to Ireland. One author called the practice "a natural extension of Ireland's pagan-derived ritual of 'waking' the dead: watching over the dead person during the night prior to burial to prevent evil spirits from entering the body." He added, "Since departure was a kind of death, the emigration ceremony was inevitably associated with waking the dead."[2]

The name for the ritual differed depending on where the emigrant lived. In parts of Galway they called it the "farewell supper." County Mayo elders named it the "feast of departure." In other areas the Irish referred to it as a "live wake" or a "convoy." In Donegal, where most of the Irish who made their way to Delaware lived, they called it "an American bottle night" or a "bottle drink."

Gift-giving was another part of the American wake. A close relative of the young man making the journey to America might give him a few loaves of "frog bread." They roasted and pulverized a frog and mixed in the powder with flour. By eating the bread during the perilous voyage, the traveler became immunized against fever, or so they thought. If a guest could not afford a physical gift, she might give the sojourner a verbal one. For example, the guest might add the affectionate "-een" to his name: "When you reach America, Mikeen, may the devil fly away with the roof of the house where you're not welcome."[3]

Authors have written volumes telling of the perilous journeys the Irish endured to emigrate to the United States; the stories need no repeating here. It is important, though, to have a flavor of the voyages to show that the emigrants lived through arduous times in pursuit of their dreams.

The du Pont family itself had a difficult voyage at the end of 1799. Captain Samuel Brooks owned the *American Eagle*, the ship that took them across the stormy Atlantic. He was perhaps a decent sailor but not a salesman; the ship had lain in port two years prior to the voyage, bereft of a single paying passenger. The lengthy time in port made the *American*

Eagle less seaworthy, so Captain Brooks needed to make repairs before leaving France, repairs he could not afford. He made only those necessary to sail. He also had problems getting the French authorities to allow the voyage. Victor du Pont stepped in with his friend, diplomat Charles Talleyrand, to get the sailing permits.

As a reward for the du Pont family's help in getting the permits, Captain Brooks allowed the family of thirteen to sail at a reduced rate. To make up the difference, he accepted more passengers; the du Ponts believed they would be the only ones. He also loaded a large amount of salt as cargo.

Victor's wife (née Gabrielle Joséphine de La Site de Pelleport) picks up the story: "This salt melted away by the minute, thanks to the water that we shipped; and then the food supply began to run low, the passengers to quarrel among themselves, the sailors to break into our trunks. The captain was unhappy about all these matters, but particularly unhappy because he didn't even know our location."

She continued: "Had it not been for the one English ship and later a second who let us know where we were and who gave us food, unquestionably we would have perished almost in sight of port."[4] A family tradition says the consumption of a large paté, made from a recipe from Irénée's wife, Sophie, saved the du Ponts. Their voyage lasted ninety days, a full month longer than most voyages the Irish took west.

It is doubtful any patés were on vessels carrying the Irish; they were lucky to have enough fresh water to slake their thirst and decent food to keep them alive.

If the emigrants were not rich enough to embark from an Irish port, they traveled to Liverpool, on the west coast of England, to transfer to a westbound ship. The rates to America from the English city were much less than from Irish ports. The voyage to England, over the Irish Sea, lasted about a day.

The ship captains who sailed from Irish ports to England needed to get as much payment as possible from each voyage, so they packed too many travelers onto their vessels. Many often had to stand for the entire trip. Since cargo, baggage, and even livestock were on the ship, the crew allowed passengers only on the main deck where they were subject to the often-inclement weather. In one case, 1400 souls, standing shoulder-to-shoulder, sailed on a Liverpool-bound vessel, where frigid seawater and "animal mire" drenched them.[5]

The unknowing emigrants also became victims of con games in Liverpool. Owners of vermin-ridden inns overcharged for stays in dirty hovels. Ticket agents sold tickets for old, leaky ships. They sold them for boats not headed for the emigrants' intended destination. The travelers faced many flimflams.

They worried about outright robbery, sometimes by their own countrymen who had preceded them to England and were unable or unwilling to get on an America-bound ship. A further concern was sickness. The passengers kept their land-based anxieties once they boarded their conveyances to the New World; the phrase "coffin ships" tells the story.

Passengers sometimes faced incompetent or drunken sailors or shipmasters, crowded conditions, under-manned crews, and leaks. They contended with shipwrecks, fights, boredom, lack of (and rotten) food. They were on the lookout for fire and pirates. Even specially constructed emigrant ships offered two square feet per passenger in steerage where only children could stand upright.[6]

Eventually the laws on both sides of the Atlantic prescribed adequate food, but in the early 19th century, such laws did not exist. The emigrants had to provide their own food, but food storage was often not available. Once the laws were in place, the captains advertised enough foodstuffs for the voyage, but carried less than promised. The travelers then had to buy food at exorbitant prices.

During storms, the crew might close hatches to the steerage decks, cutting off ventilation in the below-decks space. There was no light and little air. Steerage passengers lived with inadequate toilet facilities, the noise of children, and a high probability of disease—typhus (called "Irish fever"), cholera, consumption (tuberculosis), dysentery, and smallpox were a few of the possibilities.

One can imagine the collective sigh emanating from the steerage ranks once they heard the cry, "Land Ho!" The land in question was Newfoundland. That it was Canadian made no difference to the emigrants as they took sand from the first sounding off the Grand Banks, placing it under a baby's feet "so she might be the first who stepped on American soil."[7] Upon landing in America, the immigrant was not out of danger; the scene of Liverpool's Waterloo Docks often repeating itself on the wharves, streets, and alleyways of New York, Boston, Philadelphia, or Baltimore. Here again were the scammers, conmen, hucksters, and fraudsters, out to take full advantage of the ignorant and now even poorer Irish.

The hawkers sold tickets for travel to nonexistent interior places; they convinced the newcomers to part with what petty cash or goods they had by promising jobs, or a place to stay, or anything else nonexistent or shoddy the conjurers devised. It was the rare foreigner who kept what he carried off the ship.

The Irish who came to America under the DuPont Company's sponsorship were luckier than most. The company guaranteed men a position at the powder factory. Women worked as house servants, cooks, or in other domestic positions. The company also provided passage for relatives of their employees who did not intend to work for them, knowing that having kin nearby strengthened family ties.

For the Irish to come to America under their aegis, the DuPont Company used an organized system. First, an employee who wanted to sponsor a friend or relative notified the company of the request. Next, the company wrote to one of their Philadelphia or Delaware agents[8], requesting a ticket for passage. The agent debited money from the DuPont account and sent the ticket to the company. The employee then sent the ticket to the passenger in Ireland.

American agents sent an order to a representative in Londonderry or Liverpool, reserving a space on the next available ship. The overseas agent notified the passenger by mail when their vessel was scheduled to leave. When the ship sailed, the U.S. agent notified the company of the date and a list of all the DuPont Company passengers. The ultimate step was the passenger reuniting with their sponsor.

Soon after the newcomers arrived, the men who intended to become powdermen (also known as "crickers," referring to the body of water by which they toiled)[9] started work for the company. Their first jobs were outdoor work, which included farming; gathering black willow branches for making charcoal, one of the three ingredients of gunpowder;[10] or helping masons build the structures that dotted the mill property.

Once the man proved himself a sober and reliable worker, the company put him to work in the powder. He then became subject to the ever-present caprice of the mix that might send him "across the creek," the worker's euphemism for dying in an explosion.

As those early years went by, the musical language of the French workers E.I. put to work in the mills was replaced by the brogue spoken by the increasing numbers of families from the island of Eire.

But why Irish? E.I. du Pont first hired his countrymen from the French community in Wilmington but soon tired of their incessant demands for more money. He grew weary of their "know-it-all" attitude, telling him how to make powder. What did they know about making it? He was the one who trained for three years under Antoine Lavoisier at the powder-making factory at Essonne, France. After the failure of the seven business ideas his family had when they came to America (import/export, wool, and shipping among them), he would not fail again.

Cheap Irish labor was part of the solution. One newspaper said, "The reason given for selecting these [Irish] is that they are the only persons who will do just as they are bid, in every respect. This is absolutely necessary in this business, both for security and for excellence in workmanship. I was much struck with the affection and respect exhibited by the operatives towards their employers."

The writer continued, "Although they can occasionally get higher wages in the vicinity, yet the powder mills are never deserted, and the proprietors have never been obliged to raise their wages." He added, "On the contrary, many of the hands import numbers annually from the old country…to supply the deficiency naturally arising from the increase of the business and the departure…of the men." And he wrote, "I take pleasure in recording such instances of affectionate regard on the part of operatives in a large establishment, because it is not usual to find it in this country, and because it speaks…of the influence of kind treatment on that class of Irish, who find their way to these shores."[11]

One author gave several reasons for the high numbers of Irish workers in American manufacturing, saying there were many dangerous jobs, dirty and too onerous for skilled workers to take. He said the Irish were an underclass concentrated in industrial areas of the East, and added that immigrants tended to be young. According to the writer, "the young are often reckless and heedless of danger." He also felt that rural Irish were ignorant of the industrial perils of factory work, adding, "The Irish self-image, too, played a role for this ethnic group conceived of itself as given to daring and [is] especially endowed with adventurous qualities."[12]

Another author stated that "preferring workers with no craft background had a lengthy history among American manufacturers; arms-maker Samuel Colt once said 'the more ignorant a man was, the more brains he had for my purpose.'"[13]

Immigrants

As with most immigrants to America, citizens labeled the newcomers. They said the Irish were artistic, funny, and pious. They also said they were violent, dirty, and ignorant.[14] The Oxford English Dictionary included "bad-temper" in its definition of "Irish."[15]

E.I. du Pont ignored these epithets to hire his hard-working Irish work force, although he was not always generous regarding them. At one point, he wrote, "[I]n this quantity [of 100 Irish] there were no more than two whom I would want to work for me in the mill."[16] In 1812, he wrote that the men "are nothing but common labourers who understand nothing of the principles & nature of the work."[17] Irénée wrote those words to dissuade other powder manufacturers from enticing his workers to join their firms.

During the DuPont Company's opening years the workmen avoided disaster; the company noted few explosions. They recorded non-fatal accidents, the first reported on Saturday, August 15, 1807[18] in the drying house. Twenty-six months later, an accident happened in a pounding mill. Two years later, another pounding mill blew. They reported no injuries in these blasts.

E.I. du Pont rejected this kind of stereotyping to hire his Irish powdermen.

After the first explosion, Irénée wrote to his father, who had returned to France after accompanying his family to the New World, that it was time to make black powder.[19] "Forced by the demand to start manufacturing as soon as possible, I was obliged to use a house that was already built, sixty feet from the graining mill, to make a heated dry-house. Attached to this was another building that was formerly used in the cotton manufactory and that I use for a charcoal house, having no other." He added he knew of spontaneous lighting of charcoal at Essonne where Lavoisier taught him how to make the volatile combination, but, "My partner did think as I did; we were tired of building and we had to start."[20]

He continued, "We had taken the charcoal out of the furnace with the fire absolutely extinguished. When we stopped work in the evening,

Dalmas and I went to look at the charcoal to be sure that there was no appearance of danger; we saw none." Dalmas was Charles Dalmas, Irénée's brother-in-law, called "Jojo" by the family; E.I.'s wife, Sophie, was Charles' sister.

Du Pont wrote, "After supper Dalmas said, 'We should go back and look at the charcoal—it is too dangerous. Will you go or shall I?' Then he added, 'You are tired, I will go.'" Less than fifteen minutes after he left, the drying house exploded with a tremendous crash.

Du Pont ran the few yards to the drying house, hoping Dalmas had survived; Dalmas' cry that he made it through the explosion rewarded him. They spent the night making sure the fire didn't spread to the other mills. E.I. finished the letter by attributing the saving of the remaining buildings to the "Heaven-sent" light winds and the damp coming from the northeast that moistened the roofs.[21]

There was concern after the third explosion on October 19, 1811, the second in the pounding mill, that "some villain" had caused it. The DuPont Company offered a reward of $1,500[22] to "such person as will give sufficient information to cause the abetting or perpetrators of such villainy, to be apprehended and punished." The wrongdoer, "introduced into one of the mortars an iron ball, weighing about 1 1/2 pounds, and of about 2 inches in diameter."[23]

Three of the first four explosions, and the first fatal one, occurred in a pounding mill. Pounding, or stamping, mills incorporated the ingredients into a mixture. A cam connected to a waterwheel caused a rise and fall of wooden posts in a sequential pattern. It was old technology in the early 19th century.

John Rumm wrote that Irénée was "undoubtedly familiar with another method for incorporating powder that was replacing the pounding mill altogether in some European countries: the rolling mill."[24] He continued, "The rolling mill offered several advantages over

An ancient pounding mill.

the pounding mill: it blended the powder more thoroughly and evenly, it reduced the time needed to incorporate it to less than an hour for some grades of powder, and it was less hazardous to operate than the pounding mill." Rumm added: "The rolling mill also offered a clear savings in labor: a crew of one to two men could operate up to three mills at one time, compared with the nine-man crew needed to run the pounding mill."[25]

Calling E.I. an "unabashed Anglophobe," Rumm wrote that E.I. by then considered the roll mill a better means of mixing the ingredients because tests showed it created a superior powder. In addition, the author said that five of the explosions occurring in the years from 1809 to 1820, including the 1815 explosion that killed all nine "potsmen,"[26] happened in a pounding mill.[27] The English had banned pounding mills more than a half-century before the DuPont Company transitioned to the roll mill.[28]

A story began with two girls, dressed in ethereal white, being pursued through the powder yards by two young men. This was the story Alfred Victor du Pont, the eldest of E.I.'s sons, told of the first fatal explosion at the Brandywine powder yards. He said the workers saw a portent of the next day's disaster and believed they received the vision to warn of the impending event. Vision or not, the blast on the morning of Thursday, June 8, 1815, was all too real: they lost nine fellow workers to another pounding mill explosion. The du Ponts thought a careless workman carried a live ember from a fire at home in the cuff of his pants or on the sleeve of his coat. The explosion rent the morning air with a tremendous report "resembling that of the heaviest cannon."[29]

Killed in the explosion were Thomas Quigg, Andrew Miller, John Welch, William Foster, and Francis Leonard. Those who lingered in extreme pain were Peter Shepherd, John McCauley, and brothers Richard and Patrick Dougherty[30]. The woeful quartet of Irishmen and their families might have had the Irish proverb about doctors in their minds—*"Dearbhrathair don Bhas fios a chur ar an dochtair"*[31]—sending for the doctor is brother to death.[32] It is unlikely the du Ponts let such superstition hold sway after the explosion. They called for the medical help of Dr. Didier, who will appear again shortly.

Thomas Quig, born in 1770 in County Donegal, Ireland, was forty-five years old when he died that June morning. Like most of the Irish emigrants to the United States, he owned very little. In an accounting of his goods in an "Inventory of Close and Articles belonging to Thomas Quig decd [deceased] June 8th 1815," he possessed one coatee and summer roundabout (a jacket) valued at $1.25; a "Boddy" coat worth $5; a pair of spurs valued at $12.50; a $40 horse, and a $25 gold watch.[33]

Quig's first appearance in the petit ledgers[34] was in 1806, when he received $10 a month; payments to his account were irregular, as they were for most of the workers. For example, the ledger shows payments in 1808 of $10 on February 13, $10 on March 12, $20 in mid-May, and $60 in early August. The men could receive cash if they wanted it, but most kept their money in interest-bearing accounts with the company and drew as needed from the accounts. Before his death, Quig had amassed the princely sum of $840, showing that he had saved most of his income. Quig enlisted in the militia that protected the powder mills from potential capture by the British during the War of 1812, known as "Mr. Madison's war."

The militia was not particularly well or evenly equipped. Records show such items, under Arms and Accouterments, as "19 guns complete with straps and bayonets; 29 guns complete with no straps and bayonets; one Bayonnet; 123 cartridge boxes with belts, 2 with no belts; 50 bayonet belts and scabards; 67 belts & no scabards," and so forth.[35] On June 18, E.I. du Pont was the first signatory of the militia's rules and regulations and became captain of the unit.

Acknowledging that a committee could amend the regulations written a day later were Francis Leonard, Andrew Miller, Peter Shepherd, Patrick Dougherty (signing with an "X his mark" signifying that he was not literate)[36]. Richard Dougherty signed with "X his mark"; Michael Toner, whom we meet later, signed the same way.

"X his mark" signatures. (Hagley Museum and Library)

In the close-knit and insular Du Pont Company community, multiple names appear on multiple records. Such is the case with Thomas Quig, who at least once was a sponsor of a newborn child of another powderman and his wife. "Sponsor" was akin to "godparent." Quig was a sponsor for newborn Mary Anne Doras, daughter of Hugh and Susan Kane Doras at her baptism in February 1807.[37] A man named Thomas Quig was a sponsor a few years after the explosion, this time for the birth of Anne Toy in March 1821, to Daniel and Rose Coyle Toy; this Quig was the son of the deceased Thomas Quig. We meet the Toys in Chapter Four.

The historical record on Peter Shepherd is scant compared to that of Thomas Quig. Shepherd was a member of the South Brandywine Company of Volunteers, as shown by the record of his receiving his military cap in 1813. The unit went into the service of the United States from September 6, 1814, to January 3, 1815.[38]

As part of the militia, he received "nineteen muskets with their slings, nineteen cartouch boxes with 18 rounds of cartouch [a paper-encased cartridge] in each cartouch box, and nineteen bayonets, with their belts & scabbards,"[39] a more consistent issue than earlier. Shepherd was a non-commissioned officer or served as a quartermaster.

After being injured in the explosion, in a deposition before powdermen Laurence Curry and Patrick McGarr, Shepherd said other powdermen owed him money. He wanted the debt payments to go to his sister, Elizabeth Welch, the widow of John Welch, another victim. Shortly after the deposition, Shepherd died at his home.

John McCauley served as a corporal in E.I.'s volunteer company during the War of 1812. After his death in the 1815 accident, his service pay went to administratrix Sarah McCauley, probably his wife. In 1904, Francis A. Price recorded a list of names on tombstones in the graveyard of the First Presbyterian Church in Wilmington, and included McCauley's name. However, the cemetery no longer exists and it is not known where McCauley's remains were re-interred.

Almost no information survives on John Welch, except that he served under Victor du Pont in the militia from mid-summer of 1814 through early January 1815.[40] This is typical of the challenges faced by historians of the era. ■

▪ 2 ▪
Great Rain All Morning

> Who can speak the bitter anguish of the widow and the orphan, who…are left to mourn their irreparable loss!
> —*The American Watchman*

One difficulty historians face, particularly when studying the early days of the American Republic, is that many of the residents of the North American continent shared names. Imagine trying to research a particular John Smith or Elizabeth Jones. An example is William Foster, a worker killed in the first fatal accident at the DuPont Company mills. Michael Tepper's 1986 listing of passengers to the Port of Philadelphia[1] shows "William Foster & wf & fam" arrived after Christmas, 1808, on the *Charleston Packet*. This may have been the William Foster killed in the 1815 explosion.

After William's death, the widow Foster boarded powdermen in her home on the mill property; as long as she didn't remarry or move away she could keep her home, rent-free. Even before her husband's death, the family earned money by taking in boarders at $8 each per month. Martha Foster was one of three widows from the 1815 explosion to take advantage of this opportunity to enhance her finances.

She also enjoyed the generosity of E.I. du Pont's offer of $100 per year[2] to the families of powdermen killed in the line of duty. The extra money earned from boarding and the yearly stipend came in handy for Martha, who had one child and was pregnant with her second when William died.[3] She was the first, but far from the last, widow to give birth after losing her husband in a powder accident.

Barely seven weeks after the explosion, Martha boarded William McBride in her home. A June 1816 entry in the ledger, a page headed by the name William Foster, the "William" replaced by "Martha," and the moniker "widow," showed she earned $90 for boarding McBride for eleven months.[4] She probably didn't feed McBride, or another boarder named

William Roudey, much in the way of protein; a petit ledger entry for the purchase of "potatoes and turnips" stands out. Martha's surname before her marriage to Foster is unknown, as is her lineage. She might have been Irish, or she might have agreed to the dietary wishes of her boarders. She could have learned from her Irish neighbors how to make meals heavily laden with traditional Irish ingredients. Perhaps she served *barm brach*, bread made with sugar, spices and dried fruit, akin to a German stollen. Or maybe she, her family, and boarders were fond of black pudding, a sausage made of pig's blood, salt, lard, oatmeal, onions, and spices, then fried; or its sheep's-blood-based cousin, *drisheen*. She might have served *colcannon*, with kale or cabbage, potatoes, butter, milk, onions, and seasoning, or *crubeen*, pig's hind feet with more meat on them than trotters, the front feet.[5]

Nancy Miller was another of the trio of widows who took in boarders after her husband, Andrew, a 25-year-old Quaker, died in the explosion. Entries in the 1816 ledger included credits "by boarding hands" of $65.72 for April through June, $17.79 for July, $55.48 in October and November, and $24 for the following February. At $8 per boarder per month, three men boarded in her home. The variances show that boarders sometimes changed their housing arrangements at will.[6] DuPont-provided housing on the mill property was a necessity, as the nearest enclave of private residences, Wilmington, was four miles away and, other than foot and horse, there was no means of rapid transportation in these early years.

Before becoming a widow, Nancy Miller served the du Pont family as a domestic, employed by Sophie du Pont, Irénée's wife. She was on the domestics list with several other women—wives, sisters, or daughters of powdermen. In 1813, the company paid her for mending powder sheets, sewing towels and wagon covers, and other types of domestic work. She earned money for the Miller accounts through at least 1814, when she was one of five servants listed in the DuPont Company records.[7]

In the petit ledger for the Millers for the year 1813 is an $8 entry for Dr. Didier's bill. Dr. Pierre Didier was a Frenchman who doctored the du Ponts and the workmen and their families; $8 was his customary charge for assisting a mother at a childbirth.[8] The charge may have been for the birth of Isabella Miller. The per-birth charge didn't change in thirty years. Didier continued to deliver babies well into old age; his last recorded delivery was in 1830 as he approached his ninetieth birthday.[9]

Dr. Didier never developed a mastery of English; all his records were in French. He belonged to the close-knit French society that E.I. had found in nearby Wilmington. They had emigrated to the United States in the late eighteenth century, many because of a slave revolt in the Dominican Republic in 1791. Four hundred souls made up the Wilmington French enclave, according to one writer. He wrote that the physician's antiquated treatments reflected their provincialism. The doctor's goal was to cure the imbalance of body fluids (humors) in his patients. The physician used both vegetable and mineral substances in his treatments, mostly purgatives (laxatives) or emetics (vomit-inducing). He treated his patients with plasters and invariably prescribed barley water, regardless of the illness.[10]

Didier supplemented his medical income with other sources of revenue, including selling candles and wood and taking young boarders into his Wilmington home.

Patrick Dougherty was another victim of the 1815 blast. As he lay on his deathbed after the June 8 explosion,[11] E.I. du Pont and powderman Thomas Ritchie listened to Patrick's dying wishes. When Patrick died, the two deponents told county officials he wanted his assets to go to his brother Richard's widow. Her husband died two days before his brother of injuries sustained in the explosion. A Baltimore newspaper wrote on June 12 that Barney Dougherty (the origin of the name is unknown) and Patrick Dougherty received wounds and were "not expected to live."

Richard Dougherty was one of the first Irishmen hired by the fledgling DuPont manufacturing concern. His name first appeared in August 1803 under the name "Dawarty" with a payment of one dollar. Further payments to his account appeared for *Novembre* 8, for $2 and then another November payment, late in the month, *pour solde* [for a balance of] $44.45. Payments continued on the books, in French, for another few months, then in English.

The records show that Richard and his wife, Anne King Dougherty, had four children. The first born was Sara, baptized in June 1806 under the sponsorship of Michael Toner; next came William, who received his baptism in August 1808; third-born was James, born on September 9, 1812. Baby Elenor came along in the summer of 1814, shortly before her father began his four-month stint with the Brandywine Rangers (the militia), under Captain E.I. du Pont. Francis Leonard, another of the men killed in the 1815 explosion, served as a sponsor for the newest Dougherty. The spelling of the baby's first name may show they named her for Elenor Bradley, wife of future explosion victim Edward Bradley; she had sponsored the birth of William Dougherty in 1808.[12]

Anne King Dougherty earned $1.72 in March 1809 for her work packing powder into storage and shipping containers. In 1806, she was one of several women, spouses of powdermen, hired by Irénée to pack powder and to cut and paste labels onto the kegs.[13] Anne earned extra income by boarding workers in her home, including her brother-in-law, Patrick, at the customary $8 per month.

Anne Dougherty outlived her husband by twenty years. At her death in 1835, Anne had an estate of $134 comprising her deceased husband's savings, the money from boarding workers, and her $100 annual widow's pension. Margaret Mulrooney writes that the widow Dougherty had "the luxury of a combined sitting-dining room" in her home. The author added that the woman had goods including "her best bed, a round tea table, a cherry bureau, a walnut breakfast table… a set of china," and other table furnishings.[14]

Patrick Dougherty was Richard's younger brother by a year. He was born in Malin, County Donegal, in the province of Ulster at the northernmost tip of Ireland. He started working in the powder yards in May 1807, rising to become a pressman, squeezing out the water added to the dry mixture to reduce the chance of explosion. The press compacted loose powder into cakes that proceeded to the next step in the gunpowder manufacturing line.

The younger Dougherty's will stipulated that "in case of his death of which he was then apprehensive" his assets were to go to Richard's widow, except for part held in reserve in case his Irish nephews wanted to emigrate. Fifteen years later, James Dougherty took advantage of his uncle's generosity in providing passage expenses, and followed his extended family to America.

County Cavan in Ireland provided Irish men who came to America to work for the DuPont Company; Francis Leonard was one of these, starting to work on June 25, 1812. Tepper lists a Francis Leonard as voyaging to the New World on the *Erin* from Dublin to New York City in 1811. Leonard was from Glasstown or Port, a townland in the barony of Tullyhunco, Kildallan civil parish.[15]

At his death at 25, he had $5.50 worth of goods: a pair of shoes, a regimental roundabout, and a pair of blue pantalets, the latter two from his service in the militia. He had been AWOL (absent without leave) from his military duties at least twice.

After Leonard's death, E.I. DuPont de Nemours and Company received a strange letter from Philadelphia. The March 2, 1816, letter reads: "I take the liberty of addressing you a few lines to request of you to let me know wither my husbands one of the unfortunate sufferers who was destroyed last summer at your powder mills. I have been very anxious to hear from him this long time and it is only a few day ago I have been told that it is believed he was one of the unfortunate victims. I am in great distress of mind to know the truth concerning him, and likewise much distressed, as it respects my situation. Sir you will confer a lasting obligation in addressing a few lines to me in Knights Court in Cherry between 8 & 9 street Philada."

The letter continues: "My husband was a German and spoke broken English he went by the name of Francis Leonard when in the country, and when he was at home he went by the name of Francis Cream which was his propper name, his [stature?] short, stout, light complexion and blue eyes, he left me in May or the begginning of June last summer and I have never heard from him since but only by report lately which is said he was one that was blowed up by the explosion of powder last summer at your mill. Sir your compliance with the above request will probably alley some of the unhappy thoughts and it is to be feared, the feelings of a distressed widow."[16] The letter was "signed," Christiana "X her mark" Cream. There is no indication in the DuPont files that the company responded.

A Wilmington newspaper, in an article headlined, "Melancholy Accident," lamented, "The loss of property to the proprietors is trifling…the machinery…can go into operation in a few days. But who can speak the bitter anguish of the widow and the orphan, who…are left to mourn their irreparable loss!"[17]

Calling the deceased workers "nine of the best workmen," E.I. wrote to a French investor to say the explosion caused a cessation of production for three months.[18] In the impetus for the award of $100 pensions to families of the powdermen killed in explosions, E.I. also corresponded with Antoine Bidermann, the son of a major French stockholder (and Irénée's future son-in-law). On July 13, 1815, E.I. wrote that several of his best men had quit out of fear and discouragement and no longer wanted to work in the powder. With the harvest looming and labor scarce, Bidermann wrote back to E.I., telling him he and his father, James, would give yearly pensions to widows of the deceased.

The workers, and Irénée himself in discussion with them, had also come up with the idea to offer something for the families. Rumm writes, "The lesson of the 1815 explosion was clear: 'fair dealings' constituted the essence of mutual interest; without it, the 'republic' that Irénée sought to create in his powder yard was doomed to collapse."[19]

Collapse it did not. The nascent manufactory continued its early days' growth, producing more and more powder each year. After the end of the War of 1812, the company could return to making hunting and sporting powders for a nation teeming with hunters and gun-sport enthusiasts. As the country expanded to the west, the need for blasting powder for road and canal building, for tree-stump removal in farm fields, and coal mining, grew exponentially. The amount of all powders except those for government consumption grew from 37,000 25-pound kegs by 1810 to quadruple that in just eight years.[20]

To make that much powder, the DuPont Company hired more than 120 additional workers during the same period, bringing the total number of employees to 351.

This book centers on the workmen, but another significant story needs to be told, this one involving the first du Pont to die because of an accident at the Brandywine works.

Pierre Samuel du Pont, the *paterfamilias* of the family, was an associate of prominent government officials in pre-revolutionary France and a trusted state official in his own right. He was one of the thirteen souls on the *American Eagle* when it left La Rochelle, France, in October 1799. This French publisher, writer, economist, and cabinet official under Louis XVI returned to his native land early in the new century to attend to DuPont Company affairs there. On his return in 1815, he moved into the family residence overlooking the powder manufactory.

On the night of July 16, 1817, DuPont père awoke to the sound of the fire bell in the yard. The drying-house was afire. The seventy-seven-year-old joined in the bucket brigade toiling to keep the flames away from other powder yard buildings. He worked through the night and, after they extinguished the fire, headed straight to bed, never to rise. On August seventh, Irénée and Victor's father breathed his last.

Eight months after losing his father, Irénée faced another tremendous loss, this time of thirty-three workers and the wife of one of them. March 19, 1818, would mark the deadliest explosion ever at the Delaware gunpowder mills.

As Jonas Miller assisted in the mill that day, he could not have perceived that work on the Brandywine would be his life. Nor could he know he would suffer serious injury at least once during his long tenure in the DuPont manufactory. Or that he would sire more powder workers among his thirteen children during that span. He could not peer into a future in which he lost many friends to the whims of the volatile black powder.

Caprice was all around the barely fourteen-year-old as he picked up pieces of flesh and bone of men who minutes before were sentient human beings. Three years earlier, he may have heard the first fatal explosion at the mills, about two miles from his home, but the fates of the men killed then probably wouldn't have registered as a loss in his pre-pubescent mind. Now, though, the fast-maturing teen came face-to-face with the grim result of black powder blasts.

One victim, Michael Toner (sometimes noted as Mihel, and Tonner; the first payroll records listed him as Michael Turner), was a powder worker when production began in 1804. But in an earlier November 1, 1802 entry, Michael Turner already had $7 credited to his account. It is possible the company hired him to excavate the Eleutherian Mills[21] mill race; E.I. used men to hand dig the canal, with picks, axes, and shovels. Water from the creek, when it filled the ditch, provided the motive power for the powder-making machinery.[22] Toner's starting pay was $10 a month and, by 1807, he was earning $12. Regular raises elevated him to $27 by 1817.

As part of the company's paternalistic practices, Toner earned $14 in interest on his assets in the company accounts totaling $230 as of January 1, 1816. Interest-bearing accounts paid a handsome six percent, slightly more than U.S. Treasury notes.[23]

Toner had married Anne Gallagher in September 1809. Richard Dougherty and his wife, Anne, were witnesses. Father Patrick Kenny, who ministered to the powder makers and their families, officiated.

By the time of Michael's death, the Toners had produced a trio of children: Peter, born in 1811; Eliza, a little older than a year when her father died; and Sallie Ann, who was probably born between Peter and Eliza, perhaps between 1813 and 1815, since an every-two-years birth cycle was common then.[24]

In a strange turn of events, the tragic explosion made the Toner children orphans. Anne, after hearing the first of several detonations, scooped up her infant daughter, Eliza, and ran to the gate separating the workers' community from the powder yards. While she headed for the sound and smoke of the first blast, the storage building blew as part of the chain of blasts that occurred, despite the effort to separate the "danger buildings," those where the possibility of explosion was highest. An errant "condemned ammunition" ball from the nearby magazine struck Mrs Toner. She dropped to the ground, dead, but Eliza was unharmed. Eliza later became a nurse who cared for Lammot du Pont, Irénée's grandson[25] and a future leader of the company.

The Toner orphans were first taken in by the family of powder maker George Kidd. In September, the company credited Kidd's account with $93 "by boarding the three orphans of Tonner from March 21 to Aug. 31st, making twenty-three weeks two days @$4 [per week]."[26] The children eventually went to a Philadelphia Catholic orphanage.[27]

Because Michael Toner had worked for sixteen years at the powder yards, he had amassed a sizable estate. Among the "goods and chattels" (personal possessions) enumerated after his death were a silver watch and chain, valued at $16; a walnut bureau, worth $6; and two brass candlesticks, with a recorded value of $.75. The list of possessions took up two pages in the accounting documents, with personal property valued at over $100. Added to his company account, the assets in the hands of his administrators came to $350.[28]

Besides the rent-free housing given the powdermen, they used small plots of land for gardens and farmettes where they raised their own livestock. Michael Toner's goods included six pieces of pork, which suggests he slaughtered a pig in the season before his death,[29] leaving two hogs in the inventory. The list also included a barrel of soap and several barrels of ash; Mrs. Toner mixed the ash with animal fat to make the soap.

Another family that suffered mightily that day were the Bradys. Lost in the accident were John Sr., John Jr., Hugh, and Patrick Jr. One cannot assume "junior" was the son of "senior" of that name, as these could refer to an uncle, a nephew, or two people with the same name although unrelated.

Clues to the relationship of the four dead Bradys are scarce. Mulrooney says Patrick Brady's eldest was John, another man who died in the explosion—but was this John senior or junior? Unlike the known kinship of many of the Doughertys killed in explosions, which shows they were mostly unrelated, it is probable the quartet of Bradys were members of the same extended family. The Dick Scott collection at the Hagley Library, on a page labeled "1818" says John and Hugh were brothers and Patrick Jr. was their cousin.

A $45 annuity appears in John Brady's account six months after the accident. There was confusion as to how the company was to record the issuance of the $100 annuities on their books. Whatever uncertainty reigned in the accounting department, by the end of the year the credit side of John Brady's ledger showed an added $33.

Ann Carroll, the widow of the younger John Brady (who lived two agonizing days after the accident), later gave up her company-provided annuity by remarrying. She married powderman Owen McQuaid in September 1821. In the tight-knit Irish circle, Ann maintained her Brady ties, becoming godmother to a child of her husband's sister, Mary Brady Gagan.[30]

Little is know about Hugh Brady, but William Boyd and Thomas Morrison, administrators of Hugh's estate, listed, among other goods, a $12 silver watch, "one lot of silk handkerchiefs," and five coats and two hats, all valued at $35.[31]

A few weeks after the explosion, Father Kenny, who had married Michael Toner and Ann Gallagher, recorded the weather and solemn church services on April 5, 1818. "Great rain all morning opened passage to a great number who attended Church. 18 communicants, 4 masses ordered for Pk [Patrick] Brady's son & 1 mass in particular for John Brady—1 mass by Js Brady for Sl [soul] of Hugh Brady—3 masses for Sl of Philip Gallagher 3 masses Sl of Edward Bradley—Jas Brady paid for what I already celebrated." The masses were offered "for the Sls of all that were swept off on the 19 of March 1818 at du Pont's powder mills." Although, as Mulrooney writes, fewer than forty percent of Brandywine Catholics attended church on any given Sunday, this service was crowded because the community needed to mourn together and in public.[32]

Other members of the ill-fated Brady family appear in the DuPont Company petit ledgers. The company listed Patrick Brady Jr. and Sr. together. Not until age twenty-one did a son's account become his own. In the 1818 ledger, at the top of the page where the accountants showed the monthly wage, entries of "12+9" and "18" show that John Brady Jr.

earned $12 per month and his father, $18. The "12+9" showed regular monthly pay plus an overtime rate.

If Patrick Brady Sr. did not earn overtime, it was because he worked during his free time on his own small farm. Ledger entries include the purchase of a steer weighing 561 pounds at $.07 a pound for $40. In addition, his family earned money for peeling willow bark. Many Brandywine families provided this service for an extra dollar or two a month credited to the family treasury. One entry lists "Mowing Cherry Island 20 acres @ $1.50," for a credit of $30.[33] Twenty acres is the equivalent of fifteen of today's American football fields. The land Brady scythed is now a landfill east of Wilmington.

The sources for Edward Bradley, another victim of the 1818 explosion, present several mysteries. The words *kessymin*, *ruffins*, and *romarkin* are in the ledgers that highlight Bradley's credits and debits. From the context of the entry, we can be fairly certain that *kessymin* refers to fabric Elenor, Edward's wife, wove into clothing. Here is the entry: "Sept. 30 1815 To 3 yds brown kessymin @ $7.—for yd 21."[34] *Ruffins* may refer to a grain; "June 4 To 3 bush ruffins in Jany. and April 4," for $2.25, meaning they cost $.75 a bushel.[35] It could be another word for "roughings," possibly the detritus left after processing grain. And finally, *romarkin*, as in: "To 2 Steers of romarkin weighing 8.39# @ $58.73."[36] Were these parts of a butchered cow?

Edward and Elenor McAfferty Bradley (often spelled "McAffery" or "McCaffry") were the parents of at least four children, two of them twins. First born was James, who came into this world on June 19, 1809, when his father was in his fifth year of employment with the company. Two and a half years later, twins Anne, whose real first name may have been Nancy, and Frances, known as Fanny, were born in late November. Besides the children living in the Bradley home, two of Edward's brothers, James and John, boarded there, as did at least one other man.

Records of the Brandywine Manufacturer's Sunday School (BMSS), established by the DuPont Company in 1817 and helmed by Irénée's first-born, Victorine, show that Nancy and Fannie, daughters of Elenor Bradley, left school in 1827, Fannie after "irregular attendance." Listed in the records is scholar Edward Bradley, son of Elenor Bradley, who received premiums (prizes) for reading. He won *Anecdotes for Little Boys*, which was, like many of the books awarded to students (called scholars at the BMSS), a chapbook[37] published by the Philadelphia-based American Sunday School Union. Edward received *The History of John Robins, the Sailor*, two years after his first award and shortly before his departure for Philadelphia.[38] The books awarded to scholars had a strong moral component.[39]

After the death of her husband, Mrs. Bradley did not wait as long as Ann Carroll to remarry. In December 1819, Elenor married Owen King under the ministering of Father Kenny and the sponsorship of Michael Borrell, another powderman whom we meet in a later chapter. DuPont records name the new husband Owen; the marriage record from St. Peter's Cathedral names him Eugene. Since Eógan is Irish for Owen (and, when pronounced sounds like "Owen,") it is likely that something got mistaken in the transcription.

Because of the previous explosion of June 1815, the company had needed to hire replacement workers. Michael McLaughlin answered the call. He started with the firm four days after that accident and assisted with the reconstruction of the damaged or destroyed powder buildings. Michael (sometimes Mikel or Macil in the records) and his wife, Mary Doherty (note the different spelling of the name "Dougherty"), had twins Sara and Cornelius on October 4, 1817. The pair joined their brother Michael a week after he celebrated his third birthday.

We know nothing of Mary Doherty McLaughlin after Michael's death in the 1818 explosion, which adds mystery to events that followed. Ten years later, in March 1828, the company received a letter addressed to Victor du Pont, who had died in January of the previous year. It was from a William Johnson of Philadelphia, inquiring on behalf of Nancy McLaughlin, ostensibly Michael's cousin, who had left Ireland eight months before the date of the letter, "in order to ascertain the present condition of his estate, if it still remained unsettled, or whether any person has ever come forward to put in a claim." Johnson noted that Nancy made the request on behalf of Michael's aged mother, who had written to the company earlier requesting information on Michael and his legacy, but did not receive a response.[40]

The letter continued: "Mrs. McGlaughlin[41] has understood since that time, that a certain Henry McMenaman had come forward asserting his claim to the estate (as the only relation he had) but the fact appears to be, that the said McGlaughlin, deceased has an aged widowed mother, (and poor), still living, and also a brother." Johnson asked that Victor write as soon as convenient, saying that Nancy was eager to furnish Mrs.

McLaughlin with all information on her son, his death and his estate. "By an early complyance with the above request, you will confer a great favor, and perhaps serve the cause of humanity. Your Obdt Svt,[42] Wm. Johnson." No response could be found in the Dupont Company files.[43]

Four years later, the company responded to a letter from Ann McLaughlin, this one dated October 4, 1832. Written for Ann by her friend Mrs. Smith of Philadelphia, again to "V. du Pont," the writer mistakenly listed the explosion by which Michael died as occurring in 1822 or 1823. The note continued by stating Mrs. McLaughlin was a woman of "much good feeling but of no education," and she knew Michael's estate was small. Mrs. Smith wrote that Michael's mother resigned all claims on the money, as proven in Mrs. McLaughlin's letters to her niece, and wanted the niece to receive the cash. She added that Ann[44] would give Victor "good security for the refunding of the money in case of any other demand upon you for the same."

The company's response was quick, corrective and legal. If the claimant did not have a power of attorney, the administrators of Michael's estate, Peter Hendrickson and William Martin, could not turn over the disputed $33. The letter also specified that no Michael McLaughlin was on the payroll in the 1820s, but one had died in the 1818 explosion. Further, in the absence of a power of attorney, the administrators would have to pay out of their own pockets, and not out of the estate, if someone else came along with a valid claim . The letter concluded by saying that Ann McLaughlin's appearance with a valid document would cause the release of the estate to her. We do not know if she ever presented one or received the money from the administrators.[45]

For several families, the suffering continued after the second fatal explosion in the short history of the DuPont works. ∎

▪ 3 ▪
Seducing the Workers

*O how truly did I feel for the many poor souls thus
in an instant hurled into Eternity!*
—*Anna Wright Rumsey*

Like the Doughertys in the explosion three years before, two men suffered a week of painful agony before succumbing to their injuries. John Dunnery (Dunavee was another spelling in the pay records) and Thomas Pierce died on March 27, 1818. Dunnery had been working in the powder a scant four months and had only $3 worth of goods in his name when he died.[1] Pierce was from Baltimore, Maryland.

Imagine the double grief a pregnant woman experienced when her husband died in an accident. She lost her husband, and when she gave birth she mourned again that her child had no father. One example is Catherine Slane Finigan, the wife of powderman Hugh Finigan, who died in that spring of 1818. Like some other workers, she had developed a close relationship with her employer and his family and took the Christian name of a du Pont for her child. Enamored of Irénée's eldest daughter, Catherine named her new baby Victorine Elizabeth, born four months after her father's death. Catherine's employment with Victorine du Pont may have engendered the relationship, as Victorine paid her for washing and starching clothes. The widow Finigan later earned money peeling willow to be made into charcoal.

Another widow who faced the birth of a baby without her husband was Anne Quigley Gallagher, the wife of Philip Gallagher who had started with the company in 1814.[2] Son Philip was born to Anne on November 16, eight months after his namesake died. Catherine Slane Finigan was one of the newborn's sponsors at his baptism.

As paternalistic as the du Ponts were toward their workers, they did not pay the men on days they didn't work. David Flinn, another victim, who boarded with Michael and Anne Toner, had broken his leg in mid-

October 1817 and returned to work in early December. He received no pay during his convalescence. Records show he earned $13.85 for eleven days of work in October and nineteen in December. At his death he had amassed $119, an accumulation considerably higher than most of the men who perished in the same accident.[3]

E.I. connected powderman John Malloy, even in death, to what he interpreted as a scam. In 1819, a Captain Moffat appeared at the offices of the DuPont Company with a young woman named Mary McColgan, or perhaps Colgan. In a letter to a Philadelphia attorney, sent thirteen months after the fatal accident in March 1818, E.I. wrote that Moffat had an indenture for McColgan, a relative of Malloy. The indenture was for Capt. Moffat having paid for McColgan's trip from Ireland to America. All the men killed in the 1818 explosion had contributed at least one dollar to a fund to release McColgan from her contract; Malloy gave what was then a month's pay, ten dollars, to the McColgan fund.[4]

It seems that Moffat had somehow obtained the indenture after Malloy died and was claiming that he was still owed money for Miss McColgan's passage, even though E.I. had given him all but $20 of the fund, which E.I. had given to her. The expectation of the donors and the du Ponts was that the payment to Moffat would result in the release of McColgan from her indenture. But this appears not to have happened. E.I. wrote, "If I can be of any use myself as a witness in this case, I will willingly appear, as I consider the conduct of Moffat as highly reprehensible, after he had received our money upon the condition of letting the girl free."[5]

As with some others, the name of deceased potsman Hugh McColage presents a riddle wrapped in a mystery (with apologies to Sir Winston). The name "*McColage*" is in the petit ledgers. In the Delaware State Archives, the list of "goods and chattels" has the name "*McCalagn*," which could very well be a misspelling of "*McCalagan*." The original handwritten list of "goods and chattels" at the Hagley Museum and Library spells the name "*McCalegue*." Other spellings include "*McCalage*" and the documents written by Lammot du Pont have the name "*McCollan*."[6] Regardless of the spelling of his name, Hugh lived in the Toner household as a boarder and worked in the yards for one and a half years before his death.

Like Flinn and McColage, Michael Mooney boarded with Michael and Anne Gallagher Toner. He had begun working in the mills in early June 1813 during the War of 1812. Mooney was one of 200 men who joined the company between 1809 and 1814 as part of a hiring binge. The new employees started because of government requirements for more powder than the DuPont Company, as the major supplier of powder during the war, could produce in Eleutherian Mills. The company expanded the factory to include land called the Hagley Estate, downriver from Eleutherian Mills. The added eighty acres allowed the company to increase its powder making by two-thirds by 1814.

Mooney was more generous than other powdermen; he gave $2 to the McColgan fund (the others gave a dollar each); he donated $5 to the Catholic Church and another $3 to "the church in town";[7] and he gave a dollar to the Sunday school when the requirement for single employees was one-quarter of that. Mooney was literate— the listing of his physical assets included three book, valued at thirty-seven and a half cents.[8]

As with Michael McLaughlin, the company received letters inquiring into Mooney's estate. Two letters arrived nine and over twenty years after the 1818 explosion. The first, from attorney Samuel MacCracken, of Lancaster, Ohio, to "R. Dupont Esq.," merely asked for information about the estate of Michael Mooney on behalf of his brothers, John and Henry. Stating that he didn't want to make the siblings go through the expense of issuing a power of attorney until they knew the status of the estate, he asked the company if there were existing funds in it. On April 14, 1819, the company had passed $65 that accrued to Mooney's estate to its administrators, William Martin and Peter Hendrickson. No written response to MacCracken's request appears in the company files, not even a referral to the administrators who held the money.[9]

A second letter arrived twenty-one years after the 1818 explosion. The message, dated September 1839 and addressed to E.I. DuPont de Nemours, Esq.,[10] was a power of attorney for Elizabeth Mooney, "wid[ow] & relict" of Henry Mooney on behalf of herself and her four children. The document requested that E.I. send the assets remaining in the Mooney estate, held by administrators Hendrickson and Martin (although only Peter Hendrickson's signature is on the "goods and chattels" listing), to M.Z. Kreider, Mrs. Mooney's lawyer. There is no sign of a response.

While Mooney had $16 worth of goods when he died, refinery worker John O'Brien had $2.57. Mooney's "goods and chattels" list has four coats, seven shirts, two trunks full of clothing, and more. O'Brien owned one coat, two waistcoats, one handkerchief, one shirt and forty-seven cents in cash. He boarded with Peter and Anne Gallagher and died five months after taking the job.

Brothers Edward and Thomas Reynolds and another brother James, along with Edward's wife, Eleanor, and their daughter Mary Ann, made the perilous Atlantic voyage on the ship *Diana*, leaving their hometown of Belturbet, in Annagh Parish, County Cavan in north-central Ireland.[11] This emigration was somewhat atypical in that the usual pattern was for one family member to make the voyage and, after amassing enough money to pay for additional family voyages, send for the others. Both Edward and Thomas began working in the mills within two months of their August 1816 trek.

Thomas and James boarded with their brother Edward and sister-in-law Eleanor. Current-day Reynolds descendant Nona Kelly Smith says daughter Elizabeth was born in Ireland in 1799; she may have made the ocean voyage later than the rest of the family. Edward and Eleanor had one more child. Isabella was born the year her father died, but we don't know if the birth was in the first quarter, before her father's death, or after he died in March.[12]

Besides the money Edward and Eleanor received for boarding Thomas and James, Eleanor earned a dollar a month for doing washing for her brothers-in-law (besides performing the same task for the rest of her family). Edward left $14 to his widow and, a few months later, Eleanor received $56.17 from the estate of her late brother-in-law, Thomas.[13]

We can speculate with some certainty how James felt when he lost his two brothers, the three having faced the hardship of the ocean voyage and then the dangers of working in the powder for the brief few months the trio was together in America.

John Strain was another explosion victim who boarded with the Gallaghers. He had likely made the Atlantic voyage in 1811. According to records of the ship *Juno*, Master (Captain) Thompson at the helm, the brig landed at New York City after a fifty-six-day passage from Belfast with one hundred souls on board.[14] Strain, whose surname is a County Down variant of the name Strahan or O'Strahan, started working in the mills in late June 1817. He came from the tiny village of Dromore, twenty miles southwest of Belfast.[15]

Patrick Tollin was a powderman who did not last a full year in the employ of the DuPont Company. Starting service in the middle of August 1817, by January of the next year he was earning his regular pay of $12 a month. He worked overtime to raise his take to $21. Nancy Dougherty, no stranger to the vicissitudes of working in the powder, having suffered her husband's death in the 1815 explosion, lost her tenant Patrick when he died in the 1818 explosion. The company turned his assets over to his kin John Tollin, who, with another $229 he had amassed, left the company in early May 1818, only too aware of the dangers inherent in making black powder.[16] No one could blame those workers who moved on to safer jobs.

Peter Tungberg was listed in the petit ledgers as "Tonegeback" or "Tunegeback" in various other renditions. In an entry, "Tonegeback" is the page label but in small print at the top of the page is the name "Tunberg." Tungberg was part of the group of surviving powdermen who helped restore the mills after the June 1815 explosion; he had joined the company a few months earlier and made steady progress. He made rapid advancement through the ranks because of the loss of so many men in the 1815 explosion.[17] We will never know what piece of luck saved him in 1815 or what twist of fate ended his life in 1818.

John Torrey, David Wilson, and John Donahue were powdermen who spent only a few months in the mills before succumbing to injuries sustained in the latest explosion. Because Torrey had no assets, the DuPont Company had to pay the $11.37 in paperwork fees and other expenses required by New Castle County regulations. David Wilson had almost $100 in his account. On June 7, 1819, the company issued a check for $94.74 to attorney William Wilson on behalf of George Wilson, Joseph Wilson, Jane Wilson, James Wilson, and Theodore Wilson, siblings of the deceased.[18] Even though that was a tidy sum, it could not make up for the sudden loss of a beloved brother. John Donahue's account contained $3.69 when he died and his estate was settled six months after his death.

In Lammot du Pont's catalog of happenings in the mills from 1803 to 1856, he lists Patrick Boyle as a "boy." The records belie this description; they show him starting in mid-August 1815, at $10 a month, not a wage a boy earned in those days. By late 1816, he was earning $16 a month,[19] his wage at his death in 1818.

There is ample evidence in the records to show that Thomas Kennedy, a single powderman, died in the 1818 explosion, but, inexplicably, his name does not appear in most listings of men killed. Even Francis Gurney du Pont's detailed account of explosions does not list Kennedy. The belief that he died is somewhat supported by the taking of a personal inventory in May 1818, at about the same time as lists of goods were filed for other powdermen killed in the blast.

The bookkeepers at the DuPont Company spelled William Allison's name "Addison." He was a single powderman whose mother and father lived in the Old Country, probably in the small seaside village of Rathmullen on Lough Swilly. Lough, pronounced "loch," is the Irish word for lake but this body of water is an inlet from the North Atlantic. Nothing more is known of Allison.

The Dan Dougherty killed in the 1818 disaster could have been either Junior or Senior. The ledgers amplify the confusion. The 1817 ledger lists Dan Jr. as having started in late June that year, but leaving in early September and signing for his accumulated pay, $6.90. He boarded with Phillip and Anne Gallagher, as did several of the other men.

By the time young Dan left, his father had earned a $2 a month raise. His account was debited for the same amount as the check for Dan Junior but then was credited with that amount when the bookkeepers realized their mistake. As we have seen, it was easy to confuse people with like names. The 1818 ledger lists only Daniel Dougherty, no Junior. It appears it was Dan Senior who perished in the blast in March.

Whether William Dougherty, another man killed in the blast, was related to Daniel is unknown. The ledger shows that William was a bit of a drinker, perhaps more so than other workers. A single ledger, the one for 1817, has three entries in June alone for more than a gallon and a half of whiskey, totaling $2.25 (a quart was priced at $.30, a gallon at $1.50). No other powderman in the ledger had the cost for that much whiskey taken out of his account.[20]

Phillip Dugan was a refinery worker, hired at $13 per month in May 1816. For an unknown reason, his wage was lowered $1 in October. His pay was reduced a further $2 in 1817, perhaps because he changed jobs within the mills. In the 1818 ledger, he was back up to the $12 figure and was listed as a powderman. He may have felt that, over time, he could do better financially as a powderman than a refiner. It is not known what kind of refiner he was; two of the ingredients of powder, sulfur and saltpeter, needed refining prior to incorporation with charcoal to make black powder.

Patrick McCarren started with the DuPont Company in mid-summer 1817 at the usual $10 a month but quickly rose to making $12. He boarded with Mrs. Brady.

His surname may have been Kernan. The inventory of his possessions after his demise lists him as Kernan. In addition, the administrator of his estate received a check from the company in the name of Kernan. If his name was, indeed Kernan, or even if this was an error by some registrar along the way, he may have made the transatlantic voyage on board the *Tiffin*, sailing from Limerick, and landing in New Bedford, Massachusetts in June of 1817.[21] This debarkation fits with his start date at the mills.

The first James Cunningham to lose his life in a powder explosion worked very hard and lived frugally, as evidenced by the entries for him in the petit ledgers. In May 1816, for example, he toiled an additional nine days worth of work and earned more than double his monthly pay of $13. A year after he died in the 1818 blast, another James Cunningham, perhaps a son, signed for his accrued account of $485, about $12,700 in today's currency. The deceased Cunningham was laid to rest at Old Swede's Cemetery.

It is appropriate here to illustrate how newsmen in a hurry could mangle names by a verbal communication written or by transcription errors. Below is a verbatim account from the Saturday, March 28, 1818 edition of the *Essex Register*, a Salem, Massachusetts newspaper:

> "A gentleman who left Wilmington yesterday, had handed us the following list, (which he deems correct) of the unfortunate victims of the explosion on Thursday, last.
>
> Killed
>
> John Torry, Glendemot parish, Ireland
> William Allison, R. Mullen, do.
> Michael Town and wife, co. Donegal
> John Moony, Eunishowen
> Daniel Dougherty, do.
> Wm. Dougherty, do.
> A young man, do. not recollected
> Hugh Fennegan, Michael Mooney, David Flinn,
>   Hugh Bready, John Strain, John Dunney, places not known

Seducing the Workers

> Hugh M'Callion, Inver co.
> Philip Gallagher, do.
> John Brady, jr. Patrick Brady, John Brady, sen. Thomas
>   Kennedy, Patrick Kernagneu, co Caven
> Edward Bradley, Lever Kenny, John Donahoo, John OBrien,
>   Philip Dugan, David Wilson, places not known
> Edward and Thomas Rennels, Belterfet
> Patrick Boyle, place not known
> Peter Croney, Droghady
> A young man named Pearce, from Baltimore
> Michael McMullen, Duerg Bridge
> Peter Turnborg, not known
> One or two more not recollected
>
> Injured
>
> John Dell, Patrick Meliou, Hugh Linch, Patrick Quiet,
>   Francis Campbell, Charles Dalmas"

    Several points should be noted in the above account. First, the use of "do." This was how the papers used the interjection "ditto." So, for example, William Allison and R. Mullen were from the same parish as John Torry.

    Second, the writer of the column fractured fully one-third of the names, starting with "Michael Town and wife," (Michael Toner); "John Dunney," (Dunnery); the Rennels brothers (Edward and Thomas Reynolds); and "Peter Croney," (Peter Cooney), to name a few. We can forgive the newspaper writer, as he (most reporters were men then) wrote the piece from fourth- or fifth-hand information communicated with increasing errors as it passed from person to person.

    Notice the phrase "[name] not recollected." One report states that the conflagration killed a visitor. His host should have known his name, but the host may have died in the explosion.

    The "young man named Pearce, from Baltimore" was Thomas Pierce and, according to the *Berks and Schuylkill Journal*, he was "Listed as wounded, but died on Friday night last." The paper reported that John Dunnery died at roughly the same time.

    Note the name "Lever Kenny." There is no such name in the DuPont petit ledgers; it remains a mystery who this was; perhaps he was the visitor killed?

A few final points: John "Torry" was from Clondermot Parish, known as Glendermot. John Mooney hailed from Inishowen, Ireland's northernmost peninsula. Hugh "M'Callion" was from a small village named Inver, in County Donegal; there is no County Inver in Ireland. The "Rennels" brothers came from Belturbet, a town partly in the parish of Drumlane, but chiefly in Annagh, barony of Lower Loughtee, County Cavan, the spelling of the county from which the John Bradys came. Peter "Croney" was from Drogheda, mostly in County Louth, partially in County Meath on the east coast of the island. Duerg Bridge, from which Michael "McMullen" (McLaughlin) came, is today known as Skirts of Urney, or simply Urney, a townland in County Tyrone.[22]

Although 1818 marked the peak of a business boom, that year's powder yard explosion was a harbinger of troubled economic times. In the months after the March incident, the unraveling of the American economy began, slowly at first and then, in the following year, becoming a full-fledged panic. Interest rates climbed, businesses and banks failed — those that held on knew more stress than ever before — real estate values plummeted, prices for goods dropped precipitously, putting downward pressure on wages.

In short, as one author wrote, "The crash of 1819 was the first home-grown depression the nation had experienced and therefore all the more frightening for those who experienced it."[23] On average, wages across the nation fell 25 percent. Agricultural wages fell by 67 percent from 1818 to 1819.[24] On the Brandywine, the number of powdermen during that span dropped from 115 to 60 because of the decline in orders for powder, and the 1818 accident.[25]

Luckily, the 55 workers who left the employ of the DuPont Company would not have had a difficult time finding work elsewhere. There were more jobs open than people to fill them. Population growth in the nation was not keeping up with increases in available positions.

The early 19th century was an opportune time for factory owners to appeal for workers by offering higher wages, because of the dearth of workers in the young nation. It was common for the proprietor of a business to convince, or at least try to "steal," experienced workers to leave their current employer and work for the new owner. The DuPont Company was not immune to such efforts. Three of the men killed in the 1815 or 1818 explosions were principals in one such attempt.

Seven years before Richard Dougherty's death and ten before the deaths of Michael Toner and Hugh Finigan, the trio was drinking at nearby Buck Tavern with two other powdermen and Charles Munns, a recruiter for power mills in Richmond, Virginia. In a deposition in court dated February 6, 1809, powderman George Wallace said Munns offered Toner $20 a month to move to Virginia to work at a mill there. Wallace swore that Munns promised him $25 per month to make the same move. Toner was earning half of Munns' offer.

Munns was a continual thorn in Irénée's side. In December 1808, he had made offers to DuPont Company men Hans Peebles and Joseph Baughman, convincing the latter to steal a forty-pound brass stamper. The two gave Munns information on the company's methods for making gunpowder.

Irénée accosted Munns at Buck Tavern, near the powder mills, and gave him "a severe drubbing." A court fined E.I. $15. Du Pont friend Peter Bauduy followed Munns to Philadelphia and had him arrested. The authorities found detailed descriptions of powder manufacturing in Munns' pockets.

City officials jailed him a short time; those in New Castle did likewise upon his release, but exonerated him because he had not stolen the machinery and they could not prove he ordered the heist.

Ellis and Page, the proprietors of the Richmond mills Munns was recruiting for, denied any responsibility for his actions. The DuPont Company sued the southern firm for $10,000 but dropped the suit. E.I. wanted to punish Baughman for the theft, but Virginia authorities, eager to advance their state's ability to produce powder, refused to extradite him. Munns countersued but the case went fallow.[26]

Irénée was so perturbed by the late 1808 events that he wrote: "Our Trade is so Dangerous that very few persons wish to devote themselves to it. The Safety of our Family, the Safety of the families in our Employ, the safety of the farmers who live in our Neighborhood has imposed upon us the absolute duty, of making choice of Steady, Sober men and of establishing the most rigid discipline among our workmen in all that we have Succeeded until the Visit of Chas. Munns. What was the effect or results of His Visit?"

He outlined the results: "1. To entice away Hans Peebles who had been for Several years past busied to refine part of our materials. 2. To raise the Ideas of the whole Set of our workmen so as to put us under obligation either to submit to the presentations given them by C. Munns' offers, or to dismiss them at once."

He continued with his list: "3. To make them unruly for there is no possibility for us to maintain under the Same Severe regulations persons persuaded that other people will Treat them better than We do, although they had been perfectly satisfied to live with us for Several years back. 4. To expose us thereby to loose all our hands and be subsequently compelled to Suspend our works." And, "5. In fine to Endanger our lives, Those of all our hands and neighbors by the consequences which might have resulted from the Said C. Munns having fuddled our men."[27]

Irénée informed his father that the circumstances had one positive result. He observed that the incident might deter others from persuading his workers to leave, stating, "We have an excellent set of men, all peaceful and hard workers. I trained them all, and congratulate myself that I have been able to collect so good a staff—an invaluable and rare asset in all manufactures and in all countries, in this one." He continued, "If the first attempt to take away our men had succeeded, the men would have had an exaggerated idea of their own importance and the confusion would have been irreparable." E.I. told Pierre Samuel that, since Munns's arrest, he had restored "perfect order."[28]

Two years later, another attempted "seduction" of his workers confronted Irénée. In December 1811, the company received a note from Dr. Thomas Ewell of Washington, D.C., asking about starting a powder factory. He asked to have technical information and a superintendent sent to his location. E.I. rebuffed him. Ewell sent a second letter requesting detailed information on powder making and stated his wish to see the DuPont process for a month. E.I. ignored the request.

In August 1812, Ewell advertised in the *American Watchman*, offering $800 per year for a superintendent, $500 for foremen, and good wages to a dozen "good hands." He sent a man named Mitchell who once worked for DuPont, to meet with individual powder men in Wilmington. Mitchell spoke with Hugh Finigan and Patrick Quig, kin of Thomas Quig, offering them $500 and free housing to join the Washington concern. Finigan and Quig told Irénée of Mitchell's approach.

Irénée wrote to Ewell, denouncing the attempt and threatening to publish the written communications from him. While E.I. lost a handful of men to the Washington factory, he managed a measure of revenge by issuing a

Seducing the Workers   35

pamphlet about the affair; the title *Villainy Detected* sums up his thoughts.[29]

Author Peter Petersen writes that in January 1812 a suspicious explosion caused the loss of a part of the mills. Petersen says E.I. investigated the accident and determined someone set it as "the result of malice for the purpose of injuring us." The author surmises that the detonation resulted from the beating E.I. administered to Charles Munns in 1808.[30] This is unlikely. First, company records do not show a mill explosion occurring in January 1812. Second, it is improbable that revenge by Munns would occur four years after his conflict with the du Ponts. Maybe the author of the story that E.I. investigated the explosion got the wrong date for it.

The 1818 tragedy was the first time the local papers used the phrase "blown to atoms" to explain the effects of the powerful explosions; it was far from the last. The article did not refer to human flesh, as did so many later articles, but to a chair in which E.I.'s daughter, Evelina Gabrielle Bidermann, was sitting. The newspaper stated she was "little hurt." One wonders how the user of the furniture could escape injury in a mishap that destroyed the chair.[31]

It took two months for news of the March explosion to reach Scotland's newspapers, where the *Caledonian Mercury* told its readers the gory details. The article repeated the fiction that a picture of Napoleon in E. I.'s home was not damaged.[32]

A Wilmington newspaper set the record straight on the picture: "It might have been supposed that the real circumstance attending the late explosion on the Brandywine were, in themselves, sufficiently extraordinary & lamentable to satiate the most voracious appetite for the wonderful." Continuing, the reporter wrote, "Truth requires from us to state…there was no portrait of Napoleon Bonaparte in the house of Mr. Dupont…and consequently, that this miraculous incident, like most modern miracles, existed only in the immagination of the inventor."[33]

A Trenton newspaper lectured the instigators of the Napoleon falsehood: "It would seem…that the promulgators of it suppose that there was a specific interposition of Providence for the preservation of the picture. For ourselves, we are sorry to see such a sentiment inculcated." The article added: "More than thirty men, nearly all from Ireland, lost their lives on that deplorable occasion—and would the publishers of this paragraph insinuate that those lives were of less value in the sight of Heaven than the picture of Napoleon Bonaparte who had occasioned the death of as many millions!"[34]

Another editor repeated the false claim and added, "Would that the original had retained his station alike unhurt, amidst the political explosions and convulsions of Europe."[35]

The *Christian Messenger* of Middlebury, Vermont, cited another newspaper: "The editor…makes the following remarks. 'While the sensible and warm body is engaged in committing to the tomb the cold and lifeless corpse, death stands beside the grave and whispers to the surviving mourners, prepare to become likewise the subjects of my empire of dust and ashes.'" The paper continued: "When we see some extraordinary agent in motion beyond the power of human strength or of skill to resist, we tremble and sink into insignificance… we tremble with fear and prostrate ourselves in the dust…."

Many wondered about the cause of the 1818 explosion. When the survivors, proprietors, the press, or the public speculated, knowledge was scarce. Most who knew what happened were dead. Bias, the viewer's psychological status, the time between the event, and recollection all colored the stories related by survivors.

Again turning to Francis Gurney du Pont's rendition, we learn that one man may have carried fire, in the form of an ember, into the glazing mill. "It might be so as it is well known that the preceding day being 'St. Patrick's Day' and the workmen generally Irish, they had been frolicking all night and some of them appeared intoxicated in the morning and might in that situation have ventured in the yard without their usual care."[36]

DuPont cites another possibility, writing that one of the drunk men was the foreman of the Eleutherian Mills, a man named D'Autremont. One can only guess why he was tipsy on this Thursday morning, as he was of French origin and unlikely a St. Patrick's Day celebrant. F.G. wrote, "D'Autremont apparently instructed the glazing mill operator to give his machinery more speed, despite the workers protest that its spindle was overheating." He added, "D'Autremont fired the worker and left the yard to get another drink at the provision store; the unattended mill overheated, triggering an explosion that leveled seven buildings and killed thirty-four people."[37]

A Wilmington resident, Mrs. John (Anna Wright) Rumsey, wrote to her sister, stating another cause: "It is said the poor thoughtless creatures who were Irishmen almost to a man, had been so engrossed by the keeping of St. Patrick's Day that they neglected to grease a part of the machinery." How a person, knowing nothing of black powder manufacturing, could think this is unknown. She was willing to listen to, or read and pass on hearsay, rumor, or gossip, especially as it related to a minority group on the bottom of the social ladder.

Reports showed that the cause might have been more sinister than an accident. One worker said he saw a man running from the glazing mill seconds before the explosion. As a result, the company tightened security at the mills to ward off potential threats of sabotage.[38]

Because of this disaster, the company stopped liquor sales at the stores near the mills. The du Ponts allowed their on-duty employees to consume a ration of molasses and vinegar mixed in water, "as much as they could drink in lieu of wiskey."[39] They called the concoction "switchel." Temperance advocates were fans of the drink, as it provided the pleasurable burn of alcohol; many considered it a good thirst quencher.[40]

The substitution of switchel for whiskey did not make much of a dent in whiskey consumption in the workers' off-times. The ledgers are replete with purchases of the stuff which had a storied history in the "olde sod." Used as a legitimate medicine, uiscebeatha,[41] translated as "water of life," "[whiskey] scowereth all scurf; it sloweth age; it cutteth flegme; it pounceth the stone, it expelleth g[r]avel; it keepeth the head from whirling, the mouth from maffling, the stomach from wambling, the heart from swelling, the belly from wirtching, the guttes from rumbling…it is a sovereign liquor."[42]

If the Irish workers did not buy whiskey, they may have produced their own alcoholic drink called poitin,[43] a class of home-made drink crafted illegally in Ireland after the British banned it in 1831. They made it from grain, sugar, potato, even treacle. The sin of making poitin was told to a bishop, if confessed at all, as a village priest was not high enough in the Catholic hierarchy to receive confession of such an enormous sin.[44]

The public responded generously to the tragic reports of the 1818 explosion. Several leading citizens of nearby Philadelphia collected money for the relief of the widows and orphans. Stephen Kingston of the city wrote to E.I. to tell him that the Philadelphians had raised the handsome sum of $600. The widows Reynolds and Bradley, with four children each, collected $105; the widows with two children (Brady and Gallagher) got $55 each. Catherine Slane Finigan received $50 (compared to the two widows with two children, given that she had one child and was pregnant with another). The Toner orphans received $100, and the other Brady widow, with three children, had $80 added to her account. Fifty dollars went to Thomas Quig's kin and to the injured Hugh Lynch.

The 1818 explosion would be the worst accident ever at the Brandywine factory in terms of loss of life. Despite efforts to hire and train willing workers, reduce the availability of liquor, and improve security, the DuPont Company would lose many more lives in the years to come. ■

▪ 4 ▪
Epitaph to a Perfect Workman

> [Henry Kyle] had by his long and faithful services well
> earned the good opinion & friendship of his employers…
> a most worthy & faithful hand…much respected by all
> persons acquainted with him.
> —*The DuPont Company*

The appalling losses from the massive cusp-of-spring explosion in 1818 included not only workers who were friends of the du Ponts. They also lost several mill buildings; quantities of finished powder, estimated to be 60,000 pounds; production capabilities for a few months; men who lived through the conflagration but decided not to press their luck by remaining; and others laid off.

The company continued to produce powder in the Hagley part of the mills, as none of the buildings in this section suffered damage, or "injury," as they used the term then, from the explosion to the north. However, total production was half that of the previous year.

The years following the massive 1818 blast saw a few explosions, causing only minor injuries. In June 1820, while the company continued to use the dangerous pounding mills, one in the upper yard exploded with no injuries. Another pounding mill and the granulating mill experienced a non-injury explosion two years later. Lammot du Pont's annual summary of company activity mentions that, in late January 1822, the temperature was so low they dismissed the workers with pay for their board only. Lammot wrote, "The thermometer at noon rose to two below zero." He noted that a "freshet," a flood, leveled two upper-yard roll mills and a storm off Great Egg Harbor, New Jersey, sank ships carrying eight-ton rollers cast in a West Point, New York, foundry and destined for the DuPont mills.[1] It was during this interregnum that E.I. realized the value of the English invention of the roll mill as a replacement for the pounding mill. In June 1824, roll mill two in the Hagley yard exploded, causing a minor injury.

Roll Mill at the Hagley Museum. (Photo by Elton G. Grunden)

At the end of the summer of 1825, the glazing mill blew up, injuring three men. The accident occurred when Bob, a powder-cart horse, backed a cart into a scraper the workers used to clean their shoes; the resultant spark shot fire across the porch. An airborne building stone came down on top of workers Francis Casey and William Green, wounding them.

In the early 1830s, America experienced slave revolts (Nat Turner); sideshows (Chang and Eng, the Siamese twins);[2] religious awakenings (Lyman Beecher and Charles Finney); an epidemic of cholera; the Great Eclipse; and, according to one English author, not much fun. "I never saw the population so totally divested of gaiety; there is no trace of this feeling from one end of the Union to the other. They have no fetes, no fairs, no merrimaking, no music in the streets, no Punch, no puppet shows," wrote Fanny Trollope in 1832.[3] On the Brandywine, fewer than two hundred hard workers who labored long hours and took their jobs seriously made DuPont black powder, with employment down one-third in ten years.

Seven years had intervened since the last major (non-fatal) explosion in the Hagley yards when, on August 25, 1832, the first deadly blast in fourteen years killed two powdermen.

Patrick Holland first appears on the companys' books in the summer of 1827, after arriving in America on the ship *Israel* with his brother Thomas and a Mary Holland, perhaps a daughter of John, another sibling. She caused a minor ripple when agent John Welsh found out how old she was. He wrote to the company: "The present is to advise you of the arrival of part of the passengers I have engaged to bring you from Derry a bill of whole passages is at foot—a small difference will be observed caused by Mary Holland's being 12 yrs whereas she was represented on being under making her of course a full passenger."[4]

Despite the kerfuffle, Patrick made his way to the banks of the Brandywine and started working for the DuPont Company. His brother John had begun work in 1822 and sponsored Patrick's journey from Ireland. The brothers, each making $15.50 a month, sent money back to Eire for their families. Mulrooney writes, "By the spring of 1829, the rest of the Holland family had resolved to leave. The party that landed in Wilmington that summer included Patrick's wife, Eleanor McMackin, and their two children, John (5) and Nancy (2); a sister, Anne Holland; and the family patriarch, Patrick Holland, Sr."[5]

Like the Doughertys, Hollands flooded the area, with over thirty bearing the name living in northern Delaware by the middle of the century. Patrick and Eleanor added to their brood with the birth of James in May 1830, and Patrick two years later, eight months before his father's death.

Mulrooney says, "When several sons named their eldest sons for a common grandfather, they reinforced group and family solidarity. They also created confusion in the historical record, for the pattern typically produced several individuals with the same personal name and surname in a single generation." The author continued, "Brothers Thomas, John, and Patrick Holland, for example, all named their firstborn sons John. That their father answered to 'Patrick' points to variations in the pattern."[6] She notes evidence that Irish naming patterns varied with the island's geography.[7]

It wasn't until Patrick and Eleanor's third son came along that an heir was named Patrick, and, since this son was born after his father's death, it is likely his mother named him to honor her dead husband, not the baby's grandfather.

A tombstone placed in the ground after the 1832 explosion, now sits in the basement of St. Peter's Church in Wilmington. (The church later paved over its cemetery and moved the markers indoors.) The headstone honors Daniel Toy, about whom we know a great deal because of the diligent detective work of Reese Robinson, a Wilmington genealogist married to a Toy descendant.

Daniel, his wife Rosanna Coyle Toy and one of their Donegal-born sons, James, traveled on the schooner *Mary Ann* under the captaincy of John Beyea. It made its way from New Brunswick, Canada,[8] to Philadelphia, where, on September 19, 1817, the three Toys disembarked to their new life in America.[9] Family lore says the three-person family lived in Philadelphia for their first year in America. It is possible the family stayed there for their first three years.

The Toys left son and brother Cornelius, known as Neil, in Ireland, probably with Rosanna's family, living in Aughnish, a townland in County Donegal. Neil was four years old, James two; we do not know why they left Cornelius in Ireland, but he made his way to America when he was nineteen. The ship's passenger list shows that Neil arrived on the *Deveron* in Wilmington on July 23, 1832.[10] After fifteen years of separation from his parents and younger brother, what a reunion that must have been. He had a month with his father before the latter's untimely death in August. After his father died, Neil started working for the DuPont Company.

Daniel Toy's first day at work for the DuPont Company was in late May 1820. In August they made him a powderman. Soon after he started work in the mills, he and Rosanna added to the family. When James was six, Anne, known as Nancy, was born. Then in succession came Jane (1822), Mary (1826), and Daniel (1828). Mary would become the unluckiest of the Toy offspring, as we will see in Chapter Seven.

Before he became a powderman, Daniel and his small family roomed with the Owen Kings.[11] King, Elenor Bradley's second husband after her first died in the 1818 explosion, boarded with Mrs. Bradley in early 1819, then moved in with Mrs. Gallagher in June, then back into Mrs. Bradley's in July, and married her in December. Moving from boarding house to boarding house was a common occurrence in the small enclaves in and around the DuPont mills. Marrying the landlady was not. By late 1822 the Toys themselves were renting living space to others.[12]

Like many other workers, Daniel encouraged his children's education at the Brandywine Manufacturer's Sunday School. The firm charged unmarried workers twenty-five cents a year to support tuition at a one-room schoolhouse on the mill property for mill workers' kids and other children in the vicinity. It was not a Sunday school in the 21st century meaning of the word, although religion and moral teaching were a significant part of the curriculum. The du Ponts supported a variety of religious practices among their workers and so built the Sunday school in 1817. While single men paid a quarter, the cost for married men was double that. Daniel educated his family in 1830 at the cost of twelve and a half cents per child[13] for the entire year.

The BMSS kept meticulous records of their scholars' progress. Besides being nondenominational, there were no grade placements as we know them today. School leaders placed scholars based on their capabilities, not their age. So, for example, Mary Toy entered school at age four and a half in the ninth class, while her sister, Ann, entered the eighth class at age six. James, the older child of the Toys at ten years old, entered the second class. The instructor might have looked from his[14] lectern and seen a seventeen-year-old boy sitting next to a five-year-old. Perhaps the teen spoke only Irish when he made the move across the sea and was learning to speak English, starting at the same level as the five-year-old.

The school flourished under the leadership of Irénée's elder daughter, Victorine, who had lost her husband after eleven weeks of marriage in 1814. She attempted to galvanize students to higher learning by offering small incentives at the end of each session (semester). The inducements ran from cheaply made booklets to full-fledged, hardcover books.

For example, Mary Toy received her first premium in 1831, when she was five years old, a book entitled *Sailor's Son*. The next year she earned *The Lilly* as her premium, and in 1834, *Busy Bee* was the prize. Her siblings collected books as incentives. James, eleven years old when his sister Mary was born in 1826, earned a copy of *The Cottage Boy, or, The History of Peter Thompson*, in which the young Peter himself receives an award, a book from his uncle after the uncle queries him on the Bible.[15]

The American Sunday School Union (ASSU), based in nearby Philadelphia, published *The Cottage Boy*. Like most of the premiums given to deserving students in the BMSS, the Union laded the book with a moral and references to God. The ASSU chapbooks were efforts to send the children of the day a moral message, tinged with Christian allusions. One premium handed out in 1833 was a booklet produced by the Union entitled *Six Penny Glass of Wine*, which starts: "The following story is a relation of facts, and shows how fast a boy grows in habits of transgression; and how easily he passes from little sins to gross and dreadful crimes."[16]

But, alas, premiums didn't work for everyone. The register of those handed out in 1829 refers to one Arthur Tominey, who, "forfeits his premium for bad conduct." He gave up his October reward for the same reason. His attitude improved (whether it was because of his desire to receive awards is unknown), as his teachers awarded him the sixteen-page booklet *The Patient Pastor*, another publication of the ASSU. He later had to give up this bonus for his offensive behavior. Nine other boys relinquished their premiums for poor conduct.

Premiums for honorable conduct and scholarship weren't only in the form of books; the 1829 register shows scholars receiving pin cushions, Swiss muslin collars edged with shells, square or round band boxes, prints with shell edging, and "a monkey pasted on pasteboard."

Arthur Tominey took his time learning to behave; in both January and April 1835, the school awarded him premiums, and he appears to have kept both.[17]

In 1941, Eugene Toy, a descendant of Daniel Toy, put together an extensive Toy family tree that covered the years 1780 to 1940. Although such trees may include mistakes or misinterpretations of historical information as to names, dates of birth, and death, it remains interesting to note entries in this family tree, many supported by other documents.

The Toy family stands out in its contribution to our understanding of the history of the DuPont Company and of workers lives. For example, Daniel's son, James, married Ann Curren and together had four children before her death in 1849. He then wed Bridget McCallin (or McCallion) and they had eleven children, five of whom died young, In 1854, grandson James died after living for five months.

It was common to give the second baby of the same gender the name of a deceased child; in September 1855, James and Bridget had another son named James, who died at seven months. This James had a twin, Neal, who lived to marry and to father four children. Owen lived eighteen months and Augustus and Mary lived just a few days. A third James, Henry, Joseph, and Eugene survived and married to continue the family name.[18]

A mystery surrounds Rosanna Coyle Toy's age at death, with various sources citing her age from 98 years to 104. Reese Robinson's blog[19] addresses the question and posits several possibilities. Her most likely date of death is August 7, 1879; the discrepancy arises from when she was born. *The Daily Republican*, a Wilmington newspaper, in its August 8, 1879, issue, wrote she was born the year before the United States achieved its independence, 1775. Her glowing obituary continued, "Mrs. Toy retained her mental faculties in a remarkable degree until she passed her centennial. For the last two or three years she failed very fast, hanging on to life with but a slender thread until this morning, when the silver thread was snapped asunder, the golden bowl was broken at the fountain, the spirit took its flight to the God who gave it, and the weary worn-out body sunk to rest."[20]

Rose's tombstone gives her birth year as 1780, which would make her ninety-eight when she died. The headstone lists her death as occurring in November 1878; Robinson believes that the stone cutter either received incorrect information or confused the date with another decedent.

Whatever her age, Rosanna Toy lived a long life, surviving after Daniel's death by continuing to board powdermen in her home on the DuPont Company property, which was free of rent, and by receiving the same annuity given other widows. By 1850, Rosanna was living in the Widow's Asylum on the DuPont property, along with Margaret Holland, widow of Thomas Holland; Rosanna Connor, relict of Patrick Connor; and Catherine Baxter, Malcolm Baxter's widow. As we will see in Chapter Five, these three men died in a significant explosion in 1847, with fifteen other workers.

Using powdermen's female relatives as workers in their own right was a predominant feature of 19th-century life on the property. In 1842 Jane Toy replaced her sister Mary as a domestic in the du Pont household.

John Thomas Toy, one of Daniel's grandsons, later operated a tavern near the works called the "William Penn" or "Toy's Tavern" on Creek Road, which became the area's Democratic Party headquarters. In the early 20th century, the Toy family owned several properties on Kennett Pike, near the powder mills. Letters in the Hagley Museum and Library files show that E.I.'s great grandson, who also carried the name Irénée, wanted to buy the acreage but felt the Toys asked too much for it. The lands became part of the Tower Hill School, of which Irénée, with other du Ponts, was the founder.[21]

The day after Holland and Toy died in the 1832 explosion, E.I.'s daughter, Eleuthera wrote a letter describing her father's narrow escape. "The stones fell thickly around him, but ever present Mercy preserved him from all injury." Naming Daniel Toy as "John," she stated that both men were honorable and industrious and had families. She wrote that neither man was "mangled," and her brother Alfred thought they were weighing powder when the explosion happened. She added that the workers perished instantly and suffered no pain.

She ended her missive with the thought that E.I. and the other DuPonts who assisted after the accident were "very deeply affected by the distress occasioned, particularly Brother [Alfred] who liked the men very much and regrets for their own sake as well as for their families."

Eleuthera's wasn't the only note resulting from the incident. In a letter to the editor of Philadelphia's *National Gazette*, the writer contradicted her surmise that the men were not disfigured. He wrote that "the two men were found, horribly mangled and blackened… covered with rubbish." He further maintained, "It would, I think, be the proper duty for the proprietor of these mills, as well as all the proprietors of gunpowder mills, to have the causes of these unaccountable explosions investigated and provided against. Sir Humphrey Davy's safety lamp has saved hundreds of lives; and science, no doubt, might be applied with excellent effect to the dangers which powder mills are exposed to."[22]

The 1830s continued to be a dangerous time in the DuPont Company yards. Following the deaths of Holland and Toy in 1832, fatalities continued to occur.

"On the 20th of June, [1834] MR. HENRY KYLE, of County Derry, Ireland. He lost his life by the explosion of a powder mill at du Pont's works on the Brandywine. He had been in this employment for upwards of nine years and was not absent from work over four days during this long period. A more industrious, sober, trustworthy man never left the shore of Ireland; that country which has furnished to us so many valuable citizens. His loss is deeply regretted by his employers and fellow workmen." The brief encomium, paid for by the DuPont Company, appeared on page three of the *Delaware Gazette* on June 23, 1834; the headline: "Epitaph to a Perfect Workman."[23] Alfred du Pont lauded Kyle, saying he "exceeded any man in our employment in the qualities of industry and saving."[24]

Kyle toiled for the company for nine years; his heirs worked far longer for his money. He was the illegitimate son of Henry Kyle, of Camnish Townland, north of Dungiven in County Derry. After Henry's birth to Anne Mullin, his father, a well-off landowner, had nothing to do with either mother or son. That didn't prevent the father from working through lawyers to get his son's $3,000 in assets. He engaged attorneys in America to request legislation by Delaware lawmakers to cede the property to him. In 1843, nine years after son Henry's death, the effort remained unsuccessful.[25]

Letters in the DuPont Company files attest to the work by Kyle's mother's family to get the funds. In 1845, the administrators doled out $195.21 to each of fourteen of Henry's cousins. In today's dollars, this was equivalent to $6,800.[26]

John McGinnis became the forty-eighth worker killed in the powder yards when, on September 17, 1835, he was cleaning roll mills five and six. He was married to Ann, or Annie, and they had a daughter born the year John died; whether she came before or after her father's death is unknown.

Eleven days after this explosion, another rocked the valley, this time, in the graining mill. It killed two workers, John Vance and John Greer. According to Francis Gurney du Pont's very short rendition of the blast, Peter Boisson, one of the few Frenchmen still working in the mills, ran the mill used to size the powder particles. F.G. wrote that Boisson took sick and left the mill to what Francis said were two new workers. The petit ledgers contradict this assertion, showing that Vance's first day was in early June of the previous year.[27] Greer started in 1832.[28] Once again, though, it is possible both men started with the company earlier but in non-powder-making positions.

By this time, thirty-two years after the mills opened, the newspapers were unmoved by such a "little" blast, as one of them reported in full: "Explosion.—One of the granulating mills connected with the works of Messrs. Du Pont's exploded yesterday morning. The mill was destroyed and, we regret to add, two lives were lost."[29] Vance is in the same cemetery as John McGinnis, Old Swede's in Wilmington.

It is probable John Greer was actually named Green. In an April 12, 1836, letter, written from Letterkenny, in County Donegal, two women claiming to be sisters of the deceased asked the company to remit eight pounds sterling left in Green's estate. The sisters refer to "your kind feelings for my Dear Brother," and continued by saying that they "never wanted a father when he was at home with us."

They gave several names to whom to send the money and signed the letter "Margaret Green other ways Wilson" and "Mary Green other ways Elvin," (indicating that Wilson and Elvin were their husbands). Margaret's spouse is probably "Mr. Matthew Wilson Letterkenny Marchant County Dunnigall," one person they designated as being eligible to receive the assets.[30] No response appears in the records.

Although the DuPont Company treated its workers well compared to many other firms, labor troubles first faced the du Ponts in 1835. Although Wilmington had a surfeit of barrel-makers, or coopers, they chose this time to go on strike. The men were not DuPont employees but what we might consider today sub-contractors. The company, in the year after the founder's death, sent letters to Philadelphia and Boston requesting their coopers' aid in making barrels for the storage and shipment of gunpowder. "It is of utmost importance for us not to yield to them," the company wrote, "for if we do, we shall soon have the same difficulty with all persons directly or indirectly in our employment, and as we do not see any prospect of raising the price of powder, our business would be materially injured."[31]

The DuPont Company's paternalistic practices and awareness of the dangers of powder manufacturing kept the death toll and the effects of injury down. Throughout the 19th century and the Industrial Revolution that characterized it, fewer numbers of injured and dead were attributed to blasts on the Brandywine compared to other workplaces.

The average industrial worker labored twelve to sixteen hours a day, six days a week. This compared to the eleven hours the powdermen toiled per day in the good-weather months, and nine hours in the winter, also on a six-day-a-week schedule.

The non-DuPont worker might manage a one-hour break during the workday, while the powder-making process allowed the mill workers long breaks between attending to their duties. For example, the men working in the mixing process might get a two-hour or more break while the roll mills were incorporating the ingredients. During the breaks, they may have only had to take five or ten minutes to water the mix, reducing the chance of explosion.

The workplace provided another positive comparison. A factory worker was confined to a noisy, dirty, and cramped space with little light. Powder-mill workers enjoyed working outdoors. Frigid winter days and sweltering summer days could be tough, but means were available to mitigate those conditions—warming huts in January and the cooling waters of the Brandywine in August.

Because of high unemployment rates, other employers could easily replace workers doing a simple, monotonous task in a factory, pay a low wage, and reduce employees' bargaining power. DuPont workers received irregular but substantial pay increases.

The number of deaths in the powder mills were low by 19th century standards, but this did not mean the toll of tragedy halted its march. The next fatal explosion killed Thomas Heatherington when a roll mill went up on November 22, 1836. He was most likely the Thomas Heatherington who set off from England in the summer of 1825, arriving in Philadelphia and starting to work in the mills in mid-August.

The following three years were quiet; five explosions were recorded, including two in roll mill four, but they were minor, causing little damage and no injury. Then, two weeks before Christmas 1839, John Cole was cleaning roll mill two in the Lower Yard when it exploded. It was the first detonation in the new Lower Yard (which had started operations the year before) and Friday, the thirteenth, which no doubt caused consternation to any superstitious men working that day.

In March of the following year, the workers lost three-fourths of a day of work, and pay, because of frosty weather. Six months later, they gave up another two and a quarter days because of political meetings, or so Lammot thought, writing "then politics ran very high." At the national Whig convention, William Henry Harrison edged Henry Clay, the founder of the party and a du Pont favorite (thus the name given Henry Clay Village, a worker's enclave) to win the nomination. Harrison won the presidency, only to die a month after his inauguration, during which he gave the longest inauguration speech on record, lasting two hours.

On another note, Christopher Cowan started work in the yards after that election; Lammot labeled him "a bad fellow," and we will find out why later.

Lammot's summary of 1842 does not mention John Houtton's death, but he died when his Hagley roll mill went up on May 18. John's name appears as Houghton in the 1840 U.S. Census, when they counted but did not name others in the household. The census listed one male and one female aged twenty to thirty and one of each, forty to fifty years old. The other older woman was John's spouse, Mary Gobin. The records are unclear but it is possible that John and Mary's son, James and his wife Bridget, were the other two people listed in the census. The DuPont Company ledgers show debits to John's account for Atlantic passages for his son and daughter-in-law.[32]

Canadian Michael Borrell came to work in early April 1818, recruited after the massive accident in mid-March of that year He worked in the mills for twenty-five years, until his death in an explosion on September 21, 1843. His father was an Italian, Joseph Michael, from Milan, his mother a French-Canadian, Agathe Elizabeth Dufresne, who had given birth to Michael on September 29, 1791. They baptized him in the Basilique Notre Dame of Montreal. Two years after his arrival in Delaware he married Christiann Long, a Delawarean.[33]

During his years at the mills, Michael and Christiann had nine children. Michael was used to an extensive family: he had three brothers and five sisters. The gender mix of his offspring was the opposite, three girls and six boys.

Borrell applied for citizenship, signing first papers showing his intention to become a citizen on December 15, 1830 and, after the waiting period, made his declaration in May 1833; powderman Peter Ramo[34] attested the declaration.

From their first year of housing workers, 1823, the Borrells had several boarders, including Thomas Heatherington, Charles and Michael O'Brien, and James McClafferty, all killed in explosions.

As of April 1830, four Borrell children—Alexis, Sarah, Joseph, and Agatha—and four boarders had joined Sophia (whose twenty-second birthday was the day her father died). The name Alexis might lead the reader to think they named him for a du Pont of the same name. Michael had a brother named Alexi, so we cannot know the origin of the name for the Borrell's second child. By 1837, the household had eight children, ranging in age from one and a half to sixteen years, including Jerome, Fabian, and George, and seven boarders. The Borrells received the customary $8 a month for each boarder, so at times, Christiann earned more than her husband. They added a child, Alfred, in 1838.[35]

The names of the Borrell children pepper the Sunday school registers, with positive comments: "very attentive" (Joseph Michael); and "attentive" (Fabian, which might have been his middle name; first name, Ferdinand). Their success as scholars is evident: Sarah Jane won a copy of *The Lilly*, the same book that Mary Toy won a year earlier. From 1827 through 1835, Sarah received awards for reading more than a dozen books, including *Four Seasons*, a volume her sister Sophie earned as a premium in 1829.[36]

The Borrell's eighth child, George W., later joined the 4th Delaware Infantry during the Civil War. It was a unit attached to 2nd Brigade, 4th Division, 5th Army Corps during the Battle of Cold Harbor, Virginia, part of U.S. Grant's Overland Campaign. Wounded in action by a sniper at Petersburg on June 23, 1864, a week into the Siege of Petersburg, he died of gangrene in the left lung on July 6, in Alexandria Hospital. They buried him in Alexandria National Cemetery. His surname is etched in the headstone as Barrell. In a connection to a later Brandywine explosion, George Borrell's unit fought at the Battle of Hatcher's Run, where another explosion victim's father won the Medal of Honor.[37]

Two of George's brothers served the Union in the war, Alfred, the last child, with an unknown unit. Joseph Michael was one of the first residents of Media, Pennsylvania, to enlist after the firing on Fort Sumter in 1861. A carpenter by trade, he worked on Media's Delaware County courthouse before enlisting for a three-year stint. He may have taken sick a year later, as he resigned while his unit was at Hilton Head, South Carolina; he received an honorable discharge in November 1862. Before his discharge, he was the second lieutenant of Company G of the 97th Pennsylvania Infantry.[38]

Joseph Michael rejoined the Union force as a member of the 203rd Pennsylvania Infantry in September 1864 and, according to the National Park Service registry of this unit, entered as a private and mustered out as a first sergeant. The *Chester Times* obituary cited above said he was a captain.

Two years after Michael died, the widow Borrell, in her early forties, remarried. Peter Ramo, who earlier attested Michael's declaration that he wanted to be a citizen, became Christiann's spouse. She died in 1884 and is buried at Wilmington's Old Swede's Church.

Two theories arose for the cause of the 1843 accident that killed Michael Borrell. One was that he suffered from a toothache and came from his home where he had held his hand to the stove, from which he carried "fire in his clothes." The other was that he tried to throw a barrel out of gear and "let it fall in;" into what it may have fallen is not clear.[39] This same source adds, "Now we know almost to a certainty he was opening a barrel, cause damp saltpeter."

Michael shares the dubious distinction of being one of the two earliest gravestones in St. Joseph on the Brandywine Cemetery.[40] His kin can take heart that, ten years after his death, he became the namesake for a son born to his son, Alexis, and his wife, Catharine, a birth for which Michael's daughter, Agatha, was a sponsor.[41]

We let the DuPonts have the last word on Borrell. In letters written the day after the accident, the company wrote to a gunpowder agent in Philadelphia, lamenting the fact that they lost "the oldest hand in our employment, (Michael Borrell) a man who having been with us since 1818 had by his long and faithful services well earned the good opinion & friendship of his employers; the poor fellow had lately purchased a farm, intending it as a home for himself & family in his old age."[42]

To another correspondent in New York, "We lost yesterday at noon one of our four dust mills; the quantity of powder 675 lbs., although in the state of dust made a pretty loud crash; it is in itself an affair of but small importance for we have ample time to rebuild before frost and have such means of fabrication as to hardly feel the difference of one mill, but we lost one man, a most worthy & faithful hand; he had been with us 25 years, had attained the head of the list; being the oldest hand in the mills and was much respected by all persons acquainted with him."[43] ■

▪ 5 ▪
Blown to Atoms

> They were heard bewailing their dreadful loss, at the
> distance of more than a mile.
> —*The Cecil Whig*

Borrell was the fifty-third man who perished at the powder works: forty-three died by the 1820s, eight in the 1830s, two in the forties' first three years. The rest of the 1840s saw only three fatal accidents, but the number lost rose to seventy-five.

It was during this period the American nativist movement was incubating in large eastern cities. Fearful of the immigrant Irish and more so their Catholicism, second- and third-generation Americans responded with powerful words and stronger weapons.

Americans placed the Irish into three categories. The first was the "lace curtain" Irish, "sympathetic to Anglo-Saxon sentiment and perhaps even a little ashamed of their Celtic background." Some changed their names to make them seem less Irish.

In the second group were the "shanty Irish," who showed no interest in anything not 100 percent Irish, that did not pertain to Ireland, and who didn't bother to apply for American citizenship.

Group three, Irish Americans, wanted to reduce prejudice against them and "were convinced that the best way to do so was to become good Americans."[1] It is likely the DuPont Irish felt part of the third group. Not all applied for U.S. citizenship but many did. And, as we see throughout this book, they became good Americans.

Not a year after Michael Borrell's death, the spilling of a box of powder against a hot stove took the lives of George Russell and James McDevitt. The mishap occurred in the Lower Hagley dry house at six a.m., July 24, 1844. An eyewitness said the two raised the sluice gates that allowed the water to flow and run the machinery and were back in the building when the explosion happened. This was two months after the first (and two weeks after the second) series of deadly Kensington riots in Philadelphia where so called "native Americans" fought with, killed, and were killed by, the Irish.

DuPont Boarding Books show Russell boarded in two places. The Rent Books mention him living in a house on Hiron's Banks, another of the small communities of workers and their families. Russell wed Mary Forest in 1841. A New York newspaper wrote that Russell left a wife and two children; the story below referred to three.

A humorous story is told of a Mrs. Russell, likely George's wife, who fell ill and requested extreme unction, the sacramental anointing of a person in immediate danger of death; the name is no longer in use by the Roman Catholic Church. It has been replaced by the phrase "last rites." The priest refused to administer last rites unless Mrs. Russell agreed to have her children attend school at St. Joseph; they were then attending the Brandywine Manufacturer's Sunday School. She agreed, and the priest gave her the rites. She recovered and, with tears in her eyes, told Victorine du Pont Bauduy she would not have consented to move her children if she had known she would live.[2]

Complacency remained the order of the day for the local papers. One article said, "An explosion of one of the mills in DuPont's yard took place yesterday morning. Two men killed."[3] That's it: no names, no mention of families, just that single line. That is, in part, why we know nothing of McDevitt.

A day short of the two-year anniversary of the accident that killed Russell and McDevitt, fourteen-year veteran Archibald Watson died while cleaning his mill. In a letter to Archibald's Belfast-based brother, John, Alfred du Pont wrote that Watson "had removed the powder outside & in cleaning off the hard scales on the runners, the dust & scales took fire; there are four doors to the mill, three are 5 feet 10 inches wide, one is 2 feet 2 inches, all four were open; he unfortunately went out of the mill, after the accident, through the narrow door, the very one through which he had removed the powder from the mill, and as he had left the powder just outside of the door (contrary to orders) the fire about his clothes, set off the mill charge of 50 lbs.; this injured him so much he died within 48 hours."[4]

The head of the DuPont Company added, "In our business there is risk that must be run & myself & brothers share it with the hands; unfortunately your brother lost his life by an accident of frequent occurrence & which seldom produces any worse result than a slight burn on the wrists."[5]

As in other cases of accidental death in the 19th century at DuPont and in other settings, it was easy enough for the proprietors of manufactories to place the onus on the workers for their demise rather than admitting the structure, machinery, or something else in the owner-built environment was the culprit.

Alfred pointed out that $800 was available in Watson's accounts, two-thirds of which was, by Delaware law, to go to the four remaining children (son John died of scarlet fever in 1843) and one-third to Margaret Anderson Watson, his wife. Mrs. Watson gave up her $100 widow's annuity in November 1847 to marry Thomas Houlton. The Houlton family grew by one when Margaret gave birth to a son, named for his father, a year later. Margaret, Arch Jr., Ann, and Isabella Watson, Episcopalians, received baptisms in the Catholic Church within a few years, presumably because Thomas Houlton was Catholic. The July 1846 accident that took the life of Archibald Watson was not the last tragedy to strike the Watson family. In 1884, his namesake, a laborer at the Delaware Iron Works and a resident of the Dobbinsville neighborhood of New Castle town near Wilmington, suffered an asthma attack. He tripped on a bucket on the stairs at home and suffered fatal injuries.[6]

The ebb and flow of business was reflected in the variations in the number of workers employed at the DuPont mills. In the period 1837-1839, the number of employees had reached a peak near 500, even though the Panic of 1837 had decimated the employment rolls elsewhere. However, in 1840, that number dropped by 40 percent. By the mid-1850s, it was back up to its high for the century.

The Hagley Mills were outproducing the original Eleutherian Mills, but not by much. In 1839, the Hagley contingent produced 4,000 more kegs than those to the north.[7] This was due to Hagley having newer machinery and, perhaps, more infrastructure and manpower than the Elutherian part of the factory.

By the time of the high-fatality accident in 1847 (and partly because of it), the figures were more disparate; even the newer Lower Mills produced twice as much as the Eleutherian Mills. Lammot du Pont cited increased railroad building as the reason for the increased total in the three yards of more than 70,000 kegs of powder that year.[8]

In another "blown to atoms" article in the spring of 1847, the newspapers announced a multi-fatality explosion, this time in the press house, graining mill, and packing house in the upper powder yards. On April 14, during the Mexican-American War, eighteen men were "hurried to the grave,"[9] according to one newspaper. Another paper said the victims were "old workmen."[10] Most were. The range of ages known was forty-seven to fifty-nine.

With nary a thought for the families who might read them, the newspapers printed that the bodies were so "torn to pieces that it was impossible to recognize them." They were "so dreadfully mangled, that but four of them could be recognized by their best acquaintances." The paper added, "Only nine of them had anything like the appearance of human beings."[11] Next to later 19th-century articles, this one seems mild by comparison.

Born in October of the year before, a child named Mary Green received her baptism in the Catholic Church on April 14, 1822.[12] She was the daughter of a powderman named William Green, and Maria Baker Green. To the day, a quarter century later, she lost her father to the 1847 explosion.

After making his way to the Brandywine from the tiny village of Ballinamallardd,[13] County Fermanagh,[14] Ireland, Green had started working for the DuPont Company late in 1818. He started as a laborer, but within two years was working in the powder. In 1827, he applied for U.S. citizenship and became a citizen two years later. In the intervening years, he and his wife, Maria, she of Dutch heritage, married and started their family, which grew to five children. Mary, their second child, was born in 1821. In August 1824, another girl was born, given the name Maria. Charles, James, and William were the names of the Greens' sons.[15]

Mary Green, after attending the BMSS, taught there, as did many of the daughters of powdermen. They were, according to Mulrooney, "female, Presbyterian, and taught only for a year or two before marriage."[16] Mary also served the du Pont household as a domestic.[17]

Although the record shows that William Green owed $400 to another man at his death, he was frugal enough to buy a plot of land on Kennett Pike, near the powder yards, in 1843. He planned to build a sizable brick house on the property.

Conflict entered the life of Green after he bought the plot. He purchased it from the widow Walter, who had an arrangement with a wagoner to allow him to cross her property at will. When Green told the wagoner, James Campbell, to cease using the right of way, Campbell said he had enjoyed "right of the road" for years and that time gave him the right to continue using the route. When Green insisted, Campbell asked Alfred du Pont to look into it, a decision he may have rued. After consulting an attorney, Alfred said the right Campbell claimed ended with the death of the widow.[18]

Green was no stranger to conflagrations at the DuPont works. In the 1825 explosion of the Upper Yard glazing mill, rubble buried him, and three of his men sustained injuries. Upon being freed from the mess, he found Alfred du Pont on the scene. He is reputed to have said, "Mr. Alfred, I am sorry for your heavy loss."[19] The du Ponts thought well of Green. After his death, Sophie Madeleine du Pont wrote to her husband, Admiral Samuel Francis du Pont, her first cousin (she was the daughter of his uncle, E.I. du Pont), referring to the men who died as "picked men, Irish and true and at their head the faithful [and] invaluable Willie Green."[20]

By 1850, relicts headed thirteen percent of the powder mill households.[21] One was Elizabeth McCloskey King, widow of William King, among the eighteen men killed in the 1847 accident. He started with the company in late 1837 as a laborer; in less than a year, the company promoted him to powder cart operator, and he received a monthly wage $3.50 higher than his original $17 a month pay.

After King's death, Elizabeth and their six children, ranging in age from five to fifteen years of age,[22] continued receiving the $100 annuity. She added to their treasury by $70 in 1848, sewing wrappers onto 1,300 powder kegs. Like Ann Brady and Christiann Borrell before her, she remarried, to Fergus Ryans, who must have been Catholic, as each of the children and their mother received their baptismal rites in the Catholic Church. According to Mulrooney, "The match may even have caused a stir; Fergus had been a boarder of Elizabeth's since before her husband died, and he was seven years her junior."[23]

Another widow created by the 1847 explosion outperformed Mrs. King in wrapper and label production. Isabella Brown, widow of Samuel, sewed wrappers on 2,500 kegs, and pasted labels on 3,000 canisters. She boarded hands, earning $129. Isabella was pregnant when Samuel died, giving birth to Amelia five months after his death. It was not the first powder yard death affecting Isabella; her father, Andrew Miller had died in the 1815 explosion.

Isabella was the longest running annuitant on the Brandywine, having received, upon her death in 1894, $4,700 for the years between 1847 and 1894.[24] Her son, Samuel B. Brown, became a DuPont salesman or office worker as shown in the 1863 petit ledger. The entry lists the son with an $800 yearly salary, substantially more than the average powderman with overtime pay. Another entry shows Samuel earned $200 for expenses.

As one newspaper wrote, "No other means existed of ascertaining who were lost, and who saved, than by calling the roll (after ringing the bell) of those attached to that portion of the works. The silence which followed the calling of the unanswered names was the only evidence of the loss of the lives of those who had so often replied when they were called."[25]

Another powderman who did not answer the call in 1847 was Michael Houtton.[26] An Irishman from County Donegal, he married Mary Dougherty in 1838, three years after he started working in the powder yards.

Like other Brandywine families, the Houttons knew the deep despair of the tragic loss of children before and after Michael's death. Mary gave birth to John in late 1839, followed by another son, James, in 1841. The first child named after his father was born in October 1843 and lived for nine days. The second Michael came along two years later but lived only ten days longer than his deceased brother. Little Bridget died in August 1846, a month short of her first birthday. Yet a third son named Michael was born in May 1847 and survived but forty-nine days; he died two years after the second Michael.[27] Three months after father Michael died, only Mary, John, and James were left to grieve. A Gettysburg, Pennsylvania, newspaper article said, "Those killed have almost universally left wives and children. They were among the most valuable and successful hands attached to these great works, many of them were men of independent means."[28] This was the case for Michael Houtton, who left $400 for his wife (the company paid her in full a year after the accident) and $900 for his remaining heirs.

Unlike Michael Houtton, David Althaus was a relative newcomer to the banks of the Brandywine who had started working in the powder four years before his death. He had $114 to leave to his wife, Catherine Babby, and son, David Mathew, born one month after his father passed.

Malcolm Baxter started work in the mills in 1843, the same day as David Althaus. Living on Waggoner's Row, near the intersection of the current Delaware Route 100 and Buck Road, Baxter was a laborer and never a powder man. He lived with his wife, Catherine Elliott, whom he married in Ireland (he may have been born in Scotland in 1800) and with three children, Edward, Mary, and Jane. They came with their mother to America in 1840 on the steamship *Manchester*. The Baxter parents married in County Cork where Malcolm may have worked at the Ballincollig Royal Gunpowder Mills; the DuPont Company recruited men who worked there.

Malcolm and Catherine added to their family in the states—Isabella was born at the time her father started working in the mills, and Malcolm Jr. came along two years later. After losing her husband in the explosion of 1847, Catherine Elliott Baxter remained unmarried and died after receiving her annuity for thirty-four years.

Long after their father Malcolm's death, brothers Edward and Malcolm Jr., took opposite paths during the Civil War. Malcolm enlisted at age eighteen with the 5th Delaware Infantry, Company B, the unit captained by Lammot du Pont. Their duties comprised guard duty at the mills and service at the Fort Delaware prison, which held rebel prisoners on an island off Delaware City south of the mills. They also served on the Philadelphia, Wilmington & Baltimore Railroad line from Perryville, Maryland, to Baltimore, until August 1863, when the 5th mustered out after less than a year of service. Family lore says Malcolm Junior served as a drummer boy. Thirteen years after his death in 1903, his widow, Martha Berry Baxter, filed for a Civil War pension.[29]

After the war, Malcolm Jr. became a laborer and then a well-loved manager at the Wilmington manufactory Jackson and Sharp, the largest rolling stock (railroad car) plant in America. In 1901, the American Car and Foundry Company leased the factory.

A newspaper reported the somber occasion, "The funeral of Malcolm Baxter, assistant superintendent of the local plant of the American Car and Foundry Company, yesterday afternoon, was one of the largest that has ever been held this city. Lafayette Lodge, A.F.A.M. [Ancient Free & Accepted Masons] had charge of it. Services were conducted at the home of the deceased, No. 918 Orange Street, by Rev. Hubert W. Wells, rector of St. Andrew's Episcopal Church."

The report continued, "The shops of the company by which Mr. Baxter was employed were closed at noon, and the entire force of over 900 men attended the funeral in a body. They walked for a portion of the distance to Riverview Cemetery and took trolley cars, which had been heavily drafted in black for the occasion."[30] The paper got the cemetery wrong; Malcom, Jr., lies at Mt. Salem Cemetery.

His older brother, Edward, made his way to Nashville, Tennessee, after serving as an apprentice in the DuPont keg mill. The twenty-six-year-old convinced the managers of the Sycamore Powder Mills, outside Nashville, that his experience as a keg maker and common laborer stood him in good stead at the Confederate powder mills there. In a letter to his former teacher, Victorine du Pont Bauduy, in late November 1863, not knowing she had died in 1860, he wrote that he made "the first shell or shot for Tennessee for the Rebels." He added that since the Federals had overrun Nashville in January 1862, he recovered from the defeat, owned a store and was doing "very well."[31] Long after the war, the DuPont Company became owner of the Sycamore factory.

Edward was not the only ex-employee to toil for the Confederacy. John F. McNamara wrote a letter in early 1862 offering his labors as a powder maker for the Rebels. He claimed to have been at the DuPont powder yards for three years and requested discharge from Company D of the 12th Regiment of Virginia volunteers. This company carried the name "the Lafayette Guards."

At the bottom of the letter is the command to "report to Chief Engineer Jackson in charge of Powder works at Petersburg," one of the CSA's naval powder factories; the Confederates moved the powder works from Petersburg to Charlotte, North Carolina and later to Columbia, South Carolina, as Federal forces came near.[32] Had McNamara stayed with the 12th he might have faced George W. Borrell at the Siege of Petersburg.

Ironically, while McNamara was making gunpowder for the CSA, Peter Bauduy Garesché, a former Wilmingtonian whose father established the Eden Park powder works near the city of Wilmington, supervised him.

In 1847, the Civil War was still far away. But the enormous explosion that year devastated several more Brandywine families.

Patrick and William Connor, apparently brothers, started working at the DuPont mills in 1838, Patrick in May and William three months later. They regularly brought over family members to increase the number of Connors in Wilmington, especially during the continuing famine (*an Gorta Mor*)[33] raging in their homeland. Sadly, both men died in the April 1847 explosion, just as their family was expanding with new immigrants.

In mid-1843, "for Wm. Connor and Patrick Connor," eighteen-year-old Ellen Connor arrived on the *Provincialist* on the fifth of June; she listed her occupation as "seamstress." On the same voyage were thirty-two-year-old Hugh and fifteen-year-old John, both listed as "labourers" by Captain David Williams, who piloted the *Provincialist* between Londonderry and Philadelphia for many years.[34] Hugh Connor started with the DuPont Company that same year; William Connor paid his passage. Hugh boarded with Patrick and his wife, Rosanna A. Sweeney, and paid half his earnings to the couple.

More Connors were on the way. Three months before the two Connor men died, Andrew Craig and Company, a passenger agent, wrote "we have engaged with Connor [unknown which one] for his family of 8 & charge your a/c [account] of same say $122 he paid in cash the other two passages."[35]

Ten days after the April explosion, another DuPont agent, Robert Taylor, wrote a letter showing that Patrick, William, and John Connor paid $66 for three passengers on the *Margaret Hugg*: Eleanor McLaughlin for John Connor, Margaret McLaughlin for William, and Sally Connor for Patrick ("for" meaning "paid from the account of.") The *Margaret Hugg* sailed from an unknown port on April 1, 1847, so it is unlikely the passengers landed in time to thank William or Patrick for their sponsorship.[36]

In 1847, two more Doughertys added their names to the death roll. The list already included two who had died thirty-two years earlier, and another duo killed in the 1818 explosion. This time it was John and another Daniel Dougherty who perished.

Daniel Dougherty had made the Atlantic passage on the barque *William V George* under Master Thomas Bryson in early May 1831. He worked in the DuPont mills until mid-July and then, for an unknown reason, took a check for $14.21, his earnings up to that time, and left. He returned to the mills three years later.

Earlier that year Dougherty planned with the company to bring his wife and two children from Ireland. They arrived in the States by May 22, 1835, sailing on the brig *June Haddon* from Londonderry, Bridget for $23 and each of the children for half that. She apparently had no money when she arrived from Clonca to the port of Londonderry, as Robert Taylor's agent there advanced her one pound (worth about $5); the DuPonts decreased Daniel's accounts by $51 for the voyage and the advance.

John Dougherty was born the year of an earlier explosion, 1815, in Clonmany Parish, County Donegal, and married Mary, last name unknown. Like many of the powdermen killed in explosions, he and Daniel are buried in St. Joseph on the Brandywine Cemetery.

Although most of the Doughertys killed in powder mill explosions were from County Donegal, the majority were not related, as least not closely. That appears to be the case with John and Daniel, who had hailed from County Donegal parishes that, while near each other, face across Trawbreaga Bay. Although Daniel's tombstone reads the parish of "Clancaugh," this is likely Clonca, the same parish that was the base for other DuPont powdermen. His headstone also shows that he and his wife Bridget Bonner had at least one child, Rosanne, who died at age five, in February 1845.

Thomas Holland, another 1847 explosion victim, began work in the powder yards at the same time as his brother Patrick in 1827 and mourned Patrick's loss in the 1832 explosion. Thomas boarded with the boss, William Green, through March 1831, after which he married Margaret Travers in April. The Hollands maintained a boarding house. Thomas and Margaret then began a family, with son John being the first-born, in 1832. Nicholas followed him in 1834. They added Thomas, Eliza Ann, Hugh, Mary, and Margaret by 1844. John left home after his father's death but it is not known where he went.

The Hollands performed other jobs besides boarding hands. Thomas repaired fences; at his death, he had lots of fence posts. His extra work allowed the family to inherit more than most: Margaret received $353 and the children more than $700.[37] Margaret Holland lived forty-five years after her husband's death, to the age of eighty. She is buried at St. Joseph.

Another example of the chain migration from Ireland to America was Thomas Lynch, who lost his life in the 1847 accident. Brother Hugh preceded him to Delaware and paid for the passage of seventeen-year-old Thomas, and their parents, Hugh and Catherine. The trio sailed from Londonderry on the *Allen Kerr*, arriving in Philadelphia on May 17, 1837, "whereof Alexander Taitt is master, burthen 493 tons."[38] Thomas started working at the powder mills once the trio had made their way to Wilmington.

Six years after Thomas's arrival, he declared his intention to become a U.S. citizen, and gained citizenship in October 1844 with the attestation of Henry du Pont. About the time of his original declaration, he and Julia

McGeady married, though the papers listed her as a "McGardy."[39] They had one child, a daughter Helen (known as Ellen) born six months before losing her father.

After Thomas's death, Julia and Helen moved in with her parents, Hugh and Frances McGeady; the extended household included Julia's sisters Hannah, who sponsored Helen at her baptism, and Mary, and their brother, fifteen-year-old William. Earlier in the year he died, Thomas paid for the voyage of several in-laws. When Thomas's father, Hugh, died, he bequeathed $5 to Helen.[40]

Matthew McGarvey seems to have arrived in Delaware alone and lived as a single man. He worked in the mills for sixteen years and had amassed more than $2,000 at the time of his death in 1847. Because he was single, his brothers and sisters received portions of his estate. But it wasn't easy.

The first problem was finding Matthew's heirs. The administrators, DuPont bookkeeper Henry Belin and William Breck, sent two letters a week apart to the postmaster at the Ramelton, County Donegal, post office inquiring "whether a person named Robert McGarvey resides in your neighborhood." The letter said four heirs live in America, three sisters and a brother, and "we have learned that a Brother (Robert) resides at your place. In case the said Robert McGarvey is living, or if dead, has left heirs, it will be necessary he or they should appoint someone in the United States, in proper legal form, to secure his portion."[41]

The DuPont employees contacted a nephew, Joseph, living in Ohio; he confirmed the heirs, including Robert, whom he believed was still living in Donegal. In fact, Robert survived Matthew, but not by much, as Robert's daughters received proceeds of the estate. Each of Mathew's heirs received $424.

As we learned earlier, Delaware law in the mid-19th century did not recognize mothers of deceased persons as legitimate heirs of their estates. This did not prevent efforts to send estate proceeds to the mother of John McGinness after his death in April 1847.

Two of McGinness's sisters, Mary and Eleanor Doherty, living in Ireland, gave Londonderry attorney Arthur McCorkell a power of attorney to be their go-between with authorities in the United States. Robert Taylor of Philadelphia, acting again outside his passenger-agent role, wrote two letters to the DuPont Company. In the first, sent in September 1848, he stated that Henry Belin had settled the McGinness estate by sending checks to four heirs, brothers and sisters of the deceased powderman. Taylor, concerned with the welfare of McGinness's mother, wrote, "I think they sisters of McGinness and the mother should settle the matter among themselves."[42]

In the second letter, in February 1849, Taylor wrote, "The only difficulty which I suppose can be between Mr. McCorkell and E. and M. Doherty is in regard to part of the money which he may think the mother of the parties may be entitled to and which he might incline to give the mother contrary to their wishes.... [She] must depend on the affection of her daughters for such portion as they might choose to give her." Whether that affection benefitted the mother is unknown.

A year before the April 1847 blast, four men (and their families) were living on Wagoner's Row, south and west of the rear gate to the powder yards. The four-home building was not just for teamsters and wagoners. We have learned of the death of Malcolm Baxter in that explosion. Two brothers, Charles and Michael O'Brien also lived there. They both suffered injuries serious enough to cause their deaths in the 1847 accident.[43] A fourth worker, John McPherson, appears in Chapter Six.

Michael O'Brien's first appearance in the petit ledgers was in 1836. O'Brien married Irish-born Bridget Harrity in the summer of 1841, the union producing three children: Caroline, James, and Charles. Only eight-year-old James and four-year-old Charles appeared in the 1850 U.S. Census with their mother and with her sister-in-law, Maria, the widow of Michael's brother Charles. Maria's children, six-year-old Mary and four-year-old Catherine, lived in the same house. Maria Devine O'Brien was a member of the Devine family of powder workers; she gave birth to a son, John, born in October 1841.[44]

It is likely that Bridget O'Brien remarried eighteen years after her first husband's death, as a Bridget Harrity married John Gallagher toward the end of the Civil War.

As we have seen, the widows, or relicts, of powdermen killed in explosions received pensions of $100 every year thereafter unless they moved away from the DuPont property or remarried. One relict who did both continued to receive her annuity, at least until the company found out.

In his ledger book, Frances Gurney du Pont had a listing for John W. Barrington, killed in the 1847 accident, another example of how even those closest to the men could get their names wrong. The man in question was John Wesley or Wesley John Pennington, married to Elizabeth. Less than three months after the explosion, Elizabeth wrote to Henry du Pont: "Mr. H Dupont Sir I have been sick ever since before I received the last monny and am not well yet and I am very bad of at pressent and can not get any work to do worthwhile and I would be very much obliged to you if you could send me some money. I have moveed in Walnut street near second in the fore story yellow brick. Had to leave my brothers as I could not get along there he was not actin to me as I expected. Yours with respect, Mrs. E Pennington."[45]

The petit ledger for the years 1848 through 1849 has several entries for $10 to $16, then a December 31 entry for $79.62, with the verbiage "by annuity, balance paid her, is [illegible] amount due her, *she having got money after she was married & concealed the fact*" [italics added].[46] Nothing got past the DuPont Company accountants.

Bernard Shields, sometimes called Barry or Barney, came to the Brandywine four years before his death in 1847. After he had been in America for the better part of two years, he sent for his wife, Mary Hughes Shields, and his three Irish-born daughters, six-year-old Rose, four-year-old Bridget, and two-year-old Elizabeth. As Barney's pay rate increased, so did his family. They welcomed a boy named Peter, the first to be born in America, and later came Mary. Although Rose was six when she sailed, agent Robert Taylor charged her the full passage rate of $22 and the two younger girls at the "child" rate, half the adult rate. Taylor perhaps thought Rose was older than Shields said she was; his note to the company showed that "I have made the price of these passages at the very lowest rate." Taylor knew that the parents of earlier passengers had tried to pass off their charges at the child rate.

During the Civil War, at age seventeen, Barney's son Peter Shields joined the 5th Delaware Volunteer Regiment, as Malcolm Baxter's son Malcolm did, although Peter was a member of Company D, not Baxter's Company B. ∎

■ 6 ■
A Blast in Town

> The DuPonts ought to be linched.
> —*George Gordon*

After the 1847 explosion, peace returned to the Brandywine Valley for three years, a welcome respite. Roll mill one in the Hagley yards saw two minor mishaps but no injuries. Longer periods of calm would occur, but not yet.

On February 6, 1850, powderman Michael McLaughlin lost his life, not by explosion but to an industrial accident. He was "caught by one of the bands of the Machinery and crushed to death, we understand, almost instantly, being mangled in a shocking manner."[1] The men were normally not near the eight-ton cast-iron wheels when they were moving; McLaughlin may have been adjusting the machinery while it ran, adding water to the powder mix, or attempting to improve another dangerous mill condition.

McLaughlin had started working in the yards in August 1838. James McLaughlin, perhaps a brother, began work in the early thirties and paid, through the company, to have Michael and Mary McLaughlin come to the Brandywine. In less than a year of work as a laborer, Michael became a powderman. In 1848 he paid for the passage of another Mary McLaughlin and Kitty McLaughlin, labeled as "spinsters," the common moniker given to unmarried young women by the ship masters when making out manifests. Captain Reed noted that one of them, sixteen-year-old Kitty, had transported two boxes of goods on the ship, the *Joseph Porter*, during the voyage. We don't know the relationship between Michael, Kitty, and Mary, but likely the women were McLaughlin's daughters or nieces,[2] and sisters to each other.

The travelers were lucky to take this voyage. On a later trip from Liverpool to the States, the *Joseph Porter's* passengers received one biscuit and a paltry amount of water each day during the last half of the two-month journey. The Philadelphia Board of Health sent the emaciated passengers to the City Hospital, where two children died the following day.[3]

Two years passed before another explosion death occurred. Here we meet Christopher Cowan, whom Lammot du Pont had called "a bad fellow" in Chapter Four.

In the Hagley section of the powder operation, one man managed each pair of roll mills, now powered by more efficient and longer-lasting water turbines, instead of wooden water wheels. Manager Cowan ran mills seven and eight. Near 10:00 a.m. Thursday, March 11, 1852, he placed the charge of saltpeter, sulfur, and charcoal into the mill, without spreading it, according to Frances Gurney du Pont's memoirs.

Some observers thought Cowan had not spread out the ingredients on purpose, to blow up the mills. Two workers, John Devine and James McClafferty, or McCafferty, were hauling loaded wheelbarrows nearby, on the way to the press room, when the explosion occurred. The power of the detonation[4] tossed Cowan, now afire, into the water, otherwise uninjured. Devine and McClafferty were not so lucky. McClafferty sustained burns and compound fractures to both legs. He lasted until early afternoon. Devine suffered with burns and other injuries for four days before succumbing. During that time, they amputated his arm.

The company dismissed Cowan "for his carelessness or intentional mischief." Two years later he killed himself at a house at Bancroft's Mills, a mile or so downstream from Hagley. According to Wilmington newspapers, "Whether he [Cowan] wished to kill the two men is not known."[5]

On May 8, 1854, veteran employee Charles Devron took over mills seven and eight and was cleaning them. "A raw charge and what good powder was in the mill" burned him. Lammot duPont "used to say that he [Devron] was the only man who ever lived when exposed to a full charge in a Rolling Mill."[6]

Although Devine was a common Irish name, and John even more so, it is likely the John Devine who crossed the Atlantic from the County Londonderry parish of Tamlaght Finlagan and the townland of Glack, in 1834, is the one killed in the 1852 explosion at the age of 47.[7] Charles du Pont attested his petition for U.S. citizenship in 1846. Devine was married to Mary, and is buried in St. Joseph on the Brandywine Cemetery.

Yet another undecipherable history concerns James McClafferty. Here again, the misplacement of a single letter "l" causes much confusion. Is this actually James McCafferty? Or even McCaffery? The DuPont and other records list all three.

The 1857 petit ledger refers to the "James McClafferty Estate," but the

A Blast in Town

"l" is crossed off.[8] Meanwhile, the 1850 U.S. Census lists 60-year-old James McCafferty living with 22-year-old Grace McCafferty near several other powdermen's homes, among them Mathewson, Sweeney, Peoples, Brown, and Harkins.[9] This is very likely the James who died with John Devine. Several other references in the records point to different spellings of this powder worker.

Only three weeks later, another explosion rocked the area; it didn't happen at the mills but right in the center of Wilmington.

The 63rd annual convention of the Protestant Episcopal Church of the Diocese of Delaware had met in late May 1853 at St. Paul's Church in Georgetown, in the southern part of the state. Alexis I. du Pont served as a lay delegate, and the gathering elected Samuel Francis DuPont[10] to attend the church's national convention. Bishop Alfred Lee talked of the past year of the denomination's history, telling the congregants of his visitations to the churches of the diocese and various arcane statistics about the church's activities. The last page of the report of the convention said they would hold the next convention at Trinity Church in Wilmington on the last Wednesday in May of the following year. That would be May 31, 1854.[11]

Bishop Lee lived at Ingleside, also known as Bishopstead, a well-appointed rectory, built in 1842, at the intersection of Orange and Fourteenth streets, on the edge of downtown Wilmington, near Trinity Church. On the morning of May 31, the bishop took part in the opening service at the convention; Captain Samuel Francis du Pont, on his way to the meeting, was riding a horse nearby.[12] An enormous explosion occurred not far away, causing The Right Reverend Lee to run out of the meeting to his home, to find it a total wreck.

Debris covered the street in front of the manse, the blast destroyed nearby houses, and general chaos prevailed. One local newspaper reported, "The most shocking sight of all was the remnants of human bodies and frag-

Conestoga wagon used by E.I. du Pont de Nemours & Company to transport powder kegs to the Wilmington wharf for shipment around the world. After three powder wagons blew up in Wilmington, the DuPont Company was prohibited from using city streets to transport black powder. (Hagley Museum and Library)

ments of horses which were scattered about in every direction."[13]

The DuPont Company had a strict rule for the wagoners: when traveling in pairs or groups, they must leave the powder yards at half-hour intervals to keep at least a mile distance between them. On this day, the teamsters, employees of the company, disregarded the rules of the road and traveled but a few yards apart as they passed through Wilmington. They were on the way to the Delaware River wharf, to the company's powder magazine at Old Rocks, a few hundred yards from Old Swede's Church. No one knew the cause of the blasts. Some said the drivers were smoking; others suggested the second or third team's horses struck a spark in a trail of gunpowder that came from a hole in a keg on the first wagon. An unverified report made the rounds that some nefarious person had jumped onto the last wagon and intentionally created the blast.

Lammot du Pont arrived within twenty-two minutes and thought it could have been one of those first two causes, or it could have been incendiary or a nearby factory's sparks that ignited the powder. He referred to the Hughes Brimstone concern, where its workers were "hooping some burr stones at Tho[ma]s Hughes' establishment that a spark flew from the fire and fell into the straw on the powder." Lammot addressed thoughts the drivers were smoking or a hole in a keg caused the blast. He said there was no evidence of the former and it could not have been the latter, as the street was wet and made of clay, and he discovered no trace of powder. Lammot did not elaborate further on the possibility of incendiarism.[14]

As late as 1913, someone remembered another possible cause. That year the company celebrated the centennial of a powder wagon-train that trekked from the mills to Lake Erie. The trip had supplied powder to Admiral Perry when he defeated the British there in the War of 1812.[15] At the centennial, a Dr. Morgan reminisced about friends speaking of fractious horses causing the 1854 mishap, "and after that the DuPonts changed to mules and used them until the big wagons were dispensed with."[16]

Lammot surmised, based on evidence observed with his scientist's eyes, that the middle wagon blew first. He reckoned the hole in the street under the second wagon measured three feet deep, compared to the other two holes, which were a foot shorter.

Once Lammot arrived on the scene, a Wilmington citizen, George Gordon, "was haranguing the populace saying the Duponts ought to be linched & etc. But as soon as he saw me he stopped I supposed he thought that it was too late that the men [DuPont workers] were coming on behind me even Uncle Alexis began to think there was some danger on account of mob law."[17]

Upon arrival at the dismal scene, Bishop Lee found that, "trees were torn up by the roots, or stripped bare, and the shrubbery was wiped out. The effect of the explosion on the house was as if it had been burst out from the inside. The greater part of the front wall was thrown down, and the parts that remained standing were rent from top to bottom. The roof was broken upward as if from an inside force, and doors and windows frames burst out."[18]

The bishop's "colored" cook suffered such injuries that she may have later died, and his "young Irish nurse girl was thrown downstairs with a baby in her arms. The child was unhurt, and the nurse escaped with a few bruises."[19] Contemporary accounts did not mention the death of the cook. The consensus was the accident killed five people: the three drivers, Thomas Talley, James Chambers, and John Keys; Robert Henry, a "colored" coachman for James Price, another homeowner who lost his house; and William Simcox, a young Irish millstone maker, apprenticed to Thomas Hughes, a nearby resident and the owner of the factory whose sparks may have caused the accident.

The explosions destroyed the McLaughlin home (next to the Hughes house), but, the papers reported that "it soon became known that a child, two years of age, was buried among the ruins. Willing hands were soon busy to attempt to rescue it, and the little fellow's feet were soon discovered kicking from a heap of dust and rubbish in the cellar." The article continued, "The ruins were soon cleared from the spot, and it was found that a heavy timber had fallen across the body of the child, and thus preserved it from destruction. The little one, when extricated, was crying most vigorously, but apart from some unimportant bruises and scratches he escaped serious hurt. Those who placed the rescued child in the arms of its frantic mother describe the incident as touching in the extreme."[20]

This same source referred to the infant as being uninjured "with the exception of having its little eyes filled with dust!"[21] Another report, seventy-eight years later, told of visitors to the scene of the baby's miraculous escape stuffing $5 bills into "his chubby fist."[22]

More gruesome details followed. "The three drivers were…astride their horses at the time of the explosion. The remains of two of these men, named James Kays and John Chambers, were found horribly mutilated, and of course lifeless; the third, named Thomas Talley, has not yet been found. It is supposed his body was blown to atoms."[23]

The *Evening Bulletin* explained why so much destruction occurred: "There seem to have been two forces in operation to produce the mischief resulting from this disaster. The first was the direct force of the explosion which impelled objects in its immediate vicinity from its centre. The second was the rising of the air from all directions to supply the vacuum caused by the rapid rarefaction of the air. This is exhibited in all the objects damaged which were not in the immediate proximity of the exploding powder. All tend to the locations of the wagons as to a common centre."[24]

Damage occurred everywhere in the city. The blasts knocked houses off foundations, broke glass several blocks from the site, and brought down plaster walls and ceilings. Besides the serious damage to Bishop Lee's elegant home, those of Wilmington's wealthiest citizens—the Canbys, the McLaughlins (where they rescued the baby), the Prices—sustained damage or destruction. Many of the citizens in this part of town had to rebuild their homes.

The DuPont Company promised to pay for damages and took a charge of $34,837 on the books, resulting in a loss for the year of $32,500; had they not taken the loss, company profit would have been $2,200. They suspected some claimants repaired non-explosion related damages.[25]

Abolitionist Thomas Garrett, active in the Delaware Underground Railroad, wrote to the DuPont Company, expressing sadness at the loss of life and property. He referred to "feeling under lasting obligation to your Estimable Father [E.I.] many years since where I had lost very heavily by the failure of two cotton yarn agents, he voluntarily called on me, and offered to sustain me to the amount of several thousand dollars, if I needed it, altho I never accepted his offer… It cheered me up and gave me confidence to persevere through my difficulties." He added, "And when again at a later period in 1846 when I became embarrassed by my partners in the iron manufacture, your Alfred Dupont stepped forward, and loaned me two thousand dollars at a time that many professed friends stood off."[26]

Under the headline "Honorable," the Delaware State Journal, in the June 9 edition, said, "We understand that the Messrs. Dupont have with great promptness appointed 2 Carpenters, 2 Masons, 2 Plasterers and other gentlemen from among the best mechanics in our city, to assess the damage caused by the late explosion, in order that full and ample reparation may be made to the injured parties, without delay. This course fully accords with

A Blast in Town

the well known honorable character of the Messrs. Dupont."

And, a separate article in the same edition headlined "The Powder Explosion—Workmen have been engaged at the scene of the late explosion ever since it occurred. The Messrs. Dupont are making arrangements to repay those whose property has been injured. They have already settled a number of the claims in a very satisfactory manner. The loss of property will amount to $30,000 to $35,000."[27]

Not everyone was as generous towards the du Ponts as Garrett and the newspaper. Another of Wilmington's many papers castigated the DuPonts but saved their veiled venom for the local government, "The damages, as near as we can judge, may be restored with $50,000. This sum, more or less, we doubt not, the Messrs. du Pont will make good. But the loss of life is irreparable. If they had taken the warnings given—timely given—the calamity would not have occurred; or, if the City Council had taken our warning last winter, and prohibited the wagons coming into the city, it would have been avoided. Our lives and our property must be better guarded in the future, or the people will change the custodians thereof at the earliest moment. Joseph T. Price is himself a member of the Council; he is now a sufferer by his indifference."[28]

The newspaper reprinted a part of the law about the transport of gunpowder through the city streets: "It is asserted by many that it was not properly observed there being no canvas bags around the kegs. If such was the case, our Mayor and police should have made themselves conversant with the fact." The article printed the full Section Two of the regulations, which mentioned two items: containers of gunpowder needed to be covered while in transport, and the carriers of gunpowder should not "tarry unnecessarily" in town.

The City Council noted the uproar and approved new legislation prohibiting the transport of gunpowder through the city streets. As a result, the company built DuPont Road, then west of the city limits, to take the dangerous cargo to the port.

In Cincinnati, news of the explosion created a fear that the Ohio burg might be next. A Mr. M.D.W. Loomis, kin of the founder of the Hazard Powder Company, wrote at the end of July 1854, saying that "our citizens have become very much alarmed at our transporting the article here, through our thoroughfares." Loomis added the city's lawmakers wanted to learn the "character of the ordinance" Wilmington had enacted and asked the du Ponts to send a copy of the law now in effect in Wilmington.[29]

We know little of the wagon drivers. It is unlikely that John Keys ever knew that his wife, Margaret, was pregnant; she gave birth to John Washington Keys in late February 1855.[30]

In the Registry for Deaths and Burials that year, the "name" space where the name Thomas Talley should be is blank, but nineteen is the age given. The same record shows Keys and Chambers were born in Ireland.[31]

The story doesn't end here. In 1875, while workmen excavated the Cool Spring reservoir in Wilmington, they dug up the skeletons of horses believed to be those of the French-bred horses killed while transporting powder in the 1854 catastrophe. And, forty years after the mishap, workers digging near Fourteenth and Orange streets discovered pieces of iron in the ground, supposed to have been relics of the destroyed wagons.[32]

In February 1877, twenty-three years after the explosion, the DuPont company received a missive from a Dr. DeForest Willard of Philadelphia concerning a Mrs. Hughes. In two letters, Dr. Willard explained "her child sustained a fracture, her husband had his death hastened some year or eighteen months later and she herself was injured so as to be confined in bed for some weeks" because of the 1854 blast. Dr. Willard said she could not earn her own living and Alexis du Pont had promised at the time he would see to her care. The letter quoted Alexis as writing Mrs. Hughes "should never want as long as she lived." Saying the widow received a mere $10 from the du Ponts since the disaster, Dr. Willard asked them to give aid.[33]

A second Willard letter alluded to Mrs. Hughes' receipt of $25, stating that "I am sure you would not have regretted your generosity had you heard her expressions of gratitude." He made sure the company knew Mrs. Hughes welcomed more kindness on their part.[34] To prove his bona fides, he named three doctors in northern Delaware as references and added that "in this city I am known to most of the prominent physicians." Whether the firm responded to the second request is unknown.

No more explosions of DuPont powder occurred in Wilmington, but more, and more serious, blasts were yet to come on the Brandywine. And the du Ponts were not the only ones making black powder in or near the city.

Recall that E.I. du Pont originally employed Frenchmen from the small enclave in Wilmington in the early 19th century, but he later substituted Irish workers because the French wanted too much money and thought they knew more than he about powder making. Peter Garesché did not agree with Irénée; he continued using French workers to make

A Blast in Town

gunpowder through mid-century.

His mills were not immune to explosions. On Friday morning, August 3, 1855, one and a half tons of powder went up at the Garesché Eden Park mills, then just outside the Wilmington city limits, killing three men of French birth plus another three and injuring five powdermen.[35] After the blast, Garesché decided not to rebuild the mill and sold the assets to the du Ponts.[36] In a few short years, the Garesché name would surface again.

A week after the Eden Park mill explosion, Edward Cassiday was cleaning a roll mill at Hagley and lost his life because of burns from an explosion. Six years later, his wife Elizabeth, finding the $100 annuity too low to sustain her, boarded powdermen for the next twenty years. Cassiday was Maine-born, trained as a cabinetmaker, and the 22-year-old son of an oysterman and his wife.

Another explosion rent the air the following year, killing three DuPont workers—brothers Andrew and David Moore and collier John McPherson, who had lived on Wagoner's Row with the O'Brien brothers and Malcolm Baxter a decade before. All four of these Wagoner's Row residents died in explosions.

Andrew Moore and his wife, Martha, had a trio of offspring, one of whom, Margaret, was four months old when her father perished. The toddler died two-and-a-half years later. One can only imagine the devastation Martha Moore felt at the time of Andrew's death, with two youngsters, ages five and two, and a four-month-old, and then again when she lost Margaret.[37]

The family placed no grave marker at Andrew's burial place in Green Hill Cemetery, as they buried him in the same casket as McPherson.[38] After powder explosions, when a complete body was hard to find, relatives often buried the remains of more than one man in the same grave.

David Moore has a separate headstone in the same cemetery. He died by drowning. Frances Gurney du Pont's version of the explosion says David was near the graining mill, the site of the detonation; the blast threw him into the Brandywine. He "had no wounds upon him of any account."[39] After his death, David's wife, Anna, continued a job she had started soon after the two arrived at the mills three years earlier. She increased the Moore family accounts by sewing and mending cart and wagon covers, adding between $15 and $18 a month.

Francis du Pont blamed the 1856 blast on charcoal-maker McPherson, writing that the collier had gone "to the millwright shop to get some copper nails to repair his cutting machine," and added that the improper use of hammer and nails was the cause.[40]

The Dick Scott papers cite a different cause. In a page labeled "1856," it lists the cause as "probably due to cutting rolling mill cake or dragging the cutting machine over the floor."[41] The men made mill cake by putting roll mill slurry into two-by-three-foot forms, then pressing them to remove water from the mix.

The newspapers said McPherson and David Moore were "two worthy and useful men."[42] They made little mention of Andrew.

Five months later, as the du Pont family and the employees returned from the funeral of Irénée's eldest son, Alfred Victor, a fire started in the composition house at Hagley.[43] Alfred's younger brother, Alexis, gathered men and doused the press room roof. This was an action that Alexis often performed during mill yard emergencies.

Lammot, Alfred's second oldest son, joined powderman James Stewart to perform the same saving act on the graining mill roof. Stewart, "who labored with great pluck," told Lammot that he had better stay away, "as his life was of more value than that of Stewart."[44] Lammot fell through a decayed part of the roof into a mixing box. The building was "as dark as Erebus,"[45] and he extricated himself with the help of the men. The efforts of the men saved everything but the composition house and the sawmill. No one died in the fire, but it would not be long before another incident took five worker's lives and that of a du Pont.

Seeming to take little note of the explosions that had snuffed out the lives of so many of his workers, or perhaps responding as any son might, Francis Gurney du Pont wrote that an accident occurred on August 22, 1857, that was "the most unfortunate that ever took place on the Brandywine." It ended his father's life.

The company had scheduled demolition of a building in the yards for Monday, August 24, 1857. At the end of work the Saturday before, Alexis du Pont asked a half-dozen men to stay to help get the building ready for the impending work. While moving a large bin inside the building, the heavy box struck the stone wall and created a spark which led to fire and a minor explosion, enough to burn the men and catch their clothing on fire. Several of them jumped into the mill race a few feet away to douse the flames. When Alexis turned his gaze to the nearby press house, he saw the roof was on fire. He called to the men to form a bucket brigade, then mounted the roof and began pouring buckets of water onto the increasing flames, knowing there was enough powder in the mill to cause a serious explosion. He was right.

The resulting explosion tossed du Pont onto the drying tables north of the building, causing massive injuries: he fractured three ribs and his right thigh and sustained a perforated lung.

The men, after saving the press house, carried Alexis home, where Dr. Arthur H. Grimshaw treated him.[46] Alexis knew the wounds were mortal, so he asked that the powdermen stop by to say goodbye. All but five did; they were dead or too seriously hurt to see him.

It was well known, and we have seen, that the du Ponts would not ask their employees to perform work that they themselves would not do, despite the dangers in doing so.

Among the five, forty-seven-year-old Edward Hurst was a yard foreman with eighteen years' experience who had brought a large family from County Fermanagh on the *Caledonia* in October 1839.[47] He and wife Rebecca Hunter Hurst traveled via Liverpool with their five girls: Margaret Jane, Sarah Serena, Rebecca, Elizabeth, and Mary Ann. They added a pair of girls in America, Septima and Isabella, before having their first son, Alexander, born two days after the huge April 1847 detonation.

They added a last child, named for E.I.'s daughter, Evelina, in 1850, and suffered through her death three and a half years later. Besides appearing as a family with at least five of the children in the 1850 census, the couple boarded a half-dozen powdermen.[48]

Although the blast mortally injured Hurst, he walked home and told his wife he was not hurt.[49] He died later that day.

George Fisher, another worker who tried to move the bin, lingered for a week, suffering from burns and other injuries. His family buried him at Green Hill Cemetery. He was thirty-one and had been working at the powder yards for ten years. His wife Elizabeth continued to receive an annuity until her death at age fifty-one in 1882.

Two of Alexis's helpers were seriously injured. Michael Higgins restarted work in the mills in mid-September while Richard Hunter took a month and a half to recover from his injuries.

Catherine (Kate) McClafferty was nineteen when husband John died as a result of the 1857 explosion; their daughter, Helen (or Ellen) was born three months later. She appears to be Kate and John's only child.[50] The 1860 U.S. Census lists a Catherine McClafferty as a widow with a three-year-old daughter, Ellen. While this is likely the widow McClafferty, she may have, as many others did during these mid-century censuses, told a white lie about her age, giving it as twenty-two. A tombstone at Cathedral Cemetery in Wilmington shows a Kate McCafferty, born in 1830; if that inscription is correct, and the person buried is this Kate, she would have been 27 in 1857.[51] Here again, principals' names are tricky and confusing. A missing "l" here, an incorrect date of birth there, all add up to uncertainty.

In the ledger for 1886, "Catherine McClafferty" is one page's label; below the accounting is the following statement: "By order of Mr. Henry DuPont made October 22/1886 Mrs. Catherine McClafferty's annuities to be discontinued after December 31, 1886."[52] Given that widows of powdermen who died (before and after John McClafferty in 1857) continued to receive pensions, why, if she was still alive in 1886, would she lose hers? The petit ledger for 1891 tells why. Several pages are glued to the page for Catherine, who according to her tombstone, died May 3, 1891. On a page labeled May 5, 1891, is a bill from John A. Cannon, Furnishing Undertaker, whose facility was on the northeast corner of Sixth and Tatnall streets. The billed items include a $35 walnut coffin, grave digging expenses of $9.50, a shroud and lady attendant for $12, and a hearse and three carriages for $13. The key line items in the bill were for washing and removing the body from Delaware State Hospital, which cost $5, and conveying a daughter to the asylum and returning her to her home for $3. The bill came to $77.50. The second page glued into the ledger is the May 22 endorsement of the bill by a Mrs. O'Donnell. Catherine McClafferty lived at the hospital for the insane for an unknown period. The DuPont Company canceled Kate's annuity at the end of 1886 due to her leaving her rent-free dwelling and moving to the asylum.[53] We do not know who Mrs. Margaret X. O'Donnell was or what her relationship might have been to Kate McClafferty.

The name of Louis Vache or Vouche does not appear in the petit ledgers as, according to Frances Gurney du Pont, he started working in the yards the day of the blast that killed him.

The final fatality of the 1857 explosion was yet another Dougherty. Fifty-two-year-old Anton[54] Dougherty[55] had been in America for three years, having made the voyage unaccompanied in early 1854, sponsored by Alexis I. du Pont. He became Anthony either through the ship's master, who might not have known the name Anton, or the registrar when he arrived in the States. He was a farmer in Culdaff Glebe townland,[56] County Donegal, in northeastern Ireland.

Anton arranged through the DuPont Company to bring over his thirty-six-year-old wife, Jane McFarlane, and six children. Charles, the youngest, had never seen his father, and never would. The others were James, John, Peter, and Anthony Jr. (all of whom worked at the mills) and the only daughter, Mary Jane, who worked in the DuPont cotton mills.

They arrived the day after Anton's death. The company gave Jane a pension and a place to live in the Walker's Banks homes, a few yards downriver from the front gate of the powder works, where she took in boarders. In what may seem like a cruel detail, after Anton's death, Father John Walsh at St. Joseph sent a letter to the company: "The Late Anthony Doherty, Lewis Vache, and John McLafferty, having paid no pew rent, owed for the burying ground. Please let me know if they had any money in the office and if anything could be done towards getting something."[57]

Another tragedy hit the Doughertys a few years later when young Charles died. The 1860 U.S. Census lists him as being seven years old; he perished within a few months of being counted. When Charles died, Jane had her husband's body exhumed from the original group gravesite where other powdermen were interred and moved him to a gravesite she bought elsewhere in St. Joseph Cemetery. Father Anton and son Charles lay together. Unable to read or write, Jane accepted the misspelling of Anton's name on the tombstone as "Anthoney."

Dougherty sons James and John later joined Capt. Lammot du Pont's Company B of the 5th Delaware Volunteer Regiment and saw duty as prison guards at Fort Delaware; they would have known Malcolm Baxter Jr., another enlistee in Company B. Family history says John, named at birth Walter John, went AWOL and was next seen in Major Hugh Stirling's 7th Delaware, Co. D, for a short month of duty in mid-1864.

Another jolt to the Dougherty family occurred in a railway accident on the PW&B (Philadelphia, Wilmington and Baltimore railroad, the one Frederick Douglass used to escape slavery). On June 11, 1892, unmarried Walter Peter, then known as Peter, died while working on the railroad.[58]

John Dougherty married Mary McDermott and after seven years of marriage, they bought a house on Rising Sun Lane, near the powder yards. They added rooms, enabling them to house their family, which grew to include ten children, John's mother (Anton's widow Jane) and her son Anthony Jr., still a bachelor. Jane died in the spring of 1896 and is buried with her son Walter Peter in St. Joseph on the Brandywine Cemetery.

Yet more sorrow affected the family in later years when John died June 23, 1900, after being hit by the Royal Blue train of the Baltimore & Ohio line on a bridge over Grays Ferry Road in West Philadelphia; he was working for the B&O. Most of his children were adults at the time of his death.

In the first half of the 1880s, twenty-eight-year-old Anthony Jr., wed his mail-order bride, sixteen-year-old Ellen Jane Houghton, on the day she disembarked at Philadelphia. The couple walked straight to St. Clements Church in Philadelphia, a twenty-block walk from the wharf, and married. The union produced eleven children, two of whom died in the 1905 typhoid epidemic. It was the custom to close the eyes of the deceased using coins; Anton's two-times great granddaughter, Sarah, still has the nickels used for this purpose on two-year-old Edward, son of Anthony Jr. and Ellen.

Daughter Mary Jane married another powder Dougherty named Edward, and they, too, contributed to the growing number of Doughertys, having nine children. James married, but there was no issue from the union.

Anton's descendants continued to grow and prosper, but more Doughertys would die in the DuPont powder yards.

Two months after the 1857 explosion, in a period that saw the third and most destructive economic panic in the nation's history[59] up to that time (the others occurred in 1819 and 1837), Roseanna Sharkey Gibbons and her husband, James, welcomed their third child, William, to the family. He joined three-and-a-half-year-old Mary Ann and John, who was two days short of his second birthday. Their joy was short lived.

After a January 1859 explosion, Francis Gurney du Pont wrote, "It was thought by some that Gibbons had committed suicide"; he may have told his wife that day that "he would not trouble her long." Du Pont also maintained that, when Gibbons' brother, John, heard the explosion, he said "there goes Neal, as though he had something upon his mind"; James was also known as Neal. DuPont added that Gibbons "was either tinkering with the machinery and sent Grant for something or sent him away with the desire to save him."[60]

John Grant was the other man killed in that blast. He had married Sarah McGee on St. Patrick's Day, 1854, and they had three girls. Mary Ann came along in 1854, either conceived out of wedlock or born two months prematurely. She was two when she passed. Susan was born in 1856 and perished on the day of her birth. The last member of the family was Catherine, born in 1857; she was less than three when her father John died.

Grant hailed from "Parish Doe," according to his tombstone at St. Joseph. This could be several places in County Donegal: most likely it is Doagh in Mevagh[61] civil parish and the stone cutter etched what he heard. But it could be Doagh Beg or Doagh More, both in the civil parish of Clondavaddog.[62]

Sarah remarried between 1859 and 1865 to John Shields and gave birth to daughter May Ellen in January of the latter year.[63]

People felt the impact of the 1859 blast as far away as Philadelphia, where a writer for the *Evening Bulletin* wrote, "It is a curious circumstance that while this shock was felt with great severity at Newark, Del[aware] and at Chester, and very distinctly at Philadelphia, the people of Wilmington, although only four miles distant, knew nothing of the explosion."

The writer continued with this explanation: "The mills at Dupont's works all face the Brandywine. Their rears are constructed of heavy masonry, while the fronts are built of light wood work, in order to direct the force of an explosion towards the creek, where there are no buildings to damage. This arrangement caused the shock to come over in the direction of Philadelphia, while the heavy rear portion of the mill being in the direction of Wilmington protected that city from the violence of the concussion. The moisture in the atmosphere also assisted to convey the sound a great distance."[64]

It is possible another phenomenon was in effect. Acoustic shadow occurs when one of three atmospheric or topographical conditions is present. Intervening soil or forest or snow can muffle the noise for a time for those nearby, but persons far away on solid or open ground can hear it. People are more likely to hear sound if they are downwind rather than upwind. Or it could have been temperature inversion, "when the air near the ground becomes cooler than air higher up, causing sound waves to bend back towards the earth. In certain cases alternating rings of audibility and silence will radiate from the source as sound is retracted upwards and then down again."[65]

A week later, the *Wayne County Herald* reported on the mishap, adding "this is a hard story, but as it comes from newspaper reporters, it must be true."[66] The *Hillsborough Recorder* editorialized that, "It was thought that the preparations which have been made since the last fatal event, when one of the proprietors was killed, would tend to prevent the occurrence of these distressing disasters, but it seems there is still a wide field for improvement in safeguards."[67]

The ugly destruction of lives and property in 1859 did not end. Nine workers died when the Lower Hagley press room detonated nine months after the January 20th calamity.

We have learned that most accident causes remained unknown because all the witnesses died. Those who investigated this blast knew, or at least espoused, a cause. They found a worn and stripped pinion or bevel. A replacement was sitting on the machine shop floor, ready for installation, when the detonation happened.[68]

The men had partially loaded a horse cart with powder dust, expecting to fill the cart and taking it to the next step. The fire created by the blast jumped to another building, what Francis Gurney du Pont called a "stockhouse," in the hill above the press house. Three more mill buildings joined the chain: a glazing mill and two roll mills. This storage building contained some of the first soda powder DuPont made, thus intensifying the fire more than usual.[69]

The series of explosions blew two men into the river, one into a tree and the headless trunk of another to the opposite shore. "Of the others nothing could be ascertained."[70] The explosion did not kill the horse, although it was next to the press house. It lost an eye, had its leg broken and suffered burns; they ended its agony.

Forty-eight-year-old William Moran was foreman of the Lower Hagley yard. He had risen quite far through the ranks of the powder yards by the time he died. William had started in 1838, hired in March as a laborer. A year later, they made him a powderman. By 1844 he was a cooper. In his first year he paid $23 to agent Robert Taylor for passage of his wife, Catherine Rigby Moran,[71] from Londonderry to the States. They had at least three children:[72] Mary Ann, born in late 1839; William, age sixteen when his father died; and Elizabeth, to whom Catherine gave birth in January 1845. His family buried Moran in Green Hill Cemetery, where his wife joined him in May 1871.

Bernard Sweeney, called, as you might expect, Barney, and by the *Delaware Inquirer* newspaper, Brian, was a twenty-year-old man whose remains were buried at St. Joseph after his death in the late 1859 explosion. The 1850 census shows a Barney Sweeney married to Catherine with a five-month-old son, John, living next to the O'Brien widows, Bridget and Mary.[73] However, that Bernard Sweeney was listed as being thirty years old, which would have made him thirty-nine at death. The record is further confused by another source listing Bernard and Catherine Murray Sweeney as the parents of five-month-old John, born in March 1850, and Maria, born September 7, 1851.[74]

Another historical mystery arises in the case of Michael O'Donnell. A person with that name was baptized on November 25, 1832, by Father Carrell, a priest then presiding at St. Joseph. This Michael was the son of Michael and Sarah Byrne O'Donnell. Again, the two-year discrepancy between Michael's birth date in 1832 and the calculation of his age at death as twenty-five in 1859 is not significant for the times.

The Irish in America took advantage of a unique resource to help them find friends or relatives, fellow immigrants, with whom they had lost contact. The *Boston Pilot* printed a regular column that gave details of the person or persons sought and the seekers contact information.

In the January 5, 1861, edition of the *Pilot*, an ad sought John and Pat O'Donnell, natives of Island Parish in County Clare, who came to America in the 1850s. "Information of them will be thankfully received by their brother, Michael O'Donnell, care of Mr. Henry DuPont, Brandywine Bank, near Wilmington, New Castle County, Delaware."

The advertisement might be the result of any of several possibilities. One is that the person who placed it was the namesake of the deceased, searching for his uncles to inform them of their brother's death. Another is that John and Pat were sons of the deceased, and the advertiser's brothers. It is also possible that the DuPont Company used the deceased Michael's name to generate communication with them regarding his estate. And, least likely, Michael, before the explosion took his life, sent the particulars to the Boston paper and they had just now published it.[75]

Unanswered questions surround the final six victims of the October 1859 explosion. We know that Edward Dougherty was married to Mary, who became the executrix of his estate. Nothing more is known of him or the other men killed in the explosion: Charles Black, Ubert Jacob, Robert McIlhenny, Emile Sabar, and John Welsh. Their names remain in the company roster, perhaps waiting to be discovered by a family researcher at some future time. ■

▪ 7 ▪
No Powder for Johnny Reb

Na dein nos agus na bris nos.
—*Irish Proverb*[1]

"Last night, I heard me mother crying," Mickey Mullin told his landlady in 1860. "Where?" asked Mrs. Boisson, a powderman's widow. He replied, "Out on the rocks." When the landlady said it was an owl, Mickey retorted, "Just the same, I'm going to Ireland soon."[2] He never made it.

Thomas ("Mickey") Mullin was the only powderman who died on February 3, 1860, when roll mill thirteen blew up in the Lower Hagley yard; it was not long after he spoke with Mrs. Boisson. He started working for the DuPont Company in the early 1850s, having traveled from an Irish townland called Glenroan in the parish of Upper Bodoney, County Tyrone.

By 1860, the DuPont Company was an international concern. Although they had sold powder to the Spanish ambassador to the United States in the 1840s, the first contracted overseas direct orders negotiated by the company occurred from 1854 to 1856 during the Crimean War. The allies (England, France, the Ottoman Empire and the Kingdom of Sardinia) defeated the Russians after more than two years of battle that gave rise to the legends of the Charge of the Light Brigade, the Siege of Sevastopol, and Florence Nightingale.

During these years and into the 1860s the company was in the hands of the second and third generations of the founder's family, including Lammot and his brother Éleuthère Irénée (E.I.'s grandsons whose father was Alfred Victor du Pont), and Henry (E. I.'s second son), the senior partner. They supervised over 400 workmen, a number that dropped by 150 in 1857. Even though production went up, conscription and enlistments during the early months of the Civil War reduced the manufacturing manpower pool. Many of the remaining men worked overtime to make up for the lost workers' productivity.

On October 9, 1860, England's Prince of Wales[3] (later King Edward VII) was the first British royal to visit America, and Philadelphia, the onetime second largest city in the kingdom. The next day another single-fatality explosion in the DuPont powder yards killed Michael Gorman; he had worked for the company for seven months before his death. The blast took down five buildings in the lower yard. A roll mill blew first, then the graining mill. Destruction of the press room, the dust mill, and the pack house followed.

Years after the explosion, Francis Gurney du Pont found a piece of iron stuck in a tree 200 yards from the pack house; the iron from a metal keg had flown across the yard when the building blew.[4]

As the need for black powder grew during the Civil War, the company placed the mills on a wartime footing, with production going on twenty-four hours a day; another forty-two men would perish making powder for the Northern forces.[5]

The first explosion on the Brandywine after the war started in April 1861 occurred seven months into the struggle. Despite efforts by the du Ponts to erect mills far enough apart to lessen the chances of communication of fire or blast, this was another multi-building episode. The pressing, grinding, dusting, and drying buildings of the upper yard sustained damage or destruction.[6]

Seven months later, Charles Mulherin and Joseph Russell were in the press house when it exploded on November 11, 1861, and John Vichie was in the graining house. The three died in the explosion; one newspaper reported a woman, working in a factory across the river from the DuPont mills, died from the blast's concussion but we don't know this for sure.[7]

Mulherin had voyaged from Londonderry to Philadelphia in 1850 as a twenty-nine-year-old laborer from Dunfanaghy,[8] a town off Sheephaven Bay in Clondahorky[9] Parish, County Donegal. He came alone on the brig *Lumley* and did not appear to carry any belongings.[10] What he did for the first three years in America is unknown, but he worked in the Brandywine mills starting in March 1853. He married Frances McGinley, and the couple had four girls: Catherine, Grace, Sarah, and Margaret, and one boy, Daniel. Mulherin was 40 when his five children were left without a father.

The company listed Samuel Russell as Joseph in some of the registers; his name was either Samuel Joseph or Joseph Samuel. After his death, the du Ponts corresponded with a Mrs. Jane Russell of Ballygay, a townland near Milford in Tullyfern Parish,[11] County Donegal. They often went to extraordinary lengths to locate survivors of workers killed in explosions. In Russell's case, it took fifteen years to find an heir. The firm sent the first letter to Mrs. Russell in the summer of 1876, the year of America's Centennial celebration, "Mrs. Jane Russell has left in our hands ninety dollars in cash & an order on Wilmington Savings Fund Society for two hundred and thirty...due Aug 19, 1876—making in all Three hundred and twenty...dollars which will be paid to her on return of this certificate, accompanied by a letter from her directing where the remittance is to be made & to what address."

Given that transatlantic transit speeds for packet ships carrying mail had increased by then, the company received the response by return post one month later. Mrs. Russell requested they pay the manager of the Northern Bank branch in Ramelton, near Ballygay. Someone wrote "canceled" in red ink on the first letter, so we do not know if Mrs. Russell ever got the money.

We also don't know much about the third man killed that November. In a Hagley Library listing of all the explosions and the men lost, his name is John Vichie; that is the name Francis Gurney du Pont used. The petit ledgers show the name as "Vizier." They list, in the widows sections of the ledgers after 1861, Annie Vizier.

The mishap injured one worker; we will learn about Martin Dolan later.

Because war was raging and demand for black powder increased manyfold, the du Ponts ran the Delaware mills to their utmost capacity, but only two explosions occurred in the year and a quarter between November 1861 and February 1863. Minor accidents happened on the first day of 1862 and at the start of December that year, but these neither injured nor killed anyone. The February 25, 1863 pack house explosion made up for the gap.

She might have forgotten her reading of her school premium *Sailor's Son* in the early 1830s but not so the death of her father, Daniel Toy, in the 1832 dust mill explosion. By the early 1860s Mary Toy McKenna had her own children with their father, powderman James McKenna.

In the period since her father's death, fifty-four DuPont workmen had died in nineteen fatal blasts. Mary was used to the detonations but not the wailing and sobbing of the families. After the explosions, she would have been one of those crying until she was certain her partner had not been a victim.

All that changed on the afternoon of a snowy February 26, 1863, during the height of the war. In what Francis Gurney du Pont described as perhaps "as severe a single explosion as ever occurred on the Brandywine,"[12] Mary's husband, James, was one of the thirteen men killed. He was not in the exploding pack house; as a wheelwright, he was repairing a pump in the engine house up the hill from the pack house.[13] To lose a father and then a husband in the same type of accident seems unimaginable in modern times. But to DuPont families it must have been a hazard they were willing to face to have a good job and a supportive community.

Mary Toy McKenna, the unluckiest Toy, who lost a father and a husband in explosions. (Courtesy Reese Robinson)

James and Mary had married thirteen years before and welcomed five children during that time. First was John, born in January of the year following the marriage. Mary Ann was next in 1853. In 1856, Caroline was born; she died two years later. Then came James Jr., followed by Daniel, no doubt named for his grandfather, in 1861. At father James's death, the progeny of the McKenna-Toy union ranged in age from two to twelve.

When son James was born, he received his baptism at home because they felt he would not live. Perhaps he knew of this and responded to the "miracle" by later becoming a priest.

John, the oldest, became the administrator of his mother's estate when she passed in 1885. James and his namesake share a grave, as do siblings Daniel and Caroline, at St. Joseph.

For the fifteen years after James' death, his widow and her mother, Rosanna, received annuities (Rosanna died in 1878). During part of that time, Mary's son, twelve-year-old Daniel, worked for the du Ponts and brought in $14 a month added to his mother's account.[14] Daniel continued to work, earning $20 a month in 1877; he was by now sixteen years old. Mary was contributing more than her annual stipend to the family treasury by selling the company bundles of hoops (for powder barrels?) for nine cents a bundle.

Two Samuel Fishers were working in the pack house that day in 1863; both father and son died. The elder Samuel started in the mills in 1847, one month after that April's disaster. It didn't take long for him to earn the trust of the du Ponts, who helped send for his family in Ireland. They boarded the *Hannah Kerr* in Londonderry in early May 1848 and arrived in Philadelphia a month later. Martha Fisher, her young brood in tow, made her way to the Brandywine. Sisters Martha and Margaret and brothers James and John accompanied eight-year-old Samuel.

Samuel Jr. and brother John do not appear to have been avid students. A teacher at the BMSS in September 1859 wrote that John Fisher, Samuel Fisher, and Henry Miller, the son of Jonas Miller, "sat on the fence opposite the school till 9 o'clock instead of coming in."[15]

James Fisher later joined the Union army during the Civil War. When he found out that his father and brother were dead, James got leave from his military unit, Nield's Independent Light Artillery, in the Washington, D. C. area, for the funeral. He told his neighbors he had had a dream a few nights earlier in which he saw "father in working clothes with his sleeves rolled up bending over to kiss him." When he awoke, he experienced a premonition about the disaster.

Like Mary Toy, Martha Fisher and her family experienced twice the agony because of this explosion. Unlike Mary, who had time to grieve for her father before her husband died in the same manner, Martha lost two loved ones in the same incident.

> *Alas! Deep grief overspread the country*
> *To anticipate the death of O'Develin*[16]

The poet McNamee, after the thirteenth century Battle of Downpatrick, bemoaned the death of his king, O'Neill, and the many nobles killed, including an O'Develin. No poem was likely written in February 1863, when Hugh and Edward Devlin succumbed to their injuries from that month's explosion, but their families lamented the deaths nonetheless.

Hugh Devlin was born in Scotland in 1820. He married an Irish lass, Ann Mooney, and the duo had four Scotland-born children before sailing for the New World. In America Hugh and Ann apparently had two other children; "apparently," because the 1860 U.S. Census shows an unusual gap between the fourth child, his father's twelve-year-old namesake, and the second-to-the-last child, two-year-old William. The census shows a six-month-old baby, Alexander, living in the house.

The likely explanation for the gap is that Hugh and Ann had more children during the ten years, all of whom must have died in the intervening years. They would have been too young to leave the family home.

We don't know if Hugh and Edward were kin but, in the tight-knit Brandywine community, it is likely. They were five years apart in age and seven apart in years of powder making. Edward married Sarah Devine and they produced four children, one of whom, Josephine, was born seven months to the day after her father died.

Another victim of the February 1863 accident was Thomas Clark, who must have gone by the nickname "Clarksie," as that's the name listed in the newspapers. He was married to Elizabeth McKinney and they had one child, Alice, born in April of 1862.

This Thomas Clark was one of eight with the name who served from Delaware in the Civil War. Like other DuPont workers, he was in Lammot's company.[17]

Childbirth on the open sea was common in the 19th century. In the five years between January 1847 and December 1851, the height of the famine, there were at least 8,000 such births.[18] One of these deliveries occurred on the *Messenger*, a barque traveling from Bremen, Germany, via Galway, an Irish port city situated where the River Corrib meets the Atlantic. It was a British vessel, so it was much less comfortable for a pregnant woman than if she had traveled on an American one. U.S. ships were more regulated than their English counterparts.

For example, the U.S. Passenger Acts dictated the number of passengers America-bound ships could carry. They required foodstuff minimums for each passenger. English ships also sailed under a food-quantity regulation, but it was much less than that needed for American-flagged craft. English legislation required seven pounds per passenger per week, a near-starvation diet. The ship owners found ways around the rules if they could.

We can only imagine the discomfort Mary Noone must have suffered toward the end of the pregnancy on the cramped and dirty *Messenger*, accompanied by twenty-year-old husband, Fergus. Their first child, John, was "born on the ocean"; he entered the world with the help of Captain Thomas Moore and the female passengers.

Mary may have been less superstitious than her counterparts having children earlier in the century, although the Irish proverb that introduces this chapter means, "Neither make nor break a custom." Would she have put a horseshoe on the doorpost, cut a notch in a black cat's tail, peeled seven roods (two acres) of hazel when experiencing her first natal pain? And, once the baby was born, would she have bitten her child's nails rather than cutting them—who would want a child to grow up to be light-fingered?[19]

The Noone family arrived at the Port of Philadelphia in early May 1847 and debarked, thankful that they stood on solid ground at last. Fergus started at once working at the DuPont mills and, by 1850, rose to powderman, earning $34 a month by the time of his death thirteen years later.

Two-year-old John welcomed a brother, Michael, in 1849 and the family continued to grow, reaching six children; they added only girls to the family after Michael. And they followed the custom of births every two years with Catherine, Mary, Margaret, and Bridget joining the tribe.

Fergus, called Martin (and in the census "Faddy"), Mary and the two boys (Catherine was born in 1850) lived in one of the many communities that dotted the DuPont acreage. Their neighbors included Mary Hughes Shields, widow of Barney Shields; the widow Catherine Baxter; the widowed sisters-in-law O'Brien; widow Catherine Murray Sweeney; Sarah Kane Devine, John Devine's relict; and several soon-to-be widows, among them Ellen McGee McGinley. The Noones knew well how Fergus's life might end and the sorrow such an end would visit on the surviving family members.

By the first year of the war, Fergus earned $20 a month. That year, with powder making going on day and night, he earned as much in overtime, working at least twelve and a half hours extra each month.

The Noone family idyll came to a halt at 2:00 on that Wednesday afternoon in late February in the pack house, when Fergus met his end; 25,000 pounds of black powder exploded. Mary and the family remained living on DuPont property with the traditional free house and annuity, but their trials continued.

After paying the claimants on her husband's account, the DuPont Company credited Mary with the significant sum of $1,100.[20] She ran up a debt with the company the year Fergus died and took money out of his estate account. Sons Michael and John worked in the mills to supplement her income. Two years later she closed the annuity account; the estate account remained on the books and continued earning interest.

Tragedy struck the family a few years later when, after Mary's passing, two of her daughters died of tuberculosis (then called "consumption" and, scientifically, "phthisis pulmonalis") seven months apart.

Another non-Irish fellow began working in the yards in early January 1863, weeks before his death in the February accident. John P. Dehan had anglicized his name from Jean Pierre DeHan. He was the son of Nicholas and Catherine DeHan, born in Sotzeling, France, on June 17, 1844.[21] In 1862, when he was sixteen, he served in Company D of the 5th Delaware regiment. After his service, he worked alongside his brother, Victor, and their father at the mills.

Thomas Dougherty was ten years older than Jean Pierre when the two went "across the crick." Thomas had married Isabella A. Flynn, and they had one child, a daughter. Catherine was one and a half years old at the time of her father's demise.

Isabella buried her husband with his brother, James, who had died a decade earlier. She lived a widow for the next fifty-seven years. In 1902, while still living on the DuPont properties, she asked a company housing surveyor, George Cheney, to repair weather boards, paint the kitchen and other rooms, and fix the leaky chimney. She was living in a two-and-a-half story stone house on Breck's Lane, a quarter mile from the Hagley front gate. She complained of having to travel four hundred yards to get spring water.

Richard and Mary Foley McLaughlin, both born in Ireland, married five years before the February 1863 explosion. By the time of Richard's death, the couple had had two children, three-year-old Mary, and John, less than a year old. But, once again, the working-class McLaughlin's left little imprint, a not uncommon feature of worker's lives in the 19th century.

John Querke worked at the mills for five years before marrying Ellen Duris in 1858. They had two children, Mary Jane, born in 1859 and Ellen, born in June 1862. Again a powderman's widow needed to raise two small children without the love and help of their father.

Elizabeth Shields also married in 1858. Husband John Higgerty worked in the yards for a decade before the explosion in the pack house.

His surname could have been one of several other spellings, including Hagarty, Higgerton, and Hegarty. The Higgertys followed the same childbirth pattern as the McLaughlins and the Querkes by having two children. One, Mary Elizabeth, was less than one year old when the accident happened. The first child was three-and-a-half year-old George. Both birth certificates listed the family's surname as Hagerty.

James Credan, one of four barrel-makers working in and around the press house, left a scant historical record. In 1862 he earned eight and three-quarter cents for each of twenty-five smooth kegs[22] and another five and a half cents each for 550 rough kegs. The company signed over his $260 estate to James P. Kane, the administrator, in 1881.[23]

Credan was a working man whose biography is lost to history. The details of some who lived during this time were known through books intentionally created to tout their accomplishments, and to profit from inflated egos.

In 19th-century America, wealthy and well-known people could have a biography written in a hardback book, often with a black and white portrait. Publishers made money by selling the books to the subjects in the books, and their loved ones. These tomes are excellent historical sources, but the reader must be wary of the contents.[24] The articles were often what today we call a "puff" piece, written to extol virtues the subject might not have had.

The Delaware County, Pennsylvania, biography of John Leary is a perfect example. After telling us that John's father, William, served in the 4th Delaware Infantry, the author stated, "He participated in a number of [the] fiercest battles of the war but escaped uninjured." Other evidence shows that William served in the 5th Delaware, which seems more likely, as that was the regiment where powdermen most often served. And, as we learned earlier, the 5th saw no combat.[25]

William Leary worked at the powder mills starting in 1860; the 5th's short stint at Fort Delaware and elsewhere interrupted his tenure, but he returned, losing his life in a press house explosion in late July 1863. The detonation occurred a little before 6:00 a.m. in the Upper Hagley yard. And, as before, it destroyed other buildings nearby: graining and dust mills and roll mills three and four.

Leary left his wife, Margaret Meehan Leary, to care for the children. The 1860 census shows they had three offspring: John, Mary Ann, and Isaac, six, four, and two years old, respectively.

Besides William, another man, James Peoples, died in that explosion. He was kin to John Peoples, a company clerk whose name was on many of the documents sent to the passenger agents to bring Irish workers to the mills.

Lammot du Pont theorized the cause of the July 1863 explosion: a percussion or friction primer had gotten into loose powder in the press house. That or incendiarism, he wrote.[26] This would not be the last time arson was suspected as a cause of an explosion.

By 1863, the du Ponts, the workmen, the citizens of Wilmington, the army, and Henry Halleck, General-in-Chief, were aware of the potential for powder mill sabotage by Confederate sympathizers or spies. Major General Robert Schenck wrote to Halleck, nicknamed the not-so-complimentary "Old Brains," suggesting two artillery units training in New York transfer to guard the mills to replace the 5th Delaware, serving as prison guards at Fort Delaware. In his book, *Civil War Delaware*, author Michael Morgan wrote, "The Confederate prisoners at Fort Delaware were more restless than usual, and in June 1863, the Union authorities smelled mutiny in the area. The 5th Delaware Regiment, along with the two militia companies under Captains Lammot du Pont and Hugh Stirling, were relieved of their duty of guarding the Du Pont powder mills… and dispatched to the fort."

The author continued: "Not only did the departure of the militia companies leave the powder mills virtually defenseless, but the troop transfer also slowed production at the mills. Many of the mill workers were members of the militia companies, and some literally dropped their tools and hurried off to Fort Delaware." Mrs. Samuel F. du Pont (Sophie) wrote to her husband on June 22, "You can have no idea of the state into which the departure of the 5th Del. has thrown our settlement. The men were hurried off without any time—One who was driving a powder wagon left it en route."[27]

Henry du Pont and Delaware Governor William Cannon had sent the original suggestion. Schenck agreed, writing, "I am concerned to provide whatever defense I can for Wilmington and the powder works, in case the enemy push any force beyond the Susquehanna."[28]

In the Civil War's opening days, the du Ponts and the mills were the subjects of rumors. A letter to the editor of one of Wilmington's papers accused the company of selling ammunition to the Confederacy. "I do hope the Duponts have done making powder for Bragg and Blackguard.

They have fallen very much in my estimation since I heard of it. Do they know that it is treason to give aid and comfort to the enemy? I thought they were such strong union men. *I know it to be a fact that they have sold it to them!*"[29]

They hadn't. Although southern states bought powder from the DuPont Company after secession and the formation of the Confederacy, a company order four days after the firing on Fort Sumter prohibited shipments to the Confederate states.[30] The order did not prevent the rebels from confiscating 650,000 pounds of powder worth $110,000 from DuPont agents in the South.

Rumors abounded that secessionists in Maryland were preparing to attack the mills. DuPont security personnel captured two spies, dressed in female garb, on the yard property.[31] Whether this reference was to the reputed spies O'Keefe and Ryan is not clear. Their story occurs in September 1862.

Col. Arthur Grimshaw, whom we met before as a druggist, physician and newspaper publisher, informed an unidentified Union officer of the 4th Delaware Regiment that, "two suspicious characters supposed to be Rebel Spies" were about. The writer, accompanied by a Colonel Tevis and Lieutenant Toner, rode to O'Keefe's home; there they met his wife, who reported her husband was not home. The trio waited, and O'Keefe and companion Ryan appeared. The men denied being Southern sympathizers or spies. The Union officers transported the two men to Camp DuPont, near the mills on Kennett Pike, and confined them to separate houses.[32]

The next day, the writer sent a letter to a Major Turner, saying that O'Keefe recanted his denial and had been a captain in Hardie's Division of the CSA army. The letter said O'Keefe became dissatisfied with the war and had tendered an unaccepted resignation. He got sick leave and trekked to his wife's house in Wilmington.

Ryan continued to deny he was a spy, and both men went to Fort Delaware's prison.[33]

The du Ponts had told the government the importance of safeguarding the mills. Henry du Pont calculated they needed 800 arms to provide protection. Secretary of War Simon Cameron rejected Henry's urgent plea but suggested he contact Philadelphia regional commander Major General Robert Patterson.

The general heeded the request and sent 400 muskets; Capt. Samuel Francis du Pont, commandant of the Philadelphia Navy Yard, added more. During this early part of the war, Pennsylvania troops made up a mill guard at nearby Brandywine Springs.[34]

Someone claiming to be a relative of the du Pont family, writing a letter to the governor of Virginia two weeks after Sumter, did not help the protection efforts. Charles du Pont Bird, a Dover resident and student at Baltimore's Loyola College, wrote, "The powder mills on the Brandywine (owned by relations of mine) should be secured at all hazards. With a not very large force, if we cannot hold them, they should be destroyed. Some of the Du Ponts are friendly to the South. If it is possible to guard these works for a few weeks the stock of powder for the Southern Confederacy would be largely increased."[35] Bird sent the letter to former Virginia governor Henry A. Wise, who forwarded it to General Lee. Bird served briefly in the same regiment as John McNamara, whom we met earlier; he was the one who claimed to have worked for the du Ponts for several years and offered his services to the Confederacy.[36]

Efforts to divert DuPont powder from the Confederates were not always successful, either; British and French agents were buying powder, then re-selling to the rebel states.[37]

Only a week had gone by since the disastrous late July accident when another explosion rocked the Brandywine Valley. Patrick McGee was approaching his tenth anniversary working for the DuPont Company and was with Hugh McGinley, who had just celebrated twenty years. They were in the dust mill with non-running machinery.

F.G. du Pont theorized the men were taking off the doors of the barrels when the explosion occurred. The detonation threw McGee's body across the creek where a leg bone drove into a tree with such force the survivors had to chop it out to retrieve him.

McGee was another County Donegal resident before coming to the United States. He traveled on the *Provincialist*, the ship that had earlier dropped off forty passengers at New Castle while those remaining had had difficulty disembarking in Philadelphia. Patrick married Jane Kerrigan in early 1858. Daughter Sara was born in April 1859.

McGee was on the creek side of the mill, Hugh McGinley on the race side. McGinley, who was in his late thirties when he died, married Ellen McGee, likely kin to his partner on that ruinous day. The McGinleys lost four children, all boys, in infancy. The first-born boy, Dennis, joined two-and-half-year-old sister, Catherine, on the second day of 1853 but died by the end of the year. Another girl, given the name Frances, but known by Fannie, came along a year after Dennis's death. James was born in November 1856 and died at seventeen months of age. Hugh followed him and survived one month longer than James, succumbing to a serious case of asthma.[38] We do not know when the fourth son John was born or died. Daughters Catherine, Fannie, and Sarah lived into the 20th century.

In the years between Hugh's death and that of his wife Ellen, one of their daughters sent several requests for money due her from the estate. In the early 1890s, Sarah, going by the name Sallie, received more than $300, her share. Then, in the mid-1890s, Fannie made at least three requests of the company's bookkeepers to send money. In March 1897, she closed out her account, receiving a company check for $105.[39]

When Ellen McGinley died early in the first year of the new century, Catherine received the balance, $205, on Valentine's Day, 1901. This left Isabella Dougherty, widow of Thomas, killed in the February 1863 explosion, as the only widow continuing to receive the lifetime $100 stipend.

The cataclysm that was the American Civil War was not finished with its battlefield and sickbed carnage, nor were the DuPont powder mills done with their destruction of life and property.

Eighteen-sixty-four would be a watershed for Northern forces and a thunderstorm of epic proportions for those south of the Mason-Dixon line. The turbulence continued to strike Delaware, not in terms of battlefield havoc, but in carnage on the Brandywine. The year would prove as disastrous as the preceding one regarding the number of men killed, starting in early May.

While the Battle of Spotsylvania raged in Southwest Virginia as part of General U.S. Grant's Overland Campaign, the employees in the yards waged their own war—of production. In the earlier years, the mills produced record amounts of powder, and this period would be no exception. The year's totals became the highest ever to that time.[40] Acute production needs accompanied by overtime resulted in tired workers, which contributed to more accidents.

The first explosion in 1864 occurred May 10. The scene was the lower press house where carpenters were making repairs. As one sawed through

No Powder for Johnny Reb 95

wood and struck the underlying stone (or as some reports said, a nail), a spark ignited a conflagration. Inside the mill sat a container with 200 pounds of black powder; the fire reached the tub, causing the blast. Several newspapers and F.G. du Pont wrote that people could not hear this explosion very far away, unlike most of the others. But that did not mean it failed to kill and maim.

Because so little information is available on the men injured and killed, we must rely on the papers. Here is the report from the Georgetown, Delaware, newspaper:

"The following is a list of the casualties:

- James Kelley, horribly burned about the face and head. He lingered in great agony for a few hours, when he expired.
- Milton Engle, head and face badly burned.—He was still alive at last advice, but no hopes were entertained of his recovery. This young man was an active member of a Lodge of the Independent Order of Odd Fellows, and was among the number who are about to connect themselves with Union Encampment No. 7, whose Charter was restored to them on the evening of the dreadful catastrophe. On the Saturday night previous he had walked all the way to Chatham, Pa, to fit himself to join the Encampment. A short time before the occurrence, he conversed with a brother of the Order, and expressed the great gratification he felt at the hopes he entertained of connecting himself with the highest branch of that institution in a few hours.
- John Genn [Glenn], face and arm burned. His injuries, although very bad, are not considered serious. He will recover. [He did not]
- Thomas Dougherty, badly bruised and otherwise injured. It is feared he cannot survive.
- James Gibbons, burned about the head, face and body. Mr. Gibbons presented a horrid spectacle. He lived only a few hours.
- Martin Hynes, badly burned. No hopes are entertained of his recovery.
- A man named Patrick Tolan was badly injured.
- Three others were burned, but not seriously injured.

Medical aid was procured for the men immediately, and every effort which skill could suggest employed to save their lives. The citizens also rendered every assistance in their power to alleviate their sufferings.

We learn that the wagon of Mr. John People[s], was in the vicinity when the explosion took place, and from its effects, the driver and both of the horses were thrown violently to the earth. The driver escaped with slight bruises, and the animals were not injured.

The mill was entirely destroyed. The explosion was light and was not heard a great distance away.

Since the above was in type, we learn that Messrs. Engle, Hynes and Tolan have died. Coroner Zebley held an inquest over their bodies."[41]

An eighth man, Michael Hickey, also died.[42] The *Delaware Gazette* article, as republished in the *Chicago Tribune* editorialized, "Had the men, when they went in the building, taken the precaution to sprinkle it well with water, their lives would not have been sacrificed. It is strange that a building which has been used for the making or storing of powder until the fine dust had got into every crevice in the floor and roof and rafters, should be carelessly entered by workmen, who must have known the danger the use of their iron tools would subject them to."[43]

The next blast, on July 23, 1864, was one of irony. None of the powdermen then working for the DuPont Company died, but a former worker did. Joseph Babby, born in France, was walking on the banks of the Brandywine opposite the blast in the Lower Yard dust mill. He had quit his job at the powder mills because working in the powder scared him. A sizable piece of timber from the exploding mill flew across the creek and struck Babby in the thigh, causing a ten-inch gash. Men from the mills carried him home for treatment but to no avail, as he died from the injury.

Joseph had married Catherine Callahan in May 1852. Records show their first child, Mary, was born in February of that year, making her illegitimate. The birth record in the St. Joseph on the Brandywine Church registers by Father Walsh, the priest who baptized her, does not include the normal Latin verbiage for an illegitimate birth of a girl (filia populae).[44]

According to the newspapers, Catherine had to care for six children. The irony is that Catherine was now Mrs. Babby, the same pre-marriage name borne by Mrs. David Althaus, the widow of a man killed in the awful 1847 explosion. The third irony in this episode is that Joseph and Catherine's daughter, Mary, married William Callahan; Callahan was

Catherine's maiden name. Du Ponts married cousins; that seems to be possible for others.

By 1870, needing to supplement her income, Catherine Babby and three of her offspring worked for Joseph Bancroft and Sons, a Wilmington dye and bleaching company, a few miles downstream from the powder works. Mary, the oldest at eighteen years of age, worked alongside her fourteen-year-old sister, Rachel, and her brother, Edward, twelve years old.[45] Other than in the powder mills, where no children worked in the powder, eighty mills lining the Brandywine from Wilmington to the Pennsylvania state line employed children as young as nine years old. Little hands repaired machinery in tight places where adult hands didn't fit. Little hands got lost to industrial accidents.

The 1900 U.S. Census shows Catherine, then 70, living with her son Edward and his family on West 18th Street in Wilmington. She died ten years later; three of her seven children preceded her in death.[46]

Despite the fatal explosions, the war of production continued, at the DuPont plant, making powder for the Yankees, and in the South. ■

▪ 8 ▪
Patriotic Pissing

> The entire supply of gunpowder in the Confederacy at the beginning of the conflict, was scarcely sufficient for one month of active operations, and not a pound was being made throughout its limits.
> —George Washington Rains

Without the benefit of supply from the North, the Confederate states had to make gunpowder from scratch. The Rebels used confiscated DuPont powder at the start of the war, but that supply lasted only so long. They bought powder from the French and English, who sold to the South and transported it through the blockade, part of which was under the command of Admiral Samuel Francis du Pont.

Otherwise, the Rebels lacked the manufacturing capacity for powder making, until the CSA government found a man who became one of the South's leading figures.

The choice of Colonel George Washington Rains as a powder plant superintendent was a stroke of luck, for he built what became the second largest powder manufactory in the world. He constructed the Augusta Powder Works in Georgia by relying on a pamphlet written by English powder maker J. Fraser Baddeley in 1857.[1] The Confederate works differed from those on the banks of the Brandywine. In the South, the building arrangement came in the order of the powder-making process, so the product of one mill went to the next mill, then to its neighbor, and so on. The DuPont works used a non-linear building order.[2]

Other differences existed between the DuPont factory and the one in Augusta. The latter used a steam engine connected to a shaft running from the first composition mill to the last. The shaft turned the machinery in all twelve incorporation mills.[3] In Wilmington, each pair of mills mixed the ingredients by their own water-powered machinery. The composition percentages also differed. At the Southern mill, the ratio was 75:15:10—saltpeter, sulfur, charcoal; in the North, it was 75:12.5:12.5. The former mix may have contributed to the opinion that the Southern powder was superior to that made in the North. And it was not just Col. Rains' boss, Josiah Gorgas, and CSA President Jefferson Davis who thought so; Ulysses S. Grant praised Southern-made powder as being better than the powder his soldiers and the U.S. Navy's sailors used.[4] It was possible the difference in powders was the South's use of cottonwood for charcoal, as opposed to the willow used in the Northern mills.

Because the Confederacy had difficulty finding adequate supplies of potassium nitrate, or "nitre," used to produce powder, Col. Rains wrote a manual for the Southern citizenry on how to make it in nitre beds. While they sprinkled plain water on the nitre beds once a week, the preferred method was to use liquid manure or animal or human urine.

In a comedic battle, poetry disparaged nitre manufacturing. In late 1863, Jonathan Haralson, an agent of the Confederacy's Niter and Mining Bureau,[5] advertised in a Selma, Alabama, newspaper requesting that the women of the city "preserve all their chamber lye collected about their premises, for the purpose of making Nitre." His friend Thomas Wetmore wrote a mocking poem called "Rebel Gunpowder":

John Harrolson! John Harrolson! You are a funny creature;
You've given to this cruel war A new and curious feature.
You'd have us think while ev'ry man Is bound to be a fighter,
The women, (bless the pretty dears) Should be put to making nitre.

John Harrolson! John Harrolson! How could you get the notion,
To send your barrels 'round the town To gather up the lotion.
We think the girls do work enough In making love and kissing.
But you'll now put the pretty dears To patriotic pissing!

John Harrolson! John Harrolson! Could you not invent a meter,
Or some less immodest mode Of making our salt-petre?
The thing, it is so queer, you know—Gunpowder, like the crankey—
That when a lady lifts her shift She shoots a bloody Yankee.

John Harrolson! John Harrolson! Whate'er was your intention,
You've made another contraband Of things we hate to mention.

What good will all our fighting do, If Yanks search Venus' mountains,
And confiscate and carry off These Southern nitre fountains![6]

Not to be "outpoetried," Northern soldiers came up with their own bit of doggerel:

Jno Haralson! Jno Haralson! We read in song a story
That women in all these years, Have sprinkled fields of glory;
But never was it told before That how, midst scenes of slaughter,
Your Southern beauties dried their tears And went to making water.

No wonder, Jno, your boys were brave; who would not be a fighter
If every time he shot his gun He used his sweetheart's nitre?
And, vice verse what could make A Yankee soldier sadder,
Than dodging bullets fired from A pretty woman's bladder.

They say there was a subtle smell that lingered in the powder;
And as the smoke grew thicker, And the din of battle grew louder
That there was found in this compound This serious objection;
The soldiers could not sniff it in Without a stiff erection.[7]

Regardless of the differences in the powder or its manufacture, during its three years of operation, the Georgia works produced over three million pounds for rebel guns and did so with only one reported fatal blast. In August 1864, a temporary granulating mill blew up, killing the nine workmen inside waiting for a load of mill cake to arrive via the nearby canal, a guard standing outside, and an adolescent boy in the building next door. Like other mill operators, Col. Rains blamed the explosion on worker error (a thrown, lighted match) rather than conceding that malfunctioning machinery might have been the cause.[8]

The owners of the Sycamore Manufacturing Company near Nashville bought the Augusta machinery in 1873. The Tennessee mill was another, smaller, Confederate powder mill, the same one Malcolm Baxter's errant son, Edward, worked in during the Civil War as seen in Chapter Five. DuPont assisted with the purchase, and thus became part, and eventually full, owner of the mill. They operated it until the early 1900s.[9]

As the families of powdermen prepared for what would be the last

Christmas of the war in December 1864, several of the workers congregated in or near the upper press mill of the Hagley yards, waiting for further orders. The orders never came. Ten of the powdermen died in the mid-morning explosion that destroyed eight buildings: the press house, the graining mill, the dust mill and roll mills three through seven.

Cornelius Carr,[10] who died that winter morning, had brought his family to America in the late winter of 1846-47. Carr and his wife, Frances, known as Fanny, had traveled with their six Irish-born children on the ship *Superior*. The passage was relatively quick: a little over one month. The ship's captain listed Cornelius's occupation on the *Superior's* manifest as a farmer. Twelve-year-old Anne was the oldest child, followed, in the customary manner of a birth every two years, by William, nine; Catherine, age seven; Charles, five; three-year-old Julia; and one-year-old James.[11]

The 1850 U.S. Census compared to the manifest shows an interesting quirk in record-keeping of the era because it listed William's age as sixteen; the manifest three years earlier had listed him as being nine. Catherine's age in the manifest also increased, by seven years in the period between records; Charles' age grew by four additional years from the manifest to the census. James's age is the closest in the two documents. It appears the family fudged the ages on the manifest to save a few dollars, since the ships conveyed children at half the adult cost. Over his first few years with the DuPont Company, Cornelius repaid $122 for the family's passage.

Carr began working in the powder yards within six weeks of the family's arrival in Philadelphia, with additional short travel by smaller ship or overland to the mills. He first appeared on the payroll two weeks after the titanic explosion of April 14, 1847, that killed eighteen of his predecessors.

Within two years, he paid $24 to bring over another James Carr, this one twenty-four years old. He may have been a nephew who traveled on the same ship as Cornelius's family. Then, a year and a half later, he brought "Ann Carr and family," perhaps a niece or sister-in-law, on the *Thomas H. Perkins* at a cost of $105.[12]

In late 1850, Cornelius and Fanny purchased property in Wilmington for $1,100. The land was on Madison Street, bounded by Eighth and Ninth streets. For whatever reason—failure to keep up payments, inability to pay taxes, or having a lien on the property—by April 1864, a sheriff's advertisement announced the sale of the property.

The Carr boys served in Delaware regiments during the Civil War;

all survived the war.

Michael Hassett was another man killed in the 1864 blast ten days before Christmas. Predeceasing him was an infant son, whose name is unknown. Michael married Bridget Connell in 1858. They had three more children—Hannah in 1859, Margaret the next year, and Mary Ann in 1861. For the latter child, Bridget's last name on the birth certificate was O'Connell. Some Irish dropped the 'O' intentionally in order to sound less Irish; others' "Os" were dropped by registrars or ship masters when the person emigrated.

Like Mary Toy, Isabella Watson grieved the loss of her father and husband in explosions. She was the daughter of Archibald Watson (who had died in the 1846 explosion) and Margaret Anderson Watson, who gave birth to her in 1828. Then, in 1863, a year and a half before his death, powder worker Charles O'Neil married Isabella. When she was seventeen, she served as a domestic in the home of a wealthy railroad-car builder; rail-car building was one of the primary types of manufacturing in Wilmington during this time. We do not know if the union produced any issue before Charles's death in late 1864.[13]

The Deerys, Michael and Patrick, were brothers born twelve years apart, sons of James and Unity Deery. The family was from Clonca, the civil parish in County Donegal from which several powdermen hailed. In a misreading of his faded tombstone at St. Joseph on the Brandywine Cemetery, the Works Progress Administration published Michael's age as twenty-seven in its 1930s list of tombstone inscriptions, but he died at thirty-seven.

Thomas Gill is listed in the DuPont Company records as having started work in the mills in May, just seven months before his death in the December 1864 blast. Nothing more is known of him.

Nor is anything known about two other purported victims, Thomas Hennessy and John Dougherty.

Forty-four-year-old Dennis Collins was married to Rose, and the family consisted of two boys, Michael and John, twenty-one and eighteen, respectively, when their father died. He paid $40 in 1854 or 1855 to bring them from Ireland to America. It appears that he and Rose did not leave the young men behind for long, as Dennis started working for the company in 1854.

Edward O'Donnell and Bridget Smith married in June of 1846 but it is not known if they had children. An Edward O'Donnell sailed on the brig *Czar* from Londonderry on an unknown date. He sailed with a Sydney

O'Donnell, and their American sponsor, Michael O'Donnell, was charged an extra $1.75 for provisions proffered by the captain and $.31 for portage of their bags to the railroad station, as well as $23 each for the voyage.

After four brutal years of civil war, peace came to the nation at last on April 9, 1865. But the end of war did not mean peace on the Brandywine. Two weeks after Lee and Grant met at Appomattox, an explosion rocked the mills, this time taking three lives.

Michael Dougherty became the eleventh of his surname to die making black powder in the DuPont mills. Michael had told others he intended to quit the job in the powder "at the end of the week,"[14] which meant at the conclusion of the current shift since the mishap occurred on a Saturday.

Originally from the Irish parish of Kilkenny in County Donegal, Michael started work in the mills in the early 1850s when still a teenager. Whether he made the Atlantic voyage alone or with family is unknown. However, he had a brother, Daniel Dougherty, whom we will meet later. Michael married Rosanna and they had a daughter who died after only a year of life; Susanna lies with her father in a grave with the poetic inscription:

> He was a tender father here
> And in his life the Lord did fear
> We trust our loss will be his gain
> And that with Christ he's gone to reign[15]

John McElwee (listed in some DuPont records as "McElwell") also married a Rosanna; he and John Hughes also died in the April accident. McElwee worked for over a decade before he died. His widow, Rosanna, lived another thirty-five years, passing just days before the huge October 1890 blast. A note from a Michael Farley in the petit ledger for that year, says that Farley "wishes you to send in what money is coming to Mrs. Rosanna McElwee, as it was her desire to have it sent in. She died Wednesday morning at a quarter of 1 o'clock. As the money is to pay the funeral expenses, we wish it sent in as soon as possible."[16] It is unknown who Farley was. He was perhaps a son-in-law living at the same address as Mrs. McElwee.

Recall that E.I. du Pont's first born, Victorine, lost her husband after a few weeks of marriage and never remarried. Mary Cahill had a somewhat similar experience. She and John Hughes married February 23, 1865, near the end of the War Between the States. Two *days* after the nuptials, Mary lost her husband to an explosion in the Lower Hagley press room. She did, however, remarry fifteen months later. Father Walsh of St. Joseph on the Brandywine officiated at both her marriages; the second time she wed John Tulley.

In the 1866 petit ledger, extensive notes on the page with Mary's name tell us that, between her first husband's death and her remarriage, the firm credited her account with an annuity of $125 for fifteen months. She must have worked at willow-peeling, sewing bags, or other work for the du Ponts because through January 1870 they paid her another $120.

The bloody Civil War was over, after taking more than 600,000 lives. The bloody rampage of black powder explosions on the Brandywine continued after a brief pause.

From the time of the April blast two weeks after Lee's surrender at Appomattox, more than two years elapsed between fatal accidents in the Brandywine powder yards. The next occurrence after Dougherty, McElwee, and Hughes died happened in mid-May 1867 when a single death occurred. A married worker named James Cunningham died in this accident in a roll mill.

This second worker with the name James Cunningham had made rapid advancement in pay toward the end of the Civil War. Early in 1864, he was paid $34 per month and, by the end of the year, was making $40. He had married Mary Rosalie Thompson in 1856, but again, it is unknown if there was any issue from the marriage.

Another two years passed without a powder yard death. Then, as everyone prepared for a grand Fourth of July celebration in 1869, a blast that killed two fellow workers dashed the community's patriotic fervor.

Francis Gurney du Pont was one of many observers who erred when writing about explosions and the men involved. Misinformation on headstones of deceased powdermen was common, and James Malloy's tombstone is another case. The stone carver (or those who gave information regarding Malloy) thought Malloy hailed from Strabane, County Donegal. It was a simple mistake; Strabane town is but a river's width away from County Donegal, across the River Foyle in County Tyrone.

Malloy is buried at St. Joseph on the Brandywine Cemetery with Patrick Malloy, who died six months after James met his end. Patrick was twenty-nine, James twenty-seven at death, which could mean they were brothers. And, as we will see, Patrick may have had lingering, unseen injuries that caused his death.

James Malloy had married Margaret McCusker, who gave birth to what appears to be their only child a few days after the explosion. Given that the marriage occurred in early November the previous year, the baby was conceived before its parents' marriage or was born prematurely. It might have been the latter since Victorian-era mores were (for the most part) respected in the tight-knit Irish Catholic community of the Brandywine.[17]

The birth record has the priest's statement, "I baptized in private a son or daughter of James Molloy [another spelling of his surname] and Margaret McCusker."[18] The rite may have been private because Margaret, in mourning, might not have thought it right to have a public celebration of her child's baptism.

The 1869 explosion in the graining mill of the Hagley Yard was the first fatal one after the DuPont Company changed the annuity for the families of deceased workmen killed on duty. The stipend became $100 per year for each of the five years following the death of a husband rather than for the lifetime of the widow. James Malloy's widow, Margaret, and that of Peter Massie, Margaret Ann, were the initial widows to receive the reduced stipends. One has to wonder what both Margarets thought in 1874 when their annuities ended, but those of Ellen McGinley, Catherine McCafferty, Mary McPherson, and others continued.

Massie, a long-term employee in the mills, had served since 1843. Because he was in his sixties, he performed easier jobs than those given to younger men. Francis Gurney du Pont says Massie caused the explosion on July 1, 1869, writing that he was doing "some little work of passing powder on a sieve. He caused the explosion, for there was no machinery in the place. It was thought he tried to move a tub and thus made fire."[19] He added that Massie's body was "blown to small pieces and but little was found."

At least one newspaper took the small bit of information and ran with it: the men were "blown to a height of over one hundred feet…were horribly mutilated…fragments of flesh being scattered in all directions."[20] Not the first, nor last, gory description of the aftermath of an explosion.

In an era without newspaper photographs, the exacting description of dead bodies titillated, and sold newspapers—the pornography of death.[21] After the massive 1818 explosion, one paper had offered a reason for their reporting, stating, "We shall hereafter give such simple facts as may be useful or interesting; endeavoring to avoid the Editorial sin of spinning out horrible descriptions and racking the nerves of others for the sake of selfish profit, or the amusement of the idle."[22] Author Jamie Bronstein wrote, "But gory descriptions also conveyed other lessons. They reinforced the notion that, even in the face of the great inventions and enormous optimism of the 19th century, humans were fragile, and life was easily extinguished."[23]

A local paper reporter wrote that seven tons of powder were in the building that day but only four tons exploded, without explaining how it could happen. A few hundred yards from the epicenter, the shock wave from the blast leveled a cornfield and uprooted the stalks. In Wilmington, the usual stories of broken glass and ceramic items were legion. One newspaper report said the detonation was the worst since the powder wagons had blown up a wealthy neighborhood fifteen years earlier. "The explosion was an unusually sharp one and realized as nearly as may be the idea of 'a clap of thunder in a clear sky,'" reported another.[24]

Result of a roll mill explosion. Note the mill walls displaced but still standing. (Hagley Museum and Library)

After larger explosions, the papers said alarmed residents tried to get to high points to look north westward, toward the mills, to find if they could see anything. This case was no exception: "Over the city a dense volume of white smoke rolled, so nearly resembling the clouds as to be scarcely distinguishable from them, and the air was impregnated for a longtime afterwards with the smell of gunpowder."[25]

Closer to the scene, F.G. du Pont reported that Pat Malloy escaped the direct effect of the detonation by being near the door. When the rumbling ceased and the rest of the men gathered, they found Malloy at the corner of the mill lying down, "without a scratch on him but yelling loudly." Patrick died at the end of the year, but we do not know if the injuries he received in the July accident caused his death.

Many of the remaining workers struck for higher wages a few days after the accident. When they approached Irénée du Pont II, then in charge, he told them to go to the office and close their accounts if they were unsatisfied. Most of the hands returned to work; eight left the next day.[26]

Peter Massie's three sons worked in the DuPont mills, before and after his death. His namesake continued to work until the end of the century; he also took part as a juror in a murder trial in Wilmington in 1874.[27]

As we have seen, Sophie du Pont, E.I.'s youngest daughter received letters from the children of powdermen asking for something, usually money, to relieve them of suffering from illness or poverty. Peter Massie's son Charles's requests were less selfish.

In 1886, two years before her death, Mrs. du Pont received a series of letters from Charles, living in Baltimore. "No doubt this note will be to you a great surprise being from one so long away from you, Charlie Massie." A paragraph followed about his joining a small church called the Chapel of the Nativity in a poor section of West Baltimore. He asked Sophie to send sample booklets used in her missionary support work, pamphlets to engage donors, to help the pastor build a church.[28]

Mrs. du Pont sent the booklets, and Charles responded ten days after the original note, thanking her for sending "just what I wanted."[29] Massie and Rev. Briscoe, his pastor, met Sophie between November and March, as Massie wrote again, thanking her for seeing them during a visit to Wilmington.[30] She sent him a donation to which he responded at the end of March with a "thank you." He added a P.S.: "Mrs. DuPont I will write you & let you know how we get along."[31] If he wrote again, the du Ponts did not keep the letter(s).

Powder mill workers toiled six eleven-hour days in the three pleasant-weather seasons, nine hours in the winter, with Sundays free. They received overtime pay. They did not have to complete a full work week of sixty-six hours to receive overtime. For example, the name Darby McAteer appears many times in the petit ledgers between 1861 and his death on March 25, 1870. In 1861, the first year of the Civil War, he earned $20 a month. During one month, he was short by one and a half hours on his regular time sheet but earned an added $18 in overtime, doubling his pay. In other months, as the federal government's demands for powder zoomed up, he continued to double his usual wage.

As wages rose during the war because of decreased manpower pools owing to rising enlistments in the army, McAteer capitalized. By 1863, pay raises reached as much as 30 percent; he started at $34 per month and received $43 by the end of the year. In December, with overtime, he earned $55 a month.

In the following year, he started at $42 (I could find no reason for the dollar decrease from December) and received raises of $4 in March and $1 each in July and August. By the end of the war, his monthly wage plus overtime consistently reached $71. It is easy to see why he could provide for a family of six and make contributions of more than $5 to a Draft Club and another dollar to James Volunteers (the purpose of these groups is unclear). Darby put part of the money into real estate. In 1885, Victor du Pont,[32] administrator of McAteer's estate after the March 1870 explosion, advertised the sale of three properties in Wilmington—two brick structures and a wooden frame one. The buildings sold for $1,818,[33] money which doubtless helped Darby's widow Catherine Brogan McAteer and her four children, ranging now in age from fifteen to twenty-two.

In Francis Gurney du Pont's telling of the March blast, he mysteriously stated that "the cause of the explosion could not be determined, unless seen by the light of after events." He then said the elevators "blew the [Graining] mill."[34]

Another explosion rocked the powder yards just three weeks later. For one worker, his good luck in building a life in America ran out in April 1870. While most DuPont Irish hailed from County Donegal, Eire's northernmost county, not all did. James Donahue grew up in the townland Lisdillon, south of Derry, in Clondermot civil township.[35] (The Irish, particularly Catholics, who hated England, eliminated the "London" part of Londonderry's name.) James made the passage at age twenty-five, sailing from Liverpool to Boston on the *Diana* in 1847, captained by Fredrick Howe. Three brothers—William, Hugh, and Patrick—might have accompanied him[36] during the height of the Great Famine in Ireland.

Sorrow, despair, and desolation filled the reports from other immigrant ships voyaging as the famine reached its height. The *Cork Examiner* reprinted a *New York Sun* article about the distress of immigrants in New York. "The paupers who have recently arrived from Europe give a most melancholy account of their sufferings. Upwards of eighty individuals, almost dead with the ship fever, were landed from one ship alone, while twenty-seven of the cargo died on the passage, and were thrown into the sea. They were one hundred days tossing to and fro upon the ocean, and for the last twenty days their only food consisted of a few ounces of meal per day, and their only water was obtained from the clouds." The paper added, "The miseries which these people suffer are brought upon themselves, for *they have no business to leave their country without at least a sufficient quantity of food to feed them while making the passage.*"[37]

The editors seemed unaware that shipowners often skimped on foodstuffs, thinking their voyage would be shorter than normal, thus needing less food for passengers, or acted with extreme negligence. Captains knew they could sell stored victuals to the unsuspecting Irish at high prices, thus ensuring a handsome profit on the backs of the destitute emigrants.

To add to the misery, the winter of 1846-1847 was harder than usual, with ice causing delays for many vessels even into the spring. As an example, the *Albion*, which left Scotland for Canada in late March 1857, arrived in Quebec in early June.[38]

Boston turned away the *Mary's* passengers near this time because "the city authorities would not suffer them to be landed, owing to their destitute condition, unless the master gave bonds that they should not become a burthen to the city." Other U.S. ports rejected vessels filled with Irish and other emigrants which forced them to Canada's Grosse Isle quarantine station. Grosse Isle reported over nine thousand immigrant deaths during the 1847 arrival season.[39]

On his voyage James Donahue was lucky. That was not the case on the twenty-third anniversary of the fatal April 14, 1847 explosion. Donahue was the only worker who died in the 1870 blast, no consolation to his thirty-nine-year-old spouse, Margaret, and their ten children. Margaret Devine had sailed from Eire to Baltimore, via Liverpool, landing in 1850. She and James married in County Derry when she was but fifteen or sixteen years old. The couple had their first baby, John, a year after her arrival in the States. The other nine children arrived in the every-two-year pattern, with the last, Mary, called Mame, born in 1868.

Two of the children later married the offspring of powdermen. Catherine Grant, whose father, John, died in the January 1859 explosion, married James Donahue's namesake nine years after the death of his father. Annie Donahue married Daniel Harkins Junior, the son of a veteran powdermen who would perish in 1890.[40]

Francis Gurney du Pont wrote that James Donahue died in the 1866 (not 1870) explosion of roll mill nine, one of the so called "Eagle Mills." He noted that Donahue took the charge (powder) from this roll mill, for which he was the operator, and placed it in the stock house. Meanwhile, John Smith, overseer of roll mill ten, had taken his charge to Donahue's mill nine.

Smith later reported he observed Donahue using a copper scraper to clean the equipment. After warning Donahue to be careful, Smith left. The explosion happened moments later; Francis Gurney wrote that "the explosion occurred by Donahue striking fire with the scraper."

One author's reading of Francis's ledger book says most of the time du Pont did not record a reason. "But when a cause was given, it was invariably related to worker error rather than (for example) workplace structure."[41] DuPont's mistake in the dating of this explosion does not detract from the tragedy of a man's death.

Although 1871 saw the most explosions in any year of powder operations, no fatalities occurred. Of the twenty-six blasts reported that year, all but five happened in a roll mill. Roll mill twelve had four blasts; roll mills five and eight had three explosions each, including two just one week apart. Several other roll mills were the sites of two accidents each.

During this peaceful year (detonations yes, but no wailing at the loss of a relative or friend, no keening, no funeral following an explosion), the newspapers had fun reporting other types of explosive mishaps.

A local newspaper in Wilmington wrote that a church sexton took a lighted candle into the basement of his church, unaware that a gas pipe was leaking. "Instantly there was an explosion and now the sexton is not as well as formerly." The same paper two weeks later reported the explosion of a doughnut "placidly simmering in a kettle of lard [that] badly scalded a Chicago artist. He is now inquiring for a non-explosive doughnut."[42]

Explosions of all kinds filled the news. Most were bursts of steamboat boilers. An 1872 boiler explosion on a Mississippi River steamer burned, scalded, or drowned eighty people.[43] The papers blamed the "evil habit" of steamboat racing as the cause of an Ohio River boiler explosion in Indiana. Another boiler explosion killed a Presbyterian missionary and his family in Japan in 1870.[44]

Not only black powder mills, boilers, and doughnuts were exploding. Oil lamps were a source of explosive danger in a time before electricity came to be in common use. Mice nibbling on matches embedded in gun cotton in an Albany, New York, billiard ball factory caused an explosion that resulted in $3,000 damage.[45] In a bizarre accident in Wilmington, a boy threw a lighted firecracker into an empty barrel found on the sidewalk near an alcohol plant. The resultant blast shook houses, and Wilmingtonians heard it for some distance. The detonation tossed the boy a few feet into the air, but he recovered from his injuries. A reporter for the Wilmington Daily Commercial wrote, "The explosion was, of

Patriotic Pissing

course, owing to the fact that it was filled with fumes of alcohol, and except for the injuries to the youthful experimenter might be properly considered one of the [most] successful noises ever caused by a single fire cracker."[46]

At the same time, advertisers of goods for medicinal and other daily uses touted the safety of their products. An advertisement for Perry Davis' Pain Killer stated nothing was more painful than rheumatism, neuralgia, and sprains, but offered the concoction as "not a cheap Benzine or Petroleum product that must be kept away from fire or heat to avoid danger of explosion."[47]

Telling merchants that "appalling deaths and fires from glass lamps exploding and breaking create a great demand for this lamp," the makers of "Perkins and House's patented non-explosive metallic kerosene lamp" sold retailers on the promise of great profit: "It pays to sell it."[48]

Sewer gas explosions, paper-mill boiler eruptions, colliery accidents (one in England killing 130), exploding medicines—the list of means by which an explosion could kill was lengthy in the late 19th century.

Editors and writers also used the DuPont name to spice up their stories. For example, "There is a mighty roar going up over the county over this Alphonse-Gaston perpetuity business, which means fastening on the courthouse corridors an infestation of official barnacles that a dozen duPont explosions would fail to dislodge."[49] Alphonse and Gaston referred to a comic strip featuring two bumbling Frenchmen with a penchant for politeness.

One writer used a trading post as the scene for his story. It seems a Native American, whom the trader thought was giving him a hard time, was told if he ever appeared again with a bottle, they would throw it into the fire. The Amerind showed up a few days later, bottle in hand. The trader demanded the bottle and threw it into the stove, as promised. As the Native American headed for the door, "whang went the stove, and out came the windows, the trader following close behind. The next time the trader burns an Indian's whiskey bottle he will examine it, to see whether its contents are of 'Dupont's make' or whiskey."[50]

The papers often contributed to stereotypical thinking in the 19th century. The combination of Native Americans and whiskey was an oft-repeated cliché. So was picturing the Irish as hot-headed and buffoonish. It is also a clichè that one life lost to gunpowder explosions is one too many, but to the survivors, nothing was filled with more truth. ■

▪ 9 ▪
Explosions Are Seldom Serious, Nowadays

> "Really a valuable citizen...we hope he will speedily recover from his injuries."
> —*The Delaware Republican*

The du Ponts grieved the loss of life of their workers with the deceased's family, friends, and coworkers. They took pride that the death toll, an average two per year, was much less than the toll for canal building, mining, and manufacturing.

By 1872, Jonas Miller, whom we met in the Prolog, had worked in the powder mills for more than a half century, and had amassed a fortune of $5,000.[1] In January, he burned his hands and face trying to put out flames that arose in the Lower Hagley press room. He was leading other millwrights in unloading a heavy brass-covered plunger used in pressing, and moved too slowly when the flames, caused by a man using a pry bar which "struck fire," broke out. The others fled without injury. Since the press was not "injured," it was back in service two weeks later.[2]

Three months later, two of Miller's workmates were not so lucky. While cleaning machinery in the upper press mill in the Hagley Yard, Peter Flanigan, using a copper scraper, struck fire on what F.G. du Pont called the "tail block" of the press. The resultant explosion caused Flanigan to fall between the press and cutting machine, saving his life for the moment. Various sources differ detailing his death. F.G. says Flanigan remained living for eleven days. One newspaper, published the next day, reported that his doctor "entertains some hopes of his recovery";[3] their optimism lasted two days when they then said he was in critical condition and "is suffering, apparently, the most intense agony. Very little hopes were entertained, yesterday, of his recovery." The following day, in the same column where a writer placed a report of a non-fatal explosion elsewhere in the mills, he reported the end of Flanigan's suffering; this was only four days after the April 19, 1872 accident.

Flanigan left his widow, Mary McCusker, likely the sister of Margaret (the relict of deceased powderman James Malloy), to care for eight children, ages ten to less than a month. After Peter died, three of the children predeceased Mary. Eugene died a sudden death at age seventeen in December 1886. He must have been asthmatic or perhaps epileptic, as the newspaper said he was "apparently in his usual health" while "coasting [sledding] with several companions." The report added he was "subject to the attacks from which he died, although he looked well and hearty."[4] William, Mary's second oldest child, died at thirty-four. Her daughter, Mary Anne, also died in her thirties. William and Eugene are buried together next to their parents Peter and Mary in St. Joseph Cemetery.

The Hagley Museum and Library recorded several dozen oral interviews with workers' families in the middle and later years of the 20th century. Two interviews refer to Peter Flanigan. William F. Flanigan speaks of his grandfather Peter, saying he lived in Squirrel Run when he died in 1872.

John Schaefer made the second recording in 1988; he was the grandson of Peter's daughter, Ellen Flanigan Stewart, and, at age ten, the eldest living at home when Peter died. Schaefer says Peter and Mary had seven children, failing to mention his Uncle Patrick. He says his uncles John, Felix, and Gene worked for the DuPont Company, adding that Felix was a foreman of a group of men who built many of the stone walls dotting the New Castle County countryside. Schaefer said when there was no work in the powder mills, the company sent the men elsewhere to work on stone projects.

The second man killed in the April 1872 accident was Dennis McLaughlin, a father of six with his wife, Mary Meehan McLaughlin. McLaughlin broke both legs in the explosion, was burned, and died later that day. Like the Dougherty brothers who died in the first explosion in 1815; Daniel Dougherty and John McGinness, killed in the 1847 accident; and the Deerys, who died in 1864, McLaughlin was a native of the parish of Clonca in County Donegal.

Only four months later, on August 14, 1872, a worker whom F.G. du Pont called Patrick Burns died when the lower yard graining mill blew up. The man's name, elsewhere in Du Pont Company records, was Baun; the news reporters wrote his name as Bawn. Workers found his body thrown across the creek with a brush nearby, leading observers to think he had used it to clean machine belts resulting in sparks hitting the floor among black powder granules.

Baun had married Mary McGrath in 1864, a marriage which resulted in the birth of three children. If they read the story of his death, the paper's description would not have heartened them: "One leg was blown off, one hand was missing, and he was otherwise horribly mangled." The paper told readers, "His remains, or that part of them which could be found" would be interred the next day at St. Joseph Cemetery.[5]

On the first anniversary of the explosion that killed Peter Flanigan and Dennis McLaughlin, another blast may have cut short the lives of two powdermen. In a strange twist, one of them, Patrick Kelleher, suffered what seemed like minor injuries in this April 19, 1873 explosion. He returned to work soon after but went to the Pennsylvania Hospital in Philadelphia in July, where he died four months after the event.

Francis Gurney said Kelleher died not from his explosion injuries but from a stomach tumor found at the postmortem. F.G. noted that the mill held 7,500 pounds of powder, even after foreman John Gibbons and the men removed a load and took it to the glazing mill. The graining mill man was out of bags, so Gibbons told Kelleher to take some from the glazing mill to the graining mill. DuPont wrote that Kelleher just reached the door of the mill when the explosion occurred, setting fire to the bags he carried, which flew into the nearby trees and set them ablaze. Francis Gurney continued, "The man's clothes were set on fire but were extinguished by August Ebert, a man of very calm temperament, who by the way, was not of perfectly sound mind." Ebert's mind was sound enough to dip Kelleher into the millrace to extinguish the flames enveloping him.[6]

Another man who died as a result of the April blast was another Dougherty, this time Michael Dougherty II; he may have been the son of the Michael Dougherty killed in the February 1865 press room explosion. He was thirty-three and had worked in the powder for two years.

In writing a biography of Alfred I. du Pont, Marquis James said, "Whenever two powdermen fell to reminiscing sooner or later something would come out concerning Jonas Miller."[7] There was a lot to talk about.

We first met Jonas as a fourteen-year-old helping Victor du Pont and his guests after the 1818 explosion. Irénée, impressed by the work Jonas did, hired him as an apprentice to the head millwright, Richard Rambo. Rambo taught him well, as Jonas became a master millwright within four years.

A typewritten manuscript at the Hagley Library says Jonas's father was an illegitimate son of a nobleman or a wealthy man, and came to the North American continent "with his father…and grew up to be quite an able man and of all the Millers in this part of the world was the only branch that were worth much."[8] Editorial comment aside, Jonas's father George, says William Henry Miller, Jonas's great-grandson, came to America with his widowed mother (not his father) and two brothers,[9] who hailed from County Derry.

George worked for a brief time for the du Ponts and owned farm property in Brandywine Hundred. He operated the Blue Ball Tavern (near the extant Blue Ball Dairy Farm Museum off the current Route 202) from 1810 to 1816. Jonas and his brother George were born elsewhere, but the youngest son, Joseph, was born at the tavern. In a 2006 article in an historical archaeology journal, Heather Wholey wrote, "During [George, the father] Miller's tenure public elections were held at the inn, it became known for fine food, and it was first referred to with the name Blue Ball, in reference to a blue ball that was pulled up a pole to signal stagecoach drivers that passengers were to be picked up."[10]

Five years after starting to run the inn, George bought eighty acres nearby and, with the help of two sons, Jonas and George, cleared the forested land for farming. At age eleven, Jonas was used to hard work, a characteristic that stood him in good stead with the gunpowder mill owners three years later.[11]

Before 1823, Jonas married Jane Higgins, the daughter of Andrew Higgins, who had fought in the Revolutionary War with the Delaware Blues, about whom Henry "Lighthorse" Lee commented, "The state of Delaware furnished one regiment only; and certainly no regiment in the army surpassed it in soldiership."[12] Not only would their children carry the blood of a Revolutionary War hero, they were also kin of James G. Blaine, a Maine politician who served as speaker of the U.S. House, U.S. senator, secretary of state, and presidential candidate. Blaine was a distant relative of Jane Higgins.

Jonas and Jane, married at nineteen and fifteen years of age,[13] respectively, suffered the pangs of loss of a child six times, consoled by their seven remaining children living into adulthood. Sarah Jane was born to the couple in February 1830; she lived until at least four years of age. Father Carrell, the priest at St. Peter's in Wilmington, baptized her although Jonas and Jane were Presbyterian.

The Millers moved within the Hagley mills area several times to accommodate their ever-increasing clan. By 1842, the family was made up of at least five children including fourteen-year-old John Savage; Sarah Jane, eleven; George, five; four-year-old Catherine; and Henry, one year old. They remained in the sizable frame house near the new bridge (Rising Sun Bridge) for seven years until moving to another frame dwelling near Bogan's Store. Either this house was the Goodman House, or they moved within six months to that eponymous abode and remained there until March 1858. Jonas paid rent on a "quarry on mill property" and may have had a sideline—brick making. The records show that he paid a rent payment "in brick."

Jonas Miller's sons clearly learned the value of hard work from their father. Three of the sons, first-born John Savage, George, and William Henry, whom they called Henry, became successful businessmen, owning and operating a barley mill outside the powder mill gates in the 1880s. Two started their work careers with DuPont, although not "in the powder."

John Miller served an apprenticeship under his father and worked as a journeyman millwright for twenty-one years. Toward the end of the Civil War, in which he enlisted in the 5th Delaware and rose to the rank of sergeant, he left the mills to open a general store in Henry Clay, a DuPont neighborhood. He maintained the store for thirty-two years, turning it over in 1896 to son-in-law, Henry Gregg.[14] They demolished the store at Creek Road and Rising Sun Lane between 1912 and 1914 to make way to expand the DuPont Experimental Station.

At age nineteen, Henry became an apprentice millwright and continued working in the mills until at least 1899. In 1906, he ran for election as a Delaware state senator on the Republican ticket and served one term, moving from his district in 1910.[15] Henry, when working at the barley mill, was the most active of the three brothers. George, Jonas' second son making it to adulthood, did not work in the powder mills.

Henry, whose teacher had seen him fence-sitting with friends and not coming into the school back in September 1859, and his brother George, with James McKenna and Daniel Toy (sons or grandsons of powdermen), enrolled at St. Mary's College in Wilmington, more a high school than a college.[16]

During his half century and more working in the mills, Jonas Miller was sent by the company to work elsewhere. Entries in the DuPont Company files show he worked for Charles I. du Pont and Company, a textile mill owned by E.I.'s nephew and eldest son of E.I.'s brother, Victor. Jonas further plied his trade at Breck's Mill, downstream from the main gate of the powder yards. Charles I. du Pont owned Breck's Mill, known as Rokeby, although William Breck was the manager and former owner. (Breck married Charles's niece, Gabrielle Josephine du Pont, named for her grandmother, Victor's wife).[17] Jonas also traveled south into Delaware's middle county, Kent, to work at a sawmill in the period 1843 to 1848.[18]

As the Brandywine community prepared for a gala Fourth of July celebration in 1873, Jonas Miller and Daniel Dougherty, who would lose his eyesight in an explosion nine years hence, were among the men in the millwright shop cleaning barrels. Jonas apparently took staves off the barrels and struck another stave with an iron hammer, producing a spark. Dougherty and the others got out but, at age sixty-nine, Jonas, slower to run, caught the full force of the resultant explosion. He sustained severe burns; his fellow workers rushed him home where he suffered for three days before succumbing to the wounds.

The *Wilmington Daily Commercial*, calling him Joel Miller, told its readers that "he was injured so much that he will probably die." It said the explosion of the loose powder stripped the "flesh from his hands, arms, head, and other portions of his body." The paper erroneously reported "he was engaged in the glazing of barrels, *whatever that might be.*"[19]

Another local paper, the *Delaware Republican*, reported that the men had been tearing up the floor of the old mill building. Calling him "really a valuable citizen," the paper stated that "we hope he will speedily recover from his injuries."[20] After his death the *Republican* stated that Jonas was "highly respected by all his neighbors."[21]

Sons John and George became administrators of the estate, which included three properties in and around Wilmington. In June of the next year, an 18,000-square-foot piece of land at Rodney and 6th streets, which was divided into lots at the time of the sale, went on the block. Another thirty-one acres of farmland near Talleyville in Brandywine Hundred, including the "right to use a spring on the adjoining land of John Husbands," and another lot nearer to the powder mills in Rockland, went up for sale.[22]

Less than a week after Jonas's death, the local Independent Order Odd Fellows Brandywine Lodge elected his namesake to be the Noble Grand, or presiding officer. In the same ceremony, the son of Peter Massie, who had died in an explosion in 1869, also became an officer.[23]

Daughter Catherine married Joseph Walker and, after he died, made the westward journey to "Indian territory," i.e. Oklahoma. George traveled even farther, to California,[24] and Jonas Junior, settled in Kansas.[25] Sisters Sarah Jane and Anna Maria married apparent brothers John and James Newlin.[26] The widow Miller died two years after her husband.

The next three and a half years after the 55-year powder veteran died provided a respite from death but not destruction visited on the DuPont gunpowder factory.

In May 1875, an explosion rocked northern Delaware when two DuPont dust mills blew. The mills, driven by a single turbine, contained soda powder,[27] with more destructive force than standard black powder. In most cases, the sturdy stone used in the mill buildings (scientific name: gneiss) withstood blasts. The more powerful force of the soda powder detonation tore the mills apart and the company rebuilt them.

One local paper ended its article about the explosions with the following statement: "With the improvements which modern science has introduced, and the increased precautions taken against accident, these explosions are seldom serious, nowadays."[28] The death of another Dougherty dented the paper's optimism six months later.

That same year, in a roll mill explosion that presaged another November 30 explosion exactly forty years later, Edward Dougherty II died. He was likely the son of the Edward Dougherty who perished in the 1859 explosion. The victim in the 1875 blast married Sarah Cronin and left three children, including Catherine, who became a nun with the Sisters of Mercy in Philadelphia, and John, whom his father enjoyed for one month before the latter's death. The name of the third child is unknown.

As it was a late fall night, a theory of the mishap posited that a glass-enclosed kerosene lamp used to light the yards during night work malfunctioned, the flame from the lamp escaping its enclosure and setting two buckets of powder afire. Some observers had other theories. Dougherty, a smoker, was thought to have carried an ember from a home fire in his clothing after a dinner break, or sand attached to the shovel used to remove the powder "charge" from the wooden roller trough caused a spark.[29] Here again we see the pervasive thinking of factory owners, believing that explosions couldn't be the fault of their construction or machinery but had to be caused by careless workers.

Dougherty "was thrown violently against the wall and had his head badly cut and bruised and his leg broken."[30] He lived for a day before succumbing to the injuries.

Two more Doughertys became victims, and another had a narrow escape in an explosion six months later. On May 20, 1876, ten days after the opening of the Philadelphia Centennial exhibition (officially the International Exhibition of Arts, Manufacturers, and Products of the Soil and Mine) an explosion ripped apart the Upper Hagley press room, killing Frederick Dougherty and Patrick Dougherty II. Amos Carter and Patrick McKinney also died when four tons of powder blew.

During the powder-making process, after removing the powder slurry from the roll mill, workers transported it to the press house, where they pressed the mass to remove as much moisture as possible. They broke the resultant "cake" into smaller pieces; this was the job being performed when the explosion occurred.

Francis Gurney du Pont says a large piece of copper, had passed through the cutting

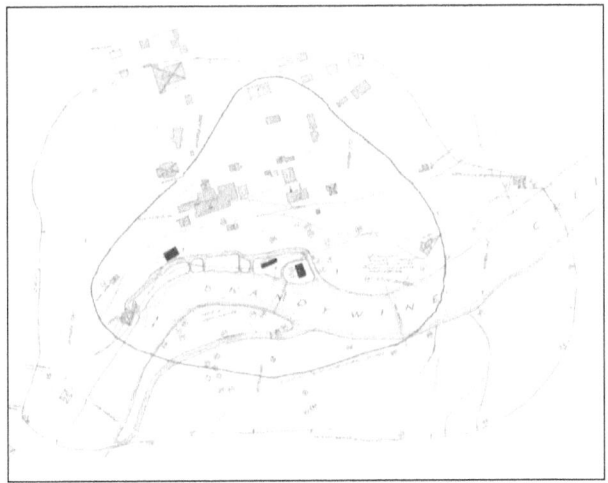

Missile map showing how far an explosion could send pieces of machinery. The outer line is several hundred yards from the epicenter. (Hagley Museum and Library)

machine, whether by accident or design he could not say.[31] He had visited the men before the explosion to ask if the press plunger operated properly. They assured him the machinery worked correctly, although they had had issues with it earlier.

The newspapers were not kind to the surviving families; their business was selling papers, not worrying what survivors might read of their loved ones, and what better way than to include the goriest of details. "They were blown into an unrecognizable mass," wrote the *Philadelphia Inquirer*.[32] "Little pieces of flesh, of bone or of clothing, are about all that can be found [of] the poor victims of this terrible explosion. A head and shoulders and part of a thigh, all blackened and swollen beyond recognition, were found in the woods, about fifty feet from the yard, and the only thing recognizable found was the head of one of the Doughertys. The other remnants are little pieces of flesh and bone," said another paper.[33]

Another description, not as graphic, said, "It is now stated that one of the four men who were blown up in the explosion at Dupont's Powder Works, has been found deeply imbedded in a bank a little distance from the scene of disaster." It added, "Some fragments of the others, of a very minute character, have since been picked up at a considerable distance, but not sufficient in their character to be identified as that of any one of the ill-fated party."[34]

The same paper reported detail that showed the reach of powder explosions. A man was hauling a wagon of lime to Wilmington from East Caln Township, in Chester County, Pennsylvania. When close to the mills, "so great was the concussion, that every mule [a total of six] fell to the ground. The driver managed to retain a perpendicular position, and soon after the occurrence he had his team upon their feet and the journey recommenced, as if nothing had happened."[35]

It was not uncommon for the news of the larger explosions on the Brandywine to make its way to far-away places such as Australia, even though it might take some time. The 1847 explosion seems to have been the first Brandywine incident to make news in Australia. In a column called "Odds and Ends from late European Papers," the October 20th edition of the *Sydney Morning Herald* that year used the by-now common phrase "blown to atoms" to tell its readers that eighteen men in Delaware had been killed by the explosion of 6,000 pounds of powder.[36] The 1847 explosion wasn't reported in Sydney until six months had gone by. The 1854 powder wagon detonations in Wilmington were not reported there until four months had passed.[37]

But, by America's Centennial year, three decades after the 1847 blast, the news of the 1876 detonation made itself known around the world much more quickly. The *Morning Herald* reported the accident just a month after it occurred and even at that significant distance, got the names right.[38]

Frederick Dougherty was a twenty-one-year-old single man who boarded with his cousin, Edward Dougherty II, (killed six months before) at Walker's Banks. Frederick continued living in the home of Edward's widow, Sarah, until his own death in the May 20 explosion.

Patrick Dougherty II had married his wife, Grace, in January 1875, and the couple produced a girl, Margaret, known as Maggie, later that same year. Eighteen seventy-six was a doubly tragic time for Grace, first losing her husband in May, then her seven-month-old daughter in July. Her neighbors in Free Park, where she lived, lovingly comforted and supported her.[39]

It was not enough. After the deaths of her spouse and baby, in October, Grace, like Jane Russell before her, returned to the old country, probably to County Donegal, from where she must have come (Patrick's headstone shows he came from there). A note in the petit ledger for the year 1876 articulated the details: "Mrs. Dougherty wishing to go to Ireland & consequently forfeiting her pension, we agreed to pay funeral expenses & bills as above & to give her in addition one hundred dollars which closes her pension claim." The company paid $66 in bills the family had accrued, including $14 to St. Joseph's Church and paid for her passage from New York to Londonderry, which cost $32.[40] It must have been a somber and lonely voyage.

Patrick McKinney was another powderman who came from the parish of Clonca (misspelled again on his tombstone), one of twelve children of a family who emigrated to America. After arrival, he paid for two of his sisters to journey from County Donegal. He was young when he died in 1876, only twenty-three, and unmarried.

McKinney's great-nephew, William Craven, provided an interview during the oral history project for the Hagley Museum in the 1980s. Craven says his uncle prevented an explosion by throwing water onto hot machinery and the company gave him a free house on the Stone Block, another small neighborhood, for life,[41] an award little used.

Amos Carter was not so lucky. On May 20 he was approaching the press house but was much closer to the mill. He was doubly unlucky; that morning he had transferred from the Lower Hagley yard to the Upper Hagley press house.

Carter, when not yet a DuPont employee, had joined Company A of the 3rd Delaware in 1864. (DuPont Company workers joined the 5th Delaware.) He did it unlike the DuPont Company workers. In what was a common enlistment method, Charles Kinney Jr., of East Dover Hundred, Kent County, paid him $300 to enlist as a substitute. Carter became one of 118,000 paid substitutes in the Northern army.

Amos, at least thirty-eight years old,[42] was above average age for enlistees in the Union forces. Most of the enlistees were half his age while some were several years older. The average age of Federal soldiers during the war was twenty-six.[43] Although his enlistment period was one year, his last pay was three months after he joined. We do not know why the short (five-foot, four-inch), hazel-eyed soldier served only three months.

In 1848, Amos had married Mary Zebley and, at his death at age 52 in 1876, they had three children: Amos Jr., Phoebe, and Henry. The Carters later moved out of company-owned housing and became homeowners in Wilmington. They found a residence in the McDowellville neighborhood, land defined by Pennsylvania Avenue, Union, and Clayton Streets named for the prominent McDowells living there.

After Carter's death, the family had difficulty paying city and school taxes. Several newspaper announcements of overdue taxes ranged from $9.24 in 1881 to $15.75 in 1909.[44] The delinquent tax rolls for 1906 listed the Carter property at 1706 Pennsylvania Avenue, now the site of an automobile dealership.[45]

Amos had also made the papers earlier, after the Civil War but before employment at the DuPont Company. While he was in his mid-forties, he was the victim of a petty crime. Dennis F. Dougherty evidently convinced the intoxicated Amos to put his feet up at the Phoenix (fire) Engine House at Twelfth and King streets. When Amos awoke, he found his boots gone. Officials charged Dougherty with the theft of the boots, returned by a police officer. The court found the defendant not guilty.[46]

As if a harbinger, on the very first full night of 1877, a three-story brick building in Wilmington, called "The Beehive" because it had so many occupying businesses, endangered the city with the largest fire in six years. The owner of the building, responsible for half of the $40,000 loss, was uninsured.

Four days later, almost to the hour, the Upper Yard graining mill exploded, killing one of the few remaining French workers, John Baptiste Minninger, born in the Alsace region of France thirty years earlier. He had worked in the mills for eighteen months. His pay was another example of a mill man working less than the required number of days in a month but still receiving overtime pay. He worked one and a half days short of a full month and received overtime pay for thirteen days in September 1876.[47]

In 1878, Joseph Bancroft & Sons, where the widow Babby and three of her children worked after Joseph Babby died, negotiated with the DuPont Company about Bancroft buildings damaged by the 1877 explosion. Bancroft proffered an amount to demolish two houses along the Brandywine, to which the du Ponts responded with a lower offer. The parties agreed on a sum of $1,000. As late as 1913, Samuel Bancroft, Jr. wrote to DuPont requesting information on the explosion.[48]

The New Year's "beehive" fire was not an omen of a dreadful year on the Brandywine after all. It was not even an augury of the rest of the seventies. Although many accidents occurred in the mills in the remainder of the decade, they recorded no fatalities. The next fatal accident did not occur until five years after John Minninger died. ∎

▪ 10 ▪
The Big One

> The report of my death was an exaggeration.
> —*Mark Twain.*

Luck was with the powdermen toiling in the DuPont mills during the first years of the 1880s. While more than eighteen explosions occurred, including three each in roll mills eight and thirteen, the first serious blast occurred in the spring of 1882. No deaths, but it was a close thing.

An older hand, fifty-two-year-old Daniel Dougherty, was working alone in roll mill five early on the morning of Monday, May 2, 1882. That afternoon the local paper reported, "The body of Dougherty torn and mangled was thrown outside the mill. The top and back of his head was a mass of bruises and sores. A physician was sent for but no hopes were entertained that he would live until the doctor arrived."[1] Another article said, "In a short time the bruised and blackened body of a man was carried out of the yard and up over the hill to a house near DuPont's church. It was that of Daniel Dougherty, and at that time he was supposed to be dead."[2]

In one of Francis Gurney du Pont's reports, he wrote that Dougherty had showed signs of "concussion of the brain" the day after the accident. He added that Dougherty "lay between life and death for seven weeks and at last got well and at this time [July 18] is about his house, but his eyes are totally destroyed. A large splinter was taken out of the back of his neck the fourth week and the eighth week one was found in his eye."[3]

Six weeks after the explosion that injured Dougherty, the people of Wilmington experienced another blast. A local paper said that "those familiar with the place designated it as 'only a puff.'"[4] The *Gazette* reporter who wrote the piece must have spoken with someone who lived in the immediate vicinity, a person now jaded by frequent explosions. The article added: "Daniel Dougherty, who was so badly injured by the explosion on May 2 is still in a critical condition, and while he may live for some time he will never be in any manner able to work again. He is totally blind, and a few days ago the wound in his head opened and a large splinter of wood worked its way out."

He lived another twenty-two years. His obituary in 1904 stated, "Mr. Dougherty was a remarkable man in several ways. Although totally blind for several years he could find his way around his home with ease and never required anyone to do any repairing around the house, as he always did it himself."[5] Although he owned half of a duplex residence in Wilmington, Dougherty rented it and continued to live on the DuPont property. The injured man received a monthly stipend of half his regular pay until five years after the accident when the company cut the $23.50 to $15.[6]

Dougherty had married Ellen Gibbons, the union resulting in ten children, one of whom died at age five. The others lived into adulthood. One daughter, Kathryn, known as Kate, figures in a humorous story told by John McGuire in the book, *Irish in America*, published in 1868 and summarized by Margaret Mulrooney.

While serving as a domestic servant, Kate took issue with something her employer's guest, a Protestant minister, had said about her Roman Catholic religion. She "accidentally" poured a tureen of hot soup on his head. She might well have lost her job, but "she valued her faith over rational economics."[7] McGuire reports that, from then on, the pastor minded his behavior.

Kate was involved in another story about religion. In the late 1890s, the Catholic daughters of Kate and her husband, powderman Charles Deery, joined a sewing group at the local Presbyterian church. When Alfred I. du Pont (whom the workers called "short-pants" because he wore knickers as a child)[8] teased Deery about his daughter's "conversion" to Protestantism, Charles told his wife. Religion was no joke to Kate, as we have seen, so ever the audacious one, she marched up to du Pont and told him off. Such was the relationship between the owners and the workers that, once again, no repercussions followed Kate's confrontation with her husband's employer on a matter of deeply held beliefs.[9]

Kate's religious views were "serious but not sanctimonious," as one author described immigrants' feelings about their religion. "The Irish abroad kept up an attachment to their faith as a way of sustaining their culture…to come to terms with the uprootedness, loneliness, insecurity, blocked social mobility and sense of alienation that so many of them experienced."[10]

Another of Daniel and Ellen Dougherty's children who lived into adulthood was the victim of yet another railroad accident. Twenty-nine-year-old William died on Christmas Eve, 1898, where the Baltimore and Ohio tracks crossed Pennsylvania Avenue in Wilmington. He was a volunteer firefighter and was responding to a fire on the hose cart of the Water Witch Fire Company when a train plowed into it.[11] The locomotive's cowcatcher struck the rear of the cart, throwing Dougherty one hundred feet into the side of a frame dwelling. The first doctor on the scene sent Dougherty to Delaware Hospital, where he died before surgeons could operate on his fractured skull. He left a wife and small child.[12]

A last note on Daniel Dougherty: one Wilmington newspaper wrote the following in his obituary: "He had the distinction of being the only man who was ever blown up in DuPont's powder mills and survived."[13] According to Francis Gurney du Pont, this may not have been true; as we learned earlier, Charles Devron had lived through an explosion after receiving a direct blast in 1854.

Two months after Daniel Dougherty's accident, another detonation shook the valley. It was not a roll mill, a dust mill or any of the other powder production buildings; it was the laboratory in the refinery where Eugene du Pont worked as head chemist. Eugene, away from the mills on July 12, 1882, had left his twenty-eight-year-old assistant, William H. Chadwick, in the lab to continue the experiments. Chadwick was heating a bottle of alcohol when the glass broke, igniting nearby benzene and powder. Since he lived a few hours after being burned over most of his body, he told those giving him care what had happened.

A news report picks up the story. "With great presence of mind he closed his eyes for an instant and started for the door, after taking one look to get his bearings. As he emerged from the building men who heard the explosion met him. They seized him, extinguished his clothing, put him in a carriage and took him home. Dr. Greenleaf was the first physician to arrive, and together with Dr. Grimshaw and others did all in their power to allay the sufferings of Mr. Chadwick." It became clear to the doctors he was dying. The newspaper reported that it was "impossible to recognize his features." His wife, Margaret, or Maggie, could not see him until they knew he would not survive.[14]

Sophie (Mrs. Samuel F.) du Pont wrote that she was conversing with Dr. Greenleaf when they heard the explosion, startling her. The doctor said it was only the purposeful firing of powder, but she became unsettled, thinking it was not the usual sound of a roll mill going up, a deafening sound she had heard dozens of times before. When they went outside to the porch, the fire bell rang. The doctor left her side and rushed to the scene.[15]

Sophie continued, "The laboratory burnt from the time of the explosion till 1 o'clock & for some time it was very uncertain if the refinery could be saved & the powder mills around. I knew it all & that my brother was on the refinery roof & my nephew in the forefront of danger & exertion—but God's mercy & good Providence saved us, as so often before from any further calamity that the loss of the young life of him, whose own carelessness caused the accident."

Mrs. du Pont included a brief biography of William H. Chadwick, writing that he was a bright boy in his early teens when his "very bad father (an English mechanic) had abandoned him." She castigated the father's second wife, calling her an "ignorant & coarse Irish woman addicted like himself to drink." She said her nephews Eugene and Lammot taught the youngster chemistry and advanced him "step by step" until he became Eugene's assistant.

Mrs. du Pont finished her letter by writing that Chadwick's death "has thrown a great gloom over all their friends & has been sensibly felt by all the community." She managed to get a discordant note into her recounting: "But Mr. Chadwick had one fault, which both Lammot & more especially Eugene, had often reproved him most seriously. He was careless through it, he had already a few years ago lost several fingers by an accident."[16]

At the request of Lammot du Pont, Chadwick had boarded with the Leithead family. He courted and married Maggie Leithead, a daughter of the family; their son was three years old when his father died.

More than three decades after William's death, Pierre Samuel du Pont, son of Lammot and Mary Belin du Pont, was sending letters and personal checks for $50 to Maggie Chadwick; the files refer to a "regular monthly payment." They show that Pierre Samuel had been sending checks to Margaret Leithead, Maggie's mother, and when she died, sent them to Mrs. Chadwick.[17] The correspondence continued into the 1920s with discussions about living in Delaware. At one point, Pierre recommended that Mrs. Chadwick buy an acoustic aid to help with her hearing.

Two non-fatal accidents marred the last days of 1882 and the first of the following year. In the former case, James Fisher instructed his son to put metal balls into a pot so James could attend to them when he returned from another job. The son placed the balls into the pot, unaware the black powder had not been cleaned from them. When James returned and placed the pot over the fire, the powder ignited, propelling the objects into his face. He suffered eye injuries from pieces, but kept his sight.[18] According to an undated newspaper article in one of the many du Pont scrapbooks, the balls in question were bullets that James was remolding to be used to put a gloss on powder. It's possible this procedure was part of the glazing process.

In January 1883, millwrights Robert Reed and Anthony Dougherty, Jr., sustained burns when roll mill two exploded while they worked on the machinery. Dougherty was the namesake of the Dougherty killed in the 1857 explosion when Alexis du Pont died.[19] Both men continued working in the mills.

Francis Gurney du Pont, known in the family as Cousin Frank, wrote that the July 13, 1883, detonation in the upper yard press mill was "the heaviest explosion we have had in years."[20] He estimated that between 6,500 and 7,000 pounds of powder blew. The newspapers lowered the reported amount to 2,500 pounds. Whatever the weight, the blast killed two men, Thomas Pearl (also written Peril) and Patrick Haley. As in 1839, when John Cole died in an explosion on Friday the thirteenth, the superstitious might have wondered what part the date played in the deaths.

Thomas Pearl had voyaged across the Atlantic from Galway, Ireland, in the summer of the war year 1863 and began working in the DuPont powder mills.[21] It is improbable that the machinery of the draft for soldiers that occurred later that summer could have worked fast enough to include Thomas in the draft drawings. An article published on August 14, 1863, was mindful of the New York City draft riots that had occurred a month before. Under the headlines "The Draft In Delaware—The State True to the Union—No Disturbance of Any Kind," Thomas Peril from Brandywine Hundred[22] was listed among the "names of the conscripts." Was this the man who died in the 1883 explosion? Once again, we see how recorded names can cause confusion these many years after an incident. Mill worker Thomas was the right age for the draft, twenty-five when he started in the mills. An argument against this being the man working at the factory is that the conscription law, passed in early March 1863, required American men between the ages of twenty and forty-five and aliens who had signed an intention to become citizens to sign up for the wartime draft by April 1. Pearl did not arrive until mid-summer and could not have registered by the deadline, nor could he have registered his wish to become an American citizen that quickly. In addition, he appears in the petit ledgers for 1863 through 1864. It is possible that he served in the militia with his fellow workers, even without having become a citizen.

Pearl married Bridget Hughes, the union producing six children. The Pearls were another family upon whom tragedy fell before the death of the patriarch. Thomas's namesake died as he approached his ninth birthday in 1875, and they lost Maggie when she was two and a half. After father Thomas's death, Bridget lost her seventeen-year-old daughter, Catherine, to consumption.

Besides her annuity, which ran through 1888, Bridget earned money by sewing bags: saltpeter bags, glazing bags, dry house bags, bags for coal, and for the grinding mill. By 1887, her fourteen-year-old son, John, brought $14 a month into the family coffers by working in the keg mill.[23]

In the 19th century many people believed in a number of superstitions involving death and bad luck. In the 1870s a local newspaper reported a "strange fancy" existed on DuPont's Banks. "It is this, that the appearance of a ghost always precedes an explosion. A few days ago a ghost, it is said, was seen by several parties, and two explosions have since followed. It is a little curious that these folks who see the ghosts do not get their friends to leave the premises; and still more strange that the ghosts do not warn those in the mills in time to avoid the danger. Unless they do so the ethereal gentry had as well remain as 'shadows unseen' to all, as we in fact believe they do."[24]

Eleven years after this article appeared, someone saw Patrick Haley's specter after the accident that killed him. Headlined a week after the explosion, "A Dead Man's Double," the July 1883 article continued, "The story of a workman living at Rising Sun caused much agitation in that place and vicinity a day or two since. He states positively that while walking on the banks of the Brandywine at midnight, he met Patrick Haley, who was blown to atoms in the recent explosion at DuPont's powder works. Haley, he says, was dressed in his working clothes, and walked past in a slow and measured tread. The man also states that neither he nor the apparition spoke as they passed each other."[25]

Patrick Haley worked for the DuPont Company for thirty years. He gained not only a sizable sum in his accounts but also an extensive family. At his death, his nine children ranged in age from twenty-three-year-old Robert, a boiler-maker in Virginia, to five-year-old Albert living at home with his seven siblings and mother Anna.

The 1880 U.S. Census shows that Robert Haley was born in Missouri, and other sons John, 17, and 16-year-old William were born in Pennsylvania, so the family must have moved east during the two years after the war. The rest of the children, starting with 13-year-old Annie, joined the family in Delaware.[26]

Seven years passed from the time of the 1883 explosion to the next fatal accident, the second-longest span between fatalities from explosions in the history of the mills. That period did not improve in the slightest the effects of the next blast.

Some of the damage resulting from the 1890 explosion, "The Big One." (Hagley Museum and Library)

Although the 1818 explosion resulted in the deaths of the most workers in the company's history in Delaware, the du Ponts, their laborers, the newspapers, and the public called the a blast in October 1890 "The Big One."

Why they called it so is no mystery; the estimated powder loss was between 25 and 150 tons. A Boston newspaper, reporting on another detonation later in the century, said, "The greatest explosion of gunpowder the world has ever known took place in the Dupont works Oct. 7, 1890."[27] Closer to home, Francis Gurney du Pont called it "the most disastrous explosion that ever happened, I will say—in the world."[28] And it may well have been. The biggest recorded explosion to that time was the Great Delft Thunderclap, as historians called the explosion of 90,000 pounds of powder, which occurred in that Dutch city in 1654.

Francis had his own theory: "As for the cause, it is hard to find. [William R.]

Green was a very careful man, and the soldering was done with a solder that melted at about 240 [degrees] and could hardly have set fire to the powder. The only plausible reason for the explosion would seem to be that Green carried fire in on his sleeve from his furnace [used to heat the soldering iron], and setting fire to the box [of powder], escaped far enough from the door for his body to remain whole."[29]

Seven of the mill buildings blew in rapid order on that foggy Tuesday afternoon. Observers believed the first to go was the magazine in which Green and William McGarvey were soldering lids onto the kegs containing prismatic powder. Known as brown or "cocoa" powder, it contained less sulfur than the regular concoction (as low as 1 percent compared to black powder's 10 to 13 percent). It formed into a specific grain shape (in this case hexagonal) to slow its burn rate and thus decrease the stress on large-bore weapons such as cannons and mortars.[30]

As witnesses would later testify in court, workmen had previously seen Green let his fire-heated soldering iron get too hot. They reported seeing sparks fly from the business end of the iron. Regardless, they thought the middle magazine of three was the first to detonate, followed in quick succession by the remaining six buildings.

The Eagle magazine, so named because it stored DuPont's Eagle brand sporting powder, was reported to have exploded with the middle magazine. Fifty yards from the Eagle storage a press room was next, followed by a drying house, a soda house, a grinding mill and a coal house.[31] The report of the Eagle magazine exploding was later shown to be in error.

Besides the mill buildings, the blast flattened fifty dwellings, making 400 powder-yard workmen and families homeless. They found temporary housing with other workers and relatives.

The DuPont Company sent men to the perimeter to guard against intrusion onto the mill property. Before they arrived, a news reporter got near the site. He reported, "All over the broad sloping hill and plain below were fragments of human beings, animals, houses and powder canisters. Here and there hands, fingers, toes, legs and a head were seen."

He added, "Dead animals were very numerous. In one place were chickens piled upon each other, all dead. In several places the fields were dotted with the bright plumage of birds, which had found death at the terrible explosion."[32] The reporter continued, writing that "the horrible sight of human bodies and those of animals mingled among this debris, was too horrible for some of the strong men who had the courage to attempt to recover the remains of some of the unfortunates. Several of the rescuers fainted away."[33]

A few onlookers got through the cordons. One man found the partial face of James Dolan, identified by his mustache, while his partner saw a torso in a tree, swinging pendulum-like. Thousands of spectators traveled to the mills by taking cars the trolley company added to the daily runs to accommodate the ghoulish citizenry.

Those who got past the protective ring sneaked into some of the fifty houses collapsed by the mammoth explosion, taking souvenirs; a curtain in a destroyed home had a four-inch square of fabric cut out. Others took desk knobs or pieces of damaged furniture or buggy-wheel spokes. One report said a resident "actually lost sixteen bushels of corn from his crib through the depredations of these relic hunting maniacs."[34] To the disgust of the remaining workmen and families, a New York paper ran an advertisement for excursions from there to Wilmington to view the ruins.[35]

One might wonder why men used a red-hot soldering iron, heated with fire, in a place that contained thousands of pounds of black powder. In his recounting, F.G. du Pont wrote, "Though soldering boxes of powder would seem to the uninitiated to be dangerous, it was really not so if carefully done."[36]

An article in a Rochester, New York, paper contradicted du Pont, saying that, "this work is extremely dangerous, and Green was the only man trusted to perform it. He was an old employee and thoroughly understood his work but it is thought his soldering iron became hot and its heat ignited the powder in spite of his carefulness."[37] Others used a different word for Green's handling of the iron, exchanging the "ful" for "less."

Three days after the "big one," in an article headlined "Mental Failure," the *Wilmington Evening Journal* said, "The explosion of Tuesday is ascribed to carelessness. *All other explosions at the DuPont Mills which have been accounted for at all have been laid to carelessness.* It seems passing belief that a man should be careless in a powder mill, but the evidence seems to make it certain that the careless handling of soldering implements by William R. Green caused the explosion of Tuesday. Green was forty years old and was a man thoroughly trustworthy, because of his character and experience." The article continued, "He had been put to work in the soldering department because he possessed those qualities, which fitted him to an eminent degree for constant and unremitting care.

In that which he was chosen for strength he was weak. In a moment of thoughtlessness, in a moment of mental aberration, in a moment, perhaps of unconsciousness, or in one of those curious lapses in which the mind fails to maintain its control over the body, he let a spark fall which sent him and his fellow workmen suddenly and violently into eternity."

The report added, "Green could not have been purposely careless," and then shifted the blame for the accident onto the du Ponts. "The only safety from such accidents is in using every possible mechanical contrivance to lessen the element of human responsibility and decrease this dreaded mind failure, mental lapse and unintentional, though fatal carelessness." And, "In this case the DuPonts should separate the soldering room from all contact, even the most remote, with the mills and, if possible, use chemicals only for sealing the powder canisters."[38] The same edition included a snide letter to the editor asking if the du Ponts minded if the writer traveled out Delaware Avenue as far as Madison Street (four miles from the site). He added, "I won't look at anything and will come back before it is dark. They have my promise that I will give no news to the papers concerning the explosion. Yours truly, Taxpayer."[39] The anonymous writer was one of those Delawareans who, because of the perceived hold the family had over the state, felt "State of DuPont" was a more apt name than "State of Delaware."

Thoughts of incendiarism lingered as a cause for the blast, harbored by Alfred du Pont, thirty miles away at the Devon Inn on Philadelphia's Main Line when the earth shook. He knew a powder explosion caused the tremors, so he raced to the scene and spent the evening of October 7th with a torchlight in hand working in the debris.

Other local events caused many to think the explosion's cause was purposeful. Ten months before, on the day after Christmas 1889, someone had set fire to new du Pont barns. Other acts followed, accompanied by threats of more violence and anonymous letters seeking resolution of grievances. A secret society of powdermen and their families called themselves the Neversweats.

The company hired the Wilkinson Detective Agency to delve into the fires. One detective, Emily Noble, befriended the Clark family. In her report, Noble quoted Mrs. Edward Clark, a conspirator, as saying that "if any member got into trouble, 50 men in Wilmington, and 100 along the Brandywine would help Neversweat members in trouble, and would right all wrongs."[40] Amongst the perceived offenses were layoffs of workers in slack times.

Besides Mrs. Clark, the conspirators included her husband, Edward, who had worked for the du Ponts since the end of the Civil War; their fifteen-year-old son, Joseph; and twenty-eight-year-old William Gibbons, one of the four sons of yard foreman John Gibbons, who served in that position for the twenty-eight years leading up to his death in 1885. William, a carpenter, was a victim of the layoffs; authorities caught and arrested him in Philadelphia. He made threatening statements to other workers about reports the company was to fire him because of drunkenness. One worker quoted him as saying, "If Frank DuPont discharges me I'll blow up every d__d mill in Hagley."[41] He was further quoted on the day of the "big one" that Francis Gurney du Pont should have been in the explosion and that "Frank DuPont ought to be in hell!"[42] The plotters received jail terms; the court sentenced Gibbons, deemed the ringleader, to an hour in the pillory and fifteen lashes,[43] punishments remarkably still in use in late 19th-century Delaware.

A week later, The *Evening Journal* told readers of what the editors thought a "strange theory." Referring to the unexploded Eagle magazine, the daily quoted Francis Gurney du Pont saying the damage would not have been greater had it blown, though it held up to one hundred tons of black powder. At the coroner's inquest, he said when "a certain amount of powder is exploded, the force of the concussion reaches a maximum, *and no matter how much more powder might be exploded this force will be no greater.*"

Aghast at this pronouncement, the newspaper stated, "The truth or falsity of this theory is a matter of much concern to the people of Wilmington.... Should the force of the concussion be in proportion to the quantity of powder exploded...houses in this city would be destroyed and the lives of the citizens imperiled."[44]

Three times as many injuries as deaths happened in "The Big One." Mrs. William McDowell almost lost an ear. Her two-year-old daughter received cuts and, the newspaper reported, "will probably die." She did not; Priscilla McDowell Warwick lived to 1950. She did, however, lose her father in a 1902 explosion. Mary and Annie Dolan, who lost their father, sustained injuries, Mary with facial cuts, Annie with internal injuries. Kate Ward was "expected to die" from facial lacerations, and three-year-old Mamie Ward "will die" because of severe cuts and bruises. Annie Harkins, who lost her father that day, sustained burns.[45]

Another injury occurred in downtown Wilmington when a sack of flour fell ten feet from the shaken shelves of a store on West 12th Street. The unfortunate Jonathan E. George stood below, and the heavy bag hit him on top of the head. Because the shock and the falling sack terrified people in the store, they could not offer any help as he lay unconscious. Someone transported him home and, although suffering severe pain, he recovered.[46]

Among the list of injured was one Hugh Ferry, described as "prostrated" by one news report and "ribs crushed" by another, died eight months after the explosion. The coroner listed the death of forty-five-year-old man as "paralysis."[47]

Local businessmen started a plan for a benefit to aid those who lost homes. If they carried through with the proposition, the papers did not report it.[48]

The explosion was the second to kill a woman and first (and only) one known to have killed a child, and it took the lives of ten powder workers. Octogenarian Roseanne Dougherty's roof fell around her. The child was her two-year-old grandson, Thomas, whom she cared for. Roseanne was the wife of Michael, who died in the February 1865 explosion, according to Hagley oral interviews.

Among the workers killed were two possible sets of brothers; John and Michael Herlihy (certain) and the (presumed) brothers Dolan, James and Martin.

The Herlihys came from Macroom Parish, twenty miles west of Cork in the south of Ireland. Their tombstones at St. Joseph Cemetery list John as twenty-three years old and Michael as twenty-six, but Michael's certificate of death lists him as being twenty-three. They might have been half-brothers, so they may have been the same age. It is possible they were twins; so reported the *Evening Journal* six days after the accident, adding that they looked much alike. The article called it "a curious circumstance" that people heard the brothers wishing they would die together and, "as if by Divine premeditation both were blown up by the powder, and killed at the same time." The story added that they interred the two in a single coffin, and "thus these were buried as they had lived."[49]

Mrs. John Horgan, the wife of another victim and sister of the Herlihys, would not have the burying of all ten men in a single grave, as the du Ponts wanted. She wanted her husband and brothers interred in a separate plot in the St. Joseph Cemetery. She got her wish. The top of the tombstone is simply inscribed "Brothers."

A few months later, the DuPont Company received a letter from Macroom.

Siblings in Ireland wanted the company to give John Horgan's widow the money in the Herlihy brothers' accounts. Patrick, Timothy, Peter, and Julia Herlihy signed the letter. The company followed their instructions, giving Mary Horgan $40 from Michael's account and $186 from John's. Mrs. Horgan received another $40 from her husband's account.[50]

John and Mary Horgan had a Christmas baby, Elizabeth, who was born ten months before her father and uncles died. No birth certificate for her existed until 1942, when Ellen Walsh attested her cousin's birth. People without a certificate often filed a Certificate of Delayed Birth Registration, which is still used in Delaware.

Mary Horgan later remarried, to a powderman named Dennis Sweeney. The 1900 census shows them living in a household with ten-year-old Lizzie Harigan (Horgan), four-year-old Mary Harigan (Horgan) and Dennis's brother-in-law, Patrick Herlihy, who had made his way to Delaware from Ireland, at DuPont's Banks.[51]

The reason for the uncertainty whether James and Martin Dolan were brothers is that their tombstones say James came from County Kildare, in the east of Ireland, and Martin hailed from Connaught Province, to the west. Many of the headstones of the immigrants to Delaware show their townland, the smallest governmental or religious division of Ireland, or at least their county within the larger province. Martin's family or the DuPont Company, which paid for his stone out of his estate, did not know exactly where he hailed from. Hannah, Martin's wife, was from County Sligo, also in the province of Connaught (now Connacht).[52]

Hannah Gibbons Dolan predeceased her spouse by ten years. The family was doubtless reeling from the loss of their mother and wife when the 1880 census enumerator called a month after she died. Daughter Annie was twenty with a listed occupation of "making house," although she later worked for the DuPont Company. The census listed second daughter Mary as "without occupation." Hannah's namesake was sixteen while that of his father was thirteen, with an occupation of "works in powder mill," and twelve-year-old Elizabeth was in school.[53] It is unclear what kind of work the thirteen-year-old was paid to do in a powder mill, although, as we have seen earlier, he could have been put to work in making powder kegs.

Missing from that page of the 1880 census was another Dolan daughter, twenty-five-year-old Catherine, who became an inmate of the almshouse in New Castle County, Delaware. The county had two almshouses, one near Hares Corner south of Wilmington, the other on Broom Street near Fourth. It is likely that Catherine was at the latter, known as "the smallpox hospital." She may have had smallpox, but they listed her cause of death as epilepsy.[54]

The Martin Dolan family took advantage of the opportunity to add to the family funds provided by the DuPont Company, which needed workers to paste labels on powder kegs. Hannah started in 1862, pasting more than 28,000 labels on cans and kegs, bringing in $70 that year. The company paid her $2.50 for each 1,000 labels.[55] Fifteen years later, when the children helped, the payments to the family increased to $386[56] in their peak year of production for 150,000 labels. Once Martin Jr., worked in the mills, he brought in wages of $15 per month at age thirteen. He left the company in 1883 to seek his fortune elsewhere, but returned in midsummer 1887, earning twice what he had made four years earlier.[57]

The 1890 explosion was the third involving Martin. F.G. du Pont, misnaming him Newton Dolan, reported in January 1861 that Dolan ran out of his graining mill after the first of three explosions, and lay near his mill for protection. A newspaper noted he jumped into the millrace. Regardless, he saved himself that day twenty-nine years before his death.[58]

Agents interviewed Martin's daughter Annie, by now working for the DuPont Company, about the explosion that killed her father. She said there was no work for her that day, so she went home. An hour later, the company told her "to get some paste ready and come to work." Before she left, the explosion occurred. After that, she refused to return to work and, since their home was in ruins, the family, or what was left of it, moved to Wilmington. Hannah, the administratrix of her father's estate, signed for the $1,115 accrued in Martin's account; the family received $175 from the DuPont Company for the value of the household goods destroyed.

Two sons of powdermen killed in the October explosion decided not to let the trauma keep them from following in their dead fathers' footsteps. Among the two dozen hands hired in the aftermath were Martin Dolan Jr., and Michael Newell.[59]

Time was up for another Dougherty, as the death toll from the 1890 disaster continued to mount. ■

▪ 11 ▪
Risky Solder

> Concerning the losses and needs of all our hands —
> we propose to them and their families and to all
> who have suffered, to bring out of chaos an orderly state
> of affairs, to restore everything except life to all;
> to nourish, protect and guide all and to do everything
> possible for man to do.
> —Eugene du Pont

The reporter from the Wilmington *Every Evening* wrote, "Within [St. Joseph's on the Brandywine Church] everything indicated the solemn features of the occasion. The plaintive chant of the Requiem for the Dead sung by the Sisters of St. Francis struck the ear with a depressing effect which was increased still more by the evidences surrounding the interior of the structure of the severe effects of the recent explosion upon the building itself." The article continued, "The heavy central chandelier hung pendent by two slight chains, tipped down in a perpendicular position, as if ready to drop at any moment upon the heads of the worshipper below. The north wall of the church is cracked in the centre from the roof to the top of one of the windows."[1] So read the newspaper report of the funeral of Patrick Dougherty V.

This Dougherty was a troublemaker, at least for some part of his life. In *Brandywine Reminiscences*, an unpublished manuscript by DuPont office worker John Macklem, he relates a story about Henry du Pont[2] and his relationship with the workers.

Macklem says Dougherty was "guilty of raising ruction on Sunday afternoons and evenings." Henry told Macklem to have Dougherty at the front gate on a Monday morning, which he did. Macklem could hear what Henry said. Henry gave Dougherty a reprimand about the previous day's disturbance, giving the powderman two choices: he could go to Father Kelly, a priest at St. Joseph, and sign a pledge to quit drinking, or he could ask Paymaster Le Carpentier for his last paycheck.

When they met later, du Pont told Dougherty to take the signed pledge to the priest for safekeeping and return to work. "This made a man out of Patrick," says Macklem, adding, "He was a good powderman and was never known to indulge in liquor thereafter."[3] In his funeral address the priest made no reference to the incident which caused Patrick's death. St. Paul's words, "I am the resurrection and the life," formed the chief subject of the speaker's remarks. At the close, mourners bore the remains to the churchyard where the services concluded, and interment made.[4]

John Newell, another long-serving powderman who died in the October 1890 explosion, had started with the company in 1853. After the blast, a farmer across the creek in Rockland found John Newell's arm in a tree; one finger was missing, and they knew that Newell had lost a digit years earlier.[5]

John and his wife Bridget made a family with five children. They did not manage money well, as shown by notes on John's petit ledger pages. Although Bridget worked for the du Ponts, probably with the willow used to make charcoal, an entry after her husband died shows they did not trust her. In May 1891, they loaned Mrs. Newell $100, "which she is to pay in a reasonable time. If she fails to do so, she is to be notified that her pension will be withheld till the note is satisfied."[6]

The eldest Newell child, Michael, working in the mills, took two years to pay an $11.62 bill. The DuPont Company rendered the invoice as early as January 1889. Inside the front cover of the 1890 ledger is a note declaring, "This bill has been rendered a number of times and must be paid now or we will have to take measures to get it. [Signed] V. Stirling."[7] The note was written on January 1, 1890. In another loose note in the same ledger, dated December 1, 1890: "This bill presented and he refused with bad language—to pay it! [Signed] V. Stirling."[8] A last entry in the same ledger showed Michael paid the bill on December 18.[9]

By the second anniversary of Newell's death, the company fulfilled his widow's annuity by forgiving the $100 loan and prepaying the remaining $200. Bridget left the Brandywine and lived out her life with her daughter's family, the Antiveilers, in Wilmington.[10]

The civil parish of Tullaghobegly[11] in Kilmacrenan Barony of County Donegal is a fir-tree shaped, elongated north and south parish made up of mountains and bogs. Daniel Harkins[12] had left the area in the late 1830s or early 1840s to go to Delaware and a lifelong position with the DuPont Company. When he arrived on the Brandywine, he boarded with Daniel

Sweeney and his wife, Mary Harkins, perhaps Daniel's sister, in the Upper Banks cluster of homes. He married Ann Sweeney ten years later, and the pair grew their family by ten in the following years. Ann hailed from County Fermanagh, probably Glenarn Parish.[13]

The Harkinses lived in Squirrel Run, a neighborhood that saw its share of death and injury over the years. Other families living in the same block were Thomas Pearl, whose father Thomas died in 1883; Dan Dougherty, son of the man injured in the 1882 explosion; and the Martin Dolan family. By the time of his death, Harkins was a widower who had lost his wife Ann in November two years earlier. The blast threw him into the race, saving his life for the time being. After a week of agony due to severe injuries, he died.

Three months after the 1890 explosion, a Michael Harkins died in an industrial accident at the Pullman Palace (railroad) Car works in Wilmington. His clothing became entangled in a whirling shaft that flung him around and threw him clear, breaking his neck. Although the newspaper said he was the son of Daniel Harkins, the death certificate listed his father as John and his mother as Margaret, both born in Ireland. Michael Harkins was thirty-two, near the age of Daniel's fifth son Michael, born in September 1865. The paper gave the accident victim's age as "about fifty."[14] Another historical mystery, perhaps solved by Shannon Connor Winward, a descendent of Daniel Harkins, who told me that Michael Joseph Harkins, Daniel's son, died in 1942.

William and Fannie Dennison McGarvey were the parents of four children when he lost his life in 1890. Isabella (Bella) was only a year old. Robert, the oldest, was eleven; daughter Fanny, seven; and second son, William, five years of age. Here was another family whose mother had to contend with raising young children in widowhood.

Between the U.S. Census of 1900 and the one taken in 1910, daughter Fannie was reported to have aged only five years. It was common practice to misstate age during census interviews for purposes of flattery. It is possible the census taker in this case was talking with someone in the household who did not know the age of their parents, spouses, or siblings. Many respondents did not know their own age.[15]

Louise du Pont Crowninshield, was a great-granddaughter of Éleuthère Irénée. Married to a member of the Boston Brahmin shipbuilding Crowninshield family,[16] she owned a home in Marblehead, Massachusetts, and kept in touch with some of the workers' families. In a 1967 oral interview, Elizabeth Beacom, a powderman's daughter, said Mrs. Crowninshield entertained Bella McGarvey in her Marblehead home. Bella was a member of a group of young women called the Willing Workers, a sewing group that Louise du Pont supported at Christ Church.

Beacom had her own connection to the 1890 blast. She noted a birthmark on her foot, in the shape of a powder burn, which was thought to result from the explosion. Her mother was seven months pregnant with her at that time.[17]

Du Pont Company, newspaper, and family records detail the life of William R. Green, whom many blamed for the 1890 explosion. Green was a literate man. Years before his death, he wrote several letters to Sophie du Pont. In one letter, he refers to speaking at "our regular monthly meeting" about bringing in an astronomy lecturer.[18] In a well-written letter in 1879, he thanked her for a basket she sent which included medicine, food, and recipes, adding that, "I gave my wife the recipes, and though she is quite a good cook, she found something new in them which she has since tried."[19]

Five years later, Sophie sent a book to the Green family boys, eleven-year-old Charles and nine-year-old William Eustis. Their father William responded that "they were very much pleased with it."[20] A week after Annie Green was born, her father sent a thank-you note to Sophie, saying that, "It [a gift] happened to be the very thing that was needed & gave my wife much pleasure to receive it."[21]

One of Green's letters to Mrs. du Pont in the Hagley Library files is a plea for a friend, Thomas Jackson of Bancroft's Banks and a worker in the Bancroft and Sons bleaching factory. Jackson's doctor urged him to leave that job for an outdoor pursuit because of ill health; he worked in a "room [that] is allways full of steam in addition to the poisonous eff[l]uvia from chemicals & while the floor is almost perpetually wet." Green told Sophie she may have remembered Jackson as the librarian in the Sunday School. "I do not expect you know of a place that would suit him or that you can immediately help him but I thought it expedient to acquaint you of him, and would ask you to remember him should you hear or know of anything better for him." He finished in the manner of all his letters to Mrs. du Pont, hoping she remained in good health.[22]

Green's last letter in the file said someone told him there were no girls "in the Institution," and he felt certain "we shall be remembered" if the establishment received girls in the future. The nature of "the

Institution" is unknown. It may have been a school that allowed only boys to attend, so the Green girls, seven-year-old Florence and three-year-old Annie, were not eligible to enroll.

The book Mrs. du Pont gave the Green boys plus the education they received both in school and at home, stood them in good stead in later life. The DuPont Company hired William's namesake (called Eustis) the year following his father's death, when he was only sixteen years old, and paid him $400 a year. By his ninth year with the company his earnings came to $1,000 a year, showing him as a valued employee, perhaps a salesman for DuPont products.[23]

As seen in Chapter Ten, the public could not get enough details about the horrific explosion. A few days after the accident that caused so many deaths, a jury convened to hear testimony about the safety practices of William R. Green. "The coroner's jury… [discovered] that William H. [the newspaper's error] Green had on more than one occasion departed from his accustomed carefulness and not only used solder not provided by the firm, but applied the soldering iron when red hot." The article continued, "Sometimes it was heated to such a degree that sparks flew from it on being taken from the fire. All of the witnesses examined in the fore noon described Green as a very careful man who took every precaution to ensure safety."[24]

The paper reported a commotion at lunchtime. The coroner sent the jurors to lunch, while keeping the witnesses in the courtroom. Powderman Timothy Toomey "rudely demanded expenses from the coroner," to which he responded that Toomey wanted to put the jury to "every inconvenience." Charles I. du Pont interceded to calm the recalcitrant witnesses.[25]

When the hearing reconvened in the afternoon, the court heard from George Dougherty, perhaps the same man who lost a two-year-old son in the collapse of Roseanne Dougherty's house. He said he told Green the iron got too hot and warned the solderer not to heat it to such a high degree. None of the witnesses believed Green's job any more risky than other work in the yards. One put it this way: "A man's life is always in danger at whatever work he does, therefore, I never thought any particular work more dangerous than another." A different powderman said he "never dreamt of danger, and would have no fear of working in any mill or magazine in the yard," but, "my wife would not hear of me going back since the day of the explosion."[26]

After deliberating, the jury came back with a verdict of accidental death. Nothing strange there, but what was strange is that five of the nine jurors agreed to the verdict. The other four may have thought the jury's recommendation that the local government pass legislation "as will prevent the storage of powder in dangerous quantities too near the limits of the city"[27] was superfluous.

The du Ponts considered Green to be "one of their best men," and had given him the important job of sealing the powder boxes, or cans. He had confided in his wife, telling her he was nervous about the soldering work and, "Someday…a speck of powder would come in contact with a spark from the hot iron, and then all would be up" with him.[28] Sadly, the details of his prediction proved hauntingly accurate.

Fall colors washed over the Brandywine Valley three more times before another accident took a life. A week before Christmas 1893, Edward Gallagher became the sole victim of an Upper Hagley yard explosion. For the third time in twenty-three years the Upper Yard graining mill was the scene of a powderman's death. Darby McAteer had died there in March 1870 and Michael Dougherty lost his life in the explosion of April 1873.

Gallagher knew firsthand the danger of working in the powder. He had experienced more than a dozen fatal explosions and succored the families of at least twenty-four of his fellow powdermen since joining DuPont in 1866. He remembered family stories about his grandfather, Philip, dying in the big 1818 explosion. He helped pick up the pieces of the dead workers, sometimes when fragments of flesh and bone were all they found. This time, it was his mortal self that others collected in buckets and baskets.

In yet another "blown to atoms" account, *Every Evening* told the story of "a roaring sound accompanied by an impact that shook buildings to their foundations and lasted at least 10 seconds," adding that "it was unusual in its distinctiveness and severe force."[29] In Wilmington, "Instinctively everyone thought of the DuPont Powder Works, and a glance in that direction immediately showed the great mass of gray smoke—a sure indication that an explosion occurred there. Slowly the mass of smoke, looking like a huge balloon moved to the southeastward until it was barely over Wilmington….Soon it dissipated and was lost to view."[30]

In announcing Gallagher's funeral, a Wilmington newspaper quoted the deputy coroner who issued a certificate of accidental death: "Mr. Palmer…found that it was useless to hold an inquest over the remains, as only the deceased knew the cause of the accident." Coroner Palmer mistakenly said, "It has not been customary to hold inquests on the bodies of persons who have been killed in the powder works. No one could ever tell the causes."[31]

After working in the mills for eight years, Gallagher had married Bridget Deery in 1874. When she came over from County Donegal, arriving in New York harbor on the *Europa* in April 1873, several family members accompanied Biddy, as they called her. She brought with her daughter Ella, or Ellen, two-and-a-half years old.

In Ireland, Bridget had been Mrs. William Kearney, sometimes represented as Carney. According to family researcher Marie Donahue Walls, Bridget either divorced Mr. Kearney or had the marriage annulled in Ireland before the voyage, or perhaps in America.[32]

Bridget married Edward Gallagher within a year and a half of setting foot on Delaware soil. She and Edward had ten children. After he died, Bridget raised children ranging in age from six-year-old Edward Junior to Sarah, eighteen. Daughter Ella married Daniel Haggerty about 1890; he was near the mill that exploded when his stepfather-in-law died, but was not hurt.[33]

Like many other young DuPont workers, Daniel Haggerty was lucky to have a job, even one as dangerous as powder making. His father-in-law died in what became the first of eight years of severe economic stress in the United States. By the time of the accident, businesses were closing at a record pace, the interest rate had reached an all-time high of 74 percent, farm foreclosures had risen, and unemployment had soared to 20 percent. In the years following the Panic of 1893. in several major industries—mining, railroad, and textiles—wages dropped by as much as half and, sometimes, the workday expanded by 25 percent.[34] In the late nineties, the Spanish-American War brought back a level of prosperity.

Another three-year hiatus in death by explosion occurred in the mid-nineties, ending in March 1897 when twenty-nine-year-old James Walker died.[35] He was working roll mills three and four in the Hagley yard. He had just gotten away from number three when it blew. A compatriot, Pierre Gentieu, said, "Thinking as a true powderman that he might save the other Mill by stopping it in time,"[36] Walker ran back and got to number four as it exploded, throwing him against the flash wall. This was a separate structure from, and parallel to, the back wall of the mill, constructed to give extra shock-wave protection wherever there was a doorway in the rear wall of a mill. The violent tossing of his body against the stone wall, made of the very dense and hard gneiss rock, fractured his skull; he lived but a short time.

He and wife Ellen and family of four children lived at Squirrel Run, but Walker left home several times, traveling to Springfield, Pennsylvania. The town he went to was not the current Springfield just across the Pennsylvania border in Delaware County, but the one in northern Chester County, now called Elverson. Ironically, at one time they called the town Blue Rock. In the area lay the headwaters of the east branch of Brandywine Creek, which melds with the west branch, the water then wending south past the DuPont mills.

Walker may have gone to test DuPont powder at a gun plant. In June 1896, the company took one day off his $40 per month pay for a trip to Springfield, but paid him two dollars from another account. The petit ledgers listed three men, with the last name Oar, working for DuPont at Springfield.[37]

After James's death, his widow Ellen supplemented her annuity by sewing bags for the graining mill, the drying house, and the coal house. The DuPont Company paid her by the day and by the unit. She received $1.50 per day and twelve and a half cents a bag in 1900, and continued sewing after her annuity ended on March 9, 1902.[38]

In an oral interview in the 1950s, powder-family descendant John E. Krauss said, "My dad used to speak very positively about the fact that when breaking a man in, he could size him up in the first couple of hours — what sort of a workman he was going to be. If a fellow who would come in and step gingerly around all the time and every little noise would panic him, it was a sign he should be watched. The fellow that came in and took it quietly and followed instructions usually turned out to be a good workman, but the other fellow, who was timid at first, after he got so he was familiar with things, then he lost his respect for the dangers. They always wanted to get rid of that type."[39]

The workers in the mills were not "that type." Robert McIlhenny, Samuel Stewart, John Moore, John Wright, and Thomas McCann were not "that type." These men knew the dangers but did not let the knowledge prevent them from performing their jobs. That didn't mean their fates were always and only in their control. And, on December 9, 1898, when the Spanish-American war was twenty-four hours from ending with the signing of the Treaty of Paris, their fates were placed in someone else's hands.

John Mulherin (possibly Mulhern) was driving a team of horses pulling a powder wagon on the narrow-gauge rail track that wove its way through the mills from the graining mill to the press house in the Upper Yard. Sam Frizzell Junior, whose father ran one of the local stores near the mill property, was carting goods on a horse cart on an intersecting road. The passage of Frizzell's cart spooked Mulherin's team, upsetting the cart and spilling its load onto the frozen ground. The wheels of Mulherin's cart, off their track, created a spark and caused a gigantic explosion which communicated first to the press room and, by the time it was over, to roll mills three through eight.

Riding in the front of the cart were Sam Stewart and Tom Knox, and in the rear, John Moore and Thomas McCann. On the porch of the nearby press house, waiting for Mulherin's load of powder, were Robert McIlhenny and John Wright. As the riders were jumping off after the derailment, the explosion occurred. The first blast sent a powder bag careening into the press house, and, after ten seconds, it too exploded.[40]

Historian Richard Stout, in commenting on the notes he had obtained from DuPont employees early in the 20th century, said, "So this little community, living apart and visiting but seldom the outside world, made of the banks of the Brandywine a kind of happy valley. Its dominant note was contentment.... One generation succeeded another in what was surely the strangest of communities."[41]

The oral histories on file at the Hagley Library show a perfect example of the secluded DuPont society. In one interview, Emily Peoples Blackwell said that her mother's brother married her father's sister.[42] Her maternal uncle was Robert McIlhenny, one man standing on the porch of the press house on December 9, 1898. Hannah Peoples, Emily's aunt, was his second wife. He had worked for the firm since 1882.

According to one newspaper, McIlhenny was one of the most popular people living on "the Banks," the name the workers used for describing the area. Of the five children born to Robert and Hannah, one, Elizabeth Mary, died at three days of age. Two other children had Certificates of Delayed Birth Registration completed for them, the information based on records authenticated by a family bible. Hannah attested at least one certificate; she lived to be over one hundred years old. Sixty-six-year-old son Robert C. McIlhenny used his certificate to get a social security number.

The seclusion of the community, though, was disappearing. The latter part of the 19th century was a time of new connections for the residents of the Brandywine Banks, as it was for many Americans. Powdermen and their families were using savings to buy properties in and around the city of Wilmington and leaving the low rents of the DuPont-provided housing.[43] In becoming more integrated with the larger community, the men joined organizations that provided a place for male companionship, and allowed them to bond with their new neighbors, exercise political pressure, and take advantage of other benefits.

Robert McIlhenny became a joiner, enrolling in four such societies: the local Columbia Lodge, AOUW; Star of Bethlehem Lodge of Orangemen; IOOF Brandywine Lodge; and the Wawaset Tribe of the IORM. It was not unusual for someone to belong to many organizations; the same individuals often made up the membership in such fraternities, particularly in smaller towns and cities.

The Ancient Order of United Workmen, AOUW, founded after the Civil War in Meadville, Pennsylvania, as a beneficiary society for white males, became the first fraternal organization to sell insurance to its members. The organization provided its members' families a death benefit. Workmen's rights and working conditions also concerned the order. Membership eventually opened to non-white men, although the founders of the group wrote into the original rules the whites-only rule could never be "altered, amended, or expunged."[44] The organization lasted into the 1950s.

The second group McIlhenny joined called itself the Orangemen, or the Loyal Orange Lodge, founded in the 1830s. Membership was limited to men over the age of eighteen who believed in a supreme being and who met other religious and patriotic requirements. It started as, and remains, a Protestant organization.[45]

McIlhenny's third society was the Odd Fellows, IOOF, which continues in existence. Historians do not know where the name originated: perhaps its membership comprised men working in jobs considered too rare in numbers to create a guild. Another source stated that, "common laboring men should associate themselves together and form a fraternity for social unity and fellowship and for mutual help was such a marked violation of the trends of the times (England in the 1700s) that they became known as 'peculiar' or 'odd,' and hence they were derided as 'Odd Fellows.'"[46]

Finally, McIlhenny was a Red Man, a member of the Improved Order of Red Men, IORM. This organization took pride in its reverence for Native Americans and their assumed rituals and customs, although, again, only white men could enroll. We do not know if McIlhenny or any of the other powder workers who joined this group became Keeper of the Wampum or Great Mishinewa. Theodore and Franklin Roosevelt became members of the IORM.[47] One of the primary benefits of such organizations was the insurance payout upon a member's death. Although Thomas McCann was not lucky in that he lost his life in the 1898 explosion, his surviving family was. The night before the blast, he paid a $1 initiation fee to join the AOUW. His mother, Sarah, his beneficiary, received $2,000; in today's dollars, the equivalent of $60,000 in buying power. It is likely that Robert McIlhenny's widow, Hannah, got the same payout, as would Samuel Stewart's relict.[48]

McCann was a thirty-one-year-old powder worker who sustained burns and injuries to his lungs and legs. He survived two days before succumbing to the wounds. Besides his membership in the AOUW, he had joined the Ancient Order of Hibernians, which today bills itself as the oldest American fraternal organization of Irish Catholics.

Three months before his death, McCann and his family, headed by his widowed mother, Sarah, buried older brother, Peter, at St. Joseph on the Brandywine Cemetery. Forty-four-year-old Peter died of pulmonary complications. Sarah, laid low by both deaths, survived her sons by a year and a half. Coincidentally, next to the newspaper announcement of the burial of Sarah, appeared a notice for Louise Gerhard, the wife of the late Henry du Pont, "the General."[49]

Samuel Stewart was another of the men riding the powder cart that upended in front of the press house that December day. He was the brother of John Stewart, who became boss of the yard on the death of John Gibbons in 1885 and who received light wounds in the explosion. Samuel had started with DuPont in 1882, hired as a farm worker. The blast threw him into the water, and it was from there the rescuers retrieved him, burned and nearly frozen to death. He lingered for three days at the Delaware Hospital before succumbing to the injuries.

Stewart was a member of the IORM's Wawaset tribe, the Odd Fellows, and the AOUW. He was a Knight of the Golden Eagle, an organization which used militaristic and Christian rituals based on Crusade legends.[50] His brothers in those organizations attended the funeral en masse and may have served as pallbearers.

Samuel Stewart and his wife, Adeline Moore Stewart, had a large family, at least until 1896 when, tragically, they lost three children within as many weeks during an epidemic of diphtheria. They had named the first girl to die for her mother and she was the youngest in the family to die from the prevalent disease; Addie was five years old when she passed November 9. Not a week later, her soon-to-be six-year-old brother, Samuel, died. A week after that misfortune, eight-year-old Wilhemina (Minnie) died. The Free Park home of the Stewarts must have been reeling by Thanksgiving, which came four days after the last child's passing.[51] It is hard to fathom what the remaining family members gave thanks for that day.

This was hardly the first time tragedy had visited the Stewart family. On May 31, 1882, Adeline gave birth to their first child, a daughter named Margaret. At age nine, she died of meningitis in 1891.[52] Then, Lydia Emma Stewart came into the family in May 1884. She must have died within the next two years, as twins named Lydia Emma and Kate joined the family in April 1886.[53] As we saw earlier, a second child of the same gender as a deceased earlier child could carry the deceased's name; this appears to be the case with the second Lydia Emma. She died seven weeks after her birth, with the cause of death listed as debility.[54]

The historical record again leaves a mystery. It shows that Lydia Emma, the second with that name and the twin of Kate, died on June 14, 1886. Another record shows that Mary, born to Samuel and Addie, died the very next day. Where did Mary come from? Were she, Kate, and the second Lydia triplets? Was Lydia known as Mary? Mary and Lydia are both listed in the death records as having been seven weeks old at death, but Lydia and Kate are "twins," not triplets, in the birth record. And they recorded Mary as a single birth. A conundrum, to be sure.

The records show another enigma, this time regarding Jennie Emma Stewart. Jennie was born in 1885. She would have been child number three born to Samuel and Addie, after Margaret and the first Lydia Emma. On the birth certificate for the twins Kate and Lydia, they are children numbers three and four. This may have been a simple clerical error by the registrar.

Another calamity hit the widow Stewart a few months after losing her husband. Her daughter, Emeline, born three months after his death, lived only seven months. The suffering this woman experienced is unimaginable. By the time of Mrs. Stewart's death in early 1900, only four of her eleven, or perhaps twelve, children were left to grieve. Robert, Jennie, Katherine, and James split the last three of her five years of annuity payments.[55]

Joining Robert McIlhenny on the press house porch at the time of the blast was pressman John Wright, known as Jack, a forty-seven-year-old who had worked for DuPont since 1870. The company credited his wife Margaret with sewing bags after his death. Her annuity lasted only two years, as she remarried and moved to Philadelphia in 1900.[56]

Survivors found Wright and McIlhenny's bodies, or what fragments remained, two hundred yards away on the bluff overshadowing the Brandywine's east side. They had both truly gone "across the creek."

John Moore, who was riding on the back of Mulherin's powder cart, and his wife, Kate Wilmot Moore, were another couple with an extensive family. One of their eight children, three-year-old Alice Mullin Moore, died in 1885, but the rest made it into adulthood. Two sisters, Helen and Christina, died while living at Farnhurst, the Delaware State Hospital, the latter for the last fifteen years of her life.

Moore and Kate had married in 1878, and a few years later she began to sew for the DuPont Company. After his death, she continued and, by 1900, was one of only two women listed in the pay books earning wages for sewing. In her second year at such toil, she earned $6 a week and rated her own petit ledger page,[57] apart from her spouse's page.

John Moore, a carpenter at the works, died at his home in the Louviers section of the company's housing, on the east side of the Brandywine, an hour after the explosion.

Nine more explosions occurred in the waning days of the century; to the community's relief, only one resulted in injury. That occurred when the keg mill blew; the other blasts were in roll mills.

And, thus, the first century in which the du Ponts made black powder on the Brandywine came to a close, with the loss of 180 lives. ■

▪ 12 ▪
A Gift of Diamonds

> The affair has thrown the little village into a state of
> sadness, as almost everyone had received a favor
> at the hands of "Little Bill."
> —*The Evening Journal*

The new century did not begin with a bang in the Brandywine neighborhood, fireworks and the clanging of pots and pans notwithstanding. No explosions occurred until the end of the second year.

One day short of the fourth anniversary of the 1898 explosion, a blast emanating from the new graining mill rocked the Hagley Yard, on the former site of the dust mill. Thirty-three-year-old William McDowell ("Little Bill" to his neighbors to distinguish him from another William McDowell, or "Big Bill") died in the conflagration. The two McDowell families lived a few houses apart on Squirrel Run. In another usual method of separating men with the same name, they listed the William who died as "William McDowell 2nd," though he was not the son of Big Bill; the two were close in age.

Little Bill was married to Matilda Devinney, who gave birth to a daughter, Anna, six years old when her father died.

When the people of Wilmington heard the explosion, they ran to 5th and Tatnall streets, the site of the city electric plant, thinking the clamor had come from there. Their arrival disabused them of the thought and they turned to the northwest to anticipate the ominous smoke cloud rising from the gunpowder mills.[1]

Once again, the local papers, in their zeal to outsell the competition, wrote the tiniest details of McDowell's death. One paper reported that, "Not one garment of the body weighing more than fifteen pounds will repose in the casket. The head has not yet been recovered and probably never will be.... [F]or several hours gangs of men were engaged in picking up pieces of the victim, using buckets in which to carry them." For greatest effect, the paper added, "Pieces of the dead man were on trees and bushes on the other side of the creek, and on the buildings and rocks inside the yard."[2]

Another news item said, "All the afternoon until dark employees climbed among rocks with tin kettles looking for portions of McDowell's body, and dragged the Brandywine, but little of it was found. Although bloodstains were seen on the snow for some distance surrounding the spot where the grinding mill stood. There has not been more than a handful of the fragments of the unfortunate man found, but they will be put in a coffin of the regular size and the vacant space will be filled with sawdust and some weighty substance and given burial."[3]

A third paper saw a little good news in the horror of McDowell's death. It reported that although the blast wrecked the house surrounding it, Joseph Haley's new piano, delivered a half hour before the explosion, had but a single scratch.[4]

McDowell was also a joiner, having memberships in the Red Men, the AOUW and the Loyal Orange Lodge. As a survivor of a United Workman, Matilda would have received the $2,000 payment. A year after her husband's death and burial in Riverview Cemetery in Wilmington, she married a man named Flinn, possibly Andrew Flinn, another powder worker.[5]

Over three years passed without an injury-producing accidental explosion. Death and serious trauma created havoc nonetheless. On June 8, 1904, an errant stone from an intentional quarry blast struck Charles Viola on the head and he died at the hospital. At almost the same time a worker, known to history only as "Italian Sam," a tinsmith, lost an arm after it became entangled in a shaft at the Henry Clay keg factory.[6] Then, on Groundhog Day, 1906, a single fatality occurred.

Forty-four-year-old Samuel J. Buchanan was the second fatal victim of the powder in the 20th century. Buchanan, favored over brother Albert with the nickname "Buck" (they called Albert "Yaba"), married Catherine Moore, who, seven years before, had lost her brother John to an explosion.

Buchanan and Andrew Moore, a relative of Samuel's fiancée, Catherine, had pledged a $200 marriage bond the week before Christmas in 1886.[7] The bond was a guarantee against legal impediments (either of the couple was already married, for example) to the upcoming nuptials.[8] Their first child was born a year later; Margaret K. Buchanan died at six years old. Elizabeth Jane was born August 23, 1889, and daughter

A Gift of Diamonds 153

Catherine Moore Buchanan came along in early 1893. The first son named Samuel James died one month after birth. Later in the nineties, Harvey Oscar (August 31, 1895) and the second Samuel James (October 4, 1897) joined the family.[9] The second Margaret K., or Maggie, was born in 1899.[10]

Sam Buchanan, killed in the February 2, 1906 explosion. (Hagley Museum and Library)

Samuel had started working in the DuPont mills in 1889. A tall, muscular man, he towered over most of the other powdermen. His workmates considered him taciturn, made so by the hard, physical labor performed in the yards. He was thoughtful and a reader and a player in Alfred I. du Pont's Tankopanicum Musical Club, known as "Al's Band" (Tankopanicum is a Native American word meaning "rushing waters of the Brandywine.") Buchanan played the bass violin, an instrument larger than a cello but smaller than a bass. Alfred called playing the bass violin "shaking hands with a bull fiddle."[11] He may have provided the instrument to Buchanan, as he did with other members, and he may have paid for music lessons. The Delaware Symphony Orchestra grew out of Al's band.[12]

Buchanan disliked dogs in the powder yards, saying that, if he went across the creek, he did not want dog bones mixed in with his. According to a great granddaughter, he was "wild and aggressive, as well as thoughtful, he was respected by everyone and earned that reputation as a hard-working employee." Buck was "fearless and incorruptible, but most of all he had guts."[13] The descendant said that despite his avidity for reading and thirst for knowledge, he "thought himself not a very smart person."[14]

The DuPont workmen had a sixth sense regarding explosions. In the event of an explosion, they "knew" whose mill building had gone up without being in the immediate vicinity. One example of this intuition comes from a Hagley oral interview with a daughter of a powder worker. Mary Braden Jackson reports that, on the morning Sam died, her father, who came home after working the overnight shift, said, "'Oh, God bless us, there goes Sam Buchanan.' And we all went out on the porch, and we run down the road, we were going to the gates, you know, everybody, all the older people to find out who it was, and sure enough it was Sam Buchanan."[15]

With headlines screaming "blown to atoms," or "blown in fragments," the newspaper told the full story of Buck Buchanan's death. One article was the same size as the description of the Brandywine Zoo's groundhog seeing his shadow, foretelling six more weeks of winter. The writer added that frigid temperatures "plunged immediately on the animal burrowing back into his den."[16]

According to later reports, a group of men had left the graining mill where the explosion occurred a few minutes before the accident, thus saving their lives. Buchanan was the only worker who remained. The mill was in the same spot as the blast that had killed "Little Bill" McDowell three years earlier. People debated how much powder blew up, some saying one ton, others, two. Whatever the quantity, it was so-called "fuse" powder, more powerful than the usual mix used for blasting. Reports came in from as far away as the DuPont plant across the Delaware River at Carneys Point, New Jersey, of hearing and feeling the effects of the blast. Those looking for the familiar cloud of billowing smoke were not disappointed. As one paper reported, "Apart from the detonation of the explosion, which was one of the sharpest and loudest in many years, the picture caused by the large sphere of smoke arising skyward, was most interesting to beholders. The ball remained intact until it reached a great height, and the sunlight brought out the smoke in fine relief. After attaining a great height, the smoke dissipated in all directions, unfolding like a mammoth umbrella."[17]

The papers reported that the Improved Order of Red Men, of which Buchanan was a member, would attend the funeral as a group. Two other stories made the papers. A fellow workman found one of Buchanan's hands in the woods a quarter mile from the site of the blast. When the worker took it to the deceased's home, where the funeral rites were about to begin, the family did not want mourners to know about the found body part so they gave it to the undertaker, John Kilmer. When he saw his chance, he surreptitiously opened the casket and "gently placed the hand with the other remains in the coffin, just as the Red Men...arrived to attend the funeral." The paper said the family found it a source of comfort that Kilmer had placed the hand with the remains.[18]

As might be expected, fifteen-year-old Elizabeth Buchanan was distraught at losing her father. In deep grief, she attributed the gift of a diamond ring given to her the day of the explosion as coming from Alfred I. du Pont's wife, Bessie Gardner du Pont.

That morning, her mother had sent Elizabeth to run an errand some distance from their home in Squirrel Run. While on the errand, she heard the explosion at eight o'clock. Close to noon, as she was returning home, she met a man and woman on the road. Elizabeth asked them where the blast had been and if it killed anyone. The woman asked the teenager, "My child, do you not know your father was killed in that explosion?" The blunt communication caused Elizabeth to swoon.

After she revived and got home, many visitors came to the house, including Mrs. du Pont. Still later the woman she had met on the road came to the Buchanan home with the admonition to Elizabeth, "You cannot do any good by crying, little one. You only weaken yourself and worry your mother more. Be a little woman, stop crying and I will give you a nice present."

On the same day, the woman sent the ring to the Buchanan home with the message, "Wear this." Newspapers confirmed Elizabeth received a ring of gold with seven diamonds, but the family "only know what the child says of who gave it to her. The little girl is still suffering seriously from nervous shock."[19] In the next day's issue, the *Morning News* cleared up the story. To give "full credit" to the donor, the paper published an article stating that she was Mrs. Frank Connable, the wife of the assistant[20] to Alfred I. du Pont.[21] Alfred mourned for days after his friend and fellow musician died.[22]

Widowed Catherine Moore Buchanan became Mrs. Percy Churchill in 1908. The 1910 U.S. Census showed her with a new daughter by Percy, eight years her junior, an Englishman and a shipyard riveter. John B. Piesuzka, the census enumerator, mistakenly gave two-year-old Gladys the last name Buchanan. Her parents divorced in 1920; the census that year showed Catherine living with her daughter, sixteen-year-old Stella, both of them working in a Morocco plant, Catherine as a "forelady," Stella as a "seasoner." Morocco leather was made into gloves, bookbindings, and like items.[23]

Three months later, two workers died, one instantly, the other surviving for a week. William McCrea had left the company six weeks before the May 1906 accident to work at the Bancroft Mills but soon returned to pick up where he left off. McCrea and David Cammock were working in roll mill fifteen when it blew.

Patrick Dougherty, the owner of a hotel at Henry Clay village, a neighborhood outside the Hagley gates, told a reporter from the *Evening*

Journal that he and McCrea had talked about what it would be like to get blown up in an explosion. Dougherty related that McCrea spoke of the danger of the work, saying it felt much greater to him after he left to work at Bancroft's. "I imagine all you know is the flash and then it is all over," Dougherty quoted his friend.[24]

The blast tore McCrea's leg off and the papers once again spared no slight detail: "His body was burned almost to a crisp."[25] Over a thousand mourners attended the funeral, held at his home on Long Row. Members of the Wawaset Tribe of the IORM and the Shepherds of Bethlehem, another organization that, unlike most others, accepted women, were in the crowd. At the coroner's inquest into McCrea's death, the jury foreman was State Representative William H. Miller, one of Jonas Miller's sons. Widow Annie McCrea later remarried a Mr. Martin.

The second May victim, forty-year-old David Cammock was preparing to return to Ireland for a visit to his homeland when he suffered injuries alongside McCrea. He had lived in Newtownards, a civil parish in County Down, east of Belfast, before embarking on the *S.S. Southwark* of the American Line. His wife, Catherine, and their ten-month-old son, David, accompanied him on the ten-day voyage. The trio disembarked at the port of Philadelphia in the first week of October 1894.

Making his way to the Brandywine, Cammock's first appearance in the ledgers occurred when the leaves on the mill's trees turned their most vivid in the following year's fall. Second son James joined the family in 1895 and another son, Robert, became the last child, born in 1898. They lost their six-and-a-half-year-old brother David to pneumonia in 1900.

Cammock and McCrea were brothers-in-law, married to the Dunbar sisters, David's Catherine and McCrea's wife, Anne. The Cammocks lived at 183 Breck's Lane, near the primary mill gate. They asked George Cheney, the company's housing man, to do repairs and updates to the home, down the street from Thomas and Isabella Dougherty, who also made repair requests. The family asked the company to extend their back porch to a tree in the yard they wanted cut down and paint applied to the kitchen woodwork. They also wanted the upstairs rooms repainted, and the fence repaired. Whether DuPont made the improvements is not known.[26]

After the explosion, the newspapers kept close tabs on David Cammock's well-being. On the day after the accident, the *Evening Journal* reported, as of 1:30 in the afternoon, Cammock was alive but in critical condition.[27]

Three days later, the *Morning News* reported that his status had worsened. "It was thought that he had good chances of recovery, but his condition has become worse." The article added, "It is doubtful whether he will survive the effects of being blown from the powder mill into the mill race along the Brandywine."[28] He died later that day. Son James told an interviewer he visited his father in the hospital but could only see his eyes, as they were the only part of his body not covered in bandages. James said while being thrown into the mill race saved his father's life in the short run, the pneumonia he caught combined with serious burns and killed him four days later.[29]

Elder Christie of the Little Band, "a religious organization formed sometime ago at DuPont's Banks," led the funeral. The Orangemen conducted a commitment ceremony graveside at Green Hill Presbyterian Church, near Cammock's home.[30]

It was customary in the early 20th century for minor children, even with one parent still living, to have a guardian appointed. In the fall of 1906, the Orphans Court did just that, appointing Patrick Cammock, probably an uncle, as James and Robert's guardian. By 1930, Robert was a DuPont chemist;[31] his brother also worked for the company. The day after the United States declared it was at war with the Empire of Japan in 1941, widowed Catherine died at seventy-eight.

A colorful, short-time worker would be the next to succumb to the powder.

On a frosty morning near the first day of spring, 1909, a ton of powder exploded in detonations of a graining mill and a glazing mill in the Hagley yards. George Whiteman, a widower who had worked six months in the powder yards, died in the conflagration.

He had been in the livery business, owning stables in Wilmington. Before buying the Hagan Brothers stable, Whiteman had been a stone dresser at the William Lea & Sons flour mill. He made grooves in the millstones used for grinding wheat.[32] Whiteman had a bustling business renting buggies and horses; he used money from the business to raise show dogs, take part in horse racing, and serve on committees devoted to promoting that sport.

Whiteman rented horse and buggy combinations to Wilmington police detectives for official work and to out-of-towners who wanted to explore the area. In one case, a couple from Philadelphia rented a team for a country drive. The *Delaware Gazette and State Journal* picks up the story: "When opposite the property of Benjamin Haley, on the Concord Pike, the wagon was overturned, and both occupants thrown to the ground. Watson sustained a fracture of the forearm and other painful injuries, while his wife was unhurt. The wagon was completely wrecked...[but] both occupants managed to extricate themselves from under the wagon and were brought to the city in a milk wagon by Mr. Haley." Whiteman had a warrant issued for their arrest on a charge of demolishing his property.[33]

In another case, Whiteman was the defendant. In mid-May 1898, Whiteman's horse became unmanageable while he drove on Washington Street in Wilmington. The horse and buggy careened into a trench where John Foard, a water department worker, was working with a pick. The horse landed on top of him and the pick was driven into his shoulder. He was knocked unconscious.

Foard told the court he could not do any heavy lifting, and he wanted $3,000 from Whiteman, who had given him $10 and paid for a physician to treat him. Foard denied that, when the doctor visited him at home, he ran upstairs and got into bed fully clothed. Dr. J.W. Crumbaugh testified that he saw him do just that. After the jury received the charge from the judge, they deliberated less than a half hour and returned a verdict in favor of Whiteman.[34]

Whiteman was an active horseman, entering his steeds in steeple chases and sulky races. He was a regular participant, both as a horseman and a shower of horses and dogs at the Wilmington Fair, which began in the late 1880s at Hazel Dell Park in South Wilmington. His horse, Dexter, ran in races but won none of them; mostly, he finished last. Another horse, Gild Edge, was also a losing proposition, winning none of the sulky races reported in the newspapers. Whiteman, however, was more successful raising dogs. He could demand $25 for the puppies of Beauty, a smooth-haired Collie, because she won first prizes. In 1890, Whiteman displayed dogs at a show that S.F. du Pont had also entered; this was not Samuel Francis, "the Admiral," but a later relative.

During that same show at the Wilmington Agricultural and Industrial Association fair, when they chose Whiteman to serve as race marshal, he showed his mettle[35] by reining in a horse. Madame Marantette, a horsewoman of repute, wanted to amaze the afternoon crowd with a display of a quartet of horses jumping together over three hurdles in a half mile. As the horses neared the first hurdle, a gray shied and balked, but the other three cleared the obstacle. "The reins attached to the gray broke and released it, at the same time getting tangled up in the second horse's legs. The sorrel kicked itself loose and ran down the track. Madame Marantette kept her seat and held the two remaining horses while Marshall George C. Whiteman went on a race for the sorrel. He caught it on the turn to the home stretch, and came up the track with it, jumping two hurdles and winning applause."[36]

George Whiteman's stables were the scene of many incidents during the 1890s: thefts of animals, buggies, whips, horse blankets, and other equine accouterments; the suspicious death of his show dog, a Cocker Spaniel named Carlo; assaults on the proprietor; and frauds. The papers reported the oddest happening in October 1889. "A strange accident occurred one evening last week at the stables of George C Whiteman, Shipley Street near Seventh. A horse belonging to Henry P. Scott was discovered with his right hind foot held firmly in its mouth. The poor brute lay in the stall in the peculiar position, quite unable to free itself. By using a pitchfork in prying open the horse's mouth, the hoof was freed. A few tooth marks around the fetlocks indicate the tightness of the lock."[37]

A later article described an arson. "Benjamin Morris and Ashburn McNitt, both colored lads, were arraigned in the municipal court this morning on a serious charge, that of attempting to fire the stables of George C. Whiteman, Numbers 717 and 719 Shipley St." Two weeks earlier, Whiteman had caught young Morris loitering in the stables so he put him in the water trough before letting him go. The boy returned to throw a brick through the door, just missing "striking an aged man sitting on a chair."

On the night of June 1, 1893, a Whiteman employee noticed smoke coming from the stables and saw a boy run out. Whiteman collared him and his companion and turned them over to the police. The newspaper reported, "Morris is the worse of the two." McNitt's mother had forbidden him to associate with Morris, but her son ignored the pleas. Young McNitt told Whiteman that Morris had said that, if he had a rifle, he would "shoot that ___ __ _ _____." He likely joined his brother at the Ferris Industrial School, the local reform school.[38]

That same year, tragedy struck the Whiteman household when George's eight-year-old namesake died. The newspapers wrote that his mother was Lulu; her full name was Margaret Lucinda Whiteman. Margaret L. Pierce and George C. Whiteman had married in 1884.[39]

The death of young George Whiteman was not the first loss experienced by the extensive family. In early 1894, toddler Katherine, twenty months old, succumbed to bronchial catarrh, a respiratory infection. Then, in 1900, the family lost another child, this time infant Edith. Born in July, she died three months later of "marasmus," or severe malnutrition.[40] The following year, the ninth baby, Frances, died from pneumonia at four months. The year after that saw the death of the oldest daughter of the clan, Helen; it is unclear how the fifteen-year-old died, as the news headline about her demise said she was a "typhoid fever victim," but the story said it was malaria. The official death certificate said "myocarditis"; either of the diseases listed in the newspaper can cause it. And, in 1907, they lost their matron when forty-year-old Margaret Whiteman died of "pulmonary embolism because of a retained placenta"[41] during the birth of the last child, Ellis. It is never easy to read of so many deaths that might have been avoidable with the help of today's modern medicine.

By 1904, the livery business was no longer good to George C. Whiteman. Officials sold the Shipley street properties and contents at a sheriff's auction for $3,000.

The 1909 explosion that killed Whiteman, had it occurred just a few minutes later, would have killed more men. Whiteman had begun work before the others, on their way to the mills for a seven o'clock start. The *Morning News* reported the story: "It is thought by many that Whiteman had begun work at this preparing to start it for the day. It is supposed that powder tossed into the cylinder Saturday night had congealed and that in breaking it up to start the machine going Whiteman used, as customary, a mallet and chisel. Perhaps a spark was drawn from this and the mill went up with a roar that scattered the remains of the unfortunate man over an area of six hundred yards in breadth or more." The article continued, "Some of the remains were picked up across the creek from the plant while other parts were found in a large field north and at least two hundred yards from the scene of the explosion. In all, two buckets full of the small pieces of the unfortunate man were collected together by boys and men sent out for that purpose or self delegated. None of the parts were recognizable excepting a small part of the upper jaw and front teeth and one eye."[42]

Several other employees sustained injuries. One worker, initially listed as dead, was Morris Curry, hospitalized with a fractured skull and burns. Three weeks after the fatal explosion, Curry developed tetanus and was in critical condition, but he overcame that "dreaded disease," as one article described it, and was released from care.[43]

Flying debris injured others. In an oral interview for the Hagley Museum, Elizabeth Beacom related that, "My mother had her washtub on two chairs. In those days they boiled their clothes in a boiler and stirred them with a broomstick. She told me to help her off with the boiler and just as we went out the door, my, it did rip.... [S]omething struck me on the back of the hand and I had a lump the size of a walnut." She added that it was her impression that most of the explosions occurred in wintertime.[44]

Residents of the nearby workers community also had narrow escapes. Pieces of the glazing barrel, which weighed between three and four thousand pounds, traveled five hundred yards and just missed falling into a dwelling. A piece of steel plate weighing twenty-five pounds flew in the front door of the Lawrence Cunningham residence as the lady of the house exited the same door. A sizable piece of shafting plowed a trench twenty feet long and three feet deep. Another piece of the barrel fell through the roof and onto the bed of John Sykes, who had just vacated it.[45]

Five months passed before another powder worker died. Unlike many Americans on the move to the open spaces of the West in the 1800s, John Mott, born in Illinois, had made his way east to Lackawanna County, Pennsylvania. Born in the early fifties, he married Pennsylvanian Emily "Emma" Edwards on Independence Day 1880. They had two sons, Frederick and Leonard, both adults when John died.[46]

Across from the graining mill on that warm summer day, several boys were pursuing their usual pastime—swimming in the gurgling Brandywine. One of them tells the story: "All of a sudden there was a flash went out of that mill. When that thing went off, we dove in that water as quick as if somebody yelled, 'Get under the water.' Man, when we came to the top you never heard such a shower of hot metal hitting the water in all your life."[47]

Morris Curry and Moses Campbell, injured in the blast, served on the coroner's jury that said the explosion was accidental. Mott was buried at the Chelten Hills Cemetery in Philadelphia.

A month later another detonation jolted the local citizenry. Questions regarding which mill blew up and how many people died flooded the telephone lines to one newspaper. It was not a mill that blew. In Rising Sun Lane, where workmen and their families lived, road builders had used dynamite to break up the earth instead of using picks and shovels or machinery.

November 11, 1909, saw the somber year's third fatal explosion and its third, fourth, and fifth deaths.

The first to die that day was twenty-three-year-old newlywed Walter McDermott, who was in charge of the Upper Yard pack house. Close to six tons of powder blew while he was inside the building. The conflagration moved to the nearby prismatic press mill and it, too, exploded. Driver George Howard Darrah and laborer Nicholas Dinesto were riding on a horse cart between the two buildings. Both died when the press house blew, their bodies blackened but not mangled. The papers used the now-trite phrase "blown to atoms" to describe McDermott's remains.[48]

Eleven months before, McDermott had wed eighteen-year-old Margaret Dodley. They had no children. The census taken the year after she lost her husband listed Margaret as a servant for the Meridith Samuel family of four in Wilmington.[49] Six years after her first husband's death, Margaret remarried and she and Joseph Keeley had two children. She died during the Spanish Flu pandemic in 1918.[50]

McDermott was buried in the New Garden Cemetery, near his wife's family's residence in Toughkenamon, Pennsylvania. Margaret lies in Wilmington's Silverbrook Cemetery.

George Howard Darrah, the driver of the horse cart, was a single nineteen-year-old boarding with Mrs. Hahn, an aunt, on Rising Sun Lane. He was from Bensalem, Pennsylvania, where the 1900 U.S. Census puts him in a household with his parents, two siblings, an uncle and both of his grandmothers.[51]

In his short life, Howard joined three organizations: the Knights of the Golden Eagle, the IORM, and the Patriotic Order Sons of America, an anti-Catholic and anti-immigration society. Founded in Philadelphia in mid-century, it was connected to the Know Nothings, a group whose members preserved secrecy by denying its existence.

Darrah's obituary indicates his burial in the Newark Union M.E. Church Cemetery in North Wilmington but neither a physical search of the grave markers nor a listing from the Delaware Genealogical Society, taken from earlier records, turned up his name.

Italian immigrants had started working for the French du Ponts in the early 1870s but, until now, none had died because of a powder explosion. Perhaps this was due to a perceived trait pointed out by one du Pont and her view of the Italians compared to the Irish. Mrs. J.B. du Pont said, "an Italian will do what he's told; whereas an Irishman is apt to get to thinking of some way to do it better. When an Irishman on a powder line gets to 'thunkin,' it's time to look for him on the other side of the creek."[52]

Charles Sicco, a worker misidentified as Charles Sickles and Charles Sisilo in news articles when George Whiteman died earlier in the year (and about whom we will learn more later) made a narrow escape from the disaster. Nicola DiNesto's luck ran out on the back of the horse cart at the end of 1909.

DiNesto[53] was living in Wilmington with his wife and four children. A few nights before the accident, he argued with his wife about continuing to work in the mills. A report said he laughed at her fear that he might die in an explosion, telling her he only had to die once and he "might as well die in the powder yards as elsewhere." Soon after the accident, Mrs. DiNesto, accompanied by her brother-in-law, Edward DiNesto, who also worked in the powder, went to the yards to ask after her husband. When she grasped the truth, "her frantic cries could be heard all over the settlement near the powder yards," and Edward led her home to grieve.[54] Edward had worked with the powder car in earlier days but was out that day with a sore throat, which saved his life.

"DuPont Officers Deny Plot Story," screamed the *Morning News* headline a week later. "People in the Vicinity and Employes are Greatly Agitated However," the sub-headline said. And, "Metal Found in Explosives—Orders from the duPont Powder Company, closing the Hagley powder yards along the Brandywine until further notice, went into effect yesterday, following the report that pieces of iron and other metals had been found in the powder in process of manufacture. These two circumstances have given rise to the rumor that there is a conspiracy in operation to destroy the company's mills along the creek."[55]

The company told the newspaper the factory closing was routine; it was normal procedure to close one of their many operations when excess powder was on hand. Powder Operations Manager Frank Connable said, "This company cannot conceive that any person would be so malicious as to deliberately put any foreign substance in its product, and the company takes pains to see that no person of such tendencies gets into its employ. The company has the utmost confidence in the loyalty of its men."[56]

Those men had other ideas, believing someone was trying to sabotage the mills. They pointed out when John Mott died three months earlier, that he had found a piece of iron in the powder on the morning of the day he died. "It is the firm belief of many employed at the yards, the exception being the managers of that department, that some miscreant is at his heinous work," opined the paper. The article continued, reporting that the worried workers said no piece of machinery could loosen and fall into the powder, as they burred and riveted every nut and every other piece of potential danger on the machines.

Later, on the evening of the November 11, 1909, explosion that snuffed out three lives, fire broke out on the third floor of the pulp keg factory, stoking the worker's fears, said the paper. Some thought the cause of the fire was matches in the waste paper used to make pulp, "and mice did the rest." The news article was adamant. "There is no possibility of it having been of incendiary origin."[57]

In a few short years, more worried rumors would spread that saboteurs were afoot in the yards. ■

▪ 13 ▪
Men at War

> The DuPont explosions over which there has been a good deal of excited speculation were very probably due to what might be called "confusional incompetency."
> —*The Charlotte Observer*

In the ensuing six years, only two explosions happened at the mills, calming sabotage fears. One injured a worker, but there were no deaths. One reason for the gap was the gradual discontinuation of manufacturing at the mills.

Under the headline "Rejuvenating Brandywine Powder Plant," *Every Evening's* June 23, 1915, edition said the "abandoned mills of [the] DuPont Company [were] being gotten in shape for use." The article continued: "It is…a fact that mills that were supposed to have been abandoned are being rebuilt and rejuvenated." Further, "When other mills were put into operation in New Jersey and other states the manufacture of explosives was gradually discontinued along the Brandywine, and a few months ago, it was understood, none was being made there."[1] The company restarted the mills, likely because of the sinking of the Lusitania by a German U-boat a month earlier. Four weeks after the article, the death toll rose again. One day short of the start of the war's first anniversary, when the Italian and Irish workers would have been on ideologically opposite sides of the conflict,[2] a powder fire killed two men in the first fatal accident in a half decade.

Why Henry M. Cazier worked in the powder is unknown. The question is of interest because he was the scion of a very wealthy family from the Kirkwood section of northern Delaware. He grew up on a large acreage called Mt. Vernon, his father Jacob's estate. Jacob inherited 3,300 acres near Glasgow, Delaware, in the middle of the 19th century, from his father, Henry. The family traced their lineage to before the 17th century, and to Matthias van Bibber, an early settler in Cecil County, Maryland. A van Bibber ancestor married Daniel Boone's youngest son, Nathan.

More than a century removed, we can speculate why the man who stood to inherit rich lands of west-central New Castle County, Delaware, worked in the yards. Perhaps he had a falling out with his family. Another explanation is that Henry wanted to prove he was his own man, not just the son of a prominent citizen. The application of Occam's Razor leads to the conclusion that Henry, called Harry, chose to work in the powder or it was the only job available to him. Whatever the reason, he was working at the mills on July 13, 1915.

Managers of the DuPont Company spent that day disavowing two early morning explosions in the mills. The blasts happened in the Glen Mills quarries, fifteen miles north of the powder mills.[3] Another newspaper said, "Officials of the powder company are at a loss to explain how the story originated that one man had been killed and three injured in an explosion at the Carneys Point [New Jersey] plant on Tuesday. The powder officials say there was no explosion, and that nobody was hurt. The names of the supposed victims were given by powder workers at Penns Grove yesterday, but officials of the company state the names and the story are 'a dream,' and have no basis of truth. No record of a man being killed has been received by the coroner of Salem County."[4] No denials came from the du Ponts regarding the mishap on the Brandywine.

Cazier had married Aubertine Grant in New York City in 1906. Prior to the marriage, while courting, they had been traveling on Concord Pike when their horse became frightened. The upending of the carriage threw both to the road, slightly injured. Two boys found the horse, with buggy still attached, and returned it to its owner, Jesse Hanby, a one-time competitor of George C. Whiteman.[5]

Aubertine was the daughter of Wilmingtonians Willard Spencer and Martha K. Grant. Neither her father nor her mother "gave her away" at the wedding; that task was performed by her grandmother, but it is not clear why. It is probable Willard and Martha were not married when Aubertine was born in 1880. The possibility is enhanced by the changing of Aubertine's last name by the Delaware State Senate in 1885; the legislation, required at the time, to change her name from Spencer to Grant, lends credence to the supposition.[6]

In the summer of 1913, Henry filed for divorce from Aubertine in the New Castle County courts. She died of tuberculosis while visiting Atlantic City four months before her former husband's death, and is buried with her mother in the Wilmington and Brandywine Cemetery.

Because of Henry's status as heir to the Cazier fortune, he was often featured in the society pages.[7] When he was eighteen, he had won the prize for excellence in Greek at the Wilmington Literary, Scientific and Military Academy.[8] Three years later, he attended the New Year's Ball at the Middletown, Delaware, Opera House, which the local paper called "the most delightful social function ever witnessed in our town."[9]

In 1910, Henry's mother hosted a sizable party that featured a ride with her on the "go slow and never arrive railroad." Mrs. Cazier decked out a part of a large hall in the mansion to resemble a baggage room. Passengers lined up at the "ticket office," where young Henry served as ticket agent. The ticket entitled them to sit in the "parlor car," where they played a game of progressive railroad euchre. One guest thanked her with an attempt at poetry:

> Departing we all with one accord exclaimed:
> All hail to the fair and charming Mrs. Cazier
> Whom we all just think a perfect dear,
> For giving us such a unique excursion,
> Which was to us all, a most pleasant diversion.
> Here's to each and everyone
> Who on Wednesday enjoy the fun,
> of that glorious Atlantic trip,
> the only thing lacking,
> was time for an ocean dip.[10]

A year later, Henry, father Jacob, and brother-in-law George Townsend Jr., a prominent Wilmington attorney, attended the annual roundup of Chincoteague ponies.[11]

On the day Cazier became a victim of the powder fire,[12] powderman John Westcott of Chestertown, Maryland, was to take his place. Westcott saved his own life by not working. Co-workers from Chestertown felt they had had enough and left the DuPont Company. Others "decided to stick it out at $90 per month."[13]

Daniel F. Shields was one of the nearby powdermen who came to the aid of the two victims. In an oral history interview with the Hagley Museum in 1958, he told of large brass jugs of "that white medicine.[14]

When somebody got burned like that, you took the cork out and poured it down. I could see me holding this fellow in the chair pouring it over his head."[15] Cazier died the following morning while being treated for burns at the Delaware Hospital.

Daniel F. Toomey, the son of local hotelier Timothy Toomey, was the foreman that day and worked with Cazier in the prismatic press house.[16] Between the fire, on the evening of the thirteenth, and his death at the hospital a few hours later, Cazier explained where he and Toomey were when the powder fired. He had climbed on top of a press; Toomey was on one side of the room. Cazier could not tell the calamity's cause.

Toomey was the father of five boys, ranging in age from five to seventeen. Their father and mother, Hannah S. Casey, wed in 1896. Mrs. Toomey, ailing before the accident, suffered a relapse and fell in and out of consciousness.

Another powderman who came to the aid of the pair of victims was Charles Lickle, who remembered Toomey staggering around with fire coming from his body. Lickle dragged him into the creek and pushed the foreman's head under the water to douse the flames.[17]

Toomey died five hours after Cazier the morning of July 14. Mrs. Toomey died of tuberculosis in April of the following year. Her oldest boy, Timothy, still in high school, got a job as an errand boy for the company.

In a week's time another explosion caused heightened fear among the residents of northern Delaware. The headlines stirred the simmering thoughts of sabotage by German agents. The eye-catching headline in a local paper shouted that the blast was "Laid to Spies."[18]

A competing newspaper, reporting on the explosion of the same buildings that had flashed before, killing Toomey and Cazier, told its readers the "wildest kind of spy rumors are in circulation. Officials deplored such rumors. They have no evidence of being stampeded or even perturbed by the glut of sensational reports."[19]

The "Laid to Spies" headline led an article that said, "It is feared that Germans, under assumed names, may have secured employment in the mill. It is a known fact that no man whose name is of a German extraction is employed by the firm without a most thorough investigation of his antecedents and character." More accounts followed. "The explosion last night was heightened this morning by the report that a squadron of United States cavalry had been rushed from Washington to Rising Sun, in the immediate vicinity of the Hagley yards. Investigation showed that a squad of 16 men of the United States engineering corps had arrived for the purpose of making an inspection and survey of roads and bridges throughout that section of the country."[20]

The DuPont Company furloughed 300 workers so they could conduct investigations of their backgrounds. Among those checked were Lawrence Cunningham and Hugh Gillespie, the latter having joined the DuPont work force days earlier. Both made it through the inquiries and were working on August twenty-ninth when the fuse mill and nearby press mill blew.[21]

Gillespie was twenty years old and single. The men normally did not work on Sundays but, because of the European war, the company requested they sign up for extra shifts, and he answered the call. It cost the inexperienced powderman his life. He came from Hazleton, Pennsylvania, where the company returned his remains for interment.

Cunningham was an experienced worker who had started with DuPont in the early nineties. He married Hannah "Jennie" Buchanan (Sam Buchanan's sister), and they had one child, a girl, Isabella May, who predeceased her father. She was born mid-May 1894 and died at eighteen months of "convulsions."[22]

One account said the two mill workers had started machinery and were leaving it when the explosion occurred. On his way out, Cunningham must have grabbed lunch, as Thomas Dunlop remembers in his 1984 oral interview: "He was found the next day with a sandwich in his mouth."[23]

Another report said workers recovered only one body, and nobody was certain which one, as it was "burned and mangled beyond recognition." The second man was "blown to atoms [again!] the only remains recovered being bits of charred flesh hanging in the branches of trees on the opposite side of Brandywine creek."[24]

In September 1915 the Bloomington, Illinois, *Daily Pantagraph* published a list of gunpowder explosions in U.S. factories since the start of the war. While the list included several DuPont sites in New Jersey, the summer explosions at the Brandywine mills did not make the list. "Since the beginning of the European war there have been nineteen explosions and fires of undetermined origin, many of them under suspicious circumstances, in government arsenals and in powder factories and plants engaged on war contracts in the United States and one in Canada, with a total of thirty-four deaths and injuries to twenty-two," the paper said.[25]

The *Pantagraph* was not the only news outlet to fret about German sabotage. The *Evening Journal* editorialized, "It is high time that the United States government exert its best efforts to apprehend and bring to justice those Teutonic spies and emissaries who are committing such diabolical offenses against the neutrality of this country." The article went on, "There have been entirely too many explosions, fires, wrecks... for them to have been due to accident and not to design. It becomes more and more apparent that there is a systematized effort to tie up the operations of or to completely destroy American plants engaged in the manufacture of war munitions."[26] The paper was correct in referring to "systematized effort." The Germans and Austrians were sending saboteurs to America's shores to wreak havoc on the nation's industries and shipping, though the United States was still neutral.

The *Journal* added, "A report that several men, believed to be spies, have been arrested by United States officials on complaint of the DuPont powder company at Chester Island, off Chester, was not known of today by officials of the DuPont company here. They said no reports of arrests or even the men's presence on the island had been received."[27]

The spy and sabotage scare continued throughout 1915, including during and after the November 30 explosion of several tons of powder in the Upper Hagley pack house, killing thirty-one (mostly young) men. Thirteen men were in their teens. Ages ranged from sixteen to fifty-seven.

In a brief commentary on the latest accident, a North Carolina newspaper said, "The police may be puzzled—it's a way the police have—over what caused the latest explosion at DuPonts, but the rest of the country emphatically isn't." To this unsubstantiated, but understandable rumor, the company and the government responded forcefully. A DuPont official, former Congressman Charles B. Landis, brother of famed Baseball Commissioner Kennesaw Mountain Landis, issued a lengthy statement denying the blast resulted from "outside planning or interference." He added it was the corporation's stand that "no fire or explosion has occurred in any one of our factories in any part of the country since the European war began that affords ground for the suspicion."[28]

Papers quoted Bruce Bielaski, the chief of the FBI's predecessor, the Bureau of Investigation, saying the Bureau would look into the matter. This was not true. He said if the explosion was part of a plot, it would be the state's responsibility to probe it; the feds would give aid if asked.[29]

The *Charlotte Observer* boasted, "The papers that did not go into hysterics over the 'German plot' in the explosion at the DuPont plant are being vindicated." After congratulating itself that its explanation in earlier editions was "about correct," the paper introduced a novel concept, saying the detonations "were very probably due to what might be called 'confusional incompetency.'" The paper did not share in the anti-German hysteria sweeping the non-combatant nation. "We ought to be sure that a crime has been committed before recklessly imputing to anyone criminal responsibility for explosions in powder works."[30] That naïveté would, in a few months, turn to virulent hate directed at the inhuman Hun.

For now, however, reports arose that flyers nailed to trees and fences in the mill area warned anyone with a Germanic-sounding name or who was of German extraction to leave the Brandywine mills by the first of the year. There were also reports of posters at the Carneys Point, New Jersey, DuPont plant. While the managers of the DuPont concern denied seeing such flyers, many others described seeing them.

At about this time, a man who roomed with two Carneys Point powder workers poured powder, thinking it was flour, into a hot frying pan. According to the vastly understated news article, "he took the wrong bag."[31]

Back on the Brandywine, the job of the remaining workers was, as always, to collect bodies of the victims or fragments of their erstwhile friends.

On the afternoon of the November 1915 accident, they discovered only one body part they could identify (by its intact clothing), the torso of the press house foreman, Alan Thaxter.

Like Henry Cazier before him, Thaxter was the son of a well-to-do family. His father, Sydney W. Thaxter, had received the Medal of Honor thirty years after his heroism at the Civil War Battle of Hatcher's Run in Virginia.[32] Sydney became a well-known and respected businessman and city leader in Portland, Maine, after the war. He and second wife, Julia St. Felix Thom Thaxter, adopted Alan in October 1888 (his first wife, Laura May Farnham, died in 1880). Alan's brother, Sydney, was five years old when Alan joined the family; in another two years, the boys welcomed brother Langton. Another son, Philip, had died of diphtheria five days short of his first birthday in 1887; his death may have been the impetus for Sydney and Julia to adopt Alan. Brother Sydney became a distinguished jurist and state supreme court justice. Langton became a roentgenologist, another name for radiologist.

The Thaxters enjoyed relationships with many respected Americans. A distant ancestor, John Thaxter, corresponded with Abigail Adams, wife of the second American president (and mother of the sixth). Father Sydney was a classmate of Justice Oliver Wendell Holmes Jr. in the Harvard Class of 1861. Brother Sydney was a member of the Class of 1904, where he would have known his Harvard colleague, Franklin Delano Roosevelt. In the remembrance book for the elder Sydney, another Maine Medal of Honor winner, Joshua Chamberlain, appears as a member of the three-person committee who put together the memorial. In the same type of book, Felix Frankfurter lauded Alan's brother Sydney as "friend[s] for half a century"; the book praised Thaxter as "one of the most distinguished jurists ever to grace the Bench of the Supreme Judicial Court of the State of Maine."[33]

In 1903, Alan enrolled as a fourth-class cadet (freshman) at the Virginia Military Institute two years after another student, George C. Marshall, had graduated. Marshall became celebrated as Army Chief of Staff during World War II and later served as Secretary State and Secretary of Defense under President Harry S Truman.[34] Thaxter, though, was no Marshall; a letter from the VMI Superintendent's Office told a correspondent that Thaxter's "academic record and military conduct are very low, so I suppose he must have been a trifler while here."[35]

Alan Thaxter, pack house foreman when it exploded November 30, 1915. This picture was taken during his one year at Trinity College in New Haven, Connecticut. (Trinity College)

Like another member of the Class of 1907, George Patton Jr., Alan Thaxter did not return to VMI after his first year.[36] He enrolled at the Holderness School in Plymouth, New Hampshire, graduating in 1907, and winning the highest award presented to a graduate, the Rector's Award for "manliness."[37] He entered the class of 1911 at Trinity College, where he blossomed.

Thaxter appeared to enjoy college life, becoming class president in his second semester on the Hartford, Connecticut campus of the former Washington College. He won election to the German Club, joined Psi Upsilon fraternity, received a nomination to the Sophomore Eating Club, and developed into a standout center on the football team.[38] Thaxter earned a varsity letter for his work as a freshman on the team.

As at VMI, he did not return for a second year at Trinity.

The 1910 *Portland City Directory* lists him as a vice president of his father's wholesale grain business, but the census enumeration that year said he was a "clerk."[39] At one point, Thaxter may have worked in Philadelphia as a broker, perhaps of grain, as he would have learned the trade while working for his father. The Hagley oral interview with Charles Lickle, the man who pushed Dan Toomey's head under water in the July accident, proposes an intriguing scenario regarding Thaxter. Lickle tells his interviewer that Thaxter took his place at the Wilmington YMCA when he, Lickle, left that residence.

An unidentified roommate told Lickle he saw Thaxter put on two pairs of socks that late November morning and identified Thaxter's foot after the explosion, recognizing the two socks.

Lickle said, "[T]hat boy's parents thought he was working for a brokerage firm in Philadelphia. He had gotten into some sort of a scrape, and he had come down here and gone to work in the Powder Mill and was killed, and they were still writing to him at the brokerage firm in Philadelphia. They were forwarding letters, and he had a friend in the brokerage firm who was forwarding letters up to his parents from Philadelphia. They thought he was in the brokerage business at the time he was killed here."[40]

This is a curious supposition, given that, after an earlier explosion at the mills, Thaxter's mother, Julia, pleaded with him to abandon powder employment. The *New York Tribune* said, "It was learned today that the mother of Allan Thaxter, the shop foreman, who lives in Portland, Me., sent her son a telegram after a minor accident at the plant a few weeks ago, begging him to resign his position and return home." Thaxter showed the message to a friend, saying, "My mother is worried over my work and has asked me to resign. He crumpled the paper in his hand and dismissed the matter," according to the *Tribune*.[41]

One newspaper said an earlier explosion blew Thaxter out of the building, but he suffered no injuries.[42] Newspapers reported that a few days before the fatal accident, Thaxter experimented with powder in his room. The *Evening Journal* said he was "mixing powder in a shaving mug when it exploded." The paper added that he joined a Bible class at the Y, where they said prayers for him at the weekly meeting the night he died, and sent a floral wreath to his mother in Portland.[43]

Every Evening wrote about Julia Thaxter's wish that her son quit working in the powder. The paper said he was a college graduate (a notion I could not confirm) and he became a bond salesman in New York[44] but then moved to Wilmington. After an explosion at the mills, the paper said his mother wrote several letters and sent a fifty-word telegram in which she reiterated her pleas, and, the paper said that "it is likely the young man would have heeded his mother's request had he lived a short time longer."[45]

Another oral interview subject says Thaxter came to the mills after being recruited from a job at the new DuPont Hotel in downtown Wilmington. William Lynch told the interviewer, "I had a fellow, a great big immense fellow about 6 ft. tall, Roger Wilson found him in the Hotel du Pont — a bell hop. And he dressed him and fixed him all up. He came from a mighty good family up in Portland, Maine."[46]

Thaxter's widowed mother (Sydney W. Thaxter died in 1908) transcribed the full text of the obituary for Alan by hand and sent it to VMI. The obit said the deceased's "charm of manners, though marked by considerable reticence and reserve, always won him friends." It added the younger employees he supervised "refer[red] to him as their 'college chum,' and one little Italian in the corps broke down entirely on learning of Mr. Thaxter's death." The eulogy continued, "Urged by his family and friends to take up a less precarious employment he refused, and stood by his post—continuing in furtherance of the task he had undertaken with not the least wavering or dread."[47]

Except for Thaxter, it took days of tedious inspection of bits of flesh and bone for the coroner to know which belonged together. Some parts were dangling in trees as distant as a quarter mile from the accident site. Day by day the coroner matched body parts on twenty of the remaining victims. Of the other ten, little could be identified.

Marge Bricotti, only seventeen years old, is the first name on the memorial to the ten buried together in Silverbrook Cemetery in Wilmington. He was born May 18, 1898.

The second name on the headstone is that of Henry Elliott, who lived in Newport, a few miles south of the Hagley yards. At first, no one came forward to name him. Then, his parents, Robert and Mary went to the funeral home where the body parts were being held. *Every Evening* said, "Both of the parents are in great distress over the loss of their son and the mother is so ill that little hope is held out for her recovery. It was for this reason that the parents could not come to this city to identify the remains, although they afterwards tried to do so but could not." Henry's cousin, George McDougle, struggled to ID the remains of the seventeen-year-old. He was unsuccessful as well.[48]

Next on the tall monument is Norman Fisher, sixteen or seventeen years old, depending on which source one uses for his birth. The death certificate recorded his date of birth as March 24, 1899, which would make his age at death the lower one. On the marker, the date is April 29, 1898, making him seventeen.

The fourth name was that of James R. Gemmill, born December 26, 1896. A laudatory article in *Every Evening* said "[He] was well known in South Wilmington and throughout the city for his prowess in the various branches of athletics and as an all around good fellow. He was one of the most valuable players on the present Madeley Second basketball team, and he was also a dependable man on both the baseball and football teams." Besides the Madeley Athletic Association, he was a member of other clubs and played on their teams. The night before the explosion, they measured him for a new uniform, his football "suit." The team manager was expecting "Jimmie" to play in every game during the forthcoming season. The group suspended the season's immediate games in reverence for Gemmill, and his teammates planned to attend the funeral en masse.[49]

Below Gemmill was the name Edward Gross, the first-born to house painter Jeremiah and Annie B. Collins Gross. Edward, at twenty-five, was older than the first three men on the monument who were all under eighteen. He was born two weeks after the colossal 1890 explosion.

Next on the granite was James M. Malloy, whose birthdate is also in dispute. The death certificate, which unkindly puts his name as "parts of James Malloy,"[50] notes that his birth was February 2, 1900, making him the youngest to die that day. The tombstone lists date of birth as the same month and day but in 1897. Meanwhile, the U.S. Census for 1910 lists his age as ten. This "Jimmy" was also a member of a local athletic outfit, the Defiance Club.[51]

James Sylvester was an Italian who had Americanized his name from Vincenzo diSilvestri, or Silvestro, and was known as Gimi. The death certificate listed him as eighteen but with no birthdate noted; the headstone lists his birthdate as November 2, 1891. Here again, either the stone mason carved the wrong date of birth or the registrar completing the official paperwork got the age incorrect.

The Smack brothers, John E. and Paul C., are the next names on the memorial. John was the younger of the two at age nineteen; his brother was twenty-two. They came from a large family in Snow Hill, Maryland, where they had worked together on their father's farm. John had signed on at the mills the day before the explosion that killed him.

The last of the ten alphabetized names on the stone is that of Elijah Springfield, born May 27, 1892. Elijah Gilton Springfield was born in Philadelphia, Pennsylvania, to William and Sarah Elizabeth and baptized at home six months later, too sick to be carried to St. Mary's Episcopal Church on Lombard Street. He recovered and later married Mildred Florence Hobson, who gave birth to Randall Elijah Springfield five weeks after his father's passing.[52] A year and a half later another tragedy, losing her only child to pneumonia, struck the widow.

Elijah Gilton Springfield, one of ten victims whose body could not be identified in the pack house explosion in 1915.

Springfield had a premonition of death, according to *Every Evening*. The paper reported he could not find employment elsewhere, so he started working in the powder, with the remark that "it would not be surprising he should be killed." He had taken the last-ditch job the previous day.[53]

A memorial service honored Springfield and the nine other unidentified men the following Tuesday, one week after the disaster. It was a "union" service, with pastors from the Baptist, Methodist, and Presbyterian churches, led by Rev. William Laird of Christ Episcopal Church. The DuPont Company presented "a handsome blanket made of roses and other flowers." The steel casket held three silver plates, the center one having the inscription "Unidentified, Hagley Yard, November 30, 1915." The other plates, placed above and below the center one, contained the etched names of the men whose bodies were unidentified.

One bright spot that faded quickly was the story of Albert Williams, who quit working in the powder mills on the Monday night before the Tuesday explosion. He was being congratulated by friends on Tuesday night for his escape from death when he learned that a trolley car accident had killed his wife.[54]

After loved ones identified the remaining nineteen victims of the explosion, they buried them in separate graves. The process could not have been pleasant. ■

14
Sabotage Jitters

> A powder mill is a bad place for work to be carried on
> in a rush and particularly so when large numbers of
> inexperienced hands are given employment.
> —*The Charlotte Observer*

Workers who had survived the 1915 blast, inured to the gore since most of them had done this before, picked up body fragments in buckets and baskets and took them to the undertaker, who placed parts that looked as if they belonged together on separate linen sheets. *Every Evening* said, "Some of the men were identified by sections of arms, which probably were tattooed or marked in some other manner. Others were identified by the hands or feet." The article continued, "The scenes about the undertaking establishment cannot be described with plain printer's ink. The families of the reported killed, coming in the hopes of finding some trace of their lost ones, were shocked. Stories of the lost ones, how they were attracted to the city by the unusually large publicity given to the prosperity of the city, were many in number.[1]

"Mothers many in years and the fathers old and gray, were seated in the parlors, not being strong enough to take the risk of going upstairs to even try to find their lost ones. Most of the men lost were young and therefore there were not many wives there, but those who were there were in deep grief."[2] In several cases, not finding bodies of those they knew worked in the mills relieved some visitors.

Someone found the remains of James Eggner. A part of his hand with a mark resembling a scar "was the only thing that was found to show to whom this belonged."[3] James was the third child of Louis and Elizabeth Gilmore Eggner.

By the 1910 census, Elizabeth had given birth to fourteen children, but only half were alive. James's brother John died of accidental poisoning.[4] He had a cold and his parents gave him medication in a bottle that formerly had laudanum in it. The remnants overwhelmed the three-month-old.[5] The family's grief must have affected two-year-old James immensely.

More losses followed. In 1905, fourteen-year-old Joseph Eggner died of tetanus. He had shot himself in the hand with a blank gun. His mother treated the wound, and for a time, he got better. But he took a turn for the worse, his jaws locked, and delirium set in. And finally "death relieved him of his suffering."[6] Joseph had earlier lost an eye when a toy rifle accidentally discharged, severing his optical nerve in one eye.[7] How the other five children died is not known.

Growing up in the Eggner household in South Wilmington sounds like something from a Victorian novel. Louis, the father, appeared in court multiple times on charges of non-support, assault, wife-beating, resisting arrest, and drunkenness. Once, a court adjudged him insane, and they sent him to Farnhurst, the state hospital for the insane. After one charge of assault, he "showed he was not accountable for his acts." After his confinement and release from the hospital, he claimed employees ill-treated him, which, according to the newspaper, "the public did not believe….Last night he attacked his wife and threatened he would saw off her head." As a result, the authorities took Louis to City Hall where he became violent and "undressed himself in his cell and destroyed his clothes. This morning he was returned to the Delaware Hospital where he will be detained."[8] It is not known how long he was detained at this time, but James's father died at Farnhurst in 1930 and is buried in the cemetery there.

James's mother Elizabeth was no stranger to the courts either. On one July 4th, officials charged her with assault and battery after she fought with a neighbor over holiday decorations. Another time, she became the victim of her daughter Nelly's attack on her. The *Evening Journal* said, "Mrs. Eggner told the court that her daughter struck her on the head with a kettle containing beer when objection was made by Mrs. Eggner to the daughter taking beer into the house." Nelly paid a fine of $25 dollars and costs.[9]

A year and a half before suffering the trauma of James's death in the November 1915 explosion, the family suffered another tragedy. James's sister, Martha, known as Mattie, married Clarence Griffith, and they had a six-week-old boy named after his father. In late April 1914, the three Griffiths died of asphyxiation in their home next to the Eggner house. Stating that "it is seldom that three members of one family have been interred at the same time in Wilmington," the *Evening Journal* added, "The three bodies will lay side-by-side, and will be interred that way."

After removal of the deceased from the dwelling, James and a companion had descended into the cellar to turn off the gas. As they climbed the stairs to the first floor because of the fumes in the basement, the friend collapsed. James picked him up and dragged him to the door. As he stepped outside, he fell, the men reviving once out of the house.

The coroner interviewed James, and quoted him as saying that, upon returning from work on the Saturday before the gas accident, his brother-in-law, Clarence, had told him the Griffiths had a new gas meter. The paper reported, "Residents in the neighborhood said that on Thursday of last week employees of the gas company tested all the pipes in the houses in Beech Street. On that day the meter in the Griffith House was changed, the one there having become jammed for some reason."[10]

William C. Wein was one of the oldest 1915 victims. While one newspaper funeral announcement gave his age as forty, he was fifty-seven. He lies with his wife, Louisa M. Kielkopf, in St. Paul's Cemetery in Odessa, Delaware. On December 4th, they shipped his remains on the same train that carried those of Harvey Place, one of the youngest casualties, to his ultimate resting place in Denton, Maryland. Place was the first child of eight born to Hattie Beer Place and John Place, who headed a Mennonite family. Harvey died three days short of his sixteenth birthday.

Philadelphian Catherine Simpson had "demanded" that her son, twenty-three-year-old Wesley, quit his dangerous job in the powder mills. Like Elijah Springfield, she was "haunted by a foreboding disaster." She grew especially adamant since Elizabeth McHenry, another resident of the City of Brotherly Love, and Wesley were to marry Christmas week.[11] Simpson's remains were identified by a gold band around a tooth, and were first thought to be those of Elijah Springfield.[12]

A Wilmington police sergeant, presumably a friend, identified Benjamin Barber.[13] The recovery of a tattooed arm aided the officer, the inking a picture of a sailor girl. Barber had moved with his wife, Ida May Queair, to Wilmington from Philadelphia. Before their move south, the Barbers lost two sons, one in 1911, a two-months-premature baby only two days old, the other stillborn in 1912. They buried both babies in Arlington Cemetery in Philadelphia. The next year, daughter Ida was born.

A grandmother identified seventeen-year-old William Leslie Timms, although he sustained mutilations in the explosion. She ID'd him by looking at his face, which had burns but none so serious as to make him unrecognizable. His parents and siblings may not have wanted to try the recognition, not knowing what they might find. They interred him at Mt. Salem Church Cemetery, the resting place of several other powdermen: Sam Stewart, James Walker, John Keys, William R. Green, Edward Hurst, William McCrea, Patrick Haley, and Jonas W. Miller.

We do not know what mark the relatives of Brian O'Conner saw to identify his remains but recognize it they did and thus they mourned him in a private funeral[14] and buried him at Cathedral Cemetery in downtown Wilmington. He died at twenty-four.

Another powderman, like Henry Cazier and Alan Thaxter, came from a socially prominent family. Clarence Pleasonton, the son of William and Sallie Pleasonton, appeared regularly in the society columns of the local papers, especially when he visited his parents at Fleming's Landing in the Thoroughfare Neck section of southern New Castle County, east of Smyrna. Not only his visits but also his returns to Wilmington featured prominently in those pages. He married Bessie Bennett who, after his death, became a stenographer with the DuPont Company.[15]

Unlike most of the men who perished that day, Pleasonton, a fireman at the works, was among a group of four *outside* the press mill. Others transported him to the hospital, but he died the following morning, never having regained consciousness. His family buried him at the Odd Fellows Cemetery in Smyrna.

Also standing outside the mill was Patrick Hanrahan, a carpenter. An Irish immigrant, Hanrahan was two weeks short of his forty-seventh birthday. They interred him at Riverview Cemetery under a tombstone with the name Benjamin Reed at the top; Benjamin died in 1870 at twenty-two. After Patrick is the name "Mary Ellen Reed, daughter of Benjamin and Sarah Reed, Born May 28, 1869. Died December 3, 1872."[16] I could not determine the relationship among the three persons named on the headstone, although it is possible the widow Sarah Reed had married Hanrahan.

Fifty-four-year-old Elmer E. Mace was driving the powder cart on the narrow-gauge rails at the time of the November explosion. Some attributed the blast to powder on the steel tracks, ignited by either the horse's hooves or the wheels of the wagon. In an oral interview in 1966, William Lynch remembers reporting he had seen boys putting powder on the track, ostensibly to see what would happen when the cart drove over it.[17]

Elma Andrews, Elmer Mace's granddaughter, says the family often talked of rumors that Elmer caused the disaster but could not corroborate the story. And if someone put black powder on the track, we cannot blame him.[18]

Elmer Mace must have been a popular man in his Wilmington neighborhood as he signed at least four statements approving the granting of liquor licenses in the city from 1894 through 1909. In those days, "respectable citizens" of the district of the applicant, six of whom had to be "substantial freeholders," needed to approve such applications.[19]

In September 1898, Mace served on a jury for a case involving the assault on a twelve-year-old girl working at a fruit stand. The defendants were three Italian men who owned the stand at Front and King streets. The neighborhood became a popular spot for the Italian community to set up businesses; in a decade's time, another powderman, Carlo Sicco, would have a fruit stand not far away. The jury acquitted the trio.

Elmer E. Mace, the driver of a wagon near the pack house explosion in 1915. (Delaware Historical Society)

Mace and his wife, Sarah B. Smith, often referred to as Sallie, married in Chester, Pennsylvania, in 1886, and their ever-growing family lived on Long Row near the DuPont grounds. The 1900 U.S. Census shows five girls and George Mace, brother to Elmer. It does not show twins William McKinley Mace and Halert Mace, born four years before the census. In a conversation with the author, Elma Andrews did not recall hearing of twins in the family, but the birth record shows a twin birth to the Maces.[20] I could find no record of the deaths of the twins, so it remains a mystery what happened to them. The census shows that five children were born to Sarah and five living (all female living at home), which muddles the picture further, as the twins' birth certificate says they were children numbers five and six.

In the early 20th century, birth was still no guarantee of someone living past their first year. The Maces also experienced the loss of Robert, a three-month-old baby in 1901; they mourned a premature death like so many powder families had before them.

Elma Andrews' mother, Elma Mace, daughter of Elmer and Sarah Mace, called her ancestors "Little People from the Mountains." She also called them the "Black Stocking Gang," as they made up part of a religious sect in which the women wore black stockings. Elma Andrews at first thought the moniker applied to dance hall girls and experienced disappointment when her mother told her she would meet the Black Stocking Gang; the women who appeared did not wear the baubles and spangles dance hall girls wore.[21]

The fourth man outside the press house was William H. Oliver; his name is not on the death lists because, although seriously hurt, he survived his injuries. *Every Evening* reported the day after the explosion that the machinist "may expire at any moment," adding that, "He was operated upon for a fracture of the skull, yesterday afternoon, and no hope is held out for his recovery. He is burned all over the body, and is badly cut, while the left arm and second finger of the left hand are broken. A bone of the left forearm was so badly broken that it had to be wired together. The right upper jaw is also fractured."[22] But the next day's paper wrote about "wonderful improvement" in his condition.

Still others died instantly. Bartholomew Kelleher, or "Battie" as they called him and his grandfather Bartholomew, started working with the du Ponts at fourteen; in his first year he earned a boy's wage of $10 a month. He then progressed over the next two years to $13. He left the company; the 1910 U.S. Census listed him as a paper maker.[23] He later returned to the company, but we don't know when. Kelleher was a forty-year-old single man who lived with his family of parents and siblings. His paternal grandmother, and perhaps his grandfather, was a native of Balleybourney, County Cork, Ireland.

Nelson Hogate, in his early fifties, was another older man who died. In 1880, fifteen-year-old laborer Hogate had worked on the acreage of farmer Joseph Sapp in Pencader Hundred, close to where Henry Cazier lived.[24] He married Sallie Rodenhiser (her real name was Sarah) in 1893.[25] The 1910 census shows Nelson and Sallie, at ages forty-six and forty-eight, respectively, with one child marked in the column labeled "Number Born" but the "Now Living" column was blank. Either the child did not live with its parents or had died.

Sallie may have been one who fudged when the census enumerator came to their doorstep in 1910; her marriage certificate shows she was thirteen years older than painter Nelson when they married. The 1870 census shows a Sarah Rodenhiser as a domestic in a household in the town of New Castle, Delaware. If this is the same person, she would have been forty-two years old when she married Nelson. It may have been easier on her mind to cheat when talking with the census enumerator from the far-distant Federal government than with the nearer county authorities filling out paperwork when she married.[26]

Fifty-six-year-old Louis M. Booker grew up in Maryland in an extensive family; his parents had thirteen children in fifteen years, so it would seem natural that he would do the same. He and his bride, Wilhemina Seward, who went by Mina, did not match his parents in child production but did have nine children.

Booker was neither a DuPont employee nor a powderman, but a carpenter subcontracted by J.M. Phillips to work on a mill building a few buildings away from the press house where the November 1915 explosion occurred. He and another carpenter were working in the roll mill when the detonation happened. Stone and timber debris covered the two men; it hardly scratched the other man but killed Booker. He broke an arm and every rib but two. He fractured his jaw, and the debris crushed his face.[27]

Another of the very young men who died in the explosion was Elmer Cumpston, just three weeks past his sixteenth birthday. His family suffered through a powder detonation tragedy a few months earlier when his uncle, Lawrence Cunningham, died in August. Elmer, at a young age, became active in the community, being a charter member of Troop 1 of the Boy Scouts who met at the Hagley Community House, now a post office and art gallery. Cumpston was the troop's bugler; they buried his bugle and scout hat with him at Silverbrook Cemetery, where also lie the remains of the ten unidentified victims. One pallbearer was fellow scout Joseph Mace, who had buried his father two days earlier.[28]

Throughout the history of the DuPont mills, the sons of men killed in explosions got jobs with the company when they became of age. With James Baird, his daughter, Rebecca, received that treatment after her father died. Rebecca's death certificate says she was a "powder worker." She was nineteen when she died of pneumonia in 1918. James and his wife, Elizabeth Short Baird, had several other children, including twins, Emily and Elsie, in 1902.

This was apparently not the first industrial accident that injured "Jamesy"

Baird. When he was thirteen or fourteen years old, he caught his arms in a yarn machine at Bancroft's Mills, a textile plant down river from the powder mills.[29]

A third man named Elmer died in the 1915 explosion. Twenty-year-old Elmer Fox, son of John and Margaret Scott Fox of 1903 Lincoln Street, lived two doors away from a house owned by Dan Dougherty, the blind worker injured in 1882. When he was sixteen, a census showed that Elmer's occupation was "rubber work" and he had been unemployed for half the previous year.[30] In an earlier census, Elmer's sister, fourteen-year-old Eliza when Elmer was five, was shown to have worked as a cigar maker.

His full name was Elmer Spruance Fox, his middle name probably in honor of the doctor who delivered him, Dr. Harry R. Spruance. They buried Fox and Benjamin Barber together, reason unknown.

Henry (Harry) Haber ("popular in Jewish circles" in Wilmington) is buried in the Lombardy Cemetery, north of the city. (Delaware Historical Society)

Prior to becoming a DuPont employee, Harry Haber worked for six years for his uncle, Louis Reches, in the latter's bakery on West Second Street, where Harry lived. Said to be "popular in Jewish circles" in the city, he left his uncle's firm, where he was a very efficient wagon driver,[31] eight days before his death. He is buried in Lombardy Cemetery north of the city.

Edward King, another of the teenagers who died, was the eighth child born to German Frederick King and his Irish wife, Catherine Flynn King, known as Katie. They buried their son at Wilmington's Cathedral Cemetery.

Also interred at Cathedral is a worker who anglicized his name from the Italian, Frederano Cafre, or possibly Ciafre (the name on his death certificate). The seventeen-year-old changed his name to Fred Jeffry in the DuPont records.

The remains of twenty-four-year-old Bryan O'Conner were the last to be identified. Although the remains were in such a state that identification seemed impossible, relatives must have found a blemish, tattoo, or other mark that they recognized. He was single, and is another victim buried at Cathedral Cemetery in Wilmington.

While James Givinney is listed in some of the rosters of men killed in the November 1915 pack house explosion, I could find no information about this man.

At the time of the 1915 explosion, the public's fear of death or injury seemed outweighed by the lure of a steady job. The *Philadelphia Inquirer* told its readers, "One of the most unbelievable features of the whole tragedy was before the searchers had begun to recover the remains of the victims, a row of fifteen men stood at the gate where applicants for employment are received," and added, "Where death still stalked they were willing to enter and risk their lives."[32]

Although potential workers lined up for the jobs opened by the explosion, survivors remained painfully aware of their losses. In an oral interview many years later, Ethel Jones Hayword put it this way: "Intermingled with the joys of our childhood, I must record some of the shadows that would come over our lovely valley when an explosion in the mills occurred. I remember when we were in school when an explosion occurred, the whole school was dismissed. I remember we all walked solemnly home, each wondering if his own dear father may have been killed. Sadly enough, we soon learned that one of our friends was without a father. A gloom soon settled over the valley when this happened, and sorrow deep and painful seemed to be felt by every family."[33]

While the community conducted funerals for men lost in the November 30, 1915, explosion, the *Oscar II* pulled away from its berth in Hoboken, New Jersey, later the embarkation site for America's doughboys heading to the European war. Called the "Peace Ark" and the "Ship of Fools" by the press, the vessel carried 150 "rainbow chasers" (another media epithet) on the way to neutral nations on the Continent. Pacifist Henry Ford and social reformer Jane Addams, trying to end the war, led the group. For a variety of reasons, the effort failed.

A few days later, DuPont Company detectives, led by Major Richard Sylvester, past head of the Washington, D.C., police department, arrested a former worker at DuPont's Carneys Point factory. The official charge was theft because they found dynamite and gunpowder in Jacob Swoboda's Penns Grove apartment, items they believed he took from the factory.

DuPont detectives had been monitoring Swoboda, known variously as Louis Hareley, Lewis Fallter, and Louis Halbert, because he quit when the company announced added security requirements. When Sylvester received information that made him suspicious of the man, the major ordered a dozen gumshoes to tail the shady character. They reported that Swoboda approached the Wilmington newspapers, saying he could get them into the local DuPont plants to expose working conditions, which he called "a great menace to the men who worked there."

In court, Swoboda admitted he had been in prison, including a four-year stint in Sing Sing and another six years at the Eastern Penitentiary in Philadelphia for receiving stolen goods. He said he was a veteran of the Spanish Civil War, and this service, according to one source, was enough to set him free. That, and no direct evidence linked him to any explosions at DuPont plants.[34]

In the next two years before U.S. entry into the European war, the roll of Italians who died in gunpowder detonations grew by three.

The first killed was John Salvagno, who Americanized his Italian name, Giovanni R. Salvagno. The thirty-year-old, born in Italy, married Catherine Catalina in May 1916. Seven weeks later, she laid her husband to rest when he died in what the papers called a grinding mill; it was a graining mill. They found his uninjured body one hundred yards from the building, indicating he must have succumbed to the shock of the explosion. The conjecture is that he had started the mill and was walking away when it blew.

Later in July 1916, war jitters increased when actual German sabotage occurred at a New Jersey munitions depot on Black Tom Island off Jersey City. In a series of blasts felt as far away as Maryland, over two million pounds of explosives lit up the New York harbor sky. As in the past, the first reports cited authorities who blamed the detonations on carelessness.

With the war continuing to rage in Europe, scares in the Carneys Point, New Jersey, and Brandywine powder plants concerned sightings of airships. In 1916, the DuPont Company made statements to the papers that cast strong doubts on the reports, one report attributing the lights seen overhead to stars. But, they said, the company planned to keep "watchful[ly] waiting in case of its return."[35] Earlier in 1916, the newspapers carried several reports that citizens had seen or heard airplanes in the skies over the DuPont plants. Federal officials queried two private plane owners whether a nefarious person could use their planes to damage the factories. The amateur flyers assured authorities they had removed integral engine parts for the winter.

The thought that German agents were sabotaging American factories continued to simmer, even in faraway Australia. The *Sydney Morning*

Herald said, "The police are investigating reports that German plotters were responsible for the explosions at the Dupont Powder Company's works."[36] It referred to the January 5, 1917, explosion that took the life of Carlo Sicco.

Sicco was born in 1859 in Rocchetta Cairo Montenotte, a small town in the province of Savona in the far northwest of Italy's Liguria region. His parents were a road maintenance supervisor (capo di cantonieri, or municipal supervisor), Giuseppe Lorenzo Sicco, and tobacco store clerk Giacinta Sovera. Giuseppe froze to death while making his rounds to check on road conditions during a late winter blizzard when Carlo was eight years old. Carlo was away performing three years of military duty at age nineteen when his mother died.[37]

Carlo was the ninth of ten children; the family lost their first child, Maria Caterina, in her first year. Their next female child, also named Maria, had the middle name Teresa. The third, Andrea Luigi, died at three and the next four lived into adulthood before the eighth child died in infancy. Carlo was born next and had one younger sister.

His older sister, Maria Magdalena, married Bartolomeo Satragno, and it was this couple who provided the link for Carlo in America. His brother-in-law found employment with the du Ponts at Hagley, and emigrated, soon making $36 a month in the mid-1870s.

Enthralled by the stories his kin told him of their lives on the Brandywine, Carlo left via the port of Le Havre, France, in April 1883, at age twenty-four, and arrived in New York on May 9 aboard the *S.S. Canada*. He took the train from New York to northern Delaware and found his way to the home of a friend from the old country, Samuel Ferraro. Lodging was unavailable at the Ferraros', so they directed him to the Walker's Banks home of Giacomo and Giovanna Persoglio. He settled in there and started working for the DuPont Company where, by his third year, he earned $40 a month.[38]

Carlo's story continued, as told by a

Carlo Sicco, left, and friend, Joseph Persoglio. (Courtesy Janine Pizano)

granddaughter, Hilda Leto Smith, who published a book about her mother, Jennie Sicco Leto, Carlo's daughter. One day, Carlo noticed a picture of a pretty young woman on the mantel in the Persoglio home. He asked who it was and, when told it was their daughter, Maria, then still living in Italy, he urged them to convince her to emigrate to America. She did and, after five months of getting to know each other, Carlo and Maria Antoinetta Persoglio married at St. Joseph on the Brandywine in October 1887. A year and a half later, Maria gave birth to their first child, Giacinta Giovanna, named for her paternal and maternal grandmothers, respectively. They called her Jennie.

Maria became restless living near the Brandywine, which often flooded and must have lapped at her back door on occasion. She was fearful of the explosions at the Hagley mills. "The Big One" in October 1890 the year before must have been particularly worrisome; after it she, Carlo, and Jennie left America in the spring of 1891. The eastbound voyage must have been a trial for Maria, as she was pregnant with a second daughter, Angelina. The baby, born in Italy in late July, died a month later. In the spring of 1892 another daughter, Adelina, was born.

In June 1893, a third daughter was born in Rochetta and bore the name Santina Maria, who became known as Sadie. A year later a third (living) sister joined the two girls when Teresa Margherita was delivered; unlike her sisters, Teresa remained in Italy her entire life. Another daughter, Palmira Isabella, or Helen, was born in 1896, but her mother died of pneumonia a week after the birth. A wet nurse raised Helen, who stayed with the nurse's family for two or three years. The family wanted to adopt her, but Carlo said no.

It must have been an arduous time for Carlo, raising four girls under the age of ten by himself. He had help from an elderly aunt who wanted him to find a wife for himself and a mother for the Sicco girls as they became adolescents. He found a wife in thirty-five-year-old Carolina Toso who married him in early 1898. Four years later, he needed, and received, proof of a clean criminal record before he could travel back to America. Nineteen years after his first westbound voyage on the *Canada*, Carlo boarded the *S.S. Lahn*, a Scottish-made ship by now flying the German flag.[39] Rather than traversing the continent to France, he traveled to Naples or Genoa to board the *Lahn*. His wife remained in Italy.

Daughter Sadie emigrated in 1903; her sister, Helen, followed in 1910.

Three months after Sadie left for America, Carlo's wife, Carolina, died in Italy. The two sisters who remained there, Teresa and Adelina, lived with an aunt in Casseine, thirty miles northeast of Rochetta Cairo.

In 1902, Carlo's father-in-law Giacomo Persoglio scheduled his retirement from the powder mills; family lore says Carlo took over the position.[40] In 1907, the Siccos vacated their Squirrel Run home and settled elsewhere in the Wilmington area. It is not known if they left on their own accord after labor unrest in the yards or if Frank Connable, manager of powder production, forced them to leave. Connable strove to "purge the Brandywine of the undesirable element," meaning workers who had made noises about unionizing.

Jennie married in late 1908 and two years later, traveled with her husband to Italy, where she gave birth to Carlo's first grandchild and her first child of twelve. On their return voyage on the *S.S. La Lorraine*, Sadie, traveling west for the second time, accompanied her sister's family.

In the summer of 1908, Carlo, now known as Charles, opened his first fruit stand but ran into trouble with the law. The *Evening Journal* reported, "That the curbs along the market district in King Street will be cleaned up and that as soon as possible was the substance of the declaration made by Judge Cochran in city court this morning and he told Chief of Police Black to bring in everyone who violated the city market ordinance regarding the keeping of fruit stands in the street. There were three men and a woman in City Court this morning, each charged with such violation."[41]

Two of the four were Siccos. Charles was the first arraigned and received a $5 fine; after fining her father, the judge dismissed the case against Jennie. The law forbade establishing such concerns on the curb without occupying the adjacent building. Charles then established a legitimate fruit stand at 307 King Street, in a building

Carlo Sicco, standing, right; Sadie Sicco, seated, center; standing behind Sadie is Jennie Sicco. Carlo left his job at the powder yards to open his store on King Street in Wilmington, but went back to working in the mills. (Courtesy Janine Pizano)

next to where they arrested him for having the illegal stand. He employed his daughters, Jennie and Sadie.

In 1911, Charles sold the business to Paul Penno, who continued to employ the Sicco women. By 1912, fifteen-year-old Helen had joined the group in running the shop. She was an unhappy young woman, and her unhappiness manifested itself in an attempted suicide by a handgun she found in the shop basement. She told her boss, Penno, that she was "tired of living." They rushed her to the hospital and, two weeks after her attempt, the paper said her condition was unchanged, though it did not mention what that condition was. She survived.[42] In 1916, Helen married Charles Boccino; her sister Sadie served as one of her bridesmaids. Helen's tragic life ended two years later when the Spanish Flu swept her up in its long tentacles.

Meanwhile, on the Brandywine, Charles continued to make gunpowder. He quit the job at least four times,[43] always returning when the du Ponts asked him back. He was in the corning, or graining, mill on that early January day when it, and another building, plus a railcar filled with powder, exploded. Workers found Sicco's body with one arm and part of one foot missing. Someone later located the arm. Charles was laid to rest in Cathedral Cemetery.

Albert A. Vannatta was the third Italian to expire in as many explosions in eight months. Like Charles Sicco nine weeks before and John Salvagno the year before, Vannatta was operating a corning mill when it blew on March 14, 1917. His mill contained one to two tons of Lesmoke powder, DuPont's brand name for its semi-smokeless powder, the same powder that had blown up and killed Sicco in January.

We know little of Vannatta; the DuPont Company destroyed many personnel records that might have shown light on his life. He was thirty-four years old and believed to be married.

The newspapers printed more column inches on the March destruction of the corning mill and surrounding houses than on the victim. They carried stories about the blast's odd effects. For example, "Christ Church, which is located only a short distance up the hill from the corning house, was apparently not injured in the least, and yet the saloon of Patrick Dougherty, probably a quarter of a mile away, in Henry Clay village, had the front nearly torn out," wrote a reporter.[44]

In the month following Vannatta's death, another explosion rocked the area, but this time it was not a powder mill. Seventeen miles northeast of Hagley, and four days after America's declaration of war against the Central Powers,[45] a massive detonation killed over 130 people at the Eddystone Ammunition plant in Pennsylvania.

The president of the corporation that owned the plant, Samuel M. Vauclain, said, "[We] are unable to account for it in any way other than the act of some maliciously inclined person or persons."[46] His claims received support when officials arrested several people in Chester, Pennsylvania; Philadelphia; and New York, where, the papers said, the police had obtained a confession. One of those apprehended was a German sailor from the ship *Prinz Eitel Frederich*. It had been interned at the Philadelphia Navy Yard and, after the United States declared war on Germany, transformed into the American troop ship *DeKalb*.[47] Investigators later determined the Eddystone disaster was an accident.

Another explosion of note occurred in December that year, but it was neither due to combat nor the accidental detonation of black powder. In the waters off Halifax, Nova Scotia, two ships collided in the Narrows, creating the largest man-made explosion in modern history until World War II.

This time the devil's potpourri included sixty-two tons of guncotton, with six times the gas-generating ability of an equal volume of black powder; a quarter million tons of TNT; 5,000,000 pounds of picric acid; and 246 tons of benzol,[48] the latest "super gasoline." Before the addition of the benzol in barrels stuffed into open spaces on the deck, the ship's cargo had the explosive power equal to one-fifth the power of "Little Boy," famously unleashed over Hiroshima.

When the *Mont-Blanc*, carrying the volatile cargo, collided with the *Imo*, the explosion, estimated to have the explosive power of 5,000,000 pounds of black powder, killed 2,000, injured another 9,000, and left over 25,000 homeless. People 250 miles away in Cape Breton felt the blast. It was so intense that observers who lived to tell the tale reported seeing the bottom of the Narrows.

Earlier in 1917, Wilmington had served as the end of a sea chase of the *Imo* by the Schmall Engineering Company of Philadelphia. The *Imo's* captain refused to pay the German-American firm's $9,000 bill for boiler repairs. Delaware officials made the captain pay for the repair and penalties, which doubled the cost. His attorney, when asked why Captain Haakon Fröm took the *Imo* on the chase, could only say he was intensely anti-German.[49]

The names Charles William Kimberley, Allan Pollitt, and William Pollitt do not appear in any formal DuPont Company listings of men killed in powder explosions. We only find mentions of these three names in the Dick Scott files at Hagley and the local newspapers. On August 21, 1918, three months before the Armistice, the trio was working in the pack house when it blew. They died in the late afternoon explosion when two tons of powder ignited.[50]

Kimberley, a fifty-year-old Englishman, lived in Free Park on the DuPont property. The son of a railroad porter in Warwick County, England, Charles had been a foreman in a stout and ale brewery there. His brother, Ernest, managed his estate and adopted his daughter, Emma, after Charles died.

William E. Politt grew up in Maryland's St. Anne's County but lived in Wilmington at the time of the accident. His cousin, twenty-two-year-old Allan Upshure Pollitt, lived with William and his family on West 3rd Street. Both men started working in the powder mills the day they died. Allan's closest blood relative was Carrie (Caroline) Pollitt, his mother, who also lived at the Third Street address. His draft card shows he was tall and slender with light brown hair and light blue eyes.[51] Seventeen-year-old Allen Pollitt and Anna B. Sannabend had wed February 7, 1913.

William, nineteen at the time of death, lies with his mother and several other family members at Riverview Cemetery in Wilmington, with a tall obelisk marking the grave. They also buried Allan at Riverview, but no marker is in place.

By the time of the next fatal accident, the Great War[52] had ended, the troops had returned home, and production at the mills had slowed. ∎

· 15 ·
The (Not So) Old Woman Who Lived in a Shoe

> She had so many children, she didn't know what to do.
> She gave them some broth without any bread
> She kissed them all fondly and sent them to bed.
> —*Mother Goose*

On December 1, 1919, another powderman died when a pair of roll mills exploded. Thirty-eight-year-old Edward C. Snyder, whose name is on few lists of explosions at the Hagley Library, was a single man from Wilkes-Barre, Pennsylvania, who was toiling in the roll mills that day.

At first, the residents thought several mills had gone up in the explosion, which caused minor damage and lots of noise. Snyder, who boarded at the home of Mrs. William Andrews on Breck's Lane, was laid to rest in Mountain Top, Pennsylvania, where his mother buried him.[1]

On January 2, 1920, the *Evening Journal* reported, "The heaviest volume of local calls ever handled in the Wilmington central office of the Diamond State[2] Telephone Company occurred between 9 A.M. and approximately 10.30 A.M. today…. It appeared from the central office as if every subscriber in Wilmington took off his receiver at the same time…it was the almost simultaneous effort on the part of nearly every telephone user in Wilmington to reach another telephone or person. The result was an overload of not only the operators, but the machinery as well."[3] The paper referred to an explosion at the yards that killed five men when the press house, the graining mill and three roll mills exploded.

One newspaper reported that 60,000 pounds of powder had blown; the paper had added an extra zero to the total. Three tons was enough to cause the usual consternation: "Those who had a clear view of the sky to the northwest saw a colossal pillar of smoke mounting high into the sky. Its upper end, at a height of nearly six thousand feet, slowly drifted away into the north."[4] The paper said temperatures that morning had dropped twenty-six degrees in the past twenty-four hours.[5]

Reports came in from as far away as West Philadelphia of tremors in the earth. Because temperatures were low and the ground frozen, the people there felt the shock more keenly than earlier explosions, as the hard earth transmitted the waves farther.

The press house was first to go. The explosion communicated to the corning mill, where one newspaper, not knowing or caring to know much about powder making, erroneously said the "product is formed into corn-like grains."[6] This second blast jarred the three roll mills, or what the papers called "wheelhouses."

On the morning of the fatal explosions, a Wilmington saloonkeeper's wife told her husband she had seen Thomas Anselmi dead in a dream. Anselmi was a regular visitor to the establishment, owned by John and Theresa Solio, at the corner of 5th and Tatnall streets. The former leather worker lived downtown close to the Solios' saloon. He had worked for DuPont only six weeks before his death.[7] Anselmi had been thirty-eight years old when the U.S. government required men to sign up for the military draft; he did his civic duty in 1918 and filled out a card two months before the end of the war. His draft card described him as being of medium height and build, with red hair and gray eyes. It listed his occupation as "bolter" at Pusey & Jones, a Wilmington shipbuilding company.[8]

Anselmi hailed from Alessandria, Italy, at the apex of a triangle with sides drawn between itself, Genoa, and Rochetta Cairo, where powdermen Carlo Sicco lived before emigrating to Delaware. Thomas married Rose Gaino after arriving in Wilmington.

We know little of thirty-one-year-old victim Antonio Grangiulio except that he apparently left a wife and two children, and was a "wheelman" (roll mill worker), living in the city of Wilmington.

The third Italian who died in the accident was Giovanni Martini, a forty-one-year-old who had signed his draft card on September 12, 1918. His description repeated Thomas Anselmi's in terms of build and height, but Martini had black hair and brown eyes. He lived with his wife, Cecilia, in Wilmington and came from Cuneo in the far west of Italy, near the French border.

Martini was a "non-declarant" on his card, meaning he was ineligible for the U.S. military draft because he had not declared an intention to become a citizen of the United States. Thomas Anselmi had

The (Not So) Old Woman Who Lived in a Shoe

also checked off this part of his draft card.[9]

The fourth man who died that January day was Noah Columbus Pinder, or "Lum" as friends and family knew him. His family included children born to two wives. Lum lived on a farm near Sudlersville, Maryland, with his first wife, Mary Rebecca Skinner Pinder, who bore two children, James H. and Elsie Elizabeth, six years apart. James died at age eleven, in 1906, of unknown causes. Mary died five years later.

Lum then married Susie Irene Smith, and they had two daughters, Margaret and Marjorie Marie. Susie filed for divorce in 1916, when Lum was forty-two and she was twenty-three.[10] After the explosion, Lum was buried with his first wife and son in Sudlersville, Maryland, the same place as powderman Louis Booker, who died in a 1915 explosion.[11]

"There was an old woman who lived in a shoe" goes the nursery rhyme. The shoe motif was front-page news in the *Philadelphia Times* of September 24, 1899, when it featured the family of Civil War veteran Samuel P. Swartwood and his fecund spouse, Mary P. Carey Swartwood of Wilkes-Barre, Pennsylvania. The article marveled at the fact that Mary was only forty-seven years old, having had her last child the week before; it included a drawing of the "remarkably well preserved" woman. And inside a drawing of a large shoe were twenty-five circles, each with a picture of a Swartwood child. Toward the toe of the boot is a portrait of Calvin, Mrs. Swartwood's seventeenth child, born in 1891. Calvin was one of the five men who died in the Hagley explosion of the press, corning, and roll mills on the second day of 1920.

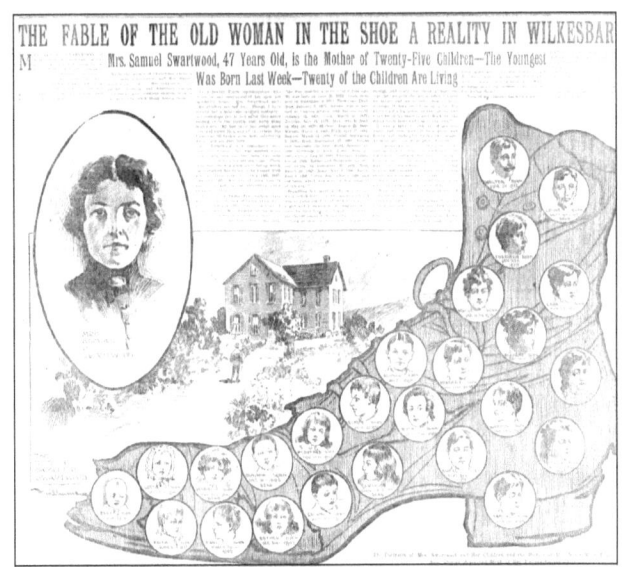

The "remarkably well preserved" Mary Swartwood and her twenty-five children. Calvin, killed in the du Pont powder mills' penultimate explosion, is pictured at the ball of the foot. (www.newspapers.com)

The *Times* piece liberally quoted Mrs.

Swartwood on the joys of marriage, of child-rearing, and of having a large household to manage. When asked what she thought of married life, she effused: "Well, I ought to know. I guess. Who was it said married life was one long, sweet dream? Grover Cleveland, wasn't it? Well, I agree with him. It has been to me. Every woman should get married, I think. I don't know much about the new woman, but if she don't believe in married life. I don't want to know anything about her. What's as happy as having children to love you and you loving them." She continued, "None of my children has been a source of grief, trouble or anxiety to me, and I think God has been especially kind to give me so many. Yes sir, you can put me down as believing in the married woman who believes in having children."[12]

The tall, brown-haired twenty-six-year-old Calvin must have agreed with his mother about marriage and children. He wed Rhoda M. Jones in August 1917, shortly after registering during the first of the three enrollment periods for the draft.

Calvin worked in the corning mill and, after the press mill blew that day, he did not have enough time to leave his post before it, too, exploded. His daughter, Mary, was two months old.[13]

On a spring day in 1920, Aubrey Carson Turner wanted to finish his job in the pack house by noon, so his friend James A. Hodge came to help. The blast that killed them was the final black powder explosion in the Hagley yards before the facility closed in 1921.

Although the newspapers reported both men were veterans, I could find no evidence that Aubrey Turner served in the military. He had signed his draft card three months before Armistice Day, so it is unlikely that this twenty-year-old son of the late George, and Annabelle Downing, Turner, their eighth child, had time to enlist or get drafted.[14] Four brothers served, one, Ralph, dying in the flu epidemic of 1918 two weeks after signing up for the Navy. He died while in training at the Great Lakes Naval facility in Chicago.[15]

Aubrey joined two fraternal organizations, the Mattahoon Tribe of the Red Men and the Diligent Council of the Junior Order of United American Mechanics, another xenophobic anti-Catholic organization, founded in Philadelphia. When he completed his draft registration card, the tall, slender man was a "chauffeur" for M. McGary & Son, a furniture store at 6th and Tatnall streets in Wilmington.

A simple military headstone stands askew in the cemetery of Green Hill Methodist Church, off Route 52, Pennsylvania Avenue, in the far west of Wilmington. It reads: "James A. Hodge, Delaware, Pvt. 1st Sn. Tn, 1 Div, May 4, 1921," the date erroneously registered in the paperwork submitted to the military for a tombstone to be sent to Mrs. Ruth Manning, 122 W. 29th Street, Wilmington. The records show the military shipped the stone January 14, 1932— twelve, not eleven, years after his death in 1920. The name of the deceased soldier on the application was "Hodge, James Andrew," so perhaps Mrs. Manning knew something the newspapers did not know, as one, in an article seeking parental information after his death, captioned his picture with that middle name.

One newspaper reported that Hodge had been working at the DuPont mills when he enlisted in the U.S. Army, a fact I could not verify. Hodge was on the *U.S.S. Huron* when it left the port of Hoboken December 5, 1917, bound for St. Nazaire, France and service with the 1st Division's 1st Sanitary Train. The 1st Division was, and remains, one of the more storied units in U.S. military history and has kept "The Big Red One" moniker to this day. Four field hospitals and four ambulance companies made up a Great War sanitary train.

Between January 15 and the first week of April 1918, Hodge was with his unit, Field Hospital No. 3, in the Asaunville region of France, training in hygiene, sanitation, nursing, ward and mess management, treatment of gassing, pathology and care of wounds, wound infection, trench foot, and first aid.

Once on hospital duty, Hodge and the rest of the enlisted medical staff bathed, clothed, and fed the wounded, changed bandages and soiled linen, emptied bedpans, administered medicines, and took vital signs. Many of the facilities were in tents with dirt or, if available, canvas flooring. If there were no ambulatory patients to help keep the wards clean, it was up to the enlisted medical staff to do so. In the middle of war, weather discomfort, and lice infestations, the field hospital men worked to avoid becoming sick themselves, particularly when the Spanish Flu[16] and a mumps contagion hit in the spring of 1918.

When the war ended on November 11, 1918, the Big Red One had progressed farther east than any other unit in the army. The unit, with its attached sanitary trains, became a part of the 3rd Army occupying Germany until late 1919. Field Hospital No. 3 lost only one man, a cook by the name of Leonard Potter, during America's brief war, and he died of disease, not combat. Doughboys of the unit would have said Potter had "gone West," a phrase comparable to the Brandywine powdermen saying their comrades had gone "across the creek."

The 1st Sanitary Train received a unit citation highlighting its work in the Cantigny sector of the battlefield, lauding the men of the unit who "performed arduous and difficult duties under conditions of great danger and hardship and gave proof of high courage, professional skill and zealous devotion to duty."[17]

James A. Hodge, killed in the last explosion at the du Pont mills. (Delaware Historical Society)

The end of war did not mean the job was over for the train or for now-Private First Class James A. Hodge. In the middle of a European winter, the unit slogged its way into Germany to give medical services to the 3rd Army, the occupation force ordered to keep the peace and make sure the Germans did not regroup into a fighting army.

Once settled in the Coblenz Bridgehead, a western Germany area designated for the troops to remain in, the army's top docs figured that at least ninety percent of the doughboys had "some degree of lice[18] infestation lingering from their last period in combat or from the long march to Germany." The medical staffs worked on a massive campaign to rid the men of vermin. Only one truck-mounted, purpose-built, army-issued steam sterilizer was available, so medics built steam-powered delousing machines. By the end of May 1919, the infestation was at less than one percent.[19]

PFC Hodge took part in the solution of another serious medical issue plaguing his brothers-in-arms. Only one-tenth of the American doughboys billeted in centralized barracks, while the remaining ninety percent lived in private homes throughout the occupation area. Sanitary facilities in many of the small farms where the soldiers lived were often inadequate and open manure pits or fields were close to the homes.

Army medics worked to rectify the situation by explaining to the German farmers the need to move the waste pits farther away from the house. With the help of army engineers the medical men improved the construction of field kitchens, screened food preparation areas from latrines, and fly-proofed latrines.[20]

On August 26, 1919, Hodge, now assigned to Headquarters Section of the field hospital of the American Forces in Germany and wearing three overseas service gold stripes on his uniform's left sleeve, boarded the *U.S.S. DeKalb* to begin his journey home. Like the ship he took to France at the start of his war service, the ship returning him home was a former German-flagged liner interned in the United States.[21]

Hodge returned to Wilmington and worked in the powder works. Nine months after experiencing war and its myriad horrors with a battleground hospital and suffering through two European winters, James A. Hodge was "blown to atoms" in a split-second black powder explosion on May 4, 1920.

After his death, the DuPont Company tried to find his next of kin. He had told friends in Wilmington, in letters he had written during his overseas service, that he came from Richmond, Virginia, and his father, James W. Hodge, was a lawyer for the Southern Railroad Company. *Every Evening* reported that he told his correspondents he was born August 5, 1898, and he had an Aunt Julia A. Hodge living at 1500 West Franklin Street in Richmond. The paper said he listed his address at the time of his enlistment as 1027 South Broad Street[22] in Virginia's capital. With all of this information leading to his kin, the company could find no one related to him.

The DuPont Company circulated far and wide their wish to find Hodge's relatives. A response of sorts came from Maysville, Kentucky, when the newspaper there reported, "Some time ago Chief of Police Harry A. Ort received a letter from the DuPont Powder Company requesting that he assist them in locating relatives of James A. Hodge, who was supposed to have lived in this section." The article continued, saying Chief Ort received a letter from a Connersville, Indiana, woman, Mrs. Laura Hodge, saying her husband had been missing from his home since April and "she fears that it was her husband killed." The paper said the DuPont Company received her information, but the result of the communication is unknown.[23]

What is clear is that James Hodge and Aubrey Turner were the last in a lengthy line of hard-working powdermen and others who gave their lives to the production of black powder at the DuPont mills on the Brandywine Creek. The creek continues its bubbling, gurgling, ever-changing path through the valley, a place no longer subject to the crash and boom, smoke and tremors, sorrows and pain of powder explosions. All that remains of people whose lives were taken are their descendants…and their stories. ■

Epilog

The stone buildings that remain on the grounds of the Hagley Museum and Library stand in silent honor to the workers who gave their lives to the making of black powder, and to their families and employers, the du Ponts. The 235-acre property is visited by many tens of thousands of parents and children every year, unaware of the tragic loss of lives that ended too soon during the nearly 120 years of powder making on the park-like acreage they walk today.

Visitors come from around the world to see the machinery that turned charcoal, sulfer, and potassium nitrate into the capricious substance that helped build the new American nation. Its roads, canals, mines, farm fields, and even its celebrations and freedoms, could not have existed without black powder.

Guests come to hear about water power and how it moved the powder-making machinery. They come to stroll the now peaceful land formerly covered with smoky, dirty, noisy factory buildings and apparatus. They take in the gently rolling landscape, traipsing over ground once trampled by boots and shoes put together with wooden pegs instead of metal because the latter could cause sparks that could turn a black, sand-like substance into instant death and destruction.

We hope that, at some point, they are reminded of the people who inhabited the long-gone wood and stone abodes where families were raised, often without fathers, brothers, sons, husbands, uncles, and nephews, and, at least twice, mothers and grandmothers.

It is impossible to think of the history of powder making in America without thinking of the name du Pont, for it was their factory in Delaware that largely provided the explosive power for the country's Industrial Revolution.

The names Watson, Buchanan, Toy, Kyle, Thaxter, Althaus, Sicco— the list goes on and on— should not be forgotten. They are the names of the people who gave their brawn, their time, and, all too often, their lives, so that others could profit from their labors. They, too, profited; many were able to buy farms and city properties to house their growing families—families who continue to serve the country to this day. ■

Appendix A

List of Persons Killed in du Pont Explosions, 1815 through 1920, by Date of Explosion, with alternate names. Various name sources are: Hagley Petit Ledgers, Francis Gurney du Pont diaries, newspapers. The names not in parentheses are those I believe are the correct names of the person.

June 8, 1815
Richard Dougherty
Patrick Dougherty
William Foster
Francis Leonard
John McCauley
Andrew Miller
Thomas Quig (Quigg)
Peter Shepherd (Sheppard)
John Welch (Welsh)

March 19, 1818
William Allison (Addison)
Patrick Boyle
Edward Bradley
Hugh Brady (Breadey)
John Brady Jr. (Bready)
John Brady Sr. (Bready)
Patrick Brady Jr. (Bready)
Patrick Brady Sr. (Bready)
Peter Cooney
James Cunningham
John Donohue (Donahue, Donahoe)
Dan Dougherty
William Dougherty
Philip Dugan (Dougan)
John Dunnery (Dunnavee)
Hugh Finigan
David Flinn (Flynn)
Philip Gallagher
Thomas Kennedy
John Malloy (Molloy, Mulloy, Melloy)
Patrick McCarran
Hugh McCollage (McCalage, McCalegue, McCollan, McColein, McCallagn, McCallagan)
Michael McLaughlin
Michael Mooney (Money)
John O'Brian
Thomas Pierce (Pearce)
Edward Reynolds (Rennels)
Thomas Reynolds (Rennels)
John Strain
Patrick Tollen (Tollan)
Anne Gallagher Toner (Tonner)
Michael Toner (Mihel, Tonner)
John Torrey
Peter Tunberg (Tonegeback, Touglarg)
David Wilson

August 25, 1832
Patrick Holland
Daniel Toy

June 24, 1834
Henry Kyle

September 17, 1835
John McGinnis (McGinness)

September 28, 1835
John Vance
John Green (Greer)

November 22, 1836
Thomas Heatherington (Hetherington)

December 13, 1839
John Cole (Coyle)

May 18, 1842
John Houghton (Houtton, Houlton)

September 21, 1843
Michael Borrell (Barrell)

July 24, 1844
James McDevitt
George Russell

July 23, 1846
Archibald Watson

April 14, 1847
David Althaus (Althouse, Oldhouse)
Malcolm Baxter
Samuel Brown
Patrick Connor (Conner)
William Connor (Conner)
Daniel Dougherty
John Dougherty
William Green
Thomas Holland
Michael Houghton (Houtton)
William King
Thomas Lynch (Linch)
Matthew McGarvey
John McGinness (McGinniss)
Charles O'Brien (O'Brian)
Michael O'Brien (O'Brian)
Wesley Pennington (Barrington)
Barnard Shields

February 6, 1850
Michael McLaughlin—industrial accident, not explosion

March 11, 1852
John Devine
James McClafferty (McLafferty, McCaffery, McCaffrey)

August 15, 1855
Edward Cassiday (Cassidy)

May 16, 1856
Andrew Moore
David Moore
John McPherso
August 22, 1857
Anthony Dougherty
Alexis I. du Pont
George Fisher
Edward Hurst
John McClafferty (McLafferty, McCaffery, McCaffrey)
Louis Vouche (Vache)

Appendix A

January 20, 1859
James Gibbons
John Grant

October 21, 1859
Charles Black
Edward Dougherty
Ubert Jacob (Jacobs)
Robert McIhenney (McIlhinney)
William Moran
Emile Sabar
Barney Sweeney
John Welsh (Welch)

February 3, 1860
Thomas Mullin (Mullen, Mullan)

October 10, 1860
Michael Gorman

November 20, 1861
Joseph Russell
John Vizier (Vichie)
Charles Mulherin (Mulhern, Mulherrin)

February 25, 1863
Thomas Clark (Clarksie, Clarke)
James Credan (Creedan)
John P. Dehan (Jean Pierre DeHan)
Edward Devlin
Hugh Devlin
Thomas Dougherty
Samuel Fisher Jr.
Samuel Fisher Sr.
John Higgerty (Higgerton, Higgarty, Hagerty)
Richard McLaughlin
James McKenna
Fergus Noone
John Querke (Quirk)

July 29, 1863
William Leary
James D. Peoples

August 8, 1863
Hugh McGinley
Patrick McGee

May 10, 1864
Milton Engle
James Gibbons
John Glenn (Genn)
Michael Hickey
Martin Hynes
James Kelly
Patrick Tolan

July 23, 1864
Joseph Babby (Babie)

December 15, 1864
Cornelius Carr
Dennis Collins
Michael Deery (Davy)
Patrick Deery (Davy)
John Dougherty
Thomas Gill
Michael Hasset
Thomas Hennessy
Edward O'Donnell
Charles O'Neil

February 25, 1865
Michael Dougherty
John Hughes
John McElwee (McElwell)

May 12, 1867
James Cunningham

July 2, 1869
Peter Massie (Massey, Masse)
James Malloy (Mulloy)

March 25, 1870
Darby McAteer

April 14, 1870
James Donahue (Donohue, Donahoo)

April 19, 1872
Peter Flanigan (Flanagan)
Dennis McLaughlin

August 14, 1872
Patrick Baun (Bawn, Burns)

April 19, 1873
Michael Dougherty

July 3, 1873
Jonas Miller

November 30, 1875
Edward Dougherty

May 20, 1876
Amos Carter

Frederick Dougherty
Patrick Dougherty
Patrick McKinney

January 5, 1877
John Minninger

July 12, 1882
William H. Chadwick

July 13, 1883
Thomas Pearl (Peril)
Patrick Haley

October 7, 1890
James Dolan
Michael Dolan
Patrick Dougherty V
Rose Dougherty
Thomas Dougherty
William R. Green
Daniel Harkins (Harkin)
John Herlihy (Herlihe)
Michael Herlihy (Herlihe)
John Horgan
William McGarvey
John Newell

December 19, 1893
Edward Gallagher

March 9, 1897
James Walker

December 9, 1898
Tom McCann

Appendix A

Samuel Stewart
John Wright (Jack)

December 8, 1902
William McDowell

June 8, 1904
Charles Viola*-fatally injured by a stone dislodged during an intentional blast in a quarry

February 2, 1906
Samuel Buchanan

May 10, 1906
William McCrea
David Cammock

March 8, 1909
George Whiteman

August 7, 1909
John Mott

November 11, 1909
Nicholas Dinesto (Nicolo, Denesta, Dinesta, Di Nesta)
Walter McDermott
Howard Darrah (George Howard Darrah)

July 13, 1915
Daniel F. Toomey
Henry M. Cazier

August 29, 1915
Lawrence Cunningham
Hugh Gillespie

November 30, 1915
James Baird
Benjamin Barber (Barker)
Louis Booker
Marge Bricotti
Elmer Cumpston (Cumston)
James Eggner (Egner)
Henry Elliot
Norman Fisher
Elmer Spruance Fox
James Gemmil
James Giviney
Edward Gross
Harry Haber
Patrick Hanrahan
Nelson Hogate
Fred Jeffry (Frederano Cafre, Ciafre)
Bartholomew Kelleher
Edward King
Elmer Mace
James Malloy
Bryan O'Connor
Harvey Place
Gimi Silvestri (James Silvester)
Wesley Hasting Simpson
John E. Smack
Paul C. Smack
Elijah Springfield
Alan Thaxter
W. Leslie Timms
William C. Wein

July 8, 1916
John Salvagno

January 5, 1917
Carlo Sicco (Charles)

March 15, 1917
Albert Vannatta

August 21, 1918
Charles Kimberley*
Allan Pollitt*
William Pollitt*

December 1, 1919
Edward C. Snyder*

January 2, 1920
Thomas Anselmi (Anselme, Anselmo)
Antonio Grangiulio (Grangville)
Giovanni Martini
Noah Columbus (Lum) Pinder (Pender)
Calvin Swartwood

May 4, 1920
Aubrey C. Turner*
James A. Hodge*

---

*This person is not found in any Hagley Library documents. Charles Viola is listed in the Dick Scott collection, but nowhere else. The other six were found in newspaper accounts. According to Hagley Library statistics, there were 288 explosions that killed 228 people. My research has uncovered three additional explosions on August 21, 1918, December 1, 1919, and May 4, 1920, in which an additional six men died (seven if we include Charles Viola, listed above in an industrial accident).

The new numbers would then be a total of 235 souls who perished. If the new numbers are accepted, then 21.6% resulted in death. These are dry, unemotional statistics. In the overall scheme of things, the stats pale when compared with the loss of life, the sorrowful tragedies of lost sons, husbands, fathers, uncles, nephews, brothers-in-law, a mother, a grandmother, a toddler, and two or three civilians (in the case of the powder wagon explosion in Wilmington in 1854).

These are the Hagley numbers:

288 explosions
228 people killed
60 explosions resulted in death (20.83%)
5 largest resulted in 107 deaths, or 46.9% of deaths
10 largest resulted in 146 deaths, or 64%

5 explosions with largest number of deaths
1818. 34
1915. 30
1847. 18
1863. 13
1890. 12

5 years with largest explosions
1871. 26
1855. 12
1857. 11
1882. 11
1880. 11

Appendix B

James Hodge's Great War

> The brutality and inhumanity of war stood
> in great contrast to what I had heard and
> read about as a youth.
> —*Reinhold Spengler*

Hodge's December 1917 voyage to France was over an ocean that, in 1917, was exceptionally stormy. One 1st Division sergeant wrote he was among those who got six meals a day—three down and three up. The typical journey to France was twelve days and, other than having to serve on "puke detail," the soldiers' worst enemy was boredom. The soldiers posted as lookouts for U-boats were successful in their work, as the German submariners sank only two eastbound troop ships in the entire war.[1]

The 1st Sanitary Train arrived at St. Nazaire aboard the *Huron*, the train part of what Winston Churchill called "this seemingly inexhaustible flood of gleaming youth in its first maturity of health and vigor," and, "the impulse of new life."[2] The unit headed for their first posting at Gondrecourt-le-Chateau, the 1st Division's training bivouac in the Lorraine region of northeastern France.

It took a week for the train, part horse-drawn, part mechanized, to reach Gondrecourt. Field Hospital No. 3 functioned as the primary medical care unit, taking over the base hospital, while they dispersed the other three field hospitals.

To understand what Private Hodge did during his two years in France and Germany, it is necessary to know how the U.S. Army organized its medical facilities in the Great War. A wounded soldier could expect to find five levels of care behind the front lines. First came the regimental aid station where medical personnel dressed wounds after litter bearers carried the injured there. Dressing stations treated those injuries requiring care beyond the aid station. The field hospital was next, then evacuation hospitals, and, finally, base hospitals.

Hodge worked in Field Hospital No. 3, the final level of care in the 1st Division (in the early months of American participation in the war, the 1st was often called "the combat division," since it was the only American unit in France at the time);[3] evacuation hospitals served under the auspices of the next highest military command. "The field hospitals, located three to four miles from the front lines, were the next portion of the sanitary train. They provided protection from the elements and more complicated treatment than the dressing stations or aid stations."[4]

It was not just the sea voyage that proved stormy; Hodge and the rest of the sanitary train arrived in the first month of a miserably frigid and wet winter in Europe. One of the biggest complaints of the doughboys in France was that, because it rained for weeks on end, boots and clothes never dried out. While the medics did not have to wear standard-issue hobnailed boots on hospital duty, this was little solace to the men who were ill-clothed, often lacking any winter clothing.[5] Supply officers in America used the flimsy excuse that soldiers in the States needed the winter gear.

Added to stateside cynicism was the fact that supplies of needless items were taking up space on France-bound ships, including floor wax, lawnmowers, bathtubs, window shades, and spittoons. At one point, General Pershing requested the suppliers stop shipping such items and told them to send ammunition, medical supplies, winter clothing, and weapons!

In April, the hospital trekked to the Cantigny[6] sector to give medical services for the first American offensive of the war. Cantigny marked a change in how the army used the four field hospitals in each train. The 1st Division's hospitals experimented with assigning specific cases to designated units based on the wound, not on location. Three units treated wounded and gassed patients, sick soldiers, and skin and venereal disease patients,[7] respectively. The fourth stayed in reserve as a recovery unit.[8]

More than one gas was used on the Western Front and each had a unique odor. Phosgene smelled like putrid fish; chlorine gas had the aroma of pineapple; and mustard gas had a rich, sweet smell. There was a fourth gas, but it was not from a gas attack. Carbon monoxide formed from the remnants of mine explosions and had no odor.

One soldier wrote, "The gas was so strong that it turned all our buttons olive green, stopped our wristwatches and turned the rats out of their holes by the score." He did not specify which gas he referred to. In the first few gas attacks, the men used face towels dipped in their own urine, as an order from higher up suggested.[9] A British Tommy outlined the effects of gas on the body: "Blindness, deafness, loss of voice, inability to swallow, choking, difficulty breathing, and burns."[10]

Appendix B

Once the gassed soldier arrived at a field hospital, they placed him into one of four categories: severely gassed (immediate or expectant); fit for duty, immediate return to unit (Minimal); fit for duty in 24 hours, return to unit (delayed); or evacuate to an army hospital.[11] If they were not a gas patient, the patients Hodge treated were injured from being on the receiving end of artillery; one author concludes that two-thirds of wounds on the Western front were from this cause.[12]

There was also the matter of "shell shock," a result of the constant bombardment of the trenches that were a primary topographical feature of battle. Treatments for the ailment ranged from disciplinary action from officers who felt the illness was the result of cowardice (or "funk") and malingering, to electric shock therapy, which was "useful…in the sense that it sometimes exposed those who had been shamming their neurosis."[13]

Hodges' field hospital worked at Froissy in a building for surgical operations and in tents. While there, they used it for gassed patients, taking in 465 of them. In June, the unit moved to Paillart, a few miles to the northeast, to care for more gas victims and others with more serious wounds. It served as a triage unit for the left flank of the division.[14] Hodge's unit then entrained in June to Montdidier-Noyon. The load there was light as the division served in a reserve capacity.

The next movement was back to Cantigny and then on to the Aisne-Marne sector. During the Battle of Soissons, Field Hospital No. 3, at Mortefontaine, got hit by an air bomb.[15] While there, the hospital treated 5,000 patients, including those from other nation's armies and disabled German soldiers. Among the injured at Soissons were Sam Ervin, later the head of the Senate Watergate investigation, and Ted Roosevelt Junior;[16] Hodge might have tended to either of them. Before their relief, the men of the field hospitals worked for five straight days providing not just medical help but also hot food and coffee.

Higher command relieved the division from the Soissons battle and it moved east, to the quiet Saizerais sector, where the field hospital worked as the triage station, and then on to Vaucouleurs.

The entire sanitary train assembled at Raulecourt to support troops fighting in the St. Mihiel offensive, followed by the Meuse-Argonne battle where the 1st Division suffered more casualties than any other. Hodge treated some of the 7,500 victims.

At the Meuse-Argonne, Field Hospital No. 3, in former German dugouts at Cheppy, performed the jobs of conducting triage and treating gas patients. They treated shock patients who could not stand transportation.[17] And recall as one author said, that "Influenza was raging throughout the United States, though the members of the First Division were unaware of it for some weeks afterward. Among the troops at the front it was negligible, though they were exposed to extremely unsettled climate conditions and undergoing great privations. There was practically no illness, they did not have time to get sick. Their greater hardship was becoming infested with lice."[18]

According to the same author, "On October 8th the hospitals at Cheppy were under shell fire for five hours. Quite a number of seriously wounded patients had accumulated owing to lack of transportation, when it was realized that the Boche was making an actual attack on the site. All possible vehicles, with any sort of capacity to accommodate men, were to proceed, and the patients evacuated. After the last load was safely on its way, a shell struck the building in which some of the worst cases had been housed."[19]

James Hodge's Field Hospital No. 3 with an ambulance company in transit. (U.S. Army Medical Department, Office of Medical History)

First Sergeant Almo E. O'Kell of Field Hospital No. 3, whom Hodge would have known, wrote in December to his wife, Pearl, in Kansas City, that, at Cheppy, "The first three days and nights not a man in the company went to sleep as we were too busy." He said the unit received a German bombing for an hour on October 4, the first bomb not exploding, the second bursting fifty feet away from the main entrance to his dugout, and the third hitting the roof, caving it in eight feet.[20]

Near the end of the war, mothers and wives of the deceased petitioned politicians to bring their soldiers home for proper burials on American soil. An organization calling itself the Purple Cross (not to be confused with the group of English children who created their own Purple Cross circle to raise money for the care and feeding of millions of war horses) lobbied the government to make sure that 55,000 soldiers' bodies were repatriated to the United States. They saw this as guaranteeing their members, cynical funeral directors, hefty profits.[21]

In French ceremonies honoring the unknown dead of the war, they laid wreaths at Bartholomae's Monument to the Dead in Paris's Père-Lachaise Cemetery, a burying ground that provided the model for the Evergreen Cemetery in Portland, Maine, where Alan Thaxter is buried.[22]

The "Coblenz Bridgehead" by the new year amounted to a quarter million doughboys in a twenty-five hundred square mile section of Germany, a space shared with a million Germans. December 1 was the first day Allied forces could enter Germany and the sanitary train did so after traversing a part of southern Luxembourg. The train's eventual destination was the German town of Dernbach, twenty miles northeast of Coblenz, where they established themselves in a large Catholic sisters hospital for the poor. Sergeant O'Kell relates in a seven-page letter, "The sisters say they can't see why we work so hard keeping the floors clean. You see it has been awful weather since we came up in a week ago," adding that it either rained or snowed the entire time.[23] Having made it through the rigors of war, Sgt. O'Kell died of peritonitis on January 12, 1919; he might have been under James Hodge's care.

Hodge continued working in Field Hospital No. 3 until the late summer of 1919. He put up with boredom on occupation duty but got leave in March and traveled to Paris on a week's furlough.[24] He might have been in the crowd when another division sponsored a carnival the following month.

The ship that took Private James Hodge to France with his unit, with six officers and eighty other enlisted men, has its own story to tell. The former name of the *USS Huron* was SS *Friedrich der Grosse*, a German ship built as a passenger liner in 1896 in Stettin, Germany, on the Baltic. Fourteen years before its internment at the port of New York, its deck was the site of Kaiser Wilhelm II's famous "Schrecklichkeit" speech, in which he compared the German Empire's military to the ancient Huns and their viciousness.

While the ship berthed in New York, German spies and idle sailors, particularly Franz von Rintelen, used it for making pencil bombs, also known as cigar bombs, small incendiaries placed on Allied ships from New York carrying supplies to Europe several years before the U.S. entry into the war. The bombs did their job: they damaged or destroyed cargoes on thirty-six ships during the war. The devices played a part in making Americans anxious about German plots to destroy factories making munitions for the Allies in the early years of the European war. Even when law enforcement officials detained suspected saboteurs, the need to prosecute on grounds other than sabotage or espionage handicapped them, as no statutes then prohibited such peacetime acts against the United States.[25]

Von Rintelen figures in another war story closer to home. One Malvin Rice, claiming to be a member of the board of the "DuPont de Nemours Powder Company," had contacted an intelligence bureau of the German government, and indicated he could help the Germans buy up large quantities of DuPont powder, thus keeping it out of the hands of their enemies. Von Rintelen had set up a dummy corporation, the Bridgeport Projectile Company, to further divert American powder from the Allies. He never met Rice, and the idea was forgotten.[26]

Before the Americans interned the German sailors aboard the *Friedrich der Grosse*, along with their ship when America entered the war, the seamen created more than seven million dollars in damage by smashing pumps and cracking cylinder casings.

The U.S. Navy repaired the damage and renamed the craft *Huron*. It was one of three troop ships the American forces had available to use at the start of its participation in the war. After the war, the Navy turned the *Huron* over to a private enterprise, which renamed it the *City of Honolulu*. They scuttled it on its maiden voyage with that name when it caught fire while transporting passengers from Los Angeles to Hawaii. A Coast Guard cutter fired two dozen cannon rounds into her and she sank with no loss of life, all the passengers and crew taken off by rescue ships.

Hodge's return trip to the States was also on a ship with a story to tell. The *DeKalb*, originally the SS *Prinz Eitel Frederich*, was interned in the Philadelphia Navy Yard when America entered the war in 1917. Soon after its commissioning in the U.S. Navy, the *DeKalb* was one of a half dozen ships that escorted General John J. "Black Jack" Pershing[27] and Captain George C. Marshall to France at the beginning of America's participation in the war.

Appendix B

She had been an auxiliary cruiser in the Imperial German Navy. Prior to the U.S. entry in the war, the *Prinz Eitel Frederich* bagged the first U.S.-flagged ship in the conflict, sinking the schooner *William P. Frye*, carrying wheat the German's thought destined for their English enemy, off the coast of Brazil.

Laden with prisoners and low on fuel and supplies, the *Frederich* entered the port at Newport News, Virginia. She overstayed her welcome and was interned, then transported, still under the German flag, to Philadelphia. When America declared war on Germany, the navy renamed her for Major General Baron Johann de Kalb, who served on George Washington's staff at Valley Forge.

The *DeKalb* made a dozen trips with returning American troops, including James Hodge, who completed the circle he began two years before, landing at Hoboken on September 5, 1919. W. Averell Harriman later bought the ship and made it into an emigrant vessel carrying steerage passengers to the New World. ■

Appendix C

Alan Thaxter's Obituary

The Portland Herald
Portland, Maine
Dec. 5, 1915

On Friday, December third all morning numberless beautiful flowers were sent to St. Luke's Cathedral as tributes of affection to the object of this brief sketch, so that the church was full of color and fragrance, as befits the symbols of youth. Dean Vernon and Canon Schuyler officiated with the full choir and the hymns sung were those specially liked by Alan Thaxter himself.

There was a very large attendance.

The bearers were Guy Stolenwerck of Wilmington, Del., Mr. Bodell of Providence, Donald Payson, Louis Runciman, Harold Payson, Dr. Van Gorden, of the Brigham Hospital, Boston, and Clinton W. Davis; the users were Howard R. Ives and Roscoe T. Holt. How well we know that with the younger generation is centered the promise of the year to come— the eager hopes and bright anticipations that need new strength and vigor for their successful fulfillment. Theirs is the age of adventure and when a young life is suddenly stricken from the list of competition for the prizes to be won by ability and industry and courage the blow falls heavily indeed. Doubly so when by temperament and disposition such a young man as Alan Thaxter adorned with remarkably lovable and sterling traits of character had drawn to himself the affection of all who knew him or with whom he had at any period of his life been associated. This is very much to affirm but in his case it was entirely and unreservedly true.

Of these were the qualities which rendered him generally popular.

Appendix C

It is not difficult to realize that in his own home his sunny disposition made him inevitably delightful and captivating.

None who stood in closest relation to him felt they needed for more blessing than they have and he was his best that centered in their affection and belief that led him to feel he must do more than his best since they were indeed all that he conceived of as his best and noblest. The younger employees who were under his direction at DuPont used to refer to him as their 'college chum' and one little Italian in the corps broke down entirely on learning of Mr. Thaxter's death.

He was a communicant of St. Luke's and was always close in touch as one of their boys with the late Bishop Cadman as well as with Dean Vernon.

At school and in college later during his business connection with a prominent brokerage firm in Providence and throughout the duration of his work at Wilmington, the reports were the same—testimonials of personal attachment and good will. His charm of manners, though marked by considerable reticence and reserve, always won him friends and friends once won were never lost. His was a splendid fearlessness. Urged by his family and friends to take up a less precarious employment he refused, and stood by his post —continuing in furtherance of the task he had undertaken with not the least wavering or dread.

In three instances recently there has come to us here in Portland the ruthless taking off of young men in their prime— at the front; one an English citizen tho counted a Portland boy. They heroically gave their lives for their respective countries. In Alan Thaxters case it was his own post he was guarding but it was the same valiant best that animated all alike.

Acknowledgements

I wrote Across the Creek for a couple of reasons. One, "I've always wanted to write a book." Cliché, I know, but in this case absolutely true. My wife, Lynn, reminded me (since I am of the age when one needs reminding, often) I have been saying that since we were married.

That wish, combined with one of the best jobs I have ever had, tour guide at the Hagley Museum, "where the DuPont story began," led me to the topic. I realized there were many tomes about the du Ponts who built the company on brains and cash, but very few on the men and women who provided the brawn, some of whom paid with their lives for the privilege.

One of my favorite phrases has to do with "standing on the shoulders of giants." There is one giant I want to highlight. Margaret Mulrooney wrote *Black Powder, White Lace: The du Pont Irish and Cultural Identity in Nineteenth-Century America,* an outstanding treatise on the lives of the men, women and children who made up the du Pont community on the banks of the Brandywine Creek (or river, as some, including me, call it). If you read just one book (other than this one) about the powdermen and their families who toiled to make black powder, it should be hers.

The primary reason for my choice of topics, though, is to honor the "little people" who make up the bulk of this book's characters. With strong backs and stronger wills, these were the souls who provided the spine for the beginning of what would become one of the best known corporations in the world. Love it, revile it, ignore it: the DuPont Company was built on the toil of ordinary people doing extraordinary things—traveling to a strange land in creaky, packed vessels; creating lives from scratch in that new land; handling volatile materials that could destroy lives in a split-second; and, if they were lucky, surviving to pick up the pieces, literally and figuratively.

To the end of honoring those who died, every one of the known powdermen and the three relatives who died in the 119 year history of the Eleutherian and Hagley Mills of the du Ponts is mentioned in the preceding pages. In some cases, in several pages. In others, just a paragraph or two.

A tip of the hat to my brother Dave, who designed the cover and the book's interior, and to his spouse, Cathy Pratt; to sister Jane for her spot-on

Acknowledgements

editorial suggestions, and brother Lee, his son Chris, and his granddaughter Blake who lent moral support throughout the three years of research and writing. The whole thing was anchored by my wife, Lynn, who provided the love and support any author would be proud and lucky to have.

A very special shout-out to my great editor, Ann McKelvie. Ann has taken my clunky manuscript and smoothed it out to make it so much more than it was when she got it.

Newspapers and the Hagley Museum and Library archives were the primary sources for the book, although I was lucky to have communicated with some knowledgeable relatives of the dead and injured powdermen. I thank Nona Kelly Smith, Janine Pizano, Sarah Dougherty, Lisa Scaglione, Reese Robinson, Nancy Van Dyke-Dickison, Elma Andrews, Ralph Walsh, Sydney Thaxter, Kathy Baker, Valerie Budischak, Patty Lindsay, Jim Walls, Shannon Connor Winward, and Victor Carre for information about their ancestors.

Among my favorite people are archivists and librarians. They are the keepers of history and they added immeasurably to this book. Among them, special thanks go to: Lucas Clawson, Hagley Library; Andrew Woods and Mary J. Manning, First Division Museum; Ed Ricci, Delaware Historical Society; Susan Kirk Ryan, Catholic Diocese of Wilmington; Stacie Petersen, World War I Museum and Memorial; Barbara Martin, Episcopal Diocese of Portland, Maine; Richard Gaarenstroom, U.S. Army Heritage and Education Center; Sanders Marble, Army Medical Department Center of History & Heritage; the late Austin Edison, Mt. Salem Church; Marge McNinch, Delaware Genealogical Society, and former archivist at the Hagley Museum and Library; Mary Laura Kludy, Virginia Military Academy Archives; and Kieran McCarthy, Cork City Council.

Much appreciation also to the library and Soda House repository staffs at the Hagley Museum and Library; the Family History Center in Wilmington; the Delaware Historical Society; the University of Delaware Library; the Brandywine branch of the New Castle County, Delaware, Library; the Maine Historical Society; the Portland, Maine, Public Library; the State of Delaware Archives; and the Archives of the United States, St. Louis and Philadelphia branches.

My gratitude also to Tedd Cocker, Anne McNally, Susan Schatz, Elton Grunden, Angelika Albright and Dr. David Cole.

All of the above relatives of powdermen and of mine, organizations and others provided invaluable information for the writing of this book; any errors are mine alone.

Please take a look at my blog at www.bluerockpublishing.com for additional information about the du Pont powder mills and the people who worked in them. And, if you are of a mind to do so, please write a brief review of your thoughts about the book. If you bought the book through a non-Internet source, you can send your review to me at info@bluerockpublishing.com. Otherwise, submit your review to the Internet place where you bought the book.

Thank you.

Bibliography

Ackerman, Karen, abs. *Tax Assessments of New Castle County 1816-1817*. Silver Spring: Family Line Publications, 1986.

Adams, Raymond D. *An Alphabetical Index to Ulster Emigration to Philadelphia 1803-1850*. Baltimore: Genealogical Publishing Co., 1992.

Adams, William Forbes. *Ireland and Irish Emigration to the New World from 1815 to the Famine*. New York: Russell & Russell, 1967.

Adolph, Anthony. *Tracing Your Irish Family History*. Buffalo: Firefly Books, 2009.

Albion, Robert G. *The Rise of New York Port (1815-1860)*. New York: Charles Scribner's Sons, 1939.

Algeo, Matthew. *The President is a Sick Man: Wherein the Supposedly Virtuous Grover Cleveland Survives Secret Surgery at Sea and Vilifies the Courageous Newspaperman Who Dared Expose the Truth*. Chicago: Chicago Review Press, 2011.

Anson, Neil. *Unknown Soldiers: The Story of the Missing of the First World War*. New York: Alfred Knopf, 2006.

Arlidge, J. T. *The Hygiene, Diseases and Mortality of Occupations*. London: Percival and Co., 1892.

Arnold, Janis Kerr. *Our Canby & Bird Scrapbook*, Unpublished manuscript. Seattle: Delaware Historical Society, 1981.

Artner, Gail Marie. *Priest and Parish in the Formative Years 1800-1840: Father Patrick Kenny of the Delaware Valley*. Master's Thesis, University of Delaware, 1968.

Assheton, Ralph, comp. *History of Explosions on Which the American Table of Distances was Based, Including Other Explosions of Large Quantities of Explosives*. Wilmington, Delaware: The Institute of Makers of Explosives, 1930.

Bacon, John U. *The Great Halifax Explosion*. New York: William Morrow, 2017.

Baddeley, J. Fraser. *Pamphlet on the Manufacture of Gunpowder, as Carried on at the Government Factory, Waltham Abbey*. Waltham Abbey: Her Majesty's Stationery Office, 1857.

Baker, Dessie. *Emigrants from Derry Port, 1847-49*. Apollo, Pennsylvania: Closson Press, 1985.

Barnes, Alexander. *In a Srange Land: The American Occupation of Germany, 1918-1923*. Atglen, Pennsylvania: Schiffer Military History, 2011.

Bauer, K. Jack. *A Maritime History of the United States*. Columbia: University of South Carolina Press, 1988.

Beckham, Polly. *A Little Cache of Green: Savings Habits of Irish Immigrant Women in 1850 Philadelphia*. Seminar Paper, University of Delaware, Unknown Date.

Bennett, David H. *The Party of Fear: The American Far Right from Nativism to the Militia Movement*. Chapel Hill, North Carolina: The University of North Carolina Press, 1988.

Bentley, Elizabeth and Deborah Carl. *Directory of Family Associations, 4th Edition*. Baltimore: Genealogical Publishing Co., 2001.

Bernstein, Peter L. *Wedding of the Waters: The Erie Canal and the Making of a Great Nation*. New York: W. W. Norton & Company, 2005.

Black, Lewis Black, Jr. *The Black Family on the Brandywine* (Self Published), 1995.

Bluett, Anthony. *Things Irish*. Dublin: Mercier Press, 1994.

Blum, Howard. *Dark Invasion: 1915, Germany's Secret War and the Hunt For the First Terrorist Cell in America*. New York: HarperCollins, 2014.

Bogert, George Dudley. *Let's Go!* San Francisco: George Dudley Bogert, 1927.

Bragg, C. L. et al. *Never for Want of Powder: The Confederate Powder Works in Augusta, Georgia*. Columbia: The University of South Carolina Press, 2007.

Bronstein, Jamie L. *Caught in the Machinery: Workplace Accidents and Injured Workers in Nineteenth-Century Britain*. Stanford, California: Stanford University Press, 2008.

Brown, Daniel James. *Under a Flaming Sky: The Great Hinckley Firestorm of 1894*. New York: Harper Perennial, 2006.

Bull, Stephen. Trench: *A History of Trench Warfare on the Western Front*. Oxford: Osprey Publishing, 2010.

Business America. *The History of the E. I. Du Pont de Nemours Powder Company*. New York: The Banker and Investor Magazine Publishing Company, 1912.

Butler, John A. *Atlantic Kingdom*. Dulles, Virginia: Brassey's Inc., 2001.

Calomiris, Ellen. *Conflict, Cooperation, Acceptance: The Italian Experience in Delaware*. Research Paper, University of Delaware, 1981.

Carr, William H. A. *The du Ponts of Delaware*. New York: Dodd, Mean, & Company, 1964.

Bibliography

Carroll, Andrew. *My Fellow Soldiers: General John Pershing and the Americans Who Helped With the Great War*. New York: Penguin Books, 2017.

Carter, Richard B., comp. *Delaware's Roll of Honor*. Dover: Delaware Heritage Commission, 2015.

Cherry, Jonathan and Brendan Scott, eds. *Cavan History and Society*. Dublin: Geography Publications, 2014.

Churchwell, Sarah. *Behold, America: The Entangled History of "America First" and "The American Dream."* New York: Basic Books, 2018.

Clark, Arthur H. *The Clipper Ship Era*. New York: G.P. Putnam's Sons, 1911.

Clark, Dennis. *The Irish in Philadelphia*. Philadelphia: Temple University Press, 1973.

Clark, Dennis. *Irish Relations, The*. East Brunswick, New Jersey: Associated University Presses, Inc., 1982.

Cockroft, Wayne. *Dangerous Energy: The Archaeology of Gunpowder and Military Explosives Manufacture*. Swindon, England: English Heritage, 2000.

Coleman, Terry. *Going to America*. Baltimore: Genealogical Publishing Company, 1987.

Conway, Alan, ed. *The Welsh in America*. Minneapolis: University of Minnesota Press, 1961.

Cooch, Francis A. *Little Known History of Newark, Delaware and its Environs*. Newark, DE: The Press of Kells, 1936.

Corley, Flora Fleming. *Confederate City: Augusta, Georgia*. 1860-1865. Columbia: University of South Carolina Press, 1960.

Crowley, John, William J. Smyth and Mike Murphy, eds. *Atlas of the Great Irish Famine, 1845-52*. Cork: Cork University Press, 2012.

Curtis, Charles M. *Old Swede's Church, Wilmington, DE 1698-1938*. Wilmington, Delaware: Delaware Tercentenary Commission, 1938.

Cutler, Carl C. *Greyhounds of the Sea: The Story of the American Clipper Ship*. New York: G.P. Putnam's Sons, 1930.

Cutler, Carl C. *Queens of the Western Ocean: The Story of Americas Mail and Passenger Sailing Lines*. Annapolis: United States Naval Institute, 1961.

Daur, Linda. *Domestic Servants at Eleutherian Mills, 1821-1842*. Eleutherian Mills-Hagley Foundation Research Report.

Day, Angelique and Patrick McWilliams, eds. *Ordnance Survey Memoirs of Ireland, Vol. 38: Parishes of County Donegal I, 1833-5, North-East Donegal*. Belfast: The Institute of Irish Studies, 1997.

Day, Angelique and Patrick McWilliams, eds. *Ordnance Survey Memoirs of Ireland, Vol. 39: Parishes of County Donegal II, 1835-6, Mid, West and South Donegal*. Belfast: The Institute of Irish Studies, 1997.

Day, Angelique. *Glimpse of Irelands Past—The Ordnance Survey Memoir Drawings: Topography and Technique*. Dublin: Royal Irish Academy, 2014.

Delaney, Mary Murray. *Of Irish Ways*. New York: Kilkenny Press, 1985.

Develin, Joseph Chubb. *The Story of an Irish Sept, the O'Develins of Tyrone, 2d Ed*. Philadelphia: College Offset Press, 1947.

Dillon, Brian. *The Great Explosion: Gunpowder, the Great War and a Disaster on the Kent Marshes*. Dublin: Penguin Books, 2015.

Dobson, David. *Ships from Ireland to Early America, 1623-1850*. Baltimore: Clearfield Publishing, 2008.

Dorian, Hugh. *The Outer Edge of Ulster: A Memoir of Social Life in Nineteenth-Century Donegal*. Breandan Mac Suibhne and David Dickson, eds. Notre Dame, Indiana: The University of Notre Dame Press, 2000.

Dorian, Max. *The du Ponts: From Gunpowder to Nylon*. Boston: Little, Brown and Company, 1961.

Drescher, Nuala McGann. *The Irish in Industrial Wilmington, 1800-1845: A History of the Life of the Irish Emigrants to the Wilmington Area in the Pre-famine Years*. Master's Thesis, University of Delaware, 1960.

Duffy, Godfrey F. *Tracing Your Donegal Ancestors*. Dublin: Flyleaf Press, 1996.

Du Pont, Bessie Gardner, trans. *The Life of Eleuthere Irenee du Pont in Contemporary Correspondence, 11 vols*. Newark, Delaware: University of Delaware Press, 1923-1926.

Du Pont, Bessie Gardner. *E.I. du Pont de Nemours and Company: A History, 1802-1902*. New York: Houghton Mifflin Company, 1920.

Dutton, William S. *DuPont: One Hundred and Forty Years*. New York: Charles Scribner's Sons, 1951.

Eagleton, Terry. *The Truth About the Irish*. New York: St. Martin's Press, 1999.

Early, Charles Montague, "Passenger Lists from 'The Shamrock or Irish Chronicle,'

1815-1816." *Journal of the American Irish Historical Society xxix (1930-31)*.
Egan, Timothy. *The Immortal Irishman: The Irish Revolutionary Who Became an American Hero*. Boston: Houghton Mifflin Harcourt, 2016.

Egerton, Douglas R. *The Wars of Reconstruction: The Brief, Violent History of America's Most Progressive Era*. New York: Bloomsbury Press, 2014.

Errigo, Joseph A. L. *History of St. Anthony's Church*. Wilmington, Delaware: Hambleton Co., 1949.

Errigo, Joseph A.L. *St. Joseph's On the Brandywine*. Wilmington, Delaware: William N. Cann, Inc., 1941.

Falley, Margaret Dickson. *Irish and Scotch-Irish Ancestral Research, Vol. I*. Baltimore: Genealogical Publishing Co., 1988.

Fanning, Charles. New Perspectives on the Irish Diaspora. Carbondale: Southern Illinois University Press, 2000.

Farris, Sally Guertler. *A Chart of Du Pont Company Expansion beyond the Banks of the Brandywine, 1859-1934*. Wilmington, Delaware: Eleutherian Mills-Hagley Foundation Research Report, 1960.

Farwell, Byron. *Over There: The United States in the Great War, 1917-1918*. New York: W.W. Norton & Company, 1999.

Fierro, Francis J. *The Italian Immigration in Wilmington*. Research paper, University of Delaware, 1979.

Filby, P. William, ed. *Passenger and Immigration Lists Bibliography 1538-1900*. Detroit: Gale Research Co., 1981.

Fisk, Catherine L. *Working Knowledge: Employee Innovation and the Rise of Corporate Intellectual Property, 1800-1930*. Chapel Hill: University of North Carolina Press, 2009.

Flayhart, William H. *The American Line (1871-1902)*. New York: W. W. Norton & Company, 2000.

Flynn, Michael. *Micks in the Census: The Search for the Residents of Flea Park (1860-1877)*, Eleutherian Mills-Hagley Foundation Research Report.

Fothergill, Gerald, "Passenger Lists to America," *The New England Historical and Genealogical Register LX (1906)*.

Frazier, Margaret M. *Delaware Advertiser 1827-1831: Genealogical Extracts*. Newhall, California: Carl Boyer III, 1987.

Freeman, Joshua. *Behemoth: A History of the Factory and the Making of the Modern World*. New York: W. W. Norton & Company, 2018.

Gabrielan, Randall. *Explosion at Morgan: The World War I Middlesex Munitions Disaster*. Charleston: The History Press, 2012.

Gallagher, Thomas. *Paddy's Lament, Ireland 1846-1847: Prelude to Hatred*. San Diego: Harcourt Brace Jovanovich, Publishers, 1982.

Gallman, J. Matthew. *Receiving Erin's Children: Philadelphia, Liverpool, and the Irish Famine Migration, 1845-1855*. Chapel Hill: The University of North Carolina Press, 2000.

General Assembly of the State of Delaware. *Laws of the State of Delaware, Revised Edition*. Wilmington: General Assembly of the State of Delaware, 1829.

General Assembly of the State of Delaware. *Laws of the State of Delaware, Vol. 16, Part I*. Dover: General Assembly of the State of Delaware, 1879.

General Assembly of the State of Delaware. *Laws of the State of Delaware, Vol. XVIII, Part 1*. Dover: General Assembly of the State of Delaware, 1887.

Gibson, George H. "Labor Piracy on the Brandywine." *Labor History* 8 (1967).

Gibson, George H., ed. *Diary of William P. Brobson, 1825-1828*. Wilmington, Delaware: The Historical Society of Delaware, 1977.

Gordon, John Steele. *An Empire of Wealth: The Epic History of American Economic Power*. New York: Harper Collins, 2004.

Green, Kara A. Briggs. *Images of America: Forty Acres*. Charleston: Arcadia Publishing, 2008.

Grenham, John. *Tracing Your Irish Ancestors. Fourth Edition*. Dublin: Gill & Macmillan, 2012.

Grier, A. O. H. *This Was Wilmington*. Wilmington, Delaware: The News-Journal Co., 1945.

Guillet, Edwin C. *The Great Migration: The Atlantic Crossing by Sailing-ship Since 1770*. Toronto: Thomas Nelson and Sons, 1937.

Hackett, J. Dominick, "Passenger Lists Published in 'The Shamrock or Irish Chronicle,' 1811," *Journal of the American Irish Historical Society xxviii (1929-1930)*.

Hancock, Harold B. *Delaware During the Civil War*. Wilmington, Delaware: Historical Society of Delaware, 1961.

Hancock, Harold B. *The Industrial Worker Along the Brandywine, 1800-1840*. Eleutherian Mills-Hagley Foundation Research Report, 1956.

Bibliography

Hancock, Harold B. *The Industrial Worker Along the Brandywine, 1840-1870*. Eleutherian Mills-Hagley Foundation Research Report, 1957.

Hancock, Harold B. *The Industrial Worker Along the Brandywine, 1870-1902*. Eleutherian Mills-Hagley Foundation Research Report, 1958.

Hancock, Harold B. and Norman B. Wilkinson. "A Manufacturer in Wartime: Du Pont, 1860-1865." *The Business History Review 40*, 2 (1966).

Hansen, Marcus Lee. The Atlantic Migration, 1607-1860: A History of the Continuing Settlement of the United States. Cambridge, Massachusetts: Harvard University Press, 1940.

Hanson, Neil. *Unknown Soldiers: The Story of the Missing of the First World War*. New York: Alfred Knopf, 2006.

Harris, Ruth-Ann and B. Emer O'Keefe, eds. *The Search for Missing Friends: Irish Immigrant Advertisements Placed in the Boston Pilot. Vol. II*. Boston: New England Historic Genealogical Society, 1991.

Harris, Ruth-Ann and B. Emer O'Keefe, eds. *The Search for Missing Friends: Irish Immigrant Advertisements Placed in the Boston Pilot. Vol. III*. Boston: New England Historic Genealogical Society, 1993.

Harris, Ruth-Ann and B. Emer O'Keefe, eds. *The Search for Missing Friends: Irish Immigrant Advertisements Placed in the Boston Pilot. Vol. IV: 1857-1860*. Boston: New England Historic Genealogical Society, 1995.

Harris, Ruth-Ann and Donald M. Jacobs, eds. *The Search for Missing Friends: Irish Immigrant Advertisements Placed in the Boston Pilot. Vol. I: 1831-1850*. Boston: New England Historic Genealogical Society, 1989.

Heald, Sarah. H. *Report on the Biographical Research for the Brandywine Manufacturers' Sunday School*. Eleutherian Mills-Hagley Foundation Research Report,1984.

Henry, Allan J. ed. and comp. *The Life of Alexis Irenee duPont*. Philadelphia: William F. Fell Co., 1945.

Henry, Allen J., ed. and comp. *Francis Gurney duPont: A Memoir.* 2 vols. Philadelphia: William F. Fell Co., 1951.

Hewett, Janet B., ed. *The Roster of Union Soldiers 1861-1865*. Wilmington, North Carolina: Broadfoot Publishing Co., 1998.

Higham, John. *Strangers in the Land: Patterns of American Nativism 1860-1925*. New York: Atheneum, 1977.

Hoffecker, Carol E. *Delaware in the War of 1812.* Bachelor's Thesis, University of Delaware, 1960.

Hoffecker, Carol E. *Wilmington, Delaware: Portrait of an Industrial City, 1830-1910.* Charlottsville: University of Virginia Press for the Eleutherian Mills-Hagley Foundation, 1974.

Holland, Dorothy Garesché. *The Garesché, De Bauduy, and Des Chapelles Families: History and Genealogy.* Saint Louis: Privately printed by the Schneider Print. Co., 1963.

Hoseth, Angela, Wade P. Catts and Rebecca Tinsman. *Status, Landscape, and Tenancy at Mount Vernon Place: Final Archaelogical Investigations of the Jacob. B. Cazier Tenancy Site #2, State Route 896, New Casle County, Delaware.* Newark, Delaware: University of Delaware, 1994.

Isenberg, Nancy. *White Trash: The 400-Year Untold History of Class in America.* New York: Viking, 2016.

Jaffin, Jonathan H. *Medical Support for the American Expeditionary Forces in France During the First World War.* Master's Degree Thesis, Fort Leavenworth, Kansas: U. S. Army Command and Staff College, 1990.

James, Marquis. *Alfred I. DuPont: The Family Rebel.* Indianapolis: The Bobbs-Merrill Company, 1941.

Johnson, Roxanne Therese. *An Analysis of the Early Record Keeping in the DuPont Company 1800-1818.* New York: Garland Publishing Co., 1989.

Jose, Polly. *Doctor Pierre Didier and Early Industrial Medicine.* Eleutherian Mills-Hagley Foundation Research Report, 1966.

Kaufmann, K. Joy. *List of Explosions in Brandywine Powder Yards, 1802-1921.* Eleutherian Mills-Hagley Foundation Research Report, 1981.

Knobel, Dale T. *Paddy and the Republic: Ethnicity and Nationality in Antebellum America.* Middletown, Connecticut: Wesleyan University Press, 1986.

Kraft, Barbara S. *The Peace Ship: Henry Ford's Pacifist Adventure in the First World War.* New York: Macmillan Publishing Co., Inc., 1978.

Kraut, Alan M. The *Huddled Masses: The Immigrant in American Society, 1880-1921.* Wheeling, Illinois: Harlan Davidson Inc., 1982.

Lancour, Harold. *A Bibliography of Ship Passenger Lists 1538-1825: Being a Guide to Published Lists of Early Immigrants to North America.* 3rd ed. New York: The New York Public Library, 1963.

Lane, Anne Kelly and David McMahon. P*eril in the Powder Mills: Gunpowder and Its*

Men. West Conshohocken, Pennsylvania: Infinity Publishing, 2004.

Laxton, Edward. *The Famine Ships: The Irish Exodus to America, 1846-1851*. London: Bloomsbury Publishing, 1996.

Lenhart, Martha K., ed. *Medical Aspects of Chemical Warfare*. Washington, D.C.: GPO, 2008.

Lewis, William D. *A Delaware Chronology 1524-1946* (Unknown Publisher), 1947.

Linn, Mott. *The E.I. duPont de Nemours and Company's Housing for Its Workers*. Senior Undergraduate Thesis, University of Delaware, 1982.

Longworth, Joyce Kettaneh and Marjorie Gregory McNinch. *The Church of Saint Joseph on the Brandywine: 1841-1994*. Wilmington, Delaware: Saint Joseph's on the Brandywine, 1995.

MacGregor, David. *Merchant Sailing Ships 1815-1850: Supremacy of Sail*. Annapolis: Naval Institute Press, 1984.

Mack, Tom. *Hidden History of Augusta*. Mt. Pleasant, South Carolina: Arcadia Publishing, 2015.

MacLaughlin, Jim and Sean Beattie, eds. *An Historical, Environmental and Cultural Atlas of County Donegal*. Cork: Cork University Press, 2013.

MacLaughlin, Jim, ed. *The Making of a Northern County*. Dublin: Four Courts Press, 2007.

MacLysaght, Edward. *Bibliography of Irish Family History*. Dublin: Irish Academic Press, 1982.

MacLysaght, Edward. *Irish Families*. Dublin: Hodges Figges & Co. Ltd., 1957.

MacLysaght, Edward. *The Surnames of Ireland*. Dublin: The Irish Academic Press Limited, 1991.

Marx, Robert F. *Shipwrecks of the Western Hemisphere 1492-1825*. New York: World Publishing Company, 1971.

McCarter, J. M. And B. F. Jackson. *Historical and Biographical Encyclopedia of Delaware*. Wilmington, Delaware: Aldine Publishing and Engraving Co., 1882.

McDermott, Donna. *E.I. duPont de Nemours and Company: The Treatment of Widows Whose Husbands Were Killed in the Powder Mill Explosions 1815-1880*. Seminar Paper, University of Delaware, 1980.

McGlinchey, Charles. *The Last of the Name*. Dublin: Arlen House, 2015.

McWilliams, Patrick. *Index to Ordnance Survey Memoirs of Ireland Series People and Places*. Dublin: The Institute of Irish Studies, 2002.

Medical Department, U.S. Army. Field Operations, *The Medical Department of the United States Army in the World War, VIII*. Washington, D.C.: GPO, 1925.

Milgram, Joseph B. Jr., and Norman P. Gentieu. "George Washington Rains—Gunpowdermaker of the Confederacy." Presentation at the ACS Civil War Association Symposium, Chicago, Illinois, September, 1961.

Miller, Kerby. *Emigrants and Exiles: Ireland and the Irish Exodus to North America*. New York: Oxford University Press, 1985.

Mitchell, Brian. *A Guide to Irish Parish Registers*. Baltimore: Genealogical Publishing Co., Inc., 1988.

Mitchell, Brian. *Finding Your Irish Ancestors: Unique Aspects of Irish Genealogy*. Baltimore: Clearfield Company, Inc., 2001.

Mitchell, Brian. *Irish Emigration Lists 1803-1806*. Baltimore: Genealogical Publishing Co., 1995.

Mitchell, Brian. *Irish Emigration Lists 1833-1839*. Baltimore: Genealogical Publishing Co., 1989.

Mitchell, Brian. *Irish Passenger Lists 1847-1871*. Baltimore: Genealogical Publishing Co., 1988.

Moffett, Cleveland. "Life and Work in the Powder-Mills." *McClure's Magazine*, June 1895.

Montgomery, Elizabeth. *Reminiscences of Wilmington in Familiar Village Tales, Ancient and New*. Philadelphia: T. K. Collins Jr., 1851.

Morgan, Michael. *Civil War Delaware: The First State Divided*. Charleston: The History Press, 2012.

Morison, Samuel Eliot, Henry Steele Commager and William E. Leuchtenburg. *The Growth of the American Republic, Seventh Edition*. New York: Oxford University Press, 1980.

Moseley, Leonard. *Blood Relations: The Rise and Fall of the duPonts of Delaware*. New York: Atheneum, 1980.

Mulrooney, Margaret M. *Black Powder, White Lace: The du Pont Irish and Cultural Identity in Nineteenth-Century America*. Hanover, New Hampshire: University Press of New England, 2002.

Murphy, Eileen M. and William J. Ralston, eds. *Fermanagh: History and Society*. Dublin: Geography Publications, 2004.

Nathan, Col. Sir Frederick L. 'The Royal Gunpowder Factory, Waltham Abbey,' in VIIth International Congress of Applied Chemistry by its Explosives Section, The Rise and Progress of the British Explosives Industry, E. A. Brayley Hodgetts, ed. London: Whittaker and Co., 1909.

Neafsey, Edward. *Surnames of Ireland*. Kansas City: Irish Genealogical Foundation, 2001.

Niles, Hezekiah. "Niles Weekly Register," Vol. IX, 1815-16.

Nolan, Willliam, Liam Ronayne, and Mairead Dunlevy, eds. *Donegal: History & Society: Interdisciplinary Essays on the History of an Irish County*. Dublin: Geography Publications, 1995.

O'Cleirigh, Nellie. *Hardship & High Living: Irish Women's Lives 1808-1923*. Dublin: Portobello Press, 2003.

O'Donnell, Vincent, ed. *O'Donnells of Tir Chonaill, 2nd Ed*. County Donegal, Ireland: O'Donnell Clan Association, 2000.

O'Grada, Cormac. *Black '47 and Beyond: The Great Irish Famine*. Princeton: Princeton University Press, 1999.

O'Keefe, B. Emer, ed. *The Search for Missing Friends: Irish Immigrant Advertisements Placed in the Boston Pilot, Vol. V: 1861-1865*. Boston: New England Historical Genealogical Society, 1996.

O'Laughlin, Michael C. *The Families of County Donegal Ireland, Vol. VIII of the Book of Irish Families, Great & Small*. Kansas City: Irish Genealogical Foundation, 2001.

Patterson, Edward M. Gunpowder *Terminology & The Incorporation Process in the Manufacture of Gunpowder and the History of the Associated Explosions*. Faversham, England: The Faversham Society, 1986.

Peden, Henry C., Jr. *The Delaware Militia in the War of 1812*. Lewes, Delaware: Colonial Roots, 2003.

Percival, Arthur. *The Faversham Gunpowder Industry*. Faversham: The Faversham Society, 1967.

Persico, Joseph. *Eleventh Month, Eleventh Day, Eleventh Hour: Armistice Day, 1918: World War I and its Violent Climax*. New York: Random House, 2005.

Peterman, Thomas J. *Catholics in Early U.S. Delmarva*. Warminster, Pennsylvania:

Cooke Publishing Co., 2006.

Pogue, Forrest C. *George C. Marshall: Education of a General, 1880-1939.* New York: Viking Press, 1963.

Pryor, Glenn H. *Worker's Lives at the DuPont Powder Mills, 1877-1912.* Master's Thesis, University of Delaware, 1977.

Reamy, Bill and Martha Reamy. *Genealogical Abstracts from Biographical and Genealogical History of the State of Delaware, 2 vols.* Westminster, Maryland: Heritage Books, 2007.

Reed, Thomas, W. Andrew McKay and Anthony Wade. *Untying the Political Knot: Delaware During the War Between the States.* Wilmington, North Carolina: Broadfoot Publishing Co., 2001.

Reilly, Ciaran, ed. *The Famine Irish: Emigration and the Great Hunger.* Dublin: The History Press, 2016.

Richards, Mary Fallon and John C. Richards. *Marriages from the Delaware Gazette 1854-59, 1861-64.* Camden, Maine: Picton Press, 1996.

Roland, Alex, W. Jeffrey Bolster, and Alexander Keyssar. T*he Way of the Ship: America's Maritime History Reenvisioned, 1600-2000.* New York: John Wiley & Sons, Inc., 2008.

Roll, David L. *George Marshall: Defender of the Republic.* New York: Dutton Caliber, 2019.

Rosenberg, Charles E. *The Cholera Years: The United States in 1832, 1849, and 1866.* Chicago: The University of Chicago Press, 1962.

Rumm, John Charles. *Mutual Interests: Managers and Workers at the Dupont Company, 1802-1915. (Volumes I and II).* Doctoral Dissertation, University of Delaware, 1989.

Runk, J. M. & Co. *Biographical and Genealogical History of the the State of Delaware.* Chambersburg, Pennsylvania: J. M Runk & Co., 1899.

Ryan, James G. *Sources for Irish Family History: A Listing of Books and Articles on the History of Irish Families.* Dublin: Flyleaf Press, 2001.

Ryan, James. *Irish Records: Sources for Family and Local History.* Lehi, Utah: Ancestry.com, 1997.

Scharf, J. Thomas. *History of Delaware: 1609-1888.* Philadelphia: L. J. Richards & Co., 1888.

Schlegel, Donald M. *Passengers from Ireland: Lists of Passengers Arriving at American Ports Between 1811 and 1817.* Baltimore: Genealogical Publishing Co., Inc., 1980.

Bibliography

Shay, Michael E. *A Grateful Heart: The History of a World War I Field Hospital*. Westport, Connecticut: Greenwood Press, 2002.

Silliman, Charles A. *The Episcopal Church in Delaware, 1785-1954*. Wilmington, Delaware: The Protestant Episcopal Church in the Diocese of Delaware, 1982.

Silliman, Charles A. *The Story of Christ Church Christiana Hundred and its People*. Wilmington, Delaware: Hambleton Company, 1960.

Sisson, William. *A Mill Village on the Brandywine: Henry Clay Village During the Nineteenth Century*. Eleutherian Mills-Hagley Foundation Research Report, 1980.

Smith, Francis Montagu. *A Handbook of the Manufacture and Proof of Gunpowder, as Carried on at the Royal Gunpowder Factory, Waltham Abbey*. London: Superintendent of Her Majesty's Stationery Office, 1870.

Smith, Hilda Leto. Jennie: *My Mother*. New London, Pennsylvania: Slipstream Press, 1996.

Soukup, Nancy Hamlin. *Women's Roles in the Du Pont Powder Mills in 1870*. Course Paper, University of Delaware, 1979.

Stapleton, Darwin H. *The Transfer of Early Industrial Technologies to America*. American Philosophical Society Memoirs, 177. Philadelphia: American Philosophical Society, 1987.

Tepper, Michael, ed. *New Immigrants*. Baltimore: Genealogical Publishing Co., Inc., 2009.

Tepper, Michael, ed. *New World Immigrants*. Baltimore: Genealogical Publishing Co., Inc., 1980.

Tepper, Michael, ed. *Passenger Arrivals at the Port of Philadelphia 1800-1819*. Baltimore: Genealogical Publishing Co., Inc., 1986.

Thomas, Richard. *The Explosions at the Royal Gunpowder Mills*. Waltham Abbey: Royal Gunpowder Mills, 2013.

Thompson, Priscilla M. *Arriving in Delaware: The Italian-American Experience*. Wilmington, Delaware: The History Store and Italo-Americans United, 1989.

Tobias, Ronald B. *Behemoth: The History of the Elephant in America*. New York: Harper Perennial, 2013.

Traxel, David. *Crusader Nation: The United States in Peace and the Great War, 1898-1920*. New York: Alfred A. Knopf, 2006.

Trustees of the Poor, New Castle County. *Emigrants Who Landed in New Castle County for the Years 1831-1841*.

Tyler, James B., III. *Paternalism in Pursuit of the Doctrine of Success: Eleuthere duPont and the DuPont Labor System, 1802-1834*. Bachelor's Thesis, Trinity College, 1969.

Uminowicz, Glenn. *Earnings and Terms of Service: Hagley Powdermen in 1850*. Seminar Paper, University of Delaware, 1979.

Union Army, The. Madison, Wisconsin: Federal Publishing Company, 1908.

Vallandigham, J. L. Et al. *History of Pencader Presbyterian Church: Historical Addresses Delivered on the Occasion of the Celebration of the 70th Anniversary of The Woman's Missionary Society of Pencader Presbyterian Church*. Glasgow, Delaware: Pencader Presbyterian Church, 1899.

Van Gelder, Arthur Pone, and Hugo Schlatter. *History of the Explosives Industry in America*. New York: Columbia University Press, 1927.

Wall, Joseph Frazier. *Alfred I. Du Pont: The Man and His Family*. New York: Oxford University Press, 1990.

Walls, Marie Donahue. *Campbell and Haggerty History*. Unpublished family history, 2007.

Walls, Marie Donahue. *Donahue*. Unpublished family history, 2004.

Wawro, Geoffrey. *Sons of Freedom: The Forgotten American Soldiers Who Defeated Germany in World War I*. New York: Basic Books, 2018.

Webb, Jenny and Anne Donaldson. *Ballincollig Royal Gunpowder Mills: A Hidden History*. Dublin: Nonesuch Publishing, 2006.

Weissenbacher, Manfred. S*ources of Power: How Energy Forges Human History*. Santa Barbara, California: ABC-CLIO, 2009.

Welbon, Henry G. *A History of Pencader Presbyterian Church (Welsh in Origin) of Glasgow, Delaware*. Glasgow, Delaware: Henry G. Welbon), 1936.

Weldin, Hannah R. Record *Book of Deaths in Brandywine Hundred and Elsewhere, 1840-1909*.

Weslager, C. A. *Delaware's Forgotten River: The Story of the Christina*. Wilmington, Delaware: Hambleton Company, Incorporated, 1947.

Whelan, Bernadette. *American Government in Ireland, 1790-1913: A History of the US Consular Service*. Manchester: Manchester University Press, 2010.

Wholey, Heather A. "The Socioeconomic Landscape of Northern Delaware's Taverns and Innkeepers: The Blue Ball Tavern and Vicinity." *Northeast Historical Archaeology* 35,

Bibliography

Article 23 (2006).

Wiggins, Kennard R. Jr. *Delaware in World War I*. Charleston: History Press, 2015.

Wilkinson, Norman B. *The Brandywine Home Front During the Civil War*. Wilmington, Delaware: The Historical Society of Delaware, 1966.

Wilkinson, Norman B. *The du Ponts Come to America, 1797-1802*. Wilmington, Delaware: Eleutherian Mills-Hagley Foundation Research Report, 1955.

Williams, William Bradford. *History of the Manufacture of Explosives for the World War*. Chicago: University of Chicago Press, 1920.

Wilson, Emerson. *Forgotten Heroes of Delaware*. Cambridge: Deltos Publishing Co., 1969.

Winkler, John K. *The Dupont Dynasty*. New York: Reynal & Hitchcock, 1935.

Witcover, Jules. *Sabotage at Big Tom: Imperial Germany's Secret War In America—1914-1917*. Chapel Hill, North Carolina: Algonquin Books, 1989.

Works Progress Administration. *Inventory of the Tombstone Inscriptions in St. Joseph's Churchyard, Henry Clay, Delaware*, typescript copy. Wilmington, Delaware: The Historical Record Survey, Works Progress Administration, 1939.

Wright, F. Edward. *Marriages, Births, Deaths and Removals of New Castle County, Delaware*. Lewes, Delaware: Colonial Roots, 2009.

Zebly, Frank R. *The Churches of Delaware*. Wilmington, Delaware: Frank R. Zebley, 1947.

Notes

Abbreviations

DHS   Delaware Historical Society

FGD   Francis Gurney du Pont

HML   Hagley Museum and Library

ISTG   Immigrant Ships Transcription Guild

LDS   Church of Jesus Christ of Latter-Day Saints, Family History Library and Local Family History Centers

LMSS   Longwood Manuscripts at the Hagley Library

PL   Petit Ledger

WMSS   Winterthur Manuscripts at the Hagley Library

A Word from the Author

1. Joyce Kettaneh Longworth and Marjorie Gregory McNinch, *The Church of Saint Joseph on the Brandywine: 1841-1994*. (Wilmington, DE: Saint Joseph's on the Brandywine), 1995.

Introduction

1. Jefferson to James Madison, April 4, 1800, *The Papers of James Madison*, 1st ser., 17 vols. [1962–91], Vol. 17, 379.

2. Jefferson to Thomas Mann Randolph, January 17, 1799, *Jefferson Papers*, 34 vols., Vol. 30, 626.

3. Also called Wilmington Blue Rock, which gives its name to the Kansas City Royal's AA-class baseball farm team in Wilmington.

4. Bessie Gardner du Pont, *The Life of E.I. Du Pont*, VI, (Newark, Delaware: University of Delaware Press), 257-258.

5. Bessie Gardner du Pont, VII, 28.

Notes

6. Several DuPont family members and company executives over the years bemoaned the dips in income during war years. They said peace time, with its building and hunting needs, to which most of their powder went, was significantly more remunerative than war sales.

Prolog

1. William P. Brobson, *Diary of William P. Brobson* (Wilmington, Delaware: Historical Society of Delaware), 1977, 32.

Chapter One

1. Pronounced "mur WRA queen."

2. Thomas Gallagher, *Paddy's Lament, Ireland 1846-1847: Prelude to Hatred* (San Diego: Harcourt Brace Jovanovich), 1982, 121.

3. Ibid., 124-125.

4. Norman Wilkinson, T*he Duponts Come to America, 1797-1802.* (Wilmington: Hagley Museum and Library, hereinafter referred to as HML) Research Paper, 1955, 14.

5. Kerby Miller, *Emigrants and Exiles: Ireland and the Irish Exodus to America* (New York; Oxford University Press), 1985, 253.

6. Ibid., 255.

7. Edwin C. Guillet, *The Great Migration: The Atlantic Crossing by Sailing-ship Since 1770* (Toronto: Thomas Nelson and Sons), 1937, 110.

8. For a list by year of the ticket agents, see https://www.hagley.org/research/digital-exhibits/business-immigration.

9. Joseph A. L. Errigo, *History of St. Anthony's Church* (Wilmington, Delaware: Hambleton Co.), 1949, 29.

10. The others were potassium nitrate, called saltpeter, and sulfur.

11. *The Daily Advertiser and Patriot*, (Brandywine Springs, Delaware), August 13, 1839.

12. Dennis Clark, *Irish Relations*, The (East Brunswick, New Jersey: Associated University Presses, Inc.), 1982, 46.

13. Joshua Freeman, *Behemoth: A History of the Factory and the Making of the Modern World.* (New York: W.W. Norton & Company), 2018, 123.

14. Anthony Bluett, *Things Irish* (Dublin: Mercier Press), 1994, 145.

15. Terry Eagleton, *The Truth About the Irish* (New York: St. Martin's Press), 1999, 17.

16. Record Group V: Library Division, Subgroup D Manuscripts & Archives Department, Series 8, Box 659.

17. John Charles Rumm, *Mutual Interests: Managers and Workers at the Dupont Company, 1802-1915. (Volumes I and II)*. Unpublished Doctoral Dissertation, University of Delaware, 1989, 19.

18. Either the DuPont record or E.I. du Pont's letter to his father had an incorrect date for this explosion; his letter to his father indicated the explosion occurred on August 18.

19. The terms "gunpowder" and "black powder," although not exactly synonymous, will be used thusly herein. Powder for guns was a subset of black powder, the other being blasting powder used for mining, canal and road building, etc.

20. John K. Winkler, *The Dupont Dynasty* (New York: Reynal & Hitchcock), 1935, 65.

21. Ibid.

22. About $30,000 of relative price worth in today's money, using the Consumer Price Index (CPI). For an excellent discussion of the various types of year-to-year dollar conversions, see https://www.measuringworth.com/index.php.

23. *American Watchman and Delaware Republican*, (Wilmington, Delaware), October 23, 1811.

24. Rumm, 17. See also Arthur Pine Van Gelder, and Hugo Schlatter. *History of the Explosives Industry in America* (New York: Columbia University Press), 1927, 15; and Oscar Guttman. *The Manufacture of Explosives*. 2 vols. (London: Whitaker and Co.) 1895.

25. Rumm, 17.

26. Ibid. Potsmen attended the powder charges that went into the pounding mills and the pounding mill machinery. Hence "pots" for the mortar pots in those mills, into which the powder composition went. Since the factory started using roll mills instead of the much more dangerous pounding mills in 1829, potsmen became powdermen, per email from Lucas Clawson, Hagley Historian and Archivist, December 10, 2019.

27. The transition from the older technology of the pounding mill to the newer (and English-created) roll mill was not the only instance when E.I. resisted an English powder-making invention. He never adopted the drencher as a safety device; in the English mills, there would be a tank of water positioned above an incorporating mill, capable

of being tipped by an explosion, thus extinguishing the flame. The mechanism could be created wherein a shaft ran from mill to mill connecting water tanks so that if one mill went up, the other mills would also be awash and, by this method, more explosions could be avoided. See Edward M. Patterson, Gunpowder Terminology & The Incorporation Process in the Manufacture of Gunpowder and the History of the Associated Explosions (Faversham, Kent, England: The Faversham Society), 1986, 2. The result of having the water tanks above the mills would not always prove to be beneficial. The mills at Waltham Abbey, England, were outfitted with such tanks after a March, 1850, explosion. Nine years later, "the weight of the tank-roof gave a lateral direction to the wave of explosion, consequently causing immense damage to the rest of the factory and to the surrounding neighborhood." See Col. Sir Frederick L. Nathan, 'The Royal Gunpowder Factory, Waltham Abbey,' in VIIth International Congress of Applied Chemistry by its Explosives Section, in The Rise and Progress of the British Explosives Industry, E.A. Brayley Hodgetts, ed. (London: Whittaker and Co.), 1909, 356. When Lammot DuPont visited the Waltham Abbey mills in 1858, he drew detailed pictures of the dousing apparatus but the company did not use it on the Brandywine.

28. Richard Thomas, *The Explosions at the Royal Gunpowder Mills* (Waltham Abbey: Royal Gunpowder Mills), 2013, 11.

29. *Carlisle Weekly Herald*, (Carlisle, Pennsylvania), June 15, 1815, http://newspapers.com, retrieved June 2, 2018.

30. In original Irish, O'Dochartaigh, a clan that served as overlords of Inishowen until 1609. See Godfrey F. Duffy, *Tracing Your Donegal Ancestors* (Dublin: Flyleaf Press), 1996.

31. Pronounced "jar braHAIR dawn bas fess arr harr ur an DOCtursh."

32. Mary Murray Delaney, *Of Irish Ways* (New York: Kilkenny Press), 1985, 169.

33. HML, LMSS, Group 5, E.I. du Pont de Nemours & Co., Series C, Special Papers, Documents, Memoirs, Drawings (1782-1881), Box 49, file Special: Mills and Magazines, Production, Supplies, Taxes, Employees 1804-1875.

34. A petit ledger was a record the DuPont Company used to track workers' pay and disbursements.

35. Delaware Public Archives Commission, Delaware Archives, Vol. 5, (Dover, DE: Public Archives Commission), 550 at https://www.google.com/books/edition/Delaware_Archives/IiRSAQAAMAAJ?hl=en&gbpv=1&dq=%2219+guns+complete+with+straps%22&pg=PA550&printsec=frontcover, 550, retrieved June 2, 2018.

36. If a person was illiterate and could not write their name, this was the format: "Richard X Dougherty," or "Richard X his mark Dougherty," the "X" signifying the signature; the name would have been written by someone else. Sometimes immigrants would sign with an 'X' even though they could write their names; often they were too deferential to contradict the registrar who had assumed they couldn't.

37. Http://www.lalley.com/index.asp?marri.htm, retrieved June 2, 2018.

38. Henry C. Peden, Jr. *The Delaware Militia in the War of 1812* (Lewes, DE: Colonial Roots), 2003, 278.

39. *Delaware Archives*, Vol. 4, (Wilmington: Starr Publishing) 1916, 418.

40. Peden, 334.

Chapter Two

1. Michael Tepper ed., *Passenger Arrivals at the Port of Philadelphia 1800-1819* (Baltimore: Genealogical Publishing Co., Inc.), 1986.

2. Relative income worth of $24,500 in today's money. See https://www.measuringworth.com/index.php.

3. The term used by the *Mechanic's Gazette and Merchants Daily Advertiser*, of Baltimore, MD in their June 19, 1815, issue, gleaned from that day's version of a wire service, was that "she was ready to be confined."

4. HML, Petit Ledger, Vol. 962, 26.

5. Bluett, 48-55.

6. HML, Petit Ledger, Vol. 962, 31, 249. The terms used in the ledgers were "by," representing credits, and "to," meaning debits. For example, an entry that said "By boarding hands" would have indicated a credit, or payment, to the widow's account.

7. Dona McDermott, *E.I. duPont de Nemours and Company: The Treatment of Widows Whose Husbands Were Killed in the Powder Mill Explosions 1815-1880*. Seminar Paper, University of Delaware, 1980, 3.

8. HML, Petit Ledger, Vol. 961, 35. A typewritten note at the Hagley Library is labeled "1815"; it is in the files of Dick Scott, a researcher who studied powder mill explosions. The note says Alexander Miller (he meant Andrew) was the father of Isabella Miller Brown and grandfather of Samuel B. Brown, of whom we learn more in a future chapter. For the Dick Scott collection, see HML, Accession 1645, Box 10.

9. Polly Jose, *Doctor Pierre Didier and Early Industrial Medicine*, HML Research Paper, 1966. Accession 1645, Box 3, No. 67.

10. Ibid, 11.

11. Either Patrick's tombstone or the deponents DuPont and Ritchie had their dates incorrect. The tombstone gives the date of death as June 11, while DuPont and Ritchie say they sat with Patrick on the 13th.

Notes

12. Https://www.lalley.com, retrieved June 3, 2018.

13. Margaret Mulrooney, *Black Powder, White Lace:The duPont Irish and Cultural Identity 19th-Century America* (Hanover, NH:The University Press of New England), 2002, 96. Mulrooney cites "Expense Account Book (1806-1809)", Accession 146, Box 10, File 149, Item 4; "Comtes avec les ouvriers (1802-1809," Accession 146, Box 9, File 148, Item 8.

14. Mulrooney, 150.

15. In the thirty-two counties of Ireland, there are more than 62,000 townlands, the smallest of the several land divisions there. The island is also divided into multiple civil and religious parishes; baronies are another division of the country, rarely used nowadays.

16. HML, Incoming Correspondence, Accession 500, Series I, Part I, Series B, Box 71.

17. *American Watchman*, (Wilmington, Delaware), June 10, 1815.

18. "Memoranda from rough draft of letter in hand writing of EIDP to Mdm. De Pusy." HML, LMSS, Group 5, Series C, Box 52.

19. Rumm, 102.

20. HML, Typewritten transcription of Lammot du Pont, *Annual Summary of DuPont Company Activity, 1803-1856*, taken from Lammot du Pont, *Powder Made by E.I. du Pont de Nemours and Company, 1803-1856*, Lammot du Pont Papers, Accession 384, Series B, Box 33, Folder 48-27.

21. This was the name given to the original 1802 factory. Over time, additional properties would be added, each with its own name. Eventually, there would be four distinct mills built on contiguous property.

22. HML, *Fabrique de Poudre-Livre des Ouvriers: 1804*, I-9-103, Longwood Lib. See also Accession 146, Box 10, Folder 2, File 150; Sums paid to hands, Accession 146, Box 9, Folder 149, File 5; and Accession 500, No. 1694 PL-2, Books A and B., 19.

23. Https://en.wikipedia.org/wiki/Treasury_Note_(19th_century), Retrieved November 14, 2019.

24. St. Peter's Cathedral Marriage Records, #36, Family History Center microfilm, Church of Jesus Christ of Latter Day Saints.

25. F.G. du Pont, *Record of Explosions, 1815-1902*, HML, LMSS, Group 5, Series C, Box 52, 7; this one of Francis Gurney du Pont's writings hereinafter referred to as FGD.

26. HML, Petit Ledger, Vol. 963, 1818, 26, 27, 94.

27. Harold Bell Hancock, *Industrial Worker Along the Brandywine, 1800-1840*. HML Research Paper, Accession 1645, 1956, 133.

28. *Papers Relative to the Men Destroyed in 1818*, HML, Accession 146, Box 6, File 76.

29. Mulrooney, 178.

30. Mulrooney, 78.

31. *List of Goods and Chattels of Hugh Brady taken this 24th of March 1818*, HML, Accession 146, Box 4, File 76.

32. Mulrooney, 67.

33. HML, Petit Ledger, Vol. 963, 184.

34. HML, Petit Ledger, Vol. 962, 1815-1817, 40.

35. Ibid., 314.

36. HML, Petit Ledger, Vol. 963, 1818, 3.

37. Chapbooks were cheap, paper-covered booklets that got the name from the fact that they were sold by chapmen, itinerant hawkers in 18th-century England.

38. *Delaware Genealogical Society Journal*. Vol. 7, No. 1, 30; and No. 2, 54. The original BMSS records are available at HML.

39. *Premium Books 1826-1873*. HML, Accession 389, Box 3, Folder 14.

40. Mrs. McLaughlin's letter could not be found in the DuPont Company archives at the Hagley Library.

41. Note the different spelling from the Dupont Company records.

42. "Your Obedient Servant," a phrase often found in letters during this time.

43. William Johnston of Philadelphia, to Victor du Pont, March 12, 1828. HML, Accession 500, Series I, Part I, Series B, Box 161.

44. Women named Nancy were often referred to as "Ann."

45. Office Copy of Letter to Miss [Ann] McLaughlin. HML, WMSS, Group 4, Series D, Box 11, Outfile, Item #W4-1586-; see also Petit Ledger, Vol. 963, 1818, 20, 341.

Chapter Three

1. *List of Goods & Chattels of John Dunnery taken this 24th of March 1818*. HML, Accession 146, Box 4, File 76.

2. St. Peter's Cathedral Marriage Records, #36, Family History Center microfilm, Church of Jesus Christ of Latter Day Saints.

3. HML, Petit Ledger, Vol. 962, 1815-1817, 207, 385.

4. HML, *Labor 3.2.18.*, Accession 500, Series I, Part II, Series N (4-7), Box 506, File 9.

5. HML, E.I. du Pont to D. P. Brown, Esq., April 15, 1819, Accession 146, Eleuthera Bradford Collection, Box 3, File 30, Copies of Letters, 1810-1834.

6. HML, Petit Ledger, Vol. 962, 1815-1817, p.232; *List of Goods & Chattel of Hugh McCalegue taken this 24th of March 1818*. HML, Accession 146, Box 4, File 76; typewritten transcription of Lammot du Pont, *Annual Summary of DuPont Company Activity, 1803-1856.*

7. This is just one example of the generosity of the men and their families to others in the community. In 1878, they and the company would give more than $113 to Mrs. Gordon, whose husband, powderman Michael, died suddenly, from apparently natural causes. The family would have been destitute without the donations. See Petit Ledger, Accession 500, No. 1000, 1878, 488.

8. Although single, the literate Mooney was a believer in education for children. Perhaps in Ireland he would have studied in a so called "hedge school," so named because it was illegal in Ireland at times to teach Catholics; in 1824, for example, of the 7,600 schools taught by lay Catholics, most of them had to be hidden away behind hedges. See Delaney, 101.

9. HML, Petit Ledger, Vol. 963, 1818, 22, 341.

10. He had died in the same Philadelphia hotel as his brother, Victor, in 1834.

11. Michael Tepper, ed., *Passenger Arrivals at the Port of Philadelphia 1800-1819* (Baltimore: Genealogical Publishing Co., Inc.), 1986. Annagh is pronounced "AN na." Cavan is pronounced "KAV en."

12. Email from Nona Kelly Smith to the author, March 28, 2019.

13. HML, Petit Ledger, Vol. 963, 1818, 44.

14. Donald M. Schlegel, *Passengers from Ireland: Lists of Passengers Arriving at American Ports Between 1811 and 1817* (Baltimore: Genealogical Publishing Co., Inc.) 1980; Michael Tepper, ed. New World Immigrants (Baltimore: Genealogical Publishing Co., Inc), 1980.

15. Schlegel, 39; Edward MacLysaght. *The Surnames of Ireland* (Dublin: The Irish Academic Press Limited), 1991.

16. HML, Petit Ledger, Vol. 963, 1818, 29.

17. HML, Petit Ledger, Vol. 962, 1815-1817, 96, 283; Vol. 963, 1818, 28.

18. HML, Petit Ledger, Vol. 962, 1815-1817, 327; Vol. 963, 1818, 31.

19. Typewritten transcription of Lammot du Pont, *Annual Summary of DuPont Company Activity, 1803-1856.*

20. Ibid, 301.

21. Schlegel, 121.

22. Samuel Lewis, A Topographical Dictionary of Ireland (London: Samuel Lewis), 1837.

23. Peter L. Bernstein, *Wedding of the Waters: The Erie Canal and the Making of a Great Nation* (New York: W. W. Norton & Company), 2005, 219.

24. Ibid, 231.

25. Rumm, 50

26. Hancock, The Industrial Worker Along the Brandywine 1800-1840, 55

27. Ibid., 56.

28. Ibid. Hancock cites "Theft of Brass Stamper by Joseph Baughman," I-12-106, "Papers Relative to Thieves, 1812-1813," File 123, and Dupont letter books, 1809-1810, X (red backed and typewritten MS), 9-33, 105-155, Longwood Library; Dupont Company Letter Books, 1808-1810, 103-104,128, 220; 1810-1813, 155 *Life of E.I. du Pont*, VIII, 138; *Munns vs. du Pont de Nemours and Company, Archives of Useful Knowledge*, II (1812), 66-75; Museum, October 22, 1808, 3.

29. Ibid., Hancock, Cites *The Affair of Thomas Ewell, 1811-1812*, I-14-167, *The Ewell Controversy*, I-3-165, and *Letters and Papers on the lawsuit of du Pont vs. Baughman, 1809*, I-12-107 Longwood Library; Bessie Gardner du Pont, Life of E.I. du Pont, VIII, 134-135.

30. Peter B. Petersen, *Effective Safety Management at du Pont: A Historical Perspective (1802-1914)*. Proceedings of the Twenty-Third Annual Meeting of the Eastern Academy of Management, 1986. HML, Accession 1645, Research Reports, Hagley ID MS1645_222, Box 7, 255-56.

31. *Newport Mercury*, (Newport, Rhode Island) March 28, 1818. http://www.newspa-

Notes

pers.com, retrieved June 2, 2018.

32. *Caledonian Mercury*, (Edinburgh, Scotland) May 18, 1818, Page 4, http://www.newspapers.com, retrieved June 2, 2018.

33. *American Watchman*, (Wilmington, Delaware) April 11, 1818.

34. *Trenton Federalist*, May 18, 1818, http://www.newspapers.com, retrieved June 2, 2018.

35. *National Messenger*, (Georgetown, Washington, D. C.) http://www.newspapers.com, retrieved June 2, 2018.

36. FGD, 9.

37. Rumm, p. 45. Cites Francis Gurney duPont, *History of Explosions*, FGDP, 1:47-54; Lammot duPont, *Rough Notes on Accidents*, entry for 1818, both at HML.

38. Joseph Frazier Wall, *Alfred I. Du Pont: The Man and His Family* (New York: Oxford University Press), 1990, 104.

39. Lammot du Pont, *Powder Made*, entries for 1808, 1837. HML, Accession 384, Box 33, Lammot duPont Papers, Series B, Technical Papers. File Labeled "Powder Made by E.I. duPont & Co., 1803-1856.

40. Https://www.atlasobscura.com/foods/switchel-new-england, retrieved January 7, 2020.

41. Pronounced "ish ke be HEH."

42. Delaney, citing 17th century Irish poet Richard Stanhurst, 85

43. Pronounced "put-CHEEN."

44. Eagleton, 13.

Chapter Four

1. Lammot du Pont, Powder Made, for the year 1822.

2. According to one newspaper, Chang had fallen in love with a woman from Wilmington. "She likes Chang well enough, but objects to marrying both." Yunte Huang. *Inseparable: The Original Siamese Twins and Their Rendezvous with American History*. (New York: Liveright Publishing Company), 2018, 212.

3. Huang, 42.

4. HML, Accession 500, Series I, Part I, Series B, Box 416; the cost for sending a child six years of age and under across the Atlantic was half the adult rate, which was the rate for anyone over that age.

5. Mulrooney, 58.

6. Mulrooney, 80.

7. Mulrooney, 232n65.

8. It is not known how or when the trio of Toys made their way to Canada from Moville, County Donegal, Ireland. "Moville-The name Maigh Bhile, from which derives Moville, signifies "the plain of the sacred tree." The word bhile, 'a sacred tree,' is usually only found in names of pre-christian religious sites. It is therefore probable that Maigh Bhile was originally the name of a pagan religious site." See Willliam Nolan, Liam Ronayne, and Mairead Dunlevy, eds. *Donegal: History & Society: Interdisciplinary Essays on the History of an Irish County* (Dublin: Geography Publications), 1995, 163.

9. Https://archive.org/details/passengerlistsof0025unit, Retrieved January 8, 2020; also Reese Robinson's "Toy" website, http://brandywinebanks.rhysr.com/the-schooner-mary-ann/#comments [private web site], retrieved January 13, 2020.

10. Https://brandywinebanks.com, retrieved January 13, 2020.

11. HML, Petit Ledger 964, p. 108. The 1820 U.S. Census shows that there were one male under ten years of age, which would have been James (assuming the census taker visited in May or June); five males ages 16-26, three males ages 26-45, three females under ten, one female age 16-26, and six unnaturalized, five in manufacturing. The five in manufacturing would have included Daniel as well as Owen, and three other powder workers.

12. HML, Petit Ledger 965, 1823-1824, 47.

13. HML, Petit Ledger 967, 1829-1832, 69.

14. Male teachers instructed the boys in the BMSS, while the girls had female instructors.

15. HML, Accession 389, Box 3, Folder 14, Premium Books.

16. Https://babel.hathitrust.org/cgi/pt?id=uc1.31175035133787&view=1up&seq=15, retrieved June 4, 2018.

17. HML, Accession 389, Box 3, Folder 14, *Premium Book*s.

18. DHS, Copy of Eugene I. Toy's T*oy Family Tree.*

Notes

19. Https://brandywinebanks.com/?s=banks, retrieved January 8, 2020.

20. *Daily Republican*, (Wilmington, Del.), 08 Aug. 1879. Chronicling America: Historic American Newspapers. Lib. of Congress. <https://chroniclingamerica.loc.gov/lccn/sn84038114/1879-08-08/ed-1/seq-4/>, retrieved January 9, 2020.

21. HML, Irénée DuPont (II) Papers, Accession 228, Series J, General Office Files, File F-339, Toy Estate, Box 118; https://www.towerhill.org/about/history, retrieved February 4, 2020.

22. *National Gazette*, (Philadelphia, Pennsylvania) August 28, 1832, http://www.newspapers.com, retrieved June 3, 2018.

23. *Delaware Gazette,* June 23, 1834, Http://www.newspapers.com, retrieved June 2, 2018.

24. Rumm, 88.

25. Mulrooney, 26.

26. Https://www.measuringworth.com/index.php, retrieved January 11, 2020.

27. HML, Petit Ledger Vol. 968, 1833-1834, 305.

28. HML, Petit Ledger Vol. 967, 1832, 448.

29. *Delaware Gazette* and *American Watchman*, Sept. 29, 1835, http://www.newspapers.com, retrieved June 2, 2018.

30. HML, LMSS, Group 5, Series A, Correspondence IN file, (1816-1844), Margaret Green Wilson and Mary Green Elvin to E.I. DuPont de Nemours & Co., April 12, 1836.

31. Hancock, *Industrial Worker, 1800-1840*, p. 72, citing HML, DuPont Company Letter Book, 1834-1836, 110-112.

32. HML, Petit Ledger Vol. 971, 1840-1841, and Vol. 972, 1842-1844.

33. "Pedigree Resource File," database, *FamilySearch* (https://familysearch.org/ark:/61903/2:2:37DD-74R), entry for Joseph Michael /Borrell/, cites sources; "Spires George Family" file (2:2:2:MMDD-372), submitted 20 November 2014. Retrieved January 13, 2020.

34. Probably Rameau.

35. HML, Boarding Books, Nos. 1695, 1697, and 1698.

36. HML, Premium Books, Accession 389, Box 3, File 14.

37. Https://www.findagrave.com/memorial/94736966/george-w-borrell, retrieved January 13, 2020. See Alan Thaxter in this volume.
38. *Chester Times*, (Chester, Pennsylvania), January 13, 1914.

39. HML, Dick Scott collection, Accession 1645, Box 10, file labeled "1843."

40. Joyce Kettaneh Longworth and Marjorie Gregory McNinch, *The Church of Saint Joseph on the Brandywine: 1841-1994* (Wilmington, Delaware: Saint Joseph on the Brandywine), 1995.

41. LDS Film #1822513—Delaware, Wilmington Catholic Diocese, St. Joseph, 1847.

42. HML, Dupont Company to F.G. Smith, September 22, 1843, LMSS, Group 10, Series A, Papers of P. S. Dupont, Box 391, File 418-2. Typewritten Source: Manuscript Letter Book of E.I. DuPont de Nemours & Co. Sept. 5 1843-June 15, 1844

43. Ibid, Dupont Company to William Kemble.

Chapter Five

1. Delaney, 272.

2. Mulrooney, 84.

3. Delaware State Journal, (Wilmington, Delaware) July 26, 1844.

4. HML, Alfred DuPont to John Watson, Belfast, Ireland, November 20, 1846, Letterbook 1846, Accession 500, Vol. 798, 179.

5. Ibid.

6. *Daily Republican*. (Wilmington, Del.), 17 Nov. 1884. Chronicling America: Historic American Newspapers. Lib. of Congress. <http://chroniclingamerica.loc.gov/lccn/sn84038114/1884-11-17/ed-1/seq-4/>; also *Delaware Gazette and State Journal*. (Wilmington, Del.), 20 Nov. 1884. Chronicling America: Historic American Newspapers. Lib. of Congress. <http://chroniclingamerica.loc.gov/lccn/sn88053046/1884-11-20/ed-1/seq-1/, both retrieved June 2, 2018.

7. About 12% more.

8. Lammot du Pont, Powder Made, for the year 1847.

9. *Cecil Whig*, (Elkton, Maryland), April 17, 1847, http://www.newspapers.com, retrieved June 2, 2018.

Notes

10. *Prairie Du Chien Patriot* (Prairie Du Chien, Wisconsin), May 4,1847, http://www.newspapers.com, retrieved June 2, 2018.

11. *American and Commercial Daily Advertiser*, (Wilmington, Delaware), April 16, 1847, http://newspapers.com, retrieved June 2, 2018.

12. Thomas J. Peterman, *Catholics in Early U.S. Delmarva* (Warminster, PA: Cooke Publishing Co.), 2006, 195n216.

13. Pronounced "ba leen a MAL ard."

14. Pronounced "fer MAN ah"

15. J. M. Runk & Co., *Biographical and Genealogical History of the the State of Delaware*, (Chambersburg, PA: J. M Runk & Co.), 1899, 630. This was a rare case where a family had both a Mary and a Maria. Typically, the names Mary and Maria were interchangeable; a person baptized as Maria could then appear in records as Mary.

16. Mulrooney, 198.

17. Linda Daur, *Domestic Servants at Eleutherian Mills, 1821-1842*, Research Paper, HML, Accession 1645, Box 5, No. 110, 1979, 11.

18. HML, Alfred V. du Pont to James Campbell, June 13, 1843, Accession 1993, Group 7-Sons of E.I. duPont, Series A-Alfred V. duPont, Box 1-Outfile: 1803-1855, Out File:1812-1847.

19. FGD, 9.

20. HML, Sophie Madeleine DuPont to Samuel Francis DuPont, April 16, 1847.

21. Mulrooney, 105.

22. United States Census, 1850; https://familysearch.org/ark:/61903/3:1:S3HY-D199-VHJ?cc=1401638&wc=95RD-RM3%3A1031311801%2C1031562801%2C1031581501, retrieved January 21, 2020. As was the custom at the time, the children were born about every two years; their ages in the 1850 census, when Elizabeth had remarried, were in the following sequence: 15, 13, 11 (all girls), and 9, 7, 5 (all boys).

23. Mulrooney, 105.

24. HML, Petit Ledger 1016, 1894, 405. It should be noted that the annuity was changed in 1869, when the $100 per annum was given for only five years. However, the older annuitants continued to receive their $100 for life.

25. *Cecil Whig*, (Elkton, Maryland), April 17, 1847, http://www.newspapers.com, retrieved June 2, 2018.

26. In different iterations Houghton, Houtton, Houlton. He might have been related to Margaret Watson's second husband, Thomas Houlton.

27. Works Progress Administration, Headstone *Inscriptions for St. Joseph on the Brandywine Cemetery*, 1934.

28. *Republican Compiler*, (Gettysburg, Pennsylvania), April 19, 1847, http://www.gendisasters.com/delaware/20199/wilmington-de-du-pont-powder-works-explosion-apr-1847, retrieved June 2, 2018.

29. Janet B. Hewett, ed., *The Roster of Union Soldiers 1861-1865* (Wilmington, North Carolina: Broadfoot Publishing Co.), 1998, 333; J. Thomas Scharf. *History of Delaware: 1609-1888* (Philadelphia: L. J. Richards & Co.), 1888, Appendix, xxiii; email correspondence between author and Lisa Scaglione, descendant of Malcolm Baxter, June 1, 2, 2018.

30. *Evening Journal*. (Wilmington, Del.), 05 Feb. 1903. *Chronicling America: Historic American Newspapers*. Lib. of Congress. <http://chroniclingamerica.loc.gov/lccn/sn85042354/1903-02-05/ed-1/seq-4/>, retrieved June 2, 2018.

31. HML, A. & E. Baxter to Respected Mistress [Victorine], Nov. 23, 1863. Accession 389, Box 6, File 21.

32. HML, Accession 828, photocopy of letter John F. McNamara to Mister Jackson, from National Archives Record Group 109-War Department Collection of Confederate Records.

33. Pronounced "ah GORshtah mors."

34. On its 1848 spring voyage, the ship docked "near Wilmington," which meant New Castle, and forty migrants disembarked seeking work at the DuPont powder works. The remaining passengers boarded the coastal steamer *Rappahannock* to complete their voyage to Philadelphia. The city denied entry to the steamer at the South Street port, so Captain Williams unloaded his passengers at the Washington Street Wharf, part of Philadelphia County but not yet part of the city. See J. Matthew Gallman, *Receiving Erin's Children: Philadelphia, Liverpool, and the Irish Famine Migration, 1845-1855* (Chapel Hill: The University of North Carolina Press), 2000, 35.

35. HML, Andrew Craig to E.I. DuPont, January 9, 1847. Accession 500, E.I. du Pont de Nemours & Co. Series I, Part 1, Series B, General Correspondence, Cox & Shellenberger-Cray & Rood, Box 70.

36. Two years later, the ship was the center of a lawsuit. See Https://supreme.justia.com/cases/federal/us/48/595/, retrieved January 27, 2020.

37. HML, Accession 500, Series I, Part II, Series N—Labor, Box 506, File 12.

38. Https://www.immigrantships.net/v11/1800v11allenkerr18370517.html.

39. Mary Fallon Richards and John C. Richards, *Marriages from the Delaware Gazette 1854-59, 1861-64* (Camden, ME: Picton Press), 1996, Vol. 3, 146. This information can also be found in the DHS Surname Index.

40. Mulrooney, p. 58; Immigrant Ships Transcribers Guild (hereinafter referred to as ISTG) at https://www.immigrantships.net/v11/1800v11/allenkerr18370517.html; Family Search at https://www.familysearch.org/ark:/61903/3:1:S3HY-D199-NK3?i=21&cc=1401638; HML, Petit Ledgers, Vols. 971 through 975, 1840-1849.

41. HML, Accession 500/501, Papers of Charles I. DuPont & Co, Series A, #2—General Correspondence, File Robert McGarvey, 1847.

42. HML, Taylor Correspondence, September 13, 1848.

43. Mulrooney, 127.

44. HML, Petit Ledger, 1835-1836, Vol. 969, 398; "United States Census, 1850," database with images, *FamilySearch* (https://familysearch.org/ark:/61903/1:1:MH81-YGC : 4 April 2020), Bridgett Obryan, Christiana Hundred, New Castle, Delaware, United States; citing family 137, NARA microfilm publication M432 (Washington, D.C.: National Archives and Records Administration, n.d.).

45. HML, Accession 500, Series I, Part I, Series B, E.I. Dupont de Nemours Co., In Correspondence Box 289. Misspellings in the original.

46. HML, Petit Ledger, Vol. 975, 262.

Chapter Six

1. *Delaware State Journal*, February 8, 1850, http://www.newsppers.com, retrieved June 2, 2018.

2. HML, Petit Ledger, Vol. 975, Flyleaf 2, February 7, 1848.

3. Gallman, 33.

4. Technically, a black powder explosion is a deflagration, or a rapid burning, not a detonation. However, detonation is the more commonly used word and will be used hereinafter. Black powder is a low explosive, burning at subsonic speed as opposed to the supersonic speed of high explosives, such as dynamite and nitroglycerin.

5. FGD, p.59; Mulrooney, 223n47; DHS, *Blue Hen's Chicken*, (Wilmington, Delaware), Friday, March 12, 1852; Delaware Journal, (Wilmington, Delaware), March 12, 1852, March 16, 1852.

6. FGD, 60.

7. Brian Mitchell, *Irish Emigration Lists 1833-1839* (Baltimore: Genealogical Publishing Co., 1989), 98.

8. HML, Petit Ledger, Vol. 980, 1857, 242.

9. "United States Census, 1850," database with images, *FamilySearch* (https://familysearch.org/ark:/61903/1:1:MHDM-671 : 4 April 2020), James Mccafferty, Christiana Hundred, New Castle, Delaware, United States; citing family 444, NARA microfilm publication M432 (Washington, D.C.: National Archives and Records Administration, n.d.).

10. Samuel Francis was the only family member to favor the capital 'D' in his name.

11. *Journal of the ... Annual Convention, Diocese of Delaware*, Episcopal Church, Diocese of Delaware Convention, The Diocese, 1842-1853.

12. DHS, Brincklé Family Papers, *Diary of Rev. Samuel Brincklé*, 123.

13. *Evening Bulletin*, (Wilmington, Delaware), Thursday, June 1, 1854.

14. HML, Accession 384, Series B, Box 27, folder 42-2; http://digital.hagley.org/1854_Wilmington_Explosion.

15. According to *Harper's Weekly*, May 2, 1914, "it was duPont powder that won that battle"; however, because the article was somewhat negative toward the du Ponts, Vice President Colonel E. J. Buckner asked for and was granted a retraction of the article.

16. HML, Accession 501, Reminiscences of Dr. James A. Morgan, P.S. du Pont Office Collection, Accession 501, Series D, (27), 1913.

17. Lammot duPont, *Notes on Accidents in Powder Mills, 1859*, HML, Accession 384/27.

18. Ralph Assheton, comp., *History of Explosions on Which the American Table of Distances was Based, Including Other Explosions of Large Quantities of Explosives* (Wilmington: The Institute of Makers of Explosives), 1930, 312.

19. *Evening Bulletin*, (Philadelphia, Pennsylvania), June 1, 1854.

20. Ibid.

21. Ibid.

22. *The Sunday Star*, (Wilmington, Delaware), July 24, 1932.

23. *Evening Bulletin*, (Wilmington, Delaware), June 1, 1854. Emphasis added.

24. Ibid.

Notes

25. It is thought a record of the cost of all explosions was kept but was destroyed in the early 20th century in the general destruction of records at the DuPont Hall of Records.

26. HML, LMSS, Group 5, Series A Corr, In File, Box 14, 1854.

27. *Delaware State Journal*, (Wilmington, Delaware), June 9, 1854.

28. *Evening Star*, (Wilmington, Delaware), June 2, 1854.

29. HML, Accession 500, Series 1, Part I-Correspondence, M.D.W Loomis to E.I. du Pont de Nemours Company, July 28, 1854.

30. HML, Accession 263, Christ Church microfilm.

31. "Delaware, Wilmington Vital Records, 1847-1954," database with images, *FamilySearch* (https://familysearch.org/ark:/61903/1:1:QKD6-V8V2 : 13 March 2018), John Keys, 31 May 1854; citing Death, Wilmington, New Castle, Delaware, United States, Public Archives, Dover; FHL microfilm 2,188,029.

32. *Evening Journal* (Wilmington, Del.), 21 June 1893. Chronicling America: Historic American Newspapers. Lib. of Congress. <https://chroniclingamerica.loc.gov/lccn/sn85042354/1893-06-21/ed-1/seq-1/>, retrieved March 11, 2020.

33. HML, Acc 500, Series I, Part I, Series B, Box 424, Correspondence of Dr. De Forest Willard of 113 So. Sixteenth St, Philadelphia, dated Feb. 19, 1877.

34. HML, Accession 500, Series I, Part I, Series B, Box 424, Correspondence of Dr. De Forest Willard, Mar. 1, 1877.

35. *New York Times*, August 4, 1855, http://www.gendisasters.com/delaware/8958/wilmington-de-powder-mill-explosion-aug-1855, retrieved June 2, 2018. The article, in a later paragraph, said fourteen hundred pounds of powder exploded.

36. *Delaware State Reporter*, Tuesday, August 14, 1855, www.newspaperarchive.com, retrieved December 8, 2018.

37. HML, Accession 263, Christ Church microfilm.

38. Ibid.

39. FGD, 61.

40. Ibid.

41. HML, Dick Scott collection, Accession 1645, Box 10.

42. *Delaware State Reporter*, (Wilmington, Delaware), May 30, 1856.

43. There is some discrepancy as to the date of this fire. According to FGD, it happened on October 24, 1856. However, Alfred Victor was laid to rest on October 6, according to the *North American* newspaper in Philadelphia, Oct. 6, 1856, https://www.findagrave.com/memorial/58461365/alfred-victor-dupont, retrieved February 1, 2020.

44. FGD, 61.

45. This Greek deity was the personification of darkness and shadows.

46. Shortly thereafter the doctor established a newspaper, *Grimshaw's Messenger*. A few years later, he became Captain Lammot DuPont's superior during the Civil War. Doctor Grimshaw was also a druggist. His newspaper contained multiple advertisements for his medical compounds such as worm lozenges. Grimshaw used the Messenger as a means of editorializing on the rise of medical "quackery," which he referred to as a "hydra-headed monster which has withstood the Herculean efforts of science and satire." He also produced and sold flavor extracts and ink in addition to authoring a history of the United States, France, and England, all of which were advertised in the paper. This multi-faceted man was also at one time the postmaster for the city of Wilmington. See https://chroniclingamerica.loc.gov/lccn/sn88053097/.

47. ISTG, https://www.immigrantships.net/v11/1800v11/caledonia18391028.html, retrieved June 2, 2018.

48. "United States Census, 1850," database with images, *FamilySearch* (https://familysearch.org/ark:/61903/1:1:MHDM-GF3 : 12 April 2016), Edward Hurst, Christiana Hundred, New Castle, Delaware, United States; citing family 462, NARA microfilm publication M432 (Washington, D.C.: National Archives and Records Administration, n.d.), retrieved June 2, 2018.

49. FGD, 63.

50. "United States Census, 1860", database with images, *FamilySearch* (https://familysearch.org/ark:/61903/1:1:M4SW-WXM : 13 December 2017), Ellen Mc Clafferty in entry for Catharine Mc Clafferty, 1860, retrieved June 2, 2018.

51. Ibid.; "Find A Grave Index," database, *FamilySearch* (https://familysearch.org/ark:/61903/1:1:QVVZ-TWDP : 27 July 2019), Kate McClafferty, 1891; Burial, Wilmington, New Castle, Delaware, United States of America, Cathedral Cemetery; citing record ID 16400149, Find a Grave, http://www.findagrave.com, retrieved June 3, 2018.

52. HML, Petit Ledger, Vol. 1008, 1886, 413.

53. HML, Petit Ledger 1014, 1891, 419. The remaining glued-in papers are Margaret X. O'Donnell's receipt for $1336.08 from DuPont; a Letter of Administration for O'Donnell for Kate's estate; and a letter saying that she had taken

out the Letter of Administration. Letters of Administration were simply the means by which an executor/executrix could manage the deceased's estate.

54. Pronounced "AN ten." According to a family history, Anton was the local Gaelic spelling of Anthony (from the Latin 'Antonius'), used in the Malin area of the Inishowen Peninsula. Anthony Dougherty, *The Family of Anton and Jane Dougherty of Henry Clay, Delaware*, unpublished manuscript (Napa, CA), 1997.

55. I am indebted to Sarah Dougherty, the great-great-granddaughter of Anton, for much of the information that follows.

56. A glebe is an area of land in addition to the parsonage house/rectory and grounds which was assigned to support the priest. He could charge rents for acreage, farm the land, or use it for other support functions.

57. John S. Walsh to John Peoples, HML, Accession 500, Incoming Correspondence, Box 400.

58. As railroad tracks increasingly stitched the nation together, rail worker deaths rose accordingly. In the Interstate Commerce Commission's first report on fatal accidents on the rails, they reported that one out of 375 workers died the year before while performing this dangerous work. These statistics far outnumber those for workers killed in black powder explosions.

59. John A. Butler, *Atlantic Kingdom: America's Contest with Cunard in the Age of Sail and Steam* (Washington: Brassey's, Inc.), 2001, 223.

60. FGD, 64.

61. Pronounced "ME va."

62. Pronounced "clot da VA dog."

63. Marie Donahue Walls. Donahue (Unpublished family history), 2004.

64. *Evening Bulletin*, (Philadelphia, Pennsylvania), January 21, 1859.

65. Brian Dillon. *The Great Explosion: Gunpowder, the Great War and a disaster on the Kent Marshes* (Dublin:Penguin Books), 2015, 169.

66. *Wayne County Herald*, (Honesdale, Pennsylvania), January 27, 1859, http://www.newspapers.com, retrieved June 18, 2018. Emphasis added.

67. *Hillsborough Recorder*, (Hillsborough, North Carolina), February 2, 1859, <https://chroniclingamerica.loc.gov/lccn/sn84026472/1859-02-02/ed-1/seq-3/>, retrieved June 18, 2018.

68. FGD, 64.

69. Soda powder has its own interesting history. Invented by Lammot DuPont just a few years before, it used sodium nitrate instead of potassium nitrate which gave the resultant powder much more force. It was the first real change in powder composition in the previous 600 years.

70. *The New York Times*, New York, NY, October 24, 1859, *http://www.gendisasters.com/delaware/11065/wilmington-de-dupont-powder-mill-explosion-oct-1859*, retrieved June 22, 2018.

71. HML, Petit Ledger, Vol. 970, 1837-1839, Flyleaf.

72. I write "at least" because DuPont petit ledgers for the years 1871 through 1890 have several references to "heiresses" Sarah Jane, apparently born in 1850 to 1851, and Margaret, who seems to have been born in the year her father died, 1859. This gap of eight years does not fit the normal pattern of the era of parents giving birth to children two years apart. Additional research would likely turn up two to four additional children.

73. "United States Census, 1850," database with images, *FamilySearch* (https://family-search.org/ark:/61903/1:1:MH81-YG3 : 4 April 2020), Barney Sweeney, Christiana Hundred, New Castle, Delaware, United States; citing family 135, NARA microfilm publication M432 (Washington, D.C.: National Archives and Records Administration, n.d.).

74. Https://www.lalley.com/index.asp?marri.htm, retrieved August 28, 2020.

75. B. Emer O'Keefe, ed. *The Search for Missing Friends: Irish Immigrant Advertisements Placed in the Boston Pilot, Vol. V: 1861-1865.* (Boston: New England Historical Genealogical Society), 1996, 2.

Chapter Seven

1. Pronounced "na JANEya noss agoose na brush noss."

2. Joseph A. L. Errigo, St. Joseph's *On the Brandywine* (Wilmington: William N. Cann, Inc.), 1941, 32.

3. The prince was a little befuddled about his visit when he told someone back home that "I met a very large interesting family name d Scrapple, and I discovered a rather delicious native food that they call biddle." *The New York Times*, (New York, New York), May 28, 2003.

4. FGD, 65.

5. Another prodigious need was cash but it could not be one of over seven thousand bank currencies in circulation nor could it be one of the five thousand types of fake bills in dubious use across the nation. It had to be a single currency, so the Federal

government printed the first national money, known as "greenbacks," so-called because they printed the reverse in green ink. To pay for the war, the Feds instituted an income tax, an effort pushed by Salmon Chase, the Secretary of the Treasury; ten years later, as Chief Justice of the Supreme Court, he found the tax unconstitutional. See John Steele Gordon, *An Empire of Wealth: The Epic History of American Economic Power* (New York: Harper Collins), 2004, 194.

6. This, according to the *Philadelphia Press*, November 23, 1860, http://www.gendisasters.com/delaware/10909/wilmington-de-dupont-powder-mill-explosion-nov-1861. Francis Gurney du Pont cites only three buildings.

7. Ibid.

8. Pronounced "don FAN a hee."

9. The second "o" is pronounced like a soft "a."

10. ISTG, Manifest of the brig Lumley, July 12, 1850, Londonderry to Philadelphia, retrieved February 7, 2020.

11. Pronounced "tully FERN."

12. FGD, 66.

13. Ibid.

14. HML, Petit Ledger, Vol. 995, 1873, 432.

15. HML, Acc 389, Box 2, Class Book folder, Nov. 1859.

16. Joseph Chubb Develin, *The Story of an Irish Sept, the O'Develins of Tyrone*, 2d Ed. (Philadelphia: College Offset Press), 1947, https://babel.hathitrust.org/cgi/pt?id=wu.89063023139&view=1up&seq=3, retrieved February 9, 2020.

17. Hewett, 339.

18. Mark Holan, *Ireland's Famine Children "Born at Sea"*, Prologue Magazine, Winter 2017–18, Vol. 49, no. 4, https://www.archives.gov/publications/prologue/2017/winter/irish-births, retrieved February 10, 2020.

19. Delaney, 112.

20. About $23,000 in today's currency. https://www.measuringworth.com/dollarvaluetoday/?amount=1100&from=1863.

21. Tombstone inscription of Jean Pierre Dehan, St. Joseph on the Brandywine Cemetery, New Castle County, Delaware. Read February 11, 2020.

22. Or "kags" as the Irish pronounced the word. See HML, Accession 2026, Box 3, Transcript of Oral Interview with William Craven, Jr., June 11, 1986, 23.

23. HML, Petit Ledger 1003, 1881, piece of paper glued to the account page for James Cre(e)dan, 442.

24. For example, a biography of one of the members of the Toy family (see Chapter Four) misspelled the name, using "Loy" throughout the article.

25. Hewitt, 361.

26. FGD, 67.

27. Michael Morgan, *Civil War Delaware: The First State Divided* (Charleston: The History Press), 2012, 77.

28. Ibid.

29. Harold B. Hancock, *Delaware During the Civil War* (Wilmington: Historical Society of Delaware), 1961, 63. Emphasis in original.

30. Ibid.

31. Ibid.

32. Unknown Union officer to Maj. L.G. Turner, Judge Advocate of the Union Army, Washington, D.C., from camp Dupont, September 21, 1862, HML, Accession 754.

33. Ibid., September 22, 1862.

34. Hancock, *Civil War*, 96.

35. Ibid, 74.

36. In late 1860, Bird sent a letter to Abraham Lincoln, imploring the President-elect to issue a letter before his inauguration denying that he would take any action to abolish slavery in the South.

37. Thomas W. Reed, Andrew McKay and Rev. Anthony Wade, *Untying the Political Knot: Delaware During the War Between the States* (Wilmington, NC: Broadfoot Publishing Co.), 2001, 19.

38. Works Progress Administration. *Inventory of the Tombstone Inscriptions in St. Joseph's Churchyard, Henry Clay, Delaware*, typescript copy. Wilmington, Delaware: The Historical Record Survey, Works Progress Administration, 1939.

39. HML, Petit Ledger Vol 1017, 1895, 434; Vol. 1018, 1896, 434.

Notes

40. Harold B. Hancock and Norman B. Wilkinson, *A Manufacturer in Wartime: Du Pont, 1860-1865*, The Business History Review 40, No. 2 (1966), 213-36. http://www.jstor.org/stable/3112330, retrieved February 12, 2020.

41. *The Weekly Union* (Georgetown, Del.), 20 May 1864. Chronicling America: Historic American Newspapers. Lib. of Congress. <http://chroniclingamerica.loc.gov/lccn/sn84038105/1864-05-20/ed-1/seq-2/>, retrieved February 14, 2020.

42. FGD, p. 68. F.G. du Pont only listed four men killed. Since his narrative was probably written concurrently with the immediate cleanup from this mishap, he probably did not go back and edit his writing after several of the men lingered before dying.

43. *Chicago Daily Tribune*. (Chicago, Ill.), 19 June 1864. Chronicling America: Historic American Newspapers. Lib. of Congress. <http://chroniclingamerica.loc.gov/lccn/sn84031490/1864-06-19/ed-1/seq-3/>, retrieved February 14, 2020.

44. St. Joseph on the Brandywine Records, Family History Center Microfilm Number 1822513, 44, Entry 4.

45. "United States Census, 1870", database with images, *FamilySearch* (https://familysearch.org/ark:/61903/1:1:M4B5-K8J : 8 June 2019), Catharine Babby, 1870, retrieved February 14, 2020.

46. "United States Census, 1900," database with images, *FamilySearch* (https://familysearch.org/ark:/61903/1:1:M31G-T37 : accessed 14 February 2020), Catherine Babby in household of Edward Babby, Wilmington Hundred, Precincts 64-65 Wilmington city Ward 7, New Castle, Delaware, United States; citing enumeration district (ED) 31, sheet 20A, family 357, NARA microfilm publication T623 (Washington, D.C.: National Archives and Records Administration, 1972.); FHL microfilm 1,240,155. Retrieved June 2, 2018.

Chapter Eight

1. J. Fraser Baddeley, *Pamphlet on the Manufacture of Gunpowder, as Carried on at the Government Factory, Waltham Abbey* (London: Her Majesties Printing Office), 1857.

2. Tom Mack, *Hidden History of Augusta* (Mt. Pleasant, South Carolina: Arcadia Publishing), 2015,

3. Joseph B. Milgram, Jr. And Norman P. Gentieu, *George Washington Rains—Gunpowdermaker of the Confederacy*. Presentation at the ACS Civil War Symposium, Chicago, IL, September, 1961.

4. Dorothy Garesché Holland, *The Garesché, De Bauduy, and Des Chapelles Families: History and Genealogy*. (Saint Louis: Privately printed by the Schneider Print. Co.),

1963, 40. Although General Grant was referring specifically to the powder made by former Wilmingtonian Peter Bauduy Garesché at the powder factories of the Confederate Navy, it is probable that the ratio cited was the same for the CSA army.

5. Later an Alabama Supreme Court Justice, one of whose former slaves became a U.S. Representative.

6. Derek Taylor, Creating Southern Thunder: *The Evolution of Confederate Gunpowder Production During the American Civil War*, The Welebaethan: A Journal of History, Vol. 46, 2019, 177.

7. Ibid, 178.

8. C. L. Bragg et al., *Never for Want of Powder: The Confederate Powder Works in Augusta, Georgia* (Columbia: The University of South Carolina Press), 2007, 95. Rains, mill owners, and mill operators were not alone in failing to shoulder any of the blame for anything they might have done to cause accidents. One industrial hygiene expert in the 19th century said it this way: "it requires no very lengthened acquaintance with workman to discover their recklessness in dangerous occupations, their neglect of cleanliness, their refusal to adopt preventive measures against evident evils, and above all, their widespread habits of intemperance." See J. T. Arlidge, *The Hygiene, Diseases and Mortality of Occupations* (London: Percival and Co., 1892), 5, https://babel.hathitrust.org/cgi/pt?id=nyp.33433075990733&view=1up&seq=9, retrieved April 15, 2020.

9. Bragg, 238.

10. Carr is a common surname in Ireland, where it often derives from the nickname, gearr, meaning short (of height). In some cases it is, ironically, thought to come from the old Welsh word Cwarr, meaning giant. From www.archives.com, retrieved February 17, 2020.

11. HML, Craig correspondence 4.23.47-general accounting list of passengers, https://www.immigrantships.net/v13/1800v13/superior18470428.html.

12. Andrew J. Catherwood to E.I. du Pont de Nemours and Company, October 24, 1850, HML, Accession. 500, Part I, Series B, Box 56, Folder "Catherwood, A.J., Phila., PA., 1847-1854."

13. Multiple tragedies occurred in other powder-making communities as well. A man by the name of Walter Luce was killed in an 1855 powder explosion in Enfield, Connecticut. As reported in another New England newspaper, the "widow Luce has lost three husbands by powder mill explosions." Article from unknown newspaper, unknown date, citing the Springfield [Massachusetts] Republican, unknown date, DuPont Scrapbook—HML, Accession 501, P. S. Du Pont Office Collection, Series D-Business Papers, (32) Scrapbooks: EIDPDNCo., history and explosions, Box 33-34, 24.

14. FGD, 69.

15. Tombstone inscription of Michael and Susanna Dougherty, St. Joseph on the Brandywine Cemetery.

16. HML Petit Ledger, Vol. 1012, 1890, 415.

17. Baptismal Records, St. Joseph on the Brandywine Roman Catholic Church, Family History Center Microfilm Number 1822512, 192.

18. Ibid.

19. FGD, 69.

20. *Pittsburgh Weekly Gazette*, (Pittsburgh, Pennsylvania), July 3, 1869, http://www.newspapers.com, retrieved June 2, 2018.

21. Jamie L Bronstein, *Caught in the Machinery: Workplace Accidents and Injured Workers in 19th-Century Britain* (Stanford, California:Stanford University Press), 2008, 72.

22. *American Watchman*, (Wilmington, Delaware), March 21, 1818; perhaps this was the first time the word "spin" was used in this context?

23. Bronstein, 72.

24. *Delaware Tribune*. (Wilmington, Delaware), 08 July 1869. Chronicling America: Historic American Newspapers. Lib. of Congress. <http://chroniclingamerica.loc.gov/lccn/sn84026822/1869-07-08/ed-1/seq-1/>, retrieved June 2, 2018.

25. Ibid.

26. FGD, 70.

27. The jury found the defendant, Aaron Woodward, not guilty of killing William T. Lukens. After Woodward's release, the authorities re-arrested him for trying to kill another man. See The *Daily Gazette*. (Wilmington, Del.), 27 Nov. 1874. Chronicling America: Historic American Newspapers. Lib. of Congress. <http://chroniclingamerica.loc.gov/lccn/sn82014805/1874-11-27/ed-1/seq-3/>, retrieved June 2, 2018.

28. HML, Charles Massie to Sophie du Pont, November 16, 1886, WMSS, Group 9, Series E-In File; Papers of Sophie M. (Mrs. S. F. Dupont Box 87—Oct. 86-June 87, Item No. W9-37115.

29. HML, Charles Massie to Sophie du Pont, November 26, 1886, WMSS, Group 9, Series E-In File; Papers of Sophie M. (Mrs. S. F. Dupont Box 87—Oct. 86-June 87, Item No. W9-37137.

30. HML, Charles Massie to Sophie du Pont, March 15, 1887, WMSS, Group 9, Series E-In File; Papers of Sophie M. (Mrs. S. F. Dupont Box 87—Oct. 86-June 87, Item No. W9-37439.

31. HML, Charles Massie to Sophie du Pont, March 30, 1887, WMSS, Group 9, Series E-In File; Papers of Sophie M. (Mrs. S. F. Dupont Box 87—Oct. 86-June 87, Item No. W9-.37470.

32. Not the brother of Éleuthère Irénée, but a later Victor du Pont. Many of the names of the early du Ponts were used by the descendants for their sons and daughters.

33. *The Morning News*, (Wilmington, Delaware), July 3, 1885, https://chroniclingamerica.loc.gov/lccn/sn84038114/1885-06-23/ed-1/seq-4/ocr/, retrieved June 2, 2018.

34. FGD, 70.

35. William Allison and John Torrey, killed in the 1818 explosion, were from this parish.

36. Marie Donahue Walls, *Genealogy of the Donahue Family*, unpublished, 2004.

37. *Cork Examiner* (Cork, Ireland), May 19, 1847, http://www.theshipslist.com/1847/america.shtml, retrieved February 20, 2020. Emphasis added.

38. Http://www.theshipslist.com/1847/america.shtml, retrieved February 20, 2020.

39. Ibid.

40. Walls, 1.

41. Bronstein, 116.

42. *Wilmington Daily Commercial*, (Wilmington, Delaware), January 25, 1871 and February 9, 1871.

43. *Middletown Transcript,* (Middletown, Delaware), 13 April 1872. Chronicling America: Historic American Newspapers. Lib. of Congress. <https://chroniclingamerica.loc.gov/lccn/sn84026820/1872-04-13/ed-1/seq-2/>, retrieved February 21, 2020.

44. *Delaware Tribune.* (Wilmington, Del.), 20 Oct. 1870. Chronicling America: Historic American Newspapers. Lib. of Congress. <https://chroniclingamerica.loc.gov/lccn/sn84026822/1870-10-20/ed-1/seq-1/>, retrieved February 21, 2020.

45. *Wilmington Daily Commercial*, (Wilmington, Delaware), June 29, 1870, www.newspapers.com, retrieved June 2, 2018.

46. *Wilmington Daily Commercial*, (Wilmington, Delaware), July 12, 1870, www.newspapers.com, retrieved June 2, 2018.

47. *The Daily Gazette.* (Wilmington, Delaware), 15 Nov. 1881. Chronicling America: Historic American Newspapers. Lib. of Congress. <https://chroniclingamerica.loc.gov/lccn/sn82014805/1881-11-15/ed-1/seq-4/>, retrieved February 21, 2020.

48. *Wilmington Daily Commercial*, (Wilmington, Delaware), November 26, 1870, https://www.newspaper.com, retrieved February 21, 2020.

49. *Philadelphia Inquirer*, (Philadelphia, Pennsylvania), December 2, 1915, https://www.newspapers.com, retrieved June 2, 2018.

50. *The Daily Comet.* (Baton Rouge, Louisiana), 04 Aug. 1855. Chronicling America: Historic American Newspapers. Lib. of Congress. <https://chroniclingamerica.loc.gov/lccn/sn83016548/1855-08-04/ed-1/seq-2/>, retrieved February 21, 2020.

Chapter Nine

1. "United States Census, 1870", database with images, *FamilySearch* (https://familysearch.org/ark:/61903/1:1:M4BP-LNG : 8 June 2019), Jonah Miller, 1870, retrieved February 21, 2020. This was Jonas, not Jonah.

2. FGD, 71; *Wilmington Daily Commercial.* (Wilmington, Del.), 15 Jan. 1872. Chronicling America: Historic American Newspapers. Lib. of Congress. <https://chroniclingamerica.loc.gov/lccn/sn84020594/1872-01-15/ed-1/seq-4/>, retrieved February 21, 2020.

3. *Wilmington Daily Commercial.* (Wilmington, Del.), 22 April 1872. Chronicling America: Historic American Newspapers. Lib. of Congress. <http://chroniclingamerica.loc.gov/lccn/sn84020594/1872-04-22/ed-1/seq-4/>, retrieved June 2, 2018

4. *Delaware Gazette and State Journal.* (Wilmington, Del.), 16 Dec. 1886. Chronicling America: Historic American Newspapers. Lib. of Congress. <http://chroniclingamerica.loc.gov/lccn/sn88053046/1886-12-16/ed-1/seq-1/>, retrieved June 2, 2018.

5. *Wilmington Daily Gazette.* (Wilmington, Del.), 14 Aug. 1872. Chronicling America: Historic American Newspapers. Lib. of Congress. <https://chroniclingamerica.loc.gov/lccn/sn84026837/1872-08-14/ed-1/seq-4/>, retrieved February 22, 2020.

6. FGD, 72.

7. Marquis James, *Alfred I. DuPont: The Family Rebel* (Indianapolis: The Bobbs-Merrill Company) 1941, 44.

8. HML, Dick Scott collection, Accession 1645, Box 10, File marked "1824."

9. Transcript of Oral Interview with William Henry Miller, recorded February 16, 1984, HML, Accession 2026, retrieved February 25, 2020.

10. Heather A. Wholey (2006) "The Socioeconomic Landscape of Northern Delaware's Taverns and Innkeepers: The Blue Ball Tavern and Vicinity," *Northeast Historical Archaeology* 35, Article 23 (2006): 65, http://orb.binghamton.edu/neha/vol35/iss1/23, retrieved February 25, 2020.

11. J. M. Runk & Co. *Biographical and Genealogical History of the the State of Delaware*, (Chambersburg, PA: J. M Runk & Co.), 1899, 492.

12. Henry Lee, 1756-1818, and Robert E. (Robert Edward) Lee. *Memoirs of the War In the Southern Department of the United States*. A new ed., with revisions, and a biography of the author, by Robert E. Lee. New York: University Pub. Co., 1869.; https://babel.hathitrust.org/cgi/pt?id=hvd.32044021148705&view=1up&seq=203, retrieved February 25, 2020.

13. "United States Census, 1850," database with images, *FamilySearch* (https://familysearch.org/ark:/61903/1:1:MH81-BH6 : 12 April 2016), Jones W Miller, Christiana Hundred, New Castle, Delaware, United States; citing family 333, NARA microfilm publication M432 (Washington, D.C.: National Archives and Records Administration, n.d.).

14. Jacqueline Hinsley, 19th Century Community Stores, HML, Eleutherian Mills-Hagley Research Report, Accession 1645, Box 6,.

15. *Evening Journal*. (Wilmington, Del.), 14 July 1910. Chronicling America: Historic American Newspapers. Lib. of Congress. <https://chroniclingamerica.loc.gov/lccn/sn85042354/1910-07-14/ed-1/seq-2/>, Retrieved February 27, 2020.

16. *Delaware Genealogical Society Journal*, Vol. 3, No. 4, October, 1986, 80.

17. Https://www.hagley.org/research/digital-exhibits/charles-i-du-pont-co, retrieved February 27, 2020.

18. HML, Accession 500, Charles I. DuPont & Co., Correspondence, In File, Box 13.

19. *Wilmington Daily Commercial*,(Wilmington, Del.), 05 July 1873. Chronicling America: Historic American Newspapers. Lib. of Congress. <https://chroniclingamerica.loc.gov/lccn/sn84020594/1873-07-05/ed-1/seq-1/>, retrieved February 27, 2020. Emphasis added.

20. *Delaware Republican* (Wilmington, Del.), 07 July 1873. Chronicling America: Historic American Newspapers. Lib. of Congress. <https://chroniclingamerica.loc.gov/lccn/sn87062253/1873-07-07/ed-1/seq-2/>, retrieved February 27, 2020.

21. *Delaware Republican*. (Wilmington, Del.), 10 July 1873. Chronicling America: Historic American Newspapers. Lib. of Congress. <https://chroniclingamerica.loc.

gov/lccn/sn87062253/1873-07-10/ed-1/seq-3/>, retrieved February 27, 2020.

22. *Delaware Republican*. (Wilmington, Del.), 17 July 1873. Chronicling America: Historic American Newspapers. Lib. of Congress. <https://chroniclingamerica.loc.gov/lccn/sn87062253/1873-07-17/ed-1/seq-3/>, AND *Delaware Republican*. (Wilmington, Del.), 01 June 1874. Chronicling America: Historic American Newspapers. Lib. of Congress. <https://chroniclingamerica.loc.gov/lccn/sn87062253/1874-06-01/ed-1/seq-3/>, retrieved February 27, 2020.

23. *Delaware Republican*. (Wilmington, Del.), 17 July 1873. Chronicling America: Historic American Newspapers. Lib. of Congress. <https://chroniclingamerica.loc.gov/lccn/sn87062253/1873-07-17/ed-1/seq-3/>, retrieved February 27, 2020.

24. George left an estate at his death in the first decade of the new century of between $70,000 and $100,000 when he died in Pasadena.

25. Jonas W. Miller, Junior, inherited a sizable farm in Kansas when his brother George died in 1909 and left the property to him.

26. Runk, 652.

27. Made of sodium nitrate, as opposed to potassium nitrate used in the standard black powder-making process.

28. *Delaware Tribune* (Wilmington, Del.), 27 May 1875. Chronicling America: Historic American Newspapers. Lib. of Congress. <https://chroniclingamerica.loc.gov/lccn/sn84026822/1875-05-27/ed-1/seq-3/>, retrieved March 2, 2020.

29. FGDP Notebook, HML, LMSS, Group 8, Series A, Box 1, p. 11. This is a different Francis Gurney DuPont notebook than previously cited.

30. Ibid.

31. FGD, 74.

32. *Philadelphia Inquirer*, Philadelphia, PA 22 May 1876, http://www.newspapers.com, retrieved March 2, 2020.

33. *News Journal*, (Wilmington, Delaware), May 20, 1876.

34. *Daily Gazette*. (Wilmington, Del.), 23 May 1876. Chronicling America: Historic American Newspapers. Lib. of Congress. <http://chroniclingamerica.loc.gov/lccn/sn82014805/1876-05-23/ed-1/seq-3/>, retrieved March 2, 2020.

35. Ibid.

36. Sydney Morning Herald, Sydney, Australia, October 20, 1847, <http://nla.gov.au/nla.news-article12891647>. retrieved August 4, 2020,

37. *South Australian Register,* Adelaide, Australia, October 9, 1854, <http://nla.gov.au/nla.news-article49205031>, retrieved August 4, 2020.

38. *Sydney Morning Herald*, Sydney, Australia, June 20, 1876, http://www.newspapers.com, retrieved June 2, 2018.

39. Because many of the residents of Free Park, so named because they, like other workmen and their families, lived rent free, also housed pigs and so the people jokingly called it Flea Park. Even the du Ponts and the newspapers of the day used that moniker.

40. HML, Petit Ledger, Vol. 998, 1876, 486.

41. Transcript of Oral Interview with William Craven Jr., HML, Accession 2026, Box 3, June 11, 1986, 4.

42. According to his enlistment papers, he stated that he was forty-one. However, his record at the Delaware archives lists him as thirty-eight. See http://archives.delaware.gov/CivilWar/volumes/volunteers_service_records_(1861-1864)_3rd_infantry_(book_2).pdf, retrieved March 2, 2020.

43. Https://www.battlefields.org/learn/articles/civil-war-facts, retrieved March 3, 2020.

44. *Daily Republican.* (Wilmington, Del.), 03 Sept. 1881. Chronicling America: Historic American Newspapers. Lib. of Congress. <http://chroniclingamerica.loc.gov/lccn/sn84038114/1881-09-03/ed-1/seq-4/> AND *Evening journal*. (Wilmington, Del.), 03 Sept. 1910. Chronicling America: Historic American Newspapers. Lib. of Congress. <http://chroniclingamerica.loc.gov/lccn/sn85042354/1910-09-03/ed-1/seq-9/>, both retrieved June 2, 2018.

45. *Evening Journal.* (Wilmington, Del.), 07 Sept. 1907. Chronicling America: Historic American Newspapers. Lib. of Congress. <http://chroniclingamerica.loc.gov/lccn/sn85042354/1907-09-07/ed-1/seq-6/>, retrieved June 2, 2018.

46. *Delaware Tribune.* (Wilmington, Del.), 20 May 1869. Chronicling America: Historic American Newspapers. Lib. of Congress. <http://chroniclingamerica.loc.gov/lccn/sn84026822/1869-05-20/ed-1/seq-3/>, retrieved June 3, 2018.

47. HML, Petit Ledger, Vol. 997, 53.

48. Irénée DuPont to Samuel Bancroft Junior, November 13, 1913, DHS, Bird Bancroft Collection, Box 8, Folder "Biographical Information," Samuel Bancroft Jr. Personal Papers.

Chapter Ten

1. Clipping from "Republican Newspaper," probably *The Delaware Republican*, May 2, 1882, HML, LMSS, Group 8, Series A, Box 1, FGDP Notebook, 42.

2. *Daily Gazette* (Wilmington, Del.), 02 May 1882. Chronicling America: Historic American Newspapers. Lib. of Congress. <https://chroniclingamerica.loc.gov/lccn/sn82014805/1882-05-02/ed-1/seq-1/>, retrieved June 3, 2018. "Supposed" in this case meaning "thought." The "house near DuPont's church" refers to Dougherty's residence in Free Park near Christ Church, a church to which the DuPonts contributed large amounts of money to build.

3. HML, LMSS, Group 8, Series A, Box 1, FGDP Notebook, p. 42.

4. *Daily Gazette* (Wilmington, Del.), 13 June 1882. Chronicling America: Historic American Newspapers. Lib. of Congress. <https://chroniclingamerica.loc.gov/lccn/sn82014805/1882-06-13/ed-1/seq-1/>, retrieved June 3, 2018.

5. *Evening Journal*, (Wilmington, Delaware), Wednesday, August 17, 1904.

6. HML, Petit Ledger, Vol. 1009, 1887, 329.

7. Mulrooney, 110, citing John McGuire, *The Irish in America* (New York: D. & J. Sadlier Co.), 1868, 335-36. The fact that it was Kate Deery, nee Dougherty, was confirmed by Ralph Walsh in conversation with the author, August 20, 2018. Ralph is a great grandson of Kate and Charles Deery.

8. Transcript of Oral Interview with Edward B. Cheney, June 5, 1958, 31, HML, Accession 2026, Box 1.

9. Mulrooney, 110.

10. Eagleton, 73.

11. Obituary of Ellen Gibbons Dougherty, *Evening journal*. (Wilmington, Del.), 24 May 1911. Chronicling America: Historic American Newspapers. Lib. of Congress. <https://chroniclingamerica.loc.gov/lccn/sn85042354/1911-05-24/ed-1/seq-2/>, retrieved June 3, 2018.

12. *Wilmington Daily Republican*. (Wilmington, Del.), 26 Dec. 1896. Chronicling America: Historic American Newspapers. Lib. of Congress. <https://chroniclingamerica.loc.gov/lccn/sn88053055/1896-12-26/ed-1/seq-1/>, retrieved March 4, 2020.

13. *Every Evening* (Wilmington, Delaware), August 17, 1904.

14. *Daily Gazette* (Wilmington, Del.), 13 July 1882. Chronicling America: Historic American Newspapers. Lib. of Congress. <https://chroniclingamerica.loc.gov/lccn/sn82014805/1882-07-13/ed-1/seq-1/>, retrieved June 3, 2018.

15. Sophie M. DuPont to Sarah Gilpin, July 21, 1882, HML, LMSS, Group 8, Series A, Box 2, File 31.

16. Ibid. Emphasis in original.

17. HML, LMSS, Group 10, Series A, Papers of PSD, Box 1311, File 804, Letters of Pierre Samuel DuPont to Margaret Chadwick.

18. FGD, 75.

19. *Daily Gazette*. (Wilmington, Del.), 13 Jan. 1883. Chronicling America: Historic American Newspapers. Lib. of Congress. <http://chroniclingamerica.loc.gov/lccn/sn82014805/1883-01-13/ed-1/seq-1/>, retrieved June 3, 2018.

20. FGD, 76.

21. *Daily Gazette* (Wilmington, Del.), 14 July 1883. Chronicling America: Historic American Newspapers. Lib. of Congress. <http://chroniclingamerica.loc.gov/lccn/sn82014805/1883-07-14/ed-1/seq-4/>, retrieved June 3, 2018.

22. *Delaware State Journal and Statesman* (Wilmington, Del.), 14 Aug. 1863. Chronicling America: Historic American Newspapers. Lib. of Congress. <http://chroniclingamerica.loc.gov/lccn/sn84038112/1863-08-14/ed-1/seq-2/>, retrieved June 3, 2018.

23. HML, Petit Ledger, Vol. 1008, 1886, 416; Vol. 1009, 1887, 28.

24. *Wilmington Daily Gazette* (Wilmington, Del.), 24 April 1872. Chronicling America: Historic American Newspapers. Lib. of Congress. <https://chroniclingamerica.loc.gov/lccn/sn84026837/1872-04-24/ed-1/seq-4/>, retrieved June 3, 2018.

25. *Delaware State Journal* (Wilmington, Del.), 19 July 1883. Chronicling America: Historic American Newspapers. Lib. of Congress. <http://chroniclingamerica.loc.gov/lccn/sn84026836/1883-07-19/ed-1/seq-3/>, retrieved June 3, 2018.

26. "United States Census, 1880," database with images, *FamilySearch* (https://familysearch.org/ark:/61903/1:1:MXCX-LXQ : 29 July 2017), Patrick Haley, Wilmington, New Castle, Delaware, United States; citing enumeration district ED 5, sheet 116B, NARA microfilm publication T9 (Washington, D.C.: National Archives and Records Administration, n.d.), FHL microfilm 1,254,118, retrieved March 5, 2020.

27. *Boston Sunday Herald*, (Boston, Massachusetts), April 28, 1898, http://www.newspapers.com, retrieved June 2, 2018.

28. HML, LMSS, Group 10, Series A, Papers of P. S. du Pont, Box 391, File 418-2, Excerpts from typed copy of F. G. du Pont's five page treatise on the explosion.

29. Ibid.

30. Https://en.wikipedia.org/wiki/Brown_powder, retrieved March 6, 2020.

31. *Evening Journal*. (Wilmington, Del.), 08 Oct. 1890. Chronicling America: Historic American Newspapers. Lib. of Congress. <http://chroniclingamerica.loc.gov/lccn/sn85042354/1890-10-08/ed-1/seq-1/>, retrieved June 4, 2018.

Notes

32. Ibid.

33. Ibid.

34. *Delaware Gazette and State Journal.* (Wilmington, Del.), 16 Oct. 1890. Chronicling America: Historic American Newspapers. Lib. of Congress. <http://chroniclingamerica.loc.gov/lccn/sn88053046/1890-10-16/ed-1/seq-3/>, retrieved March 11, 2020.

35. Transcript of Oral Interview with John Peoples, June 13, 1957, 6, HML, Accession 2026, Box 1.

36. FGD, 85.

37. Https://democratandchronicle.newspapers.com/clip/17248721/democrat_and_chronicle/, retrieved June 2, 2018.

38. *Evening Journal* (Wilmington, Del.), 10 Oct. 1890. Chronicling America: Historic American Newspapers. Lib. of Congress. <https://chroniclingamerica.loc.gov/lccn/sn85042354/1890-10-10/ed-1/seq-2/>, retrieved June 2, 2018. Emphasis added.

39. Ibid.

40. *Sunday Morning Star*, Wilmington, Delaware, August 1, 1948, http://www.newspapers.com, retrieved June 2, 2018.

41. Glenn H. Pryor W*orker's Lives at the DuPont Powder Mills, 1877-1912.* Master's Thesis, University of Delaware, 1977, 51.

42. Ibid.

43. Rumm, 179.

44. *Evening Journal*, (Wilmington, Delaware), October 16, 1890.

45. *Times*, Philadelphia, Pennsylvania, October 8, 1890, http:\\www.newspapers.com, retrieved June 2, 2018.

46. *Evening Journal* (Wilmington, Del.), 15 Oct. 1890. Chronicling America: Historic American Newspapers. Lib. of Congress. <https://chroniclingamerica.loc.gov/lccn/sn85042354/1890-10-15/ed-1/seq-1/>, retrieved June 2, 2018.

47. *Evening Journal* (Wilmington, Del.), 12 June 1891. Chronicling America: Historic American Newspapers. Lib. of Congress. <http://chroniclingamerica.loc.gov/lccn/sn85042354/1891-06-12/ed-1/seq-3/>, retrieved June 2, 2018 and "Delaware Death Records, 1855-1961," database with images, *FamilySearch* (https://familysearch.org/ark:/61903/1:1:FNP1-3XJ : 25 September 2019), Hugh Ferry, 07 Jun 1891; citing Wilmington, Delaware, United States, Hall of Records, Dover; FamilySearch digital folder 004252470, retrieved March 11, 2020.

48. *Delaware Gazette and State Journal* (Wilmington, Del.), 09 Oct. 1890. Chronicling America: Historic American Newspapers. Lib. of Congress. <http://chroniclingamerica.loc.gov/lccn/sn88053046/1890-10-09/ed-1/seq-5/>, retrieved June 2, 2018.

49. *Evening Journal* (Wilmington, Del.), 13 Oct. 1890. Chronicling America: Historic American Newspapers. Lib. of Congress. <https://chroniclingamerica.loc.gov/lccn/sn85042354/1890-10-13/ed-1/seq-3/>, retrieved June 3, 2018.

50. HML, Petit Ledger, Vol. 1014, 1891, 422.

51. "United States Census, 1900," database with images, *FamilySearch* (https://familysearch.org/ark:/61903/1:1:M315-5S4 : Mary Sweeney in household of Dennis Sweeney, Christiana Hundred (all south & west of hundred) Du Ponts Banks village, New Castle, Delaware, United States; citing enumeration district (ED) 53, sheet 10B, family 189, NARA microfilm publication T623 (Washington, D.C.: National Archives and Records Administration, 1972.); FHL microfilm 1,240,156, retrieved March 6, 2020.

52. Pronounced "CON achth."

53. "United States Census, 1880," database with images, *FamilySearch* (https://familysearch.org/ark:/61903/1:1:MXCX-LYP : 29 July 2017), Hannah Dolan in household of Martin Dolan, Christiana, New Castle, Delaware, United States; citing enumeration district ED 3, sheet 81A, NARA microfilm publication T9 (Washington, D.C.: National Archives and Records Administration, n.d.), FHL microfilm 1,254,118, retrieved June 2, 2018.

54. "Delaware, Wilmington Vital Records, 1847-1954," database with images, *FamilySearch* (https://familysearch.org/ark:/61903/1:1:QKD6-K6P2 : 13 March 2018), Catharine Dolan, 18 Dec 1881; citing Death, Wilmington, New Castle, Delaware, United States, Public Archives, Dover; FHL microfilm 2,188,029. See also Henry C. Conrad, *History of the State of Delaware*, Volume I, (Wilmington:Henry C. Conrad), 1908.

55. HML, Petit Ledger, Vol. 984, 1862, 89.

56. HML, Petit Ledger, Vol. 999, 1887, 68.

57. HML, Petit Ledger, Vol. 1005, 1883, 67;Vol. 1009, 1887, 314.

58. FGD, 65; The New York Times, New York, 24 Nov 1861. http://www.newspapers.com, retrieved June 3, 2018; and The News-Herald, Franklin, Pennsylvania, 09 Oct 1890, http://www.newspapers.com, retrieved June 2, 2018.

59. HML, Petit Ledger, Vol. 1012, 1890, 376-377.

Chapter Eleven

1. *Every Evening*, (Wilmington, Delaware), October 10, 1890.

Notes

2. It is not clear if this refers to Henry, aka The General (1812-1889), or his son, Henry, aka The Colonel (1838-1926). I'm guessing that it was the General; the Colonel was known to remove workers from the rolls at the drop of a hat.

3. John W. Macklem, *Brandywine Reminiscences*, 1936, 16-17. HML, Accession 1645, Box 6, No. 199, Unpublished typewritten manuscript.

4. *Every Evening*, (Wilmington, Delaware), October 10, 1890.

5. *Evening Journal* (Wilmington, Delaware), October 11, 1890.

6. HML, Petit Ledger, Vol. 1014, 1891, 415.

7. HML, Petit Ledger, Vol. 1012, 1890, Loose note inside front cover. Emphasis in original.

8. Ibid. Punctuation in original.

9. Ibid, 377.

10. "United States Census, 1900," database with images, *FamilySearch* (https://familysearch.org/ark:/61903/1:1:M31G-6NT :Bridget Newell in household of James P Antiveiler, Wilmington Hundred, Precincts 44-45 Wilmington city Ward 8, New Castle, Delaware, United States; citing enumeration district (ED) 35, sheet 3A, family 46, NARA microfilm publication T623 (Washington, D.C.: National Archives and Records Administration, 1972.); FHL microfilm 1,240,155, retrieved March 10, 2020.

11. Tullaghobegly, Tulacha Beigile in Irish, appears originally to have referred to an enclosed mound containing a church and graveyard in the parish of that name. The first reference to this site suggests that the original name was Tulha Logha, 'the round of the Lugh," the pagan deity who had associations with several places within the parish…suggesting that Tullaghobegly was initially a pre-christian religious site, from Nolan, p. 163. It is pronounced "Tull ah o BEG ly."

12. The name is from the Irish O'hEarcain. The ancient family were erenaghs, or a kind of parish treasurer and land overseer of Clonca Parish, Inishowen.

13. Her headstone says "Clengaren" but such a parish did not exist, and does not exist today, in County Fermanagh. Glenarn is the closest name I could find in the databases of Irish town lands. See https://www.townlands.ie/fermanagh/lurg/magheraculmoney/glenarn/, retrieved March 10, 2020.

14. *Evening Journal*. (Wilmington, Del.), 08 Jan. 1891. Chronicling America: Historic American Newspapers. Lib. of Congress. <http://chroniclingamerica.loc.gov/lccn/sn85042354/1891-01-08/ed-1/seq-3/>, retrieved March 10, 2020.

15. "United States Census, 1900," database with images, *FamilySearch* (https://familysearch.org/ark:/61903/1:1:M31R-SNB : accessed 8 April 2020), Fannie A McGarvey

in household of Fannie A McGarvey, Brandywine Hundred (all north & west of Wilmington & Great Valley turnpike & Foulk rd.), New Castle, Delaware, United States; citing enumeration district (ED) 50, sheet 6A, family 107, NARA microfilm publication T623 (Washington, D.C.: National Archives and Records Administration, 1972.); FHL microfilm 1,240,156, AND "United States Census, 1910," database with images, *FamilySearch* (https://familysearch.org/ark:/61903/1:1:MVVJ-H8Z : accessed 8 April 2020), Fannie E McGarvey, Representative District 7, New Castle, Delaware, United States; citing enumeration district (ED) ED 79, sheet 5A, family 89, NARA microfilm publication T624 (Washington D.C.: National Archives and Records Administration, 1982), roll 146; FHL microfilm 1,374,159, both retrieved June 2, 2018.

16. Jacob Crowninshield, an eighteenth century member of the family, brought from overseas the first elephant ever seen in the United States. See Ronald B. Tobias. *Behemoth: The History of the Elephant in America*. (New York: Harper Perennial), 2013, 2-6.

17. Transcript of oral interview with Elizabeth Beacom, May 29, 1967, HML, Accession 2026, Box 2, 5-6.

18. William R. Green to Mrs. du Pont, September 12, 1876, HML, WMSS, Group 9-Mrs. Samuel Francis du Pont, Series E-In File; Box 78, July 1877-1878, No. W9-32326.

19. William R. Green to Mrs. du Pont, February 17, 1879, HML, WMSS, Group 9-Mrs. Samuel Francis du Pont; Series E—In File; Box 79, 1879-June 1880 , No. W9-32487.

20. William R. Green to Mrs. du Pont, May 12, 1884, HML, WMSS, Group 9-Mrs. Samuel Francis du Pont, Series E—In File; Box 83, July 1883-June 1884, No. W9-35438.

21. William R. Green to Mrs. du Pont, October 14, 1884, HML, WMSS, Group 9-Mrs. Samuel Francis du Pont; Series E —In File; Box 84-July 1884-April 1885, No. W9-35665.

22. William R. Green to Mrs. Dupont, February 4, 1885, HML, WMSS, Group 9-In File, Box 90—undated file labeled 'Gilpin to Sloan'; No.W9-38875.

23. HML, Petit Ledger, Vol. 1014, 1891, 395; Vol. 1016, 1894, 396; Vol. 1017, 1895, 396; Vol. 1020, 1898, 396; Vol. 1022, 1900, 396.

24. *Evening Journal*. (Wilmington, Del.), 16 Oct. 1890. Chronicling America: Historic American Newspapers. Lib. of Congress. <http://chroniclingamerica.loc.gov/lccn/sn85042354/1890-10-16/ed-1/seq-3/>, retrieved March 10, 2020.

25. Ibid.

26. Ibid.

Notes

27. *Evening Journal* (Wilmington, Del.), 18 Oct. 1890. Chronicling America: Historic American Newspapers. Lib. of Congress. <https://chroniclingamerica.loc.gov/lccn/sn85042354/1890-10-18/ed-1/seq-1/>, retrieved June 2, 2018.

28. Pryor, 43.

29. *Every Evening* (Wilmington, Delaware), December 19, 1893.

30. Ibid.

31. *Evening Journal* (Wilmington, Del.), 20 Dec. 1893. Chronicling America: Historic American Newspapers. Lib. of Congress. <http://chroniclingamerica.loc.gov/lccn/sn85042354/1893-12-20/ed-1/seq-5/>, retrieved June 2, 2018.

32. Marie Donahue Walls, Campbell and Haggerty History, Unpublished family history manuscript, 3-7.

33. Ibid.

34. Matthew Algeo, *The President is a Sick Man: Wherein the Supposedly Virtuous Grover Cleveland Survives Secret Surgery at Sea and Vilifies the Courageous Newspaperman Who Dared Expose the Truth* (Chicago: Chicago Review Press), 2011, 80.

35. A fellow Orangeman, William Kirkland, wrote a poem to Walker:
    The angel of death a visit paid
    Unto our noble band,
    And took from us our brother,
    Who in our faith did stand.
    Without a moment's warning
    From earth was called away
    To Paradise, there to await
    The coming judgment day.
    An upright member of our lodge,
    A good attendant there,
    No more his presence we can see;
    His is the vacant chair.
    But ever dear his memory
    Will we forever keep,
    And mourn for our brother -
    Who in the grave now sleeps.
    Attentive to his duty,
    To his employers true,
    Our brother, full of vigor,
    His duty tried to do.
    It was attending to the same
    He met the dreadful blow
    Which called him to eternity,

His stewardship to show.
To Star of Bethlehem members
Has come a warning great,
Let each prepare to meet the call,
Lest similar be the fate.
Without a moment's warning
we may be called away;
Then let each one be ready
To meet the judgment day.
While mourning for our brother,
 Let each one keep in view,
The tide of time is rolling on,
 Our day is coming too.
We'll meet our brother by and by,
On that celestial shore,
Where one and all united are,
And parting is no more.
His body in Mt. Salem lies
To moulder in the clay;
His soul has gone to Paradise
To await the judgment day.
No more he'll roam to daily toil;
He's free from earthly strife;
 Be his the crown of victory,
Throughout eternal life.
We mourn for the widow
And children in distress,
And pray the Lord may comfort them,
And their afflictions bless.
He gives us life and takes the same
In His mysterious way;
He knows what's best for each of us
And He will lead the way.

36. HML, Accession 503, Gentieu Record Book, 13 (relabeled 11).

37. HML, Petit Ledger, Vol. 1013, 1892, 366; Vol. 1016, 1894, ; Vol. 1017, 1895, 357; Vol. 1018, 1896, 360.

38. HML, Petit Ledger, Vol. 1019, 1897, 347; Vol. 1022, 1900, 370 (which also contained reference to William and John Oar "taking care of 8" guns at Springfield); Vol. 1023, 1902, 410.

39. Transcript of Oral Interview of John E. Krauss, May 14 and 28, 1954, HML, Accession 2020, Box 1, 4.

40. James, p. 130-132. FGD writes that it was about five seconds. See FGD, 89.

Notes 273

41. HML, Notes from DuPont Employees as Obtained by Richard Stout, 1909. Eleutherian Mills-Hagley Foundation Research Report.

42. Transcript of Oral Interview of Emily Peoples Blackwell, July 6, 1970, HML, Accession 2026, Box 1, 2.

43. By this time, and since about the Civil War, the DuPonts charged their workers rent to live in company-owned housing. Rents were about $3 a month.

44. Alan Axelrod. The International Encyclopedia of Secret Societies & Fraternal Orders, (New York: Facts on File), 1999, 249.

45. Ibid.

46. Https://odd-fellows.org/history/the-name-odd-fellows/, retrieved March 15, 2020.

47. Https://en.wikipedia.org/wiki/Improved_Order_of_Red_Men#cite_ref-3, retrieved March 15, 2020.

48. *Delaware Gazette and State Journal.* (Wilmington, Del.), 15 Dec. 1898. Chronicling America: Historic American Newspapers. Lib. of Congress. <http://chroniclingamerica.loc.gov/lccn/sn88053046/1898-12-15/ed-1/seq-1/>, retrieved June 2, 2018. See Https://www.measuringworth.com/index.php.

49. *Delaware Gazette and State Journal.* (Wilmington, Del.), 15 March 1900. Chronicling America: Historic American Newspapers. Lib. of Congress. <http://chroniclingamerica.loc.gov/lccn/sn88053046/1900-03-15/ed-1/seq-5/>, retrieved June 2, 2018.

50. Axelrod, 13.

51. "Delaware Death Records, 1855-1961," database with images, *FamilySearch* (https://familysearch.org/ark:/61903/1:1:FNYV-B5H : 25 September 2019), Addie Stewart, 09 Nov 1896; Samuel Stewart, 15 Nov 1896; Minnie Stewart, 22 Nov 1896, citing Wilmington, New Castle, Delaware, United States, Hall of Records, Dover; FamilySearch digital folder 004252481, retrieved June 4, 2018.

52. "Delaware Death Records, 1855-1961," database with images, *FamilySearch* (https://familysearch.org/ark:/61903/1:1:FNP1-1ZZ : 25 September 2019), Margaret J. Stewart, 24 May 1891; citing Wilmington, New Castle, Delaware, United States, Hall of Records, Dover; FamilySearch digital folder 004252471, retrieved June 4, 2018.

53. "Delaware State Birth Records, 1861-1922," database with images, *FamilySearch* (https://familysearch.org/ark:/61903/1:1:FLJZ-ZJV : 4 September 2019), Lydia Emma Stewart, 26 Apr 1886; citing Duponts Bank, New Castle, Delaware, reference F22, Hall of Records, Dover; FHL microfilm 6,331, June 4, 2018

54. "Delaware Death Records, 1855-1961," database with images, *FamilySearch* (https://familysearch.org/ark:/61903/1:1:FNR5-TJ4 : 25 September 2019), Lydia

Stewart, 14 Jun 1886; citing Christian, New Castle, Delaware, United States, Hall of Records, Dover; FamilySearch digital folder 004252441, retrieved June 4, 2018.

55. HML, Petit Ledger, Vol. 1024, 1902, 411.

56. Margaret Wright to Frank DuPont, HML, Petit Ledger Vol. 1022, 1900, Letter pasted into page 415.

57. HML, Petit Ledger, Vol. 1008, 1886, 421.

Chapter Twelve

1. *Evening Journal.* (Wilmington, Del.), 08 Dec. 1902. Chronicling America: Historic American Newspapers. Lib. of Congress. <http://chroniclingamerica.loc.gov/lccn/sn85042354/1902-12-08/ed-1/seq-1/>, retrieved June 3, 2018.

2. *Daily Republican.* (Wilmington, Del.), 09 Dec. 1902. Chronicling America: Historic American Newspapers. Lib. of Congress. <http://chroniclingamerica.loc.gov/lccn/sn88053056/1902-12-09/ed-1/seq-1/>, retrieved June 3, 2018.

3. *Evening Journal.* (Wilmington, Del.), 09 Dec. 1902. Chronicling America: Historic American Newspapers. Lib. of Congress. <http://chroniclingamerica.loc.gov/lccn/sn85042354/1902-12-09/ed-1/seq-3/>, retrieved June 3, 2018.

4. *Delaware Gazette and State Journal.* (Wilmington, Del.), 11 Dec. 1902. Chronicling America: Historic American Newspapers. Lib. of Congress. <http://chroniclingamerica.loc.gov/lccn/sn88053046/1902-12-11/ed-1/seq-2/>, retrieved June 2, 2018.

5. E.I. DuPont de Nemours & Co.to R. H. Durham, Comptroller, December 14, 1903, HML, Petit Ledger, Vol. 1024, 1902, 415.

6. *Morning News*, (Wilmington, Delaware), June 9, 1904.

7. Marriage Records of Christ Church, Vol. 41, 57.

8. Https://www.legalgenealogist.com/2012/01/25/the-ties-that-bond/, retrieved March 12, 2020.

9. HML, Accession 263, Reel No. 1, Christ Church records.

10. "United States Census, 1900," database with images, *FamilySearch* (https://familysearch.org/ark:/61903/1:1:M315-5SL : accessed 17 March 2020), Samuel J Buchanin, Christiana Hundred (all south & west of hundred) Du Ponts Banks village, New Castle, Delaware, United States; citing enumeration district (ED) 53, sheet 10B, family 191, NARA microfilm publication T623 (Washington, D.C.: National Archives and Records Administration, 1972.); FHL microfilm 1,240,156, retrieved March 17, 2020.

Notes

11. James, 69.

12. Https://www.delawaresymphony.org/dso_events/a-i-dupont-composers-award/, retrieved March 17, 2020.

13. Ethel Ashe-Frear. *The Powderman E I du Pont de Nemours Powder Company*, https://www.faithwriters.com/article-details.php?id=180374, October 10, 2015, retrieved June 6, 2018.

14. Ibid.

15. Transcript of Oral Interview of Mary Braden Jackson, August 17, 1986, HML, Accession 2026, Box 1, 22-23.

16. *The Morning News*, (Wilmington, Delaware), February 3, 1906.

17. Ibid.

18. *Every Evening*, (Wilmington, Delaware), February 7, 1906, DHS, Bill Frank Collection, DuPont Company File, Box 13, Folder 5; *The Morning News*, (Wilmington, Delaware), February 7, 1906, http://newspapers.com, retrieved June 2, 2018. This article labeled it a "pathetic incident" intending to mean "touching," or full of pathos.

19. *Morning News*, (Wilmington, Delaware), February 8, 1906.

20. At this point, Connable was General Manager of the Powder Operations Department of the DuPont Company; he was listed as such in *Every Evening, Wilmington Daily Commercial*. (Wilmington, Del.), 12 June 1906. Chronicling America: Historic American Newspapers. Lib. of Congress. <https://chroniclingamerica.loc.gov/lccn/sn87062237/1906-06-12/ed-1/seq-8/>, retrieved March 17, 2020.

21. *Morning News*, (Wilmington, Delaware) February 9, 1906.

22. According to Marquis James, Sam Buchanan had once saved Alfred from drowning. See James, 127.

23. "United States Census, 1920," database with images, *FamilySearch* (https://familysearch.org/ark:/61903/1:1:MDW1-FL4 : accessed 17 March 2020), Catherine Buchanan, Wilmington Ward 10, New Castle, Delaware, United States; citing ED 123, sheet 1A, line 32, family 7, NARA microfilm publication T625 (Washington D.C.: National Archives and Records Administration, 1992), roll 203; FHL microfilm 1,820,203, retrieved March 17, 2020.

24. *Morning News*, (Wilmington, Delaware), May 11, 1906.

25. Ibid.

26. HML, George Cheney Hagley Property book, 73.

27. *Evening Journal*, (Wilmington, Delaware), May 11, 1906.

28. *Morning News*, (Wilmington, Delaware), May 14, 1906.

29. Transcript of Oral Interview with James Cammock, April 9, 1984, HML Accession 2026, Box 3, 21.

30. *Every Evening*, Wilmington Daily Commercial. (Wilmington, Del.), 18 May 1906. Chronicling America: Historic American Newspapers. Lib. of Congress. <http://chroniclingamerica.loc.gov/lccn/sn87062237/1906-05-18/ed-1/seq-2/>, retrieved June 2, 2018.

31. "United States Census, 1930," database with images, *FamilySearch* (https://familysearch.org/ark:/61903/1:1:CHM1-TPZ : accessed 18 March 2020), Catherine Cammock, Wilmington, New Castle, Delaware, United States; citing enumeration district (ED) ED 39, sheet 26A, line 13, family 307, NARA microfilm publication T626 (Washington D.C.: National Archives and Records Administration, 2002), roll 290; FHL microfilm 2,340,025, retrieved March 18, 2020.

32. *Delaware Gazette and State Journal*. (Wilmington, Del.), 23 Sept. 1886. Chronicling America: Historic American Newspapers. Lib. of Congress. <https://chroniclingamerica.loc.gov/lccn/sn88053046/1886-09-23/ed-1/seq-1/>, retrieved March 18, 2020.

33. *Delaware Gazette and State Journal*. (Wilmington, Del.), 24 Sept. 1891. Chronicling America: Historic American Newspapers. Lib. of Congress. <https://chroniclingamerica.loc.gov/lccn/sn88053046/1891-09-24/ed-1/seq-3/>, retrieved March 18, 2020.

34. *Delaware Gazette and State Journal*. (Wilmington, Del.), 07 Dec. 1899. Chronicling America: Historic American Newspapers. Lib. of Congress. <https://chroniclingamerica.loc.gov/lccn/sn88053046/1899-12-07/ed-1/seq-5/>, retrieved March 18, 2020.

35. "Showing ones mettle" came from the world of stone dressing, an occupation that Whiteman pursued prior to owning the stables. When dressing a stone, small flakes would fly off the stone and lodge themselves in the skin of the dresser. When someone wanted to hire a dresser, the applicant would be asked to "show his mettle," meaning show his arms; if the arms showed blue spots created by the stone chips embedded therein, the person doing the hiring would at least know that the applicant was, indeed, experienced, though not necessarily adept, at dressing the mill stones.

36. *Evening Journal*. (Wilmington, Del.), 05 Sept. 1890. Chronicling America: Historic American Newspapers. Lib. of Congress. <https://chroniclingamerica.loc.gov/lccn/sn85042354/1890-09-05/ed-1/seq-3/>, retrieved March 18, 2020.

37. *Delaware Gazette and State Journal*. (Wilmington, Del.), 10 Oct. 1889. Chronicling America: Historic American Newspapers. Lib. of Congress. <https://chroniclingamerica.loc.gov/lccn/sn88053046/1889-10-10/ed-1/seq-3/>, retrieved March 18, 2020.

38. *Evening Journal.* (Wilmington, Del.), 02 June 1893. Chronicling America: Historic American Newspapers. Lib. of Congress. retrieved March 18, 2020. The newspapers could write about heads found in trees and about being 'blown to atoms,' but found it distasteful to write that phrase.

39. *Evening Journal.* (Wilmington, Del.), 15 March 1893. Chronicling America: Historic American Newspapers. Lib. of Congress. <https://chroniclingamerica.loc.gov/lccn/sn85042354/1893-03-15/ed-1/seq-3/>, retrieved March 18, 2020.

40. *Evening Journal.* (Wilmington, Del.), 15 Oct. 1900. Chronicling America: Historic American Newspapers. Lib. of Congress. <https://chroniclingamerica.loc.gov/lccn/sn85042354/1900-10-15/ed-1/seq-4/>, retrieved March 19, 2020.

41. "Delaware Death Records, 1855-1961, "database with images, *FamilySearch* (https://familysearch.org/ark:/61903/1:1:FNYN-R3N : 25 September 2019), Margaret L. Whiteman, 19 Nov 1907; citing Wilmington, New Castle, Delaware, United States, Hall of Records, Dover; FamilySearch digital folder 004252926, retrieved March 19, 2020. For the children's deaths, see: Katherine, "Delaware, Wilmington Vital Records, 1847-1954," database with images, *FamilySearch* (https://familysearch.org/ark:/61903/1:1:QKD6-LQQB : 13 March 2018), Katharine Whiteman, 06 Jan 1895; citing Death, Wilmington, New Castle, Delaware, United States, Public Archives, Dover; FHL microfilm 2,188,030.; Edith, "Delaware, Wilmington Vital Records, 1847-1954," database with images, *FamilySearch* (https://familysearch.org/ark:/61903/1:1:QKD6-LBZG : 13 March 2018), Edith Whiteman, 13 Oct 1900; citing Death, Wilmington, New Castle, Delaware, United States, Public Archives, Dover; FHL microfilm 2,188,030; Francis, "Delaware Death Records, 1855-1961," database with images, *FamilySearch* (https://familysearch.org/ark:/61903/1:1:FNYV-SQV : 25 September 2019), Frances C. Whiteman, 24 Mar 1899; citing Wilmington, Delaware, United States, Hall of Records, Dover; FamilySearch digital folder 004252490; Helen, "Delaware Death Records, 1855-1961," database with images, *FamilySearch* (https://familysearch.org/ark:/61903/1:1:FN5W-5JQ : 25 September 2019), Helen Pierce Whiteman, 17 Sep 1901; citing Wilmington, Delaware, United States, Hall of Records, Dover; FamilySearch digital folder 004252893.

42. *Morning News*, (Wilmington, Delaware), March 9, 1909.

43. *Evening Journal.* (Wilmington, Del.), 29 March 1909. Chronicling America: Historic American Newspapers. Lib. of Congress. <http://chroniclingamerica.loc.gov/lccn/sn85042354/1909-03-29/ed-1/seq-4/>, retrieved June 2, 2018.

44. Transcript of oral interview of Elizabeth Beacom, HML, Accession 2026, Box 1, 6. Her opinion was not borne out by the facts. The top three months for explosions were April, May, and September.

45. *Morning News*, (Wilmington, Delaware), March 9, 1909.

46. "United States Census, 1900," database with images, *FamilySearch* (https://familysearch.org/ark:/61903/1:1:M33W-S2V : accessed 19 March 2020), John Mott, Lackawanna Township (part) Moosie borough, Lackawanna, Pennsylvania, United States; citing enumeration district (ED) 31, sheet 6A, family 106, NARA microfilm publication T623 (Washington, D.C.: National Archives and Records Administration, 1972.); FHL microfilm 1,241,419, retrieved April 4, 2020.

47. Transcript of Oral interview with Daniel F. Shields, March 19, 1958, HML, Accession 2026, Box 2, 7.

48. *Morning News*, (Wilmington Delaware), November 12, 1909.

49. "United States Census, 1910," database with images, *FamilySearch* (https://familysearch.org/ark:/61903/1:1:MVVK-1ND : accessed 19 March 2020), Margaret Mc Dermott in household of Meridith I Samuel, Wilmington Ward 7, New Castle, Delaware, United States; citing enumeration district (ED) ED 40, sheet 9A, family 196, NARA microfilm publication T624 (Washington D.C.: National Archives and Records Administration, 1982), roll 147; FHL microfilm 1,374,160, retrieved March 19, 2020.

50. "Delaware Death Records, 1855-1961," database with images, *FamilySearch* (https://familysearch.org/ark:/61903/1:1:FNYQ-FX6 : 25 September 2019), Margaret Keeley, 10 Oct 1918; citing Wilmington, New Castle, Delaware, United States, Hall of Records, Dover; FamilySearch digital folder 004252918, retrieved April 8, 2020.

51. "United States Census, 1900," database with images, *FamilySearch* (https://familysearch.org/ark:/61903/1:1:M39S-W7B : accessed 20 March 2020), George H Darrah in household of George J Darrah, Bensalem Township (lower district), Bucks, Pennsylvania, United States; citing enumeration district (ED) 4, sheet 10B, family 211, NARA microfilm publication T623 (Washington, D.C.: National Archives and Records Administration, 1972.); FHL microfilm 1,241,384, retrieved March 20, 2020.

52. James, 104.

53. This is the name as spelled on his headstone and in the official death records. In the DuPont record books, he is known as Nicholas Dinesta. The newspapers had several different iterations of his name.

54. *Morning News*, (Wilmington, Delaware), November 12, 1909.

55. *Morning News*, (Wilmington, Delaware), November 17, 1909.

56. Ibid.

57. Ibid.

Chapter Thirteen

1. *Every Evening*, (Wilmington, Delaware), June 23, 1915.

2. Italy joined the Allies by declaring war on Austria-Hungary in May of 1915; the Irish, of course, would have been anti-British due to the poor treatment they and their countrymen received from the English through the years and "whose hostility toward the English was particularly high at the moment of increasing clashes in Ulster", see Jules Witcover. *Sabotage at Big Tom: Imperial Germany's Secret War In America—1914-1917* (Chapel Hill, NC: Algonquin Books), 1989, 46. One Irish-American leader, Jeremiah O'Leary of the American Truth Society, insisted that his followers stand when the German anthem *Watch on the Rhine* was played. See David Traxel. *Crusader Nation: The United States in Peace and the Great War, 1898-1920*. (New York: Alfred A. Knopf), 2006, 138.

3. *Evening Journal*, (Wilmington, Delaware), July 13, 1915.

4. *Every Evening*, (Wilmington, Delaware), July 14, 1915.

5. *News Journal*, (Wilmington, Delaware), Nov. 6, 1905.

6. "New York, New York City Marriage Records, 1829-1940," database, *FamilySearch* (https://familysearch.org/ark:/61903/1:1:249D-YWJ : 10 February 2018), Henry Cazier and Aubertine Grant, 21 Dec 1906; citing Marriage, Manhattan, New York, New York, United States, New York City Municipal Archives, New York; FHL microfilm 1,558,685. See also Morning News, (Wilmington, Delaware), February 25, 1885; and https://www.findagrave.com/memorial/131008498/aubertine-grant.

7. Aubertine Grant was also well known in Wilmington and Philadelphia societies. Numerous newspaper society page mentions of her during her early twenties, prior to her marriage to Henry, can be found.

8. *The Sun*. (Wilmington, Del.), 14 June 1900. Chronicling America: Historic American Newspapers. Lib. of Congress. <http://chroniclingamerica.loc.gov/lccn/sn88053087/1900-06-14/ed-1/seq-1/>, retrieved June 3, 2018.

9. *Middletown Transcript*. (Middletown, Del.), 03 Jan. 1903. Chronicling America: Historic American Newspapers. Lib. of Congress. <http://chroniclingamerica.loc.gov/lccn/sn84026820/1903-01-03/ed-1/seq-3/>, retrieved June 3, 2018.

10. *Middletown Transcript*. (Middletown, Del.), 02 July 1910. Chronicling America: Historic American Newspapers. Lib. of Congress. <http://chroniclingamerica.loc.gov/lccn/sn84026820/1910-07-02/ed-1/seq-3/>, retrieved June 3, 2018.

11. *Middletown Transcript*. (Middletown, Del.), 29 July 1911. Chronicling America: Historic American Newspapers. Lib. of Congress. <http://chroniclingamerica.loc.gov/lccn/sn84026820/1911-07-29/ed-1/seq-3/>, retrieved June 3, 2018.

12. This incident was not an explosion, per se; it was a flash fire. In order to explode, black powder must be completely contained in a vessel of some kind, for example, a bullet. When powder is not contained it burns rapidly when ignited.

13. *Kent News*, (Chestertown, Maryland), July 17, 1915, found on https://www.findagrave.com, retrieved June 2, 2018.

14. He was probably referring to boric acid ointment, or white petrolatum. See https://jamanetwork.com/journals/jama/article-abstract/274229. In the late 19th century, treatments for burns using such things as black mud, cow dung, roasted dormice, raw egg and vinegar, pig fat, boiled beans, beeswax, honey, oak leaves, and powdered silver, were common. "The application of these salves did little that was helpful, except perhaps to ease pain temporarily, and much that was harmful. Most notably they introduced a novel assortment of pathogens and then sealed them in the wound, creating an especially inviting environment for anaerobic bacteria." See Daniel James Brown, *Under a Flaming Sky: The Great Hinckley Firestorm of 1894* (New York: Harper Perennial), 2006, 172.

15. Transcript of Oral Interview of Daniel F. Shields, March 19, 1958, HML, Accession 2026, Box 2, 6.

16. Prismatic powder, also called brown powder and cocoa powder, was a low-sulfur explosive made to burn more slowly than black powder. It was used for large artillery and ship's guns. Because of its slow burning, it caused less stress on the apparatus from which it was fired.

17. Transcript of Oral Interview of Charles Lickle, June 13, 1968, HML, Accession 2026, Box 2, 13.

18. *Every Evening*, (Wilmington Delaware), August 19, 1915.

19. *Evening Journal*. (Wilmington, Del.), 18 Aug. 1915. Chronicling America: Historic American Newspapers. Lib. of Congress. <https://chroniclingamerica.loc.gov/lccn/sn85042354/1915-08-18/ed-1/seq-13/>, retrieved March 21, 2020.

20. *Every Evening*, (Wilmington Delaware), August 19, 1915.

21. It was a press mill, according to William Frederick Lynch, see Transcript of Oral Interview of William Frederick Lynch, HML, Accession 2026, Box 2, 4. See Newark Post. (Newark, Del.), 01 Sept. 1915. *Chronicling America: Historic American Newspapers*. Lib. of Congress. <http://chroniclingamerica.loc.gov/lccn/sn88053005/1915-09-01/ed-1/seq-4/>, retrieved June 2, 2018, which says that the second mill to go was a corning, or sizing, mill. See also HML, "Explosions File" at Hagley's Soda House. According to this compendium of all of the explosions at the mills, it was the glazing and graining mills that blew.

22. "Delaware Death Records, 1855-1961," database with images, *FamilySearch* (https://familysearch.org/ark:/61903/1:1:FNRB-JMD : 25 September 2019), Bella

May Cunningham, 30 Nov 1895; citing Delaware, United States, Hall of Records, Dover; FamilySearch digital folder 004252478, retrieved March 21, 2020.

23. Transcript of Oral Interview of Thomas Dunlop, April 30, 1984, HML, Accession 2026, Box 3, 1.

24. *The News*, (Frederick, Maryland), August 30, 1915, found at http://www.gendisasters.com/delaware/5654/wilmington-de-dupont-powder-company-explosion-aug-1915, retrieved June 3, 2018.

25. *Daily Pantagraph*, (Bloomington, Illinois), September 17, 1915, http://www.newspapers.com, retrieved June 2, 2018.

26. *Evening Journal*. (Wilmington, Del.), 15 Nov. 1915. Chronicling America: Historic American Newspapers. Lib. of Congress. <https://chroniclingamerica.loc.gov/lccn/sn85042354/1915-11-15/ed-1/seq-4/>, retrieved March 21, 2020.

27. *Evening Journal*, (Wilmington, Del.), 23 June 1915. Chronicling America: Historic American Newspapers. Lib. of Congress. <https://chroniclingamerica.loc.gov/lccn/sn85042354/1915-06-23/ed-1/seq-2/>, retrieved March 21, 2020.

28. *Morning Call*, (Allentown, Pennsylvania), December 3, 1915, http://www.newspapers.com, December 3, 1915, retrieved June 2, 2018.

29. *Philadelphia Inquirer*, (Philadelphia, Pennsylvania), December 2, 1915, http://www.newspapers.com, retrieved June 2, 2018.

30. *Charlotte Observer*, (Charlotte, North Carolina), December 5, 1915, http://www.newspapers.com, retrieved June 2, 2018.

31. *Every Evening*, (Wilmington, Delaware), December 3, 1915.

32. First Hatcher's Run, occurring in late October of 1864, was also known as the Battle of Boydton Plank Road. A humorous story of Thaxter's Civil War exploits is told. About two miles from Warrenton, a Confederate camp was discovered by a scouting party and Major Thaxter volunteered to discover who was in the camp. Cautiously approaching on his horse he came at length to two soldiers asleep.

    His "Hello, there!" "What regiment?" brought no response. Moving on to a single sleeper, he asked the same question and received the answer: "The Twelfth." "The Twelfth what?" asked the major. "The Twelfth Virginia, you fool," came the response. Major Thaxter had the information he was seeking and lost no time in getting away. From http://www.ebooksread.com/authors-eng/george-thomas-little/genealogical-and-family-history-of-the-state-of-maine-volume-4-tti/page-68-genealogical-and-family-history-of-the-state-of-maine-volume-4-tti.shtml, retrieved June 4, 2018.

33. The memorial books for Sydney W. and Sydney St. Felix Thaxter can be found at the Maine Historical Society, Portland, Maine. Both are unpublished manuscripts.

The family name would itself achieve a level of fame when Alan's niece, Phyllis Thaxter (whom he never met; she was born four years after his death), acted opposite Van Johnson in the 1944 war movie, *Thirty Seconds over Tokyo*. Her last film featured her as Clark Kent's mother in Superman.

34. "S" was Truman's middle name; it stood for nothing.

35. Hunter Pendleton to Col. Joseph R. Anderson, December 4, 1915, Virginia Military Institute Archives, Lexington, Virginia. Acting Superintendent Hunter Pendleton's son married the widow of Allen [Brown] Marshall, the general's stepson, killed as a tank commander in Italy late in the Second World War. In an ironic twist, on June 12, 1864, Major General David Hunter, against the wishes of a brevet (temporary) colonel named Henry A. du Pont, ordered the colonel's artillery to bomb the VMI campus in retribution for the cadet corps' participation in the Battle of Newmarket a month earlier. A half century later, Senator Henry A. du Pont introduced a bill in the United States Senate authorizing $100,000 for VMI in restitution for the damage caused by his unit's bombing. The Institute used the money to build Jackson Hall, wherein lies a plaque honoring Henry du Pont. VMI's first superintendent, Francis H. Smith, was a lifelong friend of the colonel's father, Henry, and a fellow graduate in the elder Henry's U.S. Military Academy class.

36. Another "Rat" (freshman) in VMI's Class of 1907, was Jubal Anderson Early, a great-nephew of the famous Confederate general of the same name. Patton did not return to VMI because he had been nominated for a position in the cadet corps at West Point. Thaxter may have left because he wasn't suited to the strict discipline inculcated into the Rats, the first-year students. Or he may have become fed up with "growlie," a "a hash of various and indescribable elements that for years was the mainstay of the VMI menu." See Forrest C. Pogue. George Marshall: Education of a General, 1880-1939. (New York: Viking Press), 1963, 42.

37. *Churchman*, Vol. 96, (Hartford, Connecticut: Churchman Associates, Inc.), 1907, https://books.google.com/books?id=m9825ht3pM4C&dq=%22alan+thaxter%22+graduate+-celia&source=gbs_navlinks_s, retrieved March 23, 2020.

38. He weighed one hundred seventy pounds on a football team where no one was heavier than one hundred ninety and the average was one hundred sixty-seven. Before the 1907 season opened in October, the *Trinity Tripod* college newspaper included an encouraging article, declaring the "new material" joining the gridiron team would do well. Thaxter and his roommate received mentions as "look[ing] to be the most likely to make good."

He proved his keen football ability during the season's eight games, including a ninety-four to zero drubbing of City College of New York, beating that year's scoring record by one point (Pop Warner's Carlisle Indians defeated Albion College, ninety-three to nothing). The Trinity newspaper headline said the "contest did not even serve as a practice game." Thaxter received kudos from the newspaper sports columnists in the Amherst game, one of only two games lost that season: "The second half opened auspiciously for Trinity, as Amherst attempted a short kick-off, which Thaxter spoiled by falling on the ball on our [?] fifty yard line." Later in the game, Trinity took the ball on downs, "the feature being the good work on defense of Thaxter." In their second loss of the season, the Gold and Blue lost to the West Point cadets twelve to zero, but Thaxter received praise for his "standing off the heavy line of their opponents." In one triumph, one of the team's scoring plays was a triple forward pass, this in the year after the rules changed so a forward pass was not only legal but also not penalized fifteen yards for an incompletion, as was the rule before 1906. See Trinity Tripod, (Hartford, Connecticut), October 1, 1907, https://digitalrepository.trincoll.edu/cgi/viewcontent.cgi?article=2487&context=tripod, retrieved June 4, 2018. See also Trinity Tripod, November 5, 1907, https://digitalrepository.trincoll.edu/cgi/viewcontent.cgi?article=2480&context=tripod, retrieved June 4, 2018, and Trinity Tripod, October 15 1907, https://digitalrepository.trincoll.edu/cgi/viewcontent.cgi?article=2491&context=tripod, retrieved June 4, 2018, retrieved June 4, 2018.

39. "United States Census, 1910," database with images, *FamilySearch* (https://familysearch.org/ark:/61903/1:1:MR39-1QS : accessed 23 March 2020), Allan Thaxter in household of Julia S Thaxter, Portland Ward 7, Cumberland, Maine, United States; citing enumeration district (ED) ED 91, sheet 5A, family 95, NARA microfilm publication T624 (Washington D.C.: National Archives and Records Administration, 1982), roll 539; FHL microfilm 1,374,552, retrieved June 2, 2018.

40. Transcript of Oral Interview of Charles Lickle, June 13, 1968, HML, Accession 2026, Box 2, 13.

41. *New-York Tribune*. (New York [N.Y.]), 02 Dec. 1915. Chronicling America: Historic American Newspapers. Lib. of Congress. <https://chroniclingamerica.loc.gov/lccn/sn83030214/1915-12-02/ed-1/seq-3/> retrieved March 23, 2020.

42. *Evening Journal*. (Wilmington, Del.), 01 Dec. 1915. Chronicling America: Historic American Newspapers. Lib. of Congress. <https://chroniclingamerica.loc.gov/lccn/sn85042354/1915-12-01/ed-1/seq-2/>, retrieved March 25, 2020.

43. Ibid.

44. He worked for Bodell & Company, a providence, Rhode Island, investment bank with offices on Wall Street, and in New Haven, Boston, and Hartford. Alan was one of more than two dozen bond salesmen who covered New England for the company. His territory was his hometown of Portland.

45. *Every Evening*, (Wilmington, Delaware), December 1, 1915. On what this idea was based is unknown.

46. Transcript of oral interview with William Frederick Lynch, October 5, 1956, HML, Accession 2026, Box 2, 13.

47. *Portland Sunday Telegram*, (Portland, Maine), December 5, 1915. In another irony, a pallbearer at his Portland funeral, Guy Stollenwerck, later became assistant director at the Wayne, New Jersey, DuPont factory. In 1913, Guy was best man for his

brother, E. Carroll Stollenwerck, who was marrying Carolene Marsh Hynson. Five years after her husband's death, Carolene became the second wife of Lammot du Pont II, the youngest son of Lammot du Pont, a great grandson of Éleuthère Irénée du Pont. Carolene was the niece of Lammot's first wife, Natalie Driver Wilson. See *News Journal*, (Wilmington, Delaware), November 21, 1913, https://www.newspapers.com/clip/15414054/carolyn_marsh_hynson_marriage_to_e/, retrieved June 3, 2018, and Winkler, 315.

48. *Every Evening*, (Wilmington, Delaware), December 4, 1915.

49. *Every Evening*, (Wilmington, Delaware), December. 1, 1915.

50. "Delaware Death Records, 1855-1961," database with images, *FamilySearch* (https://familysearch.org/ark:/61903/1:1:FNTT-19Q : 24 March 2020), James Malloy, 30 Nov 1915; citing Henry Clay, New Castle, Delaware, United States, Hall of Records, Dover; FamilySearch digital folder 004252911, retrieved June 2, 2018.

51. *Every Evening*, (Wilmington, Delaware), December. 2, 1915.

52. The birth of a child soon after its father's death was not a tragedy that visited itself upon only powdermen's families. In March 1884, Lammot DuPont was killed in an accident at the works in Repauno, New Jersey; his wife, Mary Belin, gave birth to Margaretta, in May.

53. *Evening Public Ledger*. (Philadelphia [Pa.]), 02 Dec. 1915. Chronicling America: Historic American Newspapers. Lib. of Congress. <https://chroniclingamerica.loc.gov/lccn/sn83045211/1915-12-02/ed-1/seq-3/>, retrieved March 25, 2020.

54. *Every Evening*, (Wilmington Delaware), December 3, 1915.

Chapter Fourteen

1. *Every Evening*, (Wilmington, Delaware), December 1, 1915.

2. Ibid.

3. Ibid.

4. "Delaware Death Records, 1855-1961," database with images, *FamilySearch* (https://familysearch.org/ark:/61903/1:1:FNPL-XMQ : 25 September 2019), John A. Eggner, 13 Dec 1893; citing Wilmington, New Castle, Delaware, United States, Hall of Records, Dover; FamilySearch digital folder 004252474, retrieved March 24, 2020.

5. This was not the first instance of an accidental poisoning recorded in the annals of the families on the Brandywine. In 1851, E.I.'s second living daughter, Eleuthera, was asked to bring a headache remedy to her husband, Dr. Thomas Mackie Smith.

She mistakenly brought him aconite (wolfsbane), which he swallowed without looking at the label. The poison killed him within hours.

6. *Evening Journal.* (Wilmington, Del.), 17 July 1905. Chronicling America: Historic American Newspapers. Lib. of Congress. <https://chroniclingamerica.loc.gov/lccn/sn85042354/1905-07-17/ed-1/seq-1/>, retrieved March 24, 2020.

7. *Evening Republican.* (Wilmington, Del.), 26 Aug. 1902. Chronicling America: Historic American Newspapers. Lib. of Congress. <https://chroniclingamerica.loc.gov/lccn/sn88053043/1902-08-26/ed-1/seq-2/>, retrieved March 24, 2020.

8. *Wilmington Daily Republican.* (Wilmington, Del.), 02 Dec. 1898. Chronicling America: Historic American Newspapers. Lib. of Congress. <https://chroniclingamerica.loc.gov/lccn/sn88053055/1898-12-02/ed-1/seq-2/>, retrieved March 25, 2020.

9. *Evening Journal.* (Wilmington, Del.), 22 March 1918. Chronicling America: Historic American Newspapers. Lib. of Congress. <https://chroniclingamerica.loc.gov/lccn/sn85042354/1918-03-22/ed-1/seq-8/>, retrieved March 25, 2020.

10. *Evening Journal.* (Wilmington, Del.), 27 April 1914. Chronicling America: Historic American Newspapers. Lib. of Congress. <https://chroniclingamerica.loc.gov/lccn/sn85042354/1914-04-27/ed-1/seq-2/>, retrieved March 25, 2020.

11. *Evening Public Ledger.* (Philadelphia,Pennsylvania), 02 Dec., 1915. Chronicling America: Historic American Newspapers. Lib. of Congress. <https://chroniclingamerica.loc.gov/lccn/sn83045211/1915-12-02/ed-1/seq-3/>, retrieved June 4, 2018.

12. *Evening Journal.* (Wilmington, Del.), 03 Dec.,, 1915. Chronicling America: Historic American Newspapers. Lib. of Congress. <https://chroniclingamerica.loc.gov/lccn/sn85042354/1915-12-03/ed-1/seq-1/>, retrieved March 25, 2020.

13. *Evening Journal.* (Wilmington, Del.), 01 Dec. 1915. Chronicling America: Historic American Newspapers. Lib. of Congress. <https://chroniclingamerica.loc.gov/lccn/sn85042354/1915-12-01/ed-1/seq-2/>, retrieved March 25, 2020.

14. *Every Evening*, (Wilmington, Delaware), December 3, 1915.

15. R.L. Polk & Co, *Wilmington City Directory, Vol. 1918-1919*. New York: R.L. Polk & Co., 725.

16. Tombstone of Benjamin Reed, Patrick Hanrahan, and Mary Ellen Reed, at Riverview Cemetery, Section 2, Lot 24, Wilmington, Delaware.

17. Transcript of oral interview with William Lynch, October 5, 1966, HML, Accession 2026, Box 2, 13.

18. Telephone conversation between the author and Elma Andrews, December 17, 2018.

19. *Evening Journal.* (Wilmington, Del.), 29 March, 1894. Chronicling America: Historic American Newspapers. Lib. of Congress. <http://chroniclingamerica.loc.gov/lccn/sn85042354/1894-03-29/ed-1/seq-3/>, retrieved June 2, 2018.

20. "Delaware State Birth Records, 1861-1922," database with images, *FamilySearch* (https://familysearch.org/ark:/61903/1:1:FLJ7-4JF : 4 September 2019), Halert Mace, 07 Nov 1896; citing Centerville, New Castle, Delaware, reference /, Hall of Records, Dover; FHL microfilm 6,344.

21. Elma Andrews conversation, op. cit.

22. *Every Evening*, (Wilmington, Delaware), December 1, 1915.

23. One or two paper mills remained on the Brandywine. Wilmington became the paper making center of early America, but over the years, many manufacturers went out of business.

24. "United States Census, 1880," database with images, *FamilySearch* (https://familysearch.org/ark:/61903/1:1:MXCJ-TZD : 24 August 2017), Nelson Hogate in household of Joseph Sapp, Pencader, New Castle, Delaware, United States; citing enumeration district ED 27, sheet 269B, NARA microfilm publication T9 (Washington, D.C.: National Archives and Records Administration, n.d.), FHL microfilm 1,254,120, retrieved June 4, 2018.

25. "United States Census, 1880," database with images, *FamilySearch* (https://familysearch.org/ark:/61903/1:1:MXCJ-TZD : 24 August 2017), Nelson Hogate in household of Joseph Sapp, Pencader, New Castle, Delaware, United States; citing enumeration district ED 27, sheet 269B, NARA microfilm publication T9 (Washington, D.C.: National Archives and Records Administration, n.d.), FHL microfilm 1,254,120, retrieved June 4, 2018.

26. "United States Census, 1870", database with images, *FamilySearch* (https://familysearch.org/ark:/61903/1:1:M4BR-Q43 : 19 March 2020), Sarah Rodenhiser in entry for Aquilla Heizer, 1870, retrieved March 25, 2020.

27. *Every Evening*, (Wilmington, Delaware), December 1, 1915.

28. *Every Evening*, (Wilmington, Delaware), December 4, 1915.

29. Transcript of oral interview with William and Anna Baird Lloyd, June 8, 1988, HML, Accession 2026, Box 4, 15.

30. "United States Census, 1910," database with images, *FamilySearch* (https://familysearch.org/ark:/61903/1:1:MVV2-HN7 : accessed 26 March 2020), Elmer Fox in household of John W Fox, Wilmington Ward 9, New Castle, Delaware, United States; citing enumeration district (ED) ED 56, sheet 7B, family 149, NARA microfilm publication T624 (Washington D.C.: National Archives and Records Administration, 1982), roll 147; FHL microfilm 1,374,160, retrieved June 2, 2018.

Notes

31. *Every Evening*, (Wilmington, Delaware), December 1, 1915.

32. *The Philadelphia Inquirer*, (Philadelphia, Pennsylvania), December 1, 1915.

33. Transcript of oral interview with Ethel Jones Hayward, August 23, 1983, HML, Accession 2026, Box 4,12.

34. *Bridgeport Evening Farmer*. (Bridgeport, Conn.), 17 Dec. 1915. Chronicling America: Historic American Newspapers. Lib. of Congress. <https://chroniclingamerica.loc.gov/lccn/sn84022472/1915-12-17/ed-1/seq-13/>, retrieved March 27, 2020. See also https://today-in-wwi.tumblr.com/post/135362580453/arrest-in-dupont-explosion-case, retrieved March 27, 2020.

35. *Bulletin*, (Philadelphia, Pennsylvania), February 3, 1916, http://www.noufors.com/the_philadelphia_bulletin.html, retrieved June 2, 2018.

36. *Sydney Morning Herald*, January 11, 1917, https://trove.nla.gov.au/newspaper/article/15725867/1266825, retrieved June 4, 2018.

37. This and most of the other information regarding Charles Sicco was given to the author in an August, 2019 email from Janine Pizano, his great granddaughter. When possible, the specific information is annotated with its source, as researched by Ms. Pizano. Birth information: Archivio Storico Diocesano di Acqui; occupation and death information: www.antenati.beneculturi.it.

38. HML, Petit Ledger, Vol. 1008, 1886, 112.

39. Two years after Carlo's voyage, the Russian navy bought the ship and renamed it the Russ. See https://www.genealogyjourney.net/the-ships-they-came-on/, retrieved March 28, 2020.

40. On Giacomo's trip home to Italy with his wife, Giovanna, they transited through New York City. He died there before embarking on the trip. After a few months of mourning, Giovanna resumed her trip to Italy. On the sea, she got to know her son's widowed father-in-law, marrying him and living with her new husband and her son's family east of Rome.

41. *Evening Journal*. (Wilmington, Del.), 20 July 1908. Chronicling America: Historic American Newspapers. Lib. of Congress. <http://chroniclingamerica.loc.gov/lccn/sn85042354/1908-07-20/ed-1/seq-1/>.

42. *Evening Journal*, (Wilmington, Delaware), July 27, 1912.

43. Transcript of oral interview with Jennie Leto, March 5, 1983, HML, Accession 2026, Box 4, 11.

44. *Evening Journal*, (Wilmington, Delaware), March 15, 1917.

45. Germany, Austria-Hungary, the Ottoman Empire, and Bulgaria.

46. *Reading Times*, (Reading, Pennsylvania), April 11, 1917, http://www.nespapers.com, retrieved June 2, 2018.

47. *Evening Public Ledger*. (Philadelphia [Pa.]), 11 April 1917. Chronicling America: Historic American Newspapers. Lib. of Congress. <https://chroniclingamerica.loc.gov/lccn/sn83045211/1917-04-11/ed-1/seq-1/>, retrieved March 26, 2020. See the Appendix for more on this ship.

48. Benzol has been variably used as an after-shave, a coffee decaffeinater that led to the coffee product 'Sanka;' a metal degreaser; and in products like Liquid Wrench. It is no longer used in any of those products. See https://en.wikipedia.org/wiki/Benzene, retrieved April 13, 2020.

49. Bacon, 4, 107-108.

50. *Every Evening*, (Wilmington, Delaware), August 22, 1918. See also HML, Dick Scott Collection, Accession 1645, Box 10.

51. "United States World War I Draft Registration Cards, 1917-1918", database with images, *FamilySearch* (https://familysearch.org/ark:/61903/1:1:KZFG-JZC : 6 March 2020), Allan Upshure Pollitt, 1917-1918, retrieved March 29, 2020.

52. It would not be called World War I until September 1, 1939, the first day of World War II.

Chapter Fifteen

1. *Every Evening*, (Wilmington, Delaware), December 2, 1919.

2. Thomas Jefferson called Delaware a "jewel" of a state because of its strategic location in the mid-Atlantic region.

3. *Evening Journal*, (Wilmington, Delaware), January 2, 1920.

4. Another local paper said, "The main cloud was white but later it became tinged with darker smoke. The smoke held its formation and was wafted away over New Jersey like a giant cloud, the tail of it gradually drifting out of sight," emphasis added. See *Evening Journal*, (Wilmington, Delaware), January 2, 1920.

5. *Morning News*, (Wilmington, Delaware), January 3, 1920.

6. *Morning News*, (Wilmington, Delaware), January 3, 1920. The Merriam-Webster definition of "corning" is: to granulate, or to form into grains. See https://www.merriam-webster.com/dictionary/corn.

Notes 289

7. *Evening Journal*, (Wilmington, Delaware), January 3, 1920.

8. "United States World War I Draft Registration Cards, 1917-1918", database with images, *FamilySearch* (https://familysearch.org/ark:/61903/1:1:KZF2-R28 : 6 March 2020), Thomas Anselmi, 1917-1918, retrieved march 20, 2020.

9. "United States World War I Draft Registration Cards, 1917-1918", database with images, *FamilySearch* (https://familysearch.org/ark:/61903/1:1:KZF2-ZNQ : 6 March 2020), Giovanni Martin, 1917-1918, retrieved March 20, 2020.

10. *Evening Journal*, (Wilmington, Delaware), September 13, 1916; https://img5.newspapers.com/clip/17180280/the_evening_journal/, retrieved June 2, 2018.

11. One of Pinder's brothers, James, had lost a son when twelve-year-old Howard visited his uncle Lum's farm near Sudlersville. Howard and another boy were driving colts in the barnyard when one kicked him over the heart. Before the doctor had arrived, Howard died. See *Middletown Transcript*. (Middletown, Del.), 08 Aug. 1914. Chronicling America: Historic American Newspapers. Lib. of Congress.<http://chroniclingamerica.loc.gov/lccn/sn84026820/1914-08-08/ed-1/seq-7/>, retrieved June 4, 2018.

12. *Philadelphia Times*, (Philadelphia, Pennsylvania), September 24, 1899.

13. "Delaware State Birth Records, 1861-1922," database with images, *FamilySearch* (https://familysearch.org/ark:/61903/1:1:FLVH-V97 : 4 September 2019), Calvin Swartwood in entry for Mary Evelyn Swartwood, 02 Nov 1919; citing Wilmington, New Castle, Delaware, reference , Hall of Records, Dover; FHL microfilm 1,944,133, retrieved March 22, 2020.

14. "United States World War I Draft Registration Cards, 1917-1918", database with images, *FamilySearch* (https://familysearch.org/ark:/61903/1:1:KZFG-9PS : 6 March 2020), Aubrey Carson Turner, 1917-1918, retrieved March 22, 2020.

15. Tedd Cocker, *A Family of Patriots*, Friends of the Historical Riverview Cemetery Newsletter, March, 2019.

16. The flu would affect eight hundred thousand Americans at the front, killing about six percent, or forty-seven thousand. See Geoffrey Wawro, *Sons of Freedom: The Forgotten American Soldiers Who Defeated Germany in World War I*. (New York: Basic Books), 2018, 442.

17. World War Records, 1st Division, A.E.F., regular Citations, Volume 23, https://firstdivisionmuseum.nmtvault.com/jsp/viewer.jsp?doc_id=iwfd0000%2F20180924%2F00000012&page_name=668, retrieved April 1, 2020.

18. Also called 'cooties,' 'pants rabbits,' or 'seam squirrels.' The words 'lousy' and 'crummy', because lice looked like bread crumbs, became and remain slang words for anything bad or unpleasant. See Hanson, 33.

19. Ibid, 117.

20. Ibid, 124.

21. For more on James Hodge's war experiences, see the Appendix.

22. *Every Evening*, (Wilmington, Delaware), June 29, 1920.

23. *The Public Ledger.* (Maysville, Ky.), 19 Aug. 1920. Chronicling America: Historic American Newspapers. Lib. of Congress. <https://chroniclingamerica.loc.gov/lccn/sn85038022/1920-08-19/ed-1/seq-4/>, retrieved June 3, 2018.

Appendix

1. Brian Farwell, *Over There: The United States in the Great War, 1917-1918*. (New York: W.W. Norton and Company), 1999. 183. This author says there were none but this fact is contradicted by a listing in Wikipedia that lists the *USS Abraham Lincoln* troopship as having been torpedoed and sunk in May, 1918. See https://en.wikipedia.org/wiki/USS_President_Lincoln_(1907), retrieved April 18, 2020. In addition, the Tuscania with more than two thousand aboard, was sunk in 1918. Https://en.wikipedia.org/wiki/SS_Tuscania_(1914), retrieved April 18, 2020. See also Joseph Persico. Eleventh Month, Eleventh Day, Eleventh Hour (New York: Random House), 2005, 191.

2. Farwell, 19

3. After later relieving the faltering 35th Division, where Captain Harry S Truman was an artillery officer, the 1st would be called the "Immortal Division."

4. Jonathan H. Jaffin, *Medical Support for the American Expeditionary Forces in France During the First World War*. Master's Degree Thesis, U. S. Army Command and Staff College, Fort Leavenworth, KS, 1990, 82-83.

5. Michael E. Shay, *A Grateful Heart: The History of a World War I Field Hospital* (Westport, CT: Greenwood Press), 2002, 23.

6. Cantigny is north of Paris, about the same distance as Nemours, the DuPont ancestral home, is to the south of the capital.

7. If a French woman was thought to have a venereal disease, an MP was stationed outside her door, which may explain why that branch had the highest rate of VD during WWI. See Wawro, 87. Pershing was a staunch supporter of anything that would stop his men from contracting VD. During the move into Germany, he told his officers that his goal was that not a single case of a soldier with VD should arrive in the United States. The disease was not eradicated among the men; simply no man with the disease was allowed to board a U.S.-bound ship for home. See

Farwell, 147.

8. Https://www.worldwar1centennial.org/index.php/delivery-of-medical-care-on-the-battlefield.html, retrieved March 31, 2020.

9. Neil Hanson, *Unknown Soldiers: The Story of the Missing of the First World War*. (New York: Alfred Knopf), 2006, 210.

10. Joseph Persico, *Eleventh Month, Eleventh Day, Eleventh Hour: Armistice Day, 1918: World War I and its Violent Climax*. (New York: Random House), 2005, 56.

11. Martha K. Lenhart, ed., *Medical Aspects of Chemical Warfare*, (Washington, D. C.: Government Printing Office), 2008, 95.

12. Stephen Bull, *Trench: A History of Trench Warfare on the Western Front*. (Oxford: Osprey Publishing), 2010, 22.

13. Ibid.

14. Charles Lynch, Joseph Ford and Frank Weed, *The Medical Department of the United States Army in he World War, Volume VIII, Field Operations*, (Washington, D. C.: Government Printing Office), 1925, 302, at https://history.amedd.army.mil/booksdocs/wwi/fieldoperations/chapter9.html, retrieved March 31, 2020.

15. Ibid., p. 111. Hodge may or may not have known that the first American Expeditionary Force death in the war was the result of the German bombing of a field hospital in May of 1917 when Doctor William Fitzsimmons of Kansas City was killed. See Andrew Carroll, *My Fellow Soldiers: General John Pershing and the Americans Who Helped Win the Great War* (New York: Penguin Books), 2017, 137.

16. Wawro, xix.

17. Ibid, 577.

18. George Dudley Bogert, *"Let's Go!"* (San Francisco: George Dudley Bogert), 1927, 75.

19. Ibid., 23.

20. Sgt. Almo O'Kell to Pearl O'Kell, December 28, 1918, World War One Museum, Kansas City, Missouri, 1-2.

21. Hanson, 241.

22. Hanson, 328.

23. Sgt. Almo O'Kell to Pearl O'Kell, December 28, 1918, 7.

24. *Roster of Field Hospital Co., No. 3, March 31, 1919.* Field hospital Company 3 Medical Department to Hospital Company 3, 1st Sanitary Train, 1917-1921 Collection Master Rolls & Rosters, November 1912-December 1939 Robert R. McCormick Research Center Digital Collection.

25. Randall Gabrielan, *Explosion at Morgan* (Charleston: The History Press), 2012, 36.

26. Franz Von Rintelen, *The Dark Invader: War-Time Reminiscences of a German Naval Intelligence Officer*, http://gutenberg.net.au/ebooks08/0801121h.html; retrieved March 31, 2020.

27. The original epithet was "Nigger Jack," the hateful term used by West Point cadets whom he was teaching because Pershing, at one time earlier in his career, had been an officer in a contingent of African-American troops of the 10th Cavalry Regiment, the legendary "Buffalo Soldiers."

Index

Adams, Abigail, 171
Addams, Jane, 185
Albion, 109
Alexandria National Cemetery (Alexandria, Virginia), 50
Allen Kerr, 61
Allison, William, 30, 31
Althaus, Catherine Babby, 57, 96
Althaus, David, 57
American Eagle, 2-3, 17
American Sunday School Union (ASSU), 22, 43
Ancient Order of HIbernians, 148
Ancient Order of United Workmen, AOUW, 147, 148, 152
Anderson, Margaret, see Watson, Margaret Anderson
Anselmi, Rose Gaino, 194
Anselmi, Thomas, 194-195
Arlington Cemetery (Philadelphia), 179
Augusta, Georgia, Confederate powder mill, 98, 100
Babby, Catherine, See Althaus, Catherine Babby
Babby, Catherine Callahan, 57, 96-97, 122-123
Babby, Joseph, 96, 123
Baddeley, J. Fraser, 98
Baird, Elizabeth Short, 183
Baird, James, 183-184
Baker, Maria, see Green, Maria Baker
Barber, Benjamin, 179, 184
Barber, Ida May Queair, 179
Bauduy, Peter, 34
Baughman, Joseph, 34
Baun, Mary McGrath, 114
Baun, Patrick, 113-114
Baxter, Catherine Elliott, 45, 58, 88
Baxter, Edward, 59
Baxter, Malcolm Jr., 58-59, 64, 77
Baxter, Malcolm, 57-58, 63, 73

Beacom, Elizabeth, 141, 161
Bidermann, Antoine, 16
Bielaski, Bruce, 170
Bird, Charles du Pont, 93
Black Tom Island, 186
Black, Charles, 81
Blaine, James G., 115
Boisson, Peter, 46-47
Bonaparte, Napoleon, 35-36
Bonner, Bridget, see Dougherty, Bridget Bonner
Booker, Louis, 183, 195
Booker, Wilhemina (Mina) Seward, 183
Borrell, Christiann Long, 49-51, 54
Borrell, George W., 50, 59
Borrell, Joseph Michael, 50
Borrell, Michael, 22, 49-52
Boyle, Patrick, 28, 30
Bradley, Edward, 15, 20-21, 31, 42
Bradley, Elenor McAfferty, 15, 21, 22, 37, 42
Brady, Ann Carroll, 20, 31, 37
Brady, Hugh, 20
Brady, John Jr., 20, 31
Brady, John Sr., 20, 31
Brady, Patrick Jr., 19, 20, 21, 31
Brandywine Manufacturer's Sunday School (BMSS), 21, 42-43, 53, 55, 86, 141
Bricotti, Marge, 174
Brobson, William P., xiv
Brogan, Catherine, see McAteer, Catherine Brogan
Brown, Isabella Miller, 13, 56-57
Brown, Samuel, 56
Buchanan, Catherine Moore, 152, 155
Buchanan, Elizabeth, 154-155
Buchanan, Hannah (Jennie), see Cunningham, Hannah (Jennie) Buchanan
Buchanan, Samuel, 152-154
Cahill, Mary, see Hughes, Mary Cahill

Callahan, Catherine, See Babby, Catherine Callahan
Caledonia, 75
Cameron, Secretary of War Simon, 92
Cammock, Catherine Dunbar, 156
Cammock, David, 156-157
Campbell, James, 56
Campbell, Moses, 161
Cannon, Governor William, 91
Carr, Cornelius, 101
Carr, Frances (Fanny), 101
Carroll, Ann, see Brady, Ann Carroll
Carter, Mary Zebley, 122
Carter, Amos, 119, 121-122
Carey, Mary P., see Swartwood, Mary P. Carey
Cassiday, Edward, 73
Casey, Hannah S., see Toomey, Hannah S. Casey
Cassiday, Elizabeth, 73
Catalina, Catherine, see Salvagno, Catherine Catalina
Cathedral Cemetery (Wilmington, Delaware), 76, 180, 184, 190
Cazier, Aubertine Grant, 166
Cazier, Henry, 165-168, 171, 180
Chadwick, Maggie Leithead, 127
Chadwick, William, 126-127
Chamberlain, Joshua, 172
Chambers, James, 69, 72
Charleston Packet, 12
Chelten Hills Cemetery (Philadelphia, Pennsylvania), 161
Churchill, Percy, 155
Civil War, xi, 50, 58, 59, 63, 64, 82, 83, 86, 87, 91, 94, 100, 101, 104, 107, 116, 134, 171
Clark, Edward, 134
Clark, Elizabeth McKinney, 87
Clark, Joseph, 134
Clark, Mrs Edward, 133-134
Clark, Thomas, 87
Clay, Henry, 49
Cole, John, 48, 128

Collins, Dennis, 102
Collins, Rose, 102
Colt, Samuel, 6
Connable, Frank, 162, 188-189
Connable, Mrs. Frank, 155
Connell, Bridget, see Hassett, Bridget Connell
Connor, Patrick, 45, 59-60
Connor, Rosanna A. Sweeney, 45, 60
Connor, William, 58-59
Cooney, Peter, 31
Cowan, Christopher, 49, 66
Coyle, Rosanna, see Toy, Rosanna Coyle
Cream, Christiana, 16
Credan, James, 90
Crimean War, xi, 82
Cronin, Sarah, see Dougherty, Sarah Cronin
Crowninsheld, Louise du Pont, 140
Cumpston, Elmer, 183
Cunningham, Hannah (Jennie) Buchanan, 169
Cunningham, James (1818), 30
Cunningham, James (1867), 104
Cunningham, Lawrence, 161, 169, 183
Cunningham, Mary Rosalie Thompson, 103
Curry, Morris, 160, 161
Czar, 102
D'Autremont, 36
Dalmas, Charles, 8, 31
Darrah, Howard, 162
De Grouchy, Alphonse, xiv
De Grouchy, Emmanuel, xiv
De Tousard, Colonel Louis, ix
Dearborn, Henry, x
Deery, Bridget, see Gallagher, Bridget Deery
Deery, Michael, 102, 113
Deery, Patrick, 102, 113
Dehan, John, 89
Dekalb, U.S.S., 191, 199, 212-213
Delaware State Hospital, 76, 150, 178
Denesta, Nicholas, 162, 163
Dennison, Fannie, see McGarvey, Fannie Dennison

Index

Denton Cemetery (Denton, Maryland), Maryland, 179
Deveron, 42
Devine, John, 66-67, 88
Devine, Margaret, see Donahue, Margaret Devine
Devine, Maria, see O'Brien, Maria Devine
Devine, Sarah Kane, 88
Devinney, Matilda, see McDowell, Matilda Devinney
Devlin, Ann Mooney, 86-87
Devlin, Edward, 86-87
Devlin, Hugh, 85-86
Diana, 27, 108
Didier, Dr. Pierre, 9, 13-14
Dodley, Margaret, see McDermott, Margaret Dodley
Doherty, Mary, see McLaughlin, Mary Doherty
Dolan, Hannah Gibbons, 136
Dolan, James, 132, 136
Dolan, Martin, 83, 136-137, 140
Donahue, James, 108-109
Donahue, John, 28
Donahue, Margaret Devine, 109
Dougherty, Anne King, 14-15
Dougherty, Anthony, 76-78
Dougherty, Bridget Bonner, 61
Dougherty, Dan (1818), 29, 30
Dougherty, Daniel (1847), 59, 112,
Dougherty, Daniel (injured, 1882), 116, 124-126
Dougherty, Edward, 81, 118
Dougherty, Edward II, 112, 118, 120
Dougherty, Ellen Gibbons, 125
Dougherty, Fred, 119, 120-121
Dougherty, Grace, 121
Dougherty, Isabella A. Flynn, 89
Dougherty, Jane McFarlane, 77
Dougherty, John (1847), 61
Dougherty, John (1864), 102
Dougherty, Kathryn (Kate), 125
Dougherty, Mary, 57

Dougherty, Mary, see Houtton, Mary Dougherty
Dougherty, Michael, vi, 103, 114
Dougherty, Michael II, 114
Dougherty, Nancy, 28
Dougherty, Patrick (1815), 14, 15
Dougherty, Patrick II, 119, 120
Dougherty, Patrick V, 138
Dougherty, Richard, 10, 14, 18, 32
Dougherty, Rosanne, 135, 141
Dougherty, Sarah Cronin, 118, 121
Dougherty, Thomas (toddler), 135
Dougherty, Thomas, 89, 95
Dougherty, William, 29
Dugan, Philip, 30, 31
Dunnery, John, 24, 31
Dunbar, Anne, see, McRea, Anne Dunbar
Dunbar, Catherine, see Cammock, Catherine Dunbar
DuPont, Alexis I., 50, 67, 69, 72, 74, 75, 76, 128
DuPont, Alfred V., 9, 45, 46, 53, 54, 56, 70, 74, 82, 85, 133,
DuPont, Bessie Gardner, 153
DuPont, Charles I., 116, 141
DuPont, Eleuthera, 44
DuPont, Eleuthère Irénée, xiii, ix, x, xiv, 5-9, 10, 11, 12, 14, 15, 16, 17, 18, 25, 26, 33-35, 37, 45, 74, 82, 114
DuPont, Evelina, 35, 75
DuPont, Francis Gurney, 28, 36, 47, 63, 66, 73, 74, 76, 78. 80, 83, 84, 85, 93, 95, 104, 105, 106, 108, 109, 110, 113, 114, 115, 119, 124, 126, 128, 130, 132, 134, 137, 184, 201
DuPont, Gabrielle Josephine, 3, 117
DuPont, Henry, 76
DuPont, Irénée, 45, 106
DuPont, Pierre Samuel, ix, xiii, 17, 34
DuPont, Samuel Francis, 56, 67, 93, 98
DuPont, Sophie (Mrs. Samuel Francis), 55, 90, 106, 125, 126, 140,

DuPont, Victor, xiii, xiv, 3, 9, 11, 17, 22, 23, 114, 117
DuPont, Victorine, 21, 24, 43, 53, 59, 103
Duris, Ellen, see Querke, Ellen Duris
E.I. du Pont de Nemours and Company, vi, vii, viii, xi, 1, 5, 7, 8, 9, 12, 13, 15, 17, 20, 21, 23, 25, 26, 27, 28, 29, 32, 33, 37, 38, 40, 41, 43, 45, 46, 52, 54, 57, 59, 61, 67, 69, 71, 75, 76, 80, 81, 92, 95, 100, 101, 104, 112, 120, 121, 129, 130, 135, 136, 138, 141, 144, 149, 164, 165, 166, 168, 169, 175, 184, 185, 189, 190, 198, 215
Eddystone Ammunition Plant, 191
Edward, Prince of Wales, 83
Eggner, Elizabeth, 177, 178
Eggner, James, 177-178
Eggner, Louis, 177-178
Elliott, Catherine, see Baxter, Catherine Elliott
Elliot, Henry, 174
Engle, Milton, 95, 96
Erin, 15
Ervin, Sam, 209
Ewell, Thomas, 34
Farnhurst Cemetery, 178
Farnhurst, See Delaware State Hospital
Ferry, Hugh, 135
Finigan, Catherine Slane, 24, 37
Finigan, Hugh, 24, 32, 34
First Presbyterian Cemetery (Wilmington, Delaware), 11
Fisher, Elizabeth, 75
Fisher, George, 75
Fisher, Martha, 86
Fisher, Samuel Jr., 86
Fisher, Samuel Sr., 86
Fisher, Norman, 174-175
Flanagan, Mary McCusker, 113
Flanagan, Peter, 112-113
Flinn, David, 24, 30
Flynn, Isabella A., see Dougherty, Isabella A. Flynn
Foley, Mary, see McLaughlin, Mary Foley

Ford, Henry, 185
Forest, Mary, see Russell, Mary Forest
Foster, Martha, 12-13
Foster, William, 9, 12
Fox, Elmer, 184
Frankfurter, Felix, 172
Friederich Der Grosse, 211, 212
French Revolution, ix, 17
Frizzell, Sam Jr., 146
Gaino, Rose, see Anselmi, Rose Gaino
Gallagher, Anne, see Toner, Anne Gallagher
Gallagher, Anne Quigley, 24
Gallagher, Bridget Deery, 144
Gallagher, Edward, 143-144
Gallagher, Philip, 20, 24, 30
Garesché, Peter, 72-73
Garesché, Peter Bauduy, 59
Garrett, Thomas, 70, 71
Gemmil, James, 175
George, Jonathan E., 135
Gibbons, Hannah, see Dolan, Hannah Gibbons
Gibbons, James, (1859) 78, (1864) 95
Gibbons, Roseanna Sharkey, 78
Gill, Thomas, 102
Gillespie, Hugh, 169
Giviney, James, 184-185
Glenn, John, 95
Gobin, Mary, see Houtton, Mary Gobin
Gordon, George, 65
Gorman, Michael, 83
Grangiulio, Antonio, 194
Grant, Aubertine, see Cazier, Aubertine Grant
Grant, General Ulysses S., 99
Grant, John, 78-79
Grant, Sarah McGee, 78-79
Green Hill Cemetery (Wilmington, Delaware), 73, 75, 80, 157
Green, John, 46-47
Green, Maria Baker, 55
Green, William, 40, 55-56, 61
Green, William R., 132-133, 142-143, 180

Index

Grimshaw, Dr. Arthur H., 75, 92, 126
Gross, Edward, 175
Haber, Harry, 184
Haley, Patrick, 128, 129-130, 180
Halleck, General Henry, 91
Hannah Kerr, 86
Hanrahan, Patrick, 180
Haralson, Jonathan (Harrolson), 99-100
Harkins, Ann Sweeney, 140
Harkins, Daniel, 139-140
Harrison, Wiliam Henry, 49
Harrity, Bridget, see O'Brien, Bridget Harrity
Hassett, Bridget Connell, 102
Hassett, Michael, 102
Heatherington, Thomas, 48, 50
Hennessy, Thomas, 102
Herlihy, John, 135
Herlihy, Michael, 135
Hickey, Michael, 96
Higgerty, Elizabeth Shields, 89-90
Higgerty, John, 89-90
Higgins, Jane, see Miller, Jane Higgins
Hobson, Mildred Florence, see Springfield, Mildred Florence Hobson
Hodge, James, 196-199, 207-213
Hodge, Laura, 199
Hogate, Nelson, 182-183
Hogate, Sarah (Sallie) Rodenhiser, 182-183
Holland, Patrick, 40-41
Holland, Eleanor McMackin, 41
Holland, Margaret Travers, 61
Holland, Thomas, 61
Holmes, Oliver Wendell Jr., 171-172
Horgan, John, 135-136
Horgan, Mary, 135-136
Houtton Michael, 57
Houtton, John, 49
Houtton, Mary Dougherty, 57
Houtton, Mary Gobin, 49
Hughes, Bridget, see Pearl, Bridget Hughes
Hughes, John, 103-104
Hughes, Mary Cahill, 103-104

Hughes, Mary, see Shields, Mary Hughes
Hughes, Thomas, 68, 69
Hunter, Rebecca, see Hurst, Rebecca Hunter
Huron, U.S.S., 197, 207, 211, 212
Hurst, Edward, 75, 180
Hurst, Rebecca Hunter, 75
Hyne, Martin, 95, 96
Imo, 191
Improved Order of Red Men, IORM, 147, 148, 152, 154, 156, 162, 196
Independent Order of Odd Fellows, IOOF, 95, 118, 147, 180
Israel, 40
Jacob, Ubert, 81
Jefferson, Thomas, ix, x
Jeffry, Fred, 184
Joseph Porter, 65
June Haddon, 60
Junior Order of United American Mechanics, 196
Juno, 27
Kane, Sarah, see Devine, Sarah Kane
Kelleher, Bartholomew, 182
Kelly, James, 95
Kennedy, Thomas, 28, 29, 30
Kenny, Father, 18, 20, 22
Kerrigan, Jane, see McGee, Jane Kerrigan
Keys, John, 69, 71-72, 180
Keys, Margaret, 72
Kielkopf, Louisa M., see Wein, Louisa M. Kielkopf
Kimberley, Charles, 192
King, Anne, see Dougherty, Anne King
King, Edward, 184
King, Elizabeth McCloskey, 56
King, Owen, 22, 42
King, William, 56
Kinney, Charles Jr., 121
Knights of the Golden Eagle, 148, 162
Kyle, Henry, 39, 46
Landis, Charles B., 170
Lavoisier, Antoine, ix, x, 6,7
Leary, Margaret Meehan, 90
Leary, William, 90

Lee, Bishop Alfred, 67, 69, 70
Leithead, Maggie, see Chadwick, Maggie Leithead
Leonard, Francis, 10, 14, 15-16
Lickle, Charles, 168, 173
Long, Christiann, see Borrell, Christiann Long
Lombardy Cemetery (Wilmington, Delaware), 184
Loyal Orange Lodge (Orangemen), 147, 152, 157
Lumley, 83
Lynch, Julia McGeady, 61-62
Lynch, Thomas, 61
Mace, Elmer, 180-182, 183
Mace, Sarah B. Smith, 181
Malloy, Margaret McCusker, 104, 105, 113
Malloy, James, 104-105
Malloy, John, 25
Marantette, Madame, 158-159
Margaret Hugg, 60
Marshall, George C., 172, 212
Martini, Cecilia, 194
Martini, Giovanni, 194
Massie, Charles, 107
Massie, Margaret Ann, 105
Massie, Peter, 105, 107, 118
McAfferty, Elinor, see Bradley, Elinor McAfferty
McAteer, Catherine Brogan, 108
McAteer, Darby, 107-108
McCann, Thomas, 145, 146, 148
McCarren, Patrick, 29-30
McCauley, John, 9, 11
McClafferty, Catherine (Kate), 75-76
McClafferty, James, 50, 66
McClafferty, John, 75-76
McCloskey, Elizabeth, see King, Elizabeth McCloskey
McColgan, Mary, 25, 26
McCollage, Hugh, 25
McCrea, Anne Dunbar, 156

McCusker, Margaret, see Malloy, Margaret McCusker
McCrea, William, 155-156
McCusker, Mary, see Flanagan, Mary McCusker
McDermott, Margaret Dodley, 162
McDermott, Walter, 162
McDevitt, James, 53
McDowell, Matilda Devinney, 151, 152
McDowell, William, 151-152
McElwee, John, 103
McElwee, Rosanna, 103
McFarlane, Jane, see Dougherty, Jane McFarlane
McGarvey, Fannie Dennison, 140
McGarvey, Matthew, 62
McGarvey, William, 131, 140
McGeady, Julia, see Lynch, Julia McGeady
McGee, Ellen, see McGinley, Ellen McGee
McGee, Jane Kerrigan, 93
McGee, Patrick, 92, 93
McGee, Sarah, see Grant, Sarah McGee
McGinley, Ellen McGee, 88, 94, 105
McGinley, Frances see Mulherin, Frances McGinley
McGinley, Hugh, 93-94
McGinness, John, 62-63
McGinnis, John, 46, 47
McGrath, Mary, see Baun, Mary McGrath
McIlhenny, Hannah Peoples, 146, 148
McIlhenny, Robert (1859), 81
McIlhenny, Robert (1898), 145-147
McKenna, James, 84-86
McKenna, Mary Toy, 42, 43, 50, 84-86
McKinney, Elizabeth, see Clark, Elizabeth McKinney
McKinney, Patrick, 119, 121
McLaughlin, Dennis, 113, 114
McLaughlin, Mary Doherty, 22-23
McLaughlin, Mary Foley, 89
McLaughlin, Mary Meehan, 113
McLaughlin, Michael (1818), 22
McLaughlin, Michael (1850), 65

Index

McLaughlin, Richard, 89
McMackin, Eleanor, see Holland, Eleanor McMackin
McNamara, John F., 59, 93
McNitt, Ashburn, 159
McPherson, John, 73, 74
McQuaid, Owen, 20
Meehan, Margaret, see Leary, Margaret Meehan
Meehan, Mary, see McLaughlin, Mary Meehan
Messenger, 87, 88
Miller, Andrew, 9, 56
Miller, George, 115, 117, 119
Miller, Isabellla, see Brown, Isabella Miller
Miller, Jane Higgins, 115-116
Miller, John Savage, 116
Miller, Jonas, xiii, xiv, 18, 86, 112, 114-118, 156, 180
Miller, Nancy, 13
Miller, William Henry, 86, 116
Minninger, John, 122, 123
Moffat, Captain, 25
Mont-Blanc, 191
Mooney, Ann, see Devlin, Ann Mooney
Mooney, Michael, 25, 26, 30
Moore, Adeline, see Stewart, Adeline Moore
Moore, Andrew, 73
Moore, Anna, 73
Moore, Catherine, see Buchanan, Catherine Moore
Moore, David, 73, 74
Moore, John, 145, 146, 150
Moore, Kate Wilmot, 150
Moore, Martha, 73
Moran, Catherine Rigby, 80
Moran, William, 80
Morris, Benjamin, 159
Mott, John, 161
Mt. Salem Cemetery (Wilmington, Delaware), 59, 180
Mulherin, Charles, 83

Mulherin, Frances McGinley, 83
Mullin, Thomas "Mickey", 82
Munns, Charles, 32-35
Murray, Catherine, see Sweeney, Catherine Murray
New Garden Cemetery (Toughkenamon, Pennsylvania), 162
Newark Union Cemetery (Wilmington, Delaware), 162
Newell, Bridget, 139
Newell, John, 139
Noble, Emily, 133
Noone, Fergus, 88
Noone, Mary, 87-89
O'Brian, John, 26
O'Brien, Bridget Harrity, 63
O'Brien, Charles, 63
O'Brien, Maria Devine, 63
O'Brien, Michael, 63
O'Conner, Bryan, 184
O'Donnell, Bridget Smith, 102
O'Donnell, Edward, 102
O'Kell, Sgt. Almo E., 210, 211
O'Neill, Charles, 102
O'Neill, Isabella Watson, 54, 102
Odd Fellows Cemetery (Smyrna, Delaware), 180
Old Swede's Cemetery (Wilmington, Delaware), 47, 51, 68
Patriotic Order Sons of America, 162
Patton, George S., 172
Pearl, Bridget Hughes, 129
Pearl, Thomas, 128-129, 140
Peebles, Hans, 33
Pierce, Thomas, 24
Pennington, Elizabeth, 64
Pennington, Wesley, 64
Peoples, Hannah, see McIlhenny, Hannah Peoples
Peoples, James, 91
Perry, Admiral Matthew, 68
Pershing, General John, 208, 212
Persoglio, Maria Antonietta, see Sicco, Maria Antonietta Persoglio

Pierce, Margaret Lucinda, see Whiteman, Margaret Lucinda Pierce
Pinder, Mary Rebecca Skinner, 195
Pinder, Susie Irene Smith, 195
Pinder, Noah Columbus (Lum), 195
Place, Harvey, 179
Pleasonton, Clarence, 180
Pollitt, Allan, 191, 192
Pollitt, Anna B. Sannabend, 192
Pollitt, William, 192
Prinz Eitel Friedrich, 191, 212-213
Provincialist, 60, 93
Queair, Ida May, see Barber, Ida May
Querke, Ellen Duris, 89, 90
Querke, John, 89, 90
Quig, Thomas, 10, 11, 12, 29, 37
Quigley, Anne, see Gallagher, Anne Quigley
Rains, Colonel George Washington, 98, 99, 100
Ramo (Rameau), Peter, 49, 51
Reynolds, Edward, 27, 31
Reynolds, Eleanor, 27, 37
Reynolds, Thomas, 27, 31
Rice, Malvin, 212
Rigby, Catherine, see Moran, Catherine Rigby
Riverview Cemetery (Wilmington, Delaware), 59, 152, 180, 192
Rodenhiser,, Sarah (Sallie), see Hogate, Sarah (Sallie) Rodenhiser
Roosevelt, Franklin Delano, 148, 172
Roosevelt, Theodore, 172
Roosevelt, Theodore, Jr., 210
Russell, George, 52, 53
Russell, Jane, 84, 121
Russell, Joseph, 83, 84
Russell, Mary Forest, 53
Ryans, Fergus, 56
Sabar, Emile, 81
Salvagno, Catherine Catalina, 186
Salvagno, John, 186, 190
Sannabend, Anna B., see Pollitt, Anna B. Sannaband
Schenk, Major General Robert, 91

Seward, Wilhemina (Mina), see Booker, Wilhemina (Mina)
Sharkey, Roseanna, see Gibbons, Roseanna Sharkey
Shepherd, Peter, 9, 11
Shields, Barnard, 64, 88
Shields, Elizabeth, see Higgerty, Elizabeth Shields
Shields, Mary Hughes, 64
Short, Elizabeth, see Baird, Elizabeth Short
Sicco, Carlo, 163, 181, 187-190
Sicco, Carolina Toso, 188
Sicco, Marie Antoinetta Persoglio, 187, 188
Sicco, Palmira Isabella (Helen), 188, 190
Silverbrook Cemetery (Wilmington, Delaware), 162, 174, 183
Silvestri, Gimi, 175
Simcox, Willliam, 69
Simpson, Wesley, 179
Skinner, Mary Rebecca, see Pinder, Mary Rebecca Skinner
Slane, Catherine, see Finigan, Catherine Slane
Smack, John, 175
Smack, Paul, 175
Smith, Bridget, see O'Donnell, Bridget Smith
Smith, Sarah B., see Mace, Sarah B. Smith
Smith, Susie Irene, see Pinder, Susie Irene Smith
Snyder, Edward C., 191
Spanish Influenza, 162, 190, 197
Springfield, Elijah, 176, 179
Springfield, Mildred Florence Hobson, 176
St. Joseph's on the Brandywine Cemetery, 51, 61, 64, 77, 78, 79, 80, 85, 102, 104, 113, 135, 138, 148
St. Paul's Cemetery (Odessa, Delaware), 179
St. Peter's Cemetery (Wilmington, Delaware), 41

Index

Stewart Samuel, 146, 148-149, 180
Stewart, James, 74
Stewart, Adeline Moore, 148
Stolenwerck, Guy, 214
Strain, John, 27, 30
Sudlersville Cemetery (Sudlersville, Maryland), 195
Superior, 101
Swartwood, Calvin, 195-196
Swartwood, Mary P. Carey, 194-195
Sweeney, Ann, see Harkins, Ann Sweeney
Sweeney, Barney, 80
Sweeney, Catherine Murray, 80
Sweeney, Rosanna A., see Connor, Rosanna A. Sweeney
Swoboda, Jacob, 185
Sycamore Manufacturing Company, 59, 100
Sylvester, Major Richard, 185
Talley, Thomas, 69, 72
Tankopanicum Musical Club (Al's Band), 153
Thaxter, Alan, 171-174, 211, 214-215
Thaxter, Julia St. Felix, 171, 173, 174
Thaxter, Sydney W., 171, 172, 174
Thomas H. Perkins, 101
Thompson, Mary Rosalee, see Cunningham, Mary Rosalee
Tiffin, 30
Timms, William, 179
Tollin, Patrick, 27-28
Tominey, Arthur, 43-44
Toner, Anne Gallagher, 18, 19, 20, 25, 31,
Toner, Michael, 10, 14, 18-19, 20, 24-25, 31, 33
Toomey, Hannah S. Casey, 168
Torrey, John, 28
Toso, Carolina, see Sicco, Carolina Toso
Toy, Daniel, 11, 41, 42, 44, 45, 84, 116
Toy, Mary, see McKenna, Mary Toy
Toy, Rosanna Coyle, 11, 41, 44
Travers, Margaret, see Holland, Margaret Travers
Trollope, Fanny, 40

Tunberg, Peter, 28
Turner, Aubrey, 196, 199
Vance, John, 46-47
Vannatta, Albert, 189
Vauclain, Samuel M., 190
Vichie, John, 83-84
Viola, Charles, 152
Virginia Military Institute (VMI), 172, 174
Von Rintelen, Franz, 211-212
Vouche, Louis, 76
Wake, American, 1-2
Wake, Irish, 1
Walker, James, 144-146, 181
Walker, Ellen, 145
War of 1812, x, 10, 11, 17, 25, 68
Watson, Archibald, 53, 54, 102
Watson, Isabella, see O'Neill, Isabella Watson
Watson, Margaret Anderson, 54
Wein, Louisa M. Kielkopf, 179
Wein, William, 179
Welch, John, 9, 11
Welsh, John, 81
Wetmore Thomas, 99
Whiteman, George, 157-160, 163, 166
Whiteman, Margaret Lucinda Pierce, 159, 160
Wilhelm, Kaiser II, 211
Willard, Dr. DeForest, 72
William V George, 60
Wilmington and Brandywine Cemetery (Wilmington, Delaware), 167
Wilmot, Kate, see Moore, Kate Wilmot
Wilson, David, 28, 30
World War I, 197, 207-213
Wright, Margaret, 150
Wright, John (Jack), 150
Zebley, Mary, see Carter, Mary Zebley

Thank you for reading! I would love to know what you think about the book. You can leave a review on the website where you bought the book. If you bought the book elsewhere, you can email me directly at *dtempleton312@gmail.com*. I appreciate your taking time to let me know your thoughts.

www.ingramcontent.com/pod-product-compliance
Lightning Source LLC
Chambersburg PA
CBHW021053080526
44587CB00010B/236